IDEOLOGY
AND
THE
DEVELOPMENT
OF
SOCIOLOGICAL
THEORY

PRENTICE-HALL SOCIOLOGY SERIES

Neil J. Smelser,
Editor

Irving M. Zeitlin

Indiana University
Bloomington, Indiana

IDEOLOGY
AND
THE
DEVELOPMENT
OF
SOCIOLOGICAL
THEORY

PRENTICE-HALL, INC.
Englewood Cliffs, New Jersey

Library of Congress Catalog Card No. 68–23814

Printed in the United States of America

Current printing (last digit):

10   9   8   7   6   5   4

PRENTICE-HALL INTERNATIONAL, INC., *London*
PRENTICE-HALL OF AUSTRALIA, PTY. LTD., *Sydney*
PRENTICE-HALL OF CANADA, LTD., *Toronto*
PRENTICE-HALL OF INDIA PRIVATE LTD., *New Delhi*
PRENTICE-HALL OF JAPAN, INC., *Tokyo*

FOR Esther, Ruthie, Michael, Bethie, and Jeremy

Preface

Much of classical sociology arose within the context of a debate—first with eighteenth-century thought, the Enlightenment, and later with its true heir in the nineteenth century, Karl Marx.

From this perspective, the Enlightenment appears as the least arbitrary and most appropriate point of departure in the study of the origins of sociological theory. The eighteenth-century thinkers began more consistently than any of their predecessors to study the human condition in a methodical way, consciously applying what they considered to be scientific principles of analysis to man, his nature, and society.

But there are still other reasons for beginning with the thinkers of the Enlightenment: they upheld *reason* as the critical measure of social institutions and their suitability for man's nature. Man, they believed, is essentially rational and his rationality can lead him to freedom. They believed, too, in the perfectibility of man. Being infinitely perfectible meant that by criticizing and changing social institutions man could create for himself ever greater degrees of freedom, which, in turn, would enable him increasingly to actualize his potentially creative powers. These powers were inhibited and repressed by the existing institutions so long as they remained unreasonable and hence not in accord with man's basic nature.

The thinkers of the Enlightenment were therefore *critical* as well as scientific. Their major premises, the rationality and perfectibility of man, eventually inspired the French revolutionaries;

and after the Revolution many of the most influential thinkers in Europe attributed the causes of that great upheaval to the *Philosophes* and their ideas and attempted to repudiate and discredit them.

The response to the theories of the Enlightenment and the French Revolution has been treated by historians under the headings of Romanticism and the Conservative Reaction. This reaction constitutes an exceedingly interesting and important phase in the development of social theory, for it was in this general context, as we shall see, that sociology in the more formal sense emerged. In this first section of the book, Hegel's historical synthesis, the rise of positivism as a reaction to "negative" philosophy, and the thought of Saint-Simon and Comte, the founders of sociology, are given special attention.

From Saint-Simon and Hegel, and particularly one aspect of the latter's philosophy—negative-critical thinking—it is apparent that Marx and his work is a logical next step. Marx's social thought is treated as a kind of intellectual watershed, for more than any of his contemporaries he revived and synthesized in his work both tendencies of Enlightenment thought: the critical-revolutionary and the scientific.

Marx's contribution to sociological thinking, it will be argued, is one of the most important of the late nineteenth century—perhaps the most important. This is true, I believe, not only because of the immensely rich ideas he himself advanced but also because his work provoked a response that accounts, in a large measure, for the character of Western sociology. My discussion of Marx, then, sets the stage for the intense debate with his ghost, the major theme of this book.

In a series of essays the theories of Weber, Pareto, Mosca, Michels, Durkheim, and Mannheim are examined primarily in relation to Marxian thought. Hopefully, this approach achieves a number of purposes: It provides a sophisticated critique of Marx's social thought; it indicates the extent to which the assumptions, concepts, and specific theories of subsequent thought were shaped by the debate with Marxism; and, finally, it brings into relief the polemical aspects and ideological elements of classical sociological theory. This study is therefore conceived as a critical examination of the development of sociological theory—and, more particularly, of its ideological elements.

I. M. Z.

Contents

PART I

THE ENLIGHTENMENT

Chapter 1   Philosophical Foundations   3

Chapter 2   Montesquieu   11

Chapter 3   Rousseau   23

PART II

POST-REVOLUTIONARY THOUGHT

Chapter 4   The Romantic-Conservative Reaction   35

Chapter 5   Bonald and Maistre   43

Chapter 6   Saint-Simon   56

Chapter 7   Auguste Comte   70

PART **III**

THE MARXIAN WATERSHED

Chapter 8   Philosophical Orientations   83

Chapter 9   From Social Philosophy to Social Theory   93

Chapter 10   Marx's Sociology of Alienated Labor   103

PART **IV**

THE DEBATE WITH MARX'S GHOST

Chapter 11   Max Weber   **111**

Chapter 12   Vilfredo Pareto   159

Chapter 13   Gaetano Mosca   195

Chapter 14   Robert Michels   218

Chapter 15   Émile Durkheim   234

Chapter 16   Karl Mannheim   281

Epilogue   321

Index   323

PART I

THE
ENLIGHTENMENT

1

The Enlightenment:
The Philosophical Foundations

More than the thinkers of any preceding age the men of the Enlightenment held firmly to the conviction that the mind could comprehend the universe and subordinate it to human needs. Reason became the god of these philosophers who were enormously inspired by the scientific achievements of the preceding centuries. These achievements led them to a new conception of the universe based on the universal applicability of natural laws; utilizing the concepts and techniques of the physical sciences, they set about the task of creating a new world based on reason and truth. Truth became the central goal of the intellectuals of this age but not truth founded on revelation, tradition, or authority; rather, it was reason and observation that were to be the twin pillars of truth.

If science revealed the workings of natural laws in the physical world, then perhaps similar laws could be discovered in the social and cultural world. Thus the *Philosophes* investigated all aspects of social life; they studied and analyzed political, religious, social, and moral institutions, subjected them to merciless criticism from the standpoint of reason, and demanded to change the unreasonable ones. More often than not, traditional values and institutions were found to be irrational. This was another way of saying that the prevailing institutions were contrary to man's nature and thus inhibitive of his growth and development;

unreasonable institutions prevented men from realizing their potential. There-fore these thinkers waged constant war against the irrational, and *criticism* became their major weapon. They fought what they considered to be super-stition, bigotry, or intolerance; they struggled against censorship and de-manded freedom of thought; they attacked the prerogatives of the feudal classes and their restraints upon the industrial and commercial classes; and, finally, they tried to secularize ethics. They were very knowledgeable of the positive intellectual achievements up to their time, but they were also critical, skeptical, and secular. Basically, it was their faith in reason *and* science which provided so strong an impetus to their work and led them to be humanitarian, optimistic, and confident.

Some students of the Enlightenment have argued, however, that "the *Philosophes* were nearer the Middle Ages, less emancipated from the precon-ceptions of medieval Christian thought, than they quite realized or we have commonly supposed."[1] Rather than their positive achievements, and their affirmations, it is their negations which have impressed us and which have prompted us to attribute a modern character to their work. The *"Philosophes* demolished the Heavenly City of St. Augustine only to rebuild it with more up-to-date materials."[2] Ernst Cassirer, perhaps the greatest contemporary historian of eighteenth-century philosophy, shares this view to a certain degree. "Far more than the men of the epoch were aware," writes Cassirer, "their teachings were dependent on the preceding centuries." They "ordered, sifted, developed, and clarified this heritage rather than contributed and gave currency to new and original ideas."[3] Nevertheless, as Cassirer has patiently shown, the Enlightenment did produce a completely original *form* of philo-sophic thought, for it was only with respect to content that it remained dependent upon the preceding centuries. To be sure, it continued to build on the foundations of seventeenth-century thought—Descartes, Spinoza, Leibniz, Bacon, Hobbes, and Locke—and reworked their major ideas; yet, in this very reworking a new meaning and a new perspective appears. Philosophizing becomes something different from what it was before.

The eighteenth-century thinkers had lost faith in the closed, self-sufficient, metaphysical systems of the preceding century; they had lost patience with a philosophy confined to definite immutable axioms and deductions from them. More so than ever before, philosophy is to become the activity by which the fundamental form of all natural and spiritual phenomena can be discovered. "Philosophy is no longer to be separated from science, history, jurisprudence, and politics; it is rather to be the atmosphere in which they can exist and be

---

[1] Carl Becker, *The Heavenly City of the Eighteenth-Century Philosophers* (New Haven: Yale University Press, 1932) , p. 29.

[2] *Ibid.*, p. 31.

[3] The remainder of the quotations in this chapter are taken from Ernst Cassirer, *The Philosophy of the Enlightenment* (Princeton, New Jersey: Prince-ton University Press, 1951) . This citation is found on p. vi; the other page numbers will be noted in parentheses after the extract.

effective." (p. vii.) Investigations and inquiries are emphasized; Enlightenment thought is not merely reflective, nor is it satisfied to deal solely with axiomatic truths. It attributes to thought a creative and critical function, "the power and the task of shaping life itself." (p. viii.) Philosophy is no longer merely a matter of abstract thinking; it acquires the practical function of criticizing existing institutions to show that they are unreasonable and unnatural. It demands that these institutions and the entire old order be replaced by a new one that is more reasonable, natural, and hence necessary. And the fulfillment of the new order is the demonstration of its truth. Enlightenment thinking, then, has a *negative* and *critical* as well as a positive side. It is not so much the particular doctrines, axioms, and theorems which lend it a new and original quality; rather, it is the process of criticizing, doubting and tearing down—as well as building up. This unity of the "negative" and "positive" tendencies is eventually split; and after the French Revolution, as we shall see, they manifest themselves as separate and conflicting philosophical principles.

The Mind of the Enlightenment

For the Enlightenment thinkers all aspects of man's life and works were subject to critical examination—the various sciences, religious revelation, metaphysics, aesthetics, etc. These thinkers felt and sensed the many mighty forces impelling them along, but they refused to abandon themselves to these forces. Self-examination, an understanding of their own activity, their own society, and their own time, was an essential function of thought. By knowing, understanding, and recognizing the main forces and tendencies of their epoch, men could determine the direction and control the consequences of these forces. Through reason and science man could attain ever greater degrees of freedom and, therefore, ever greater degrees of perfection. Intellectual progress, an idea that permeated the thinking of that age, was to serve constantly to further man's general progress.

Unlike the seventeenth-century thinkers, for whom explanation was a matter of strict, systematic deduction, the *Philosophes* constructed their ideal of explanation and understanding on the model of the contemporary natural sciences. They turned not to Descartes but primarily to Newton, whose method was not pure deduction but analysis. Newton was interested in "facts," in the data of experience; his principles, the goal of his investigations, rested to a significant degree on experience and observation—in short, on an empirical basis. Newton's research was based on the assumption of universal order and law in the material world. Facts are not a chaotic, haphazard jumble of separate elements; quite to the contrary, they appear to fall into patterns and exhibit definite forms, regularities, and relationships. Order is immanent in the universe, Newton believed, and is discovered not by abstract principles but by observation and compilation of data. This is the methodology most characteristic of eighteenth-century thought, and it is this emphasis which distinguishes it from that of the seventeenth-century Continental philosophers. Condillac, for example, in his *Treatise on Systems* (basing himself on Locke), explicitly justifies this methodology and criticizes the great systems of the seventeenth century for having failed to adhere to it. Facts, the phenomena of the real world, were, for all practical purposes, ignored by the seventeenth-century rationalists. Single ideas and concepts were elevated to the status of dogma. The rational spirit dominated knowledge completely. Thus Condillac argues the necessity for a new method which unites the "positive" and scientific as well as the rational. One must study the phenomena themselves if their immanent forms and connections are to be known. Condillac, D'Alembert, and others now call for this new method as a prerequisite to intellectual progress. The logic of this method is indeed new for it is "neither the logic of the scholastic nor of the purely mathematical concept; it is rather the 'logic' of the facts." (p. 9.)

By observing the actual practice of science, the *Philosophes* concluded that the synthesis of the "positive" and the "rational" was not an unattainable ideal but one fully realizable. The natural sciences were proving themselves; their progress could be clearly perceived as the result of the triumphal march of the new scientific method. In the course of a century and a half, science had made a number of significant advances and then with Newton a truly qualitative step forward: The complex multiplicity of natural phenomena was reduced to, and comprehended as, the workings of a single universal law. This was an impressive victory for the new method. The *Philosophes* observed that Newton's general law of attraction was not the exclusive result of theorizing nor of sporadic experimentation or observation unguided by theory; its discovery was the fruit of the rigorous application of the scientific method. Newton completed what others had begun. Newton retained, used, and substantiated the method employed before him by Kepler and Galileo, the main feature of which was the *interdependence* of its analytical and synthetic aspects.

Employing Galileo's discovery that falling bodies accelerate at a constant rate, and Kepler's observation that there existed a fixed relationship between the distance of a planet from the sun and the speed of its revolution, Newton arrived at the law that the sun attracted planets to itself at a rate directly proportional to their mass and inversely proportional to the square of the distance between them. Eventually, he was able to demonstrate that all bodies of the universe took their positions and movement through the force of gravitation. Moreover, the force which held the planets in orbit also made objects fall to the ground. The law was operative throughout the universe. The finite universe had become an infinite machine eternally moving by its own power and mechanisms. External causation accounted for its operation, which was apparently devoid of purpose or meaning. Space, time, mass, motion, and force were the essential elements of this mechanical universe which could be comprehended in its entirety by applying the laws of science and mathematics. This conception had an incalculable impact on the intellectuals of the Enlightenment. Here was a magnificent triumph of reason *and* observation, the new method which takes observed facts and advances an interpretation which accounts for what is observed, so that if the interpretation is correct it can guide observers in their quest for new facts.

What is new and original about Enlightenment thought, therefore, is the whole-hearted adoption of the methodological pattern of Newton's physics; and what is even more important for our consideration of the philosophical foundations of sociological theory is the fact that immediately with its adoption it was generalized and employed in realms other than the mathematical and physical. It became an indispensable tool in the study of all phenomena. "However much individual thinkers and schools differ in their results," writes Cassirer, "they agree in this epistemological premise. Voltaire's *Treatise on Metaphysics*, d'Alembert's *Preliminary Discourse*, and Kant's *Inquiry Concerning the Principles of Natural Theology and Morality* all concur on this point." (p. 12.) Here again this may be contrasted with the seventeenth-century rationalists' understanding of the term "reason." For Descartes, Spinoza, and Leibniz, to select the most typical thinkers of that period, reason was the realm of "eternal verities"—truth held in common by man and God. This is not the view of the eighteenth century which, Cassirer maintains, "takes reason in a different and more modest sense. It is no longer the sum total of 'innate ideas' given prior to all experience, which reveal the absolute essence of things. Reason is now looked upon rather as an acquisition than as a heritage. It is not the treasury of the mind in which the truth like a minted coin lies stored; it is rather the original intellectual force which guides the discovery and determination of truth. . . . The whole eighteenth century understands reason in this sense; not as a sound body of knowledge, principles, and truths, but as a kind of energy, a force which is fully comprehensible only in its agency and effects." (p. 13.)

Reason bows neither to the merely factual, the simple data of experience, nor to the "evidence" of revelation, tradition, or authority. Reason together with observation is a facility for the acquisition of truth. Even the authors of the *Encyclopedia* viewed its function from this standpoint: not merely to provide knowledge and information but also and primarily to change the traditional mode of thinking—*"pour changer la façon commune de penser."* (p. 14.) The change did indeed become increasingly manifest, and analysis was now applied to psychological and even sociological phenomena and problems. In these realms, too, it had become clear that reason is a powerful instrument when employed in that special method—analysis into separate elements as well as synthetic reconstruction.

The eighteenth-century thinkers were aware of two philosophical and intellectual tendencies of the previous century that had remained relatively separate from each other and thus without any significant reciprocal influence: rational philosophy, on the one hand, and empirical philosophy on the other. Descartes had a fundamental influence in founding the first movement, while Galileo used experimentation and Bacon explained its particular virtues. One way, then, of viewing the special contribution of the Enlightenment is to see its sustained effort at bringing together these distinct philosophical approaches into one unified methodology. The *Philosophes* believed that they had synthesized the best elements of both philosophical movements. Empirical philosophy had a very profound impact upon their thinking and from that standpoint the influence of John Locke, the great exponent of empiricism, was almost as great as that of Newton. Since Locke's work tended to challenge certain prevailing ideas and since later his own approach was to be challenged by others, it will be useful to review briefly his theory of the origin of ideas.

In his famous *Essay Concerning Human Understanding* Locke held, in opposition to certain of his contemporaries, that ideas are not innate in the human mind. Quite the contrary, at birth the mind is a *tabula rasa*—that is, in a blank and empty state; only through experience do ideas enter it. The function of the mind is to collect the impressions and materials provided by the senses. In this view, the role of the mind is essentially a passive one, with little or no creative or organizing function. Clearly, this lent great support to the empirical and experimental methods: knowledge could be increased only by extending the experiences of the senses. Moreover, Locke further supported the scientists' method of focusing on measurable qualities, and ignoring the other aspects of the things they were investigating, by advancing a classification of the qualities of matter into primary and secondary: extension, number, and motion could be directly and immediately experienced; on the other hand, color and sound had no existence outside of the observer's mind. Subsequently, Locke's epistemology led to idealism and skepticism among English philosophers and to materialism among the French.

In England, Bishop Berkeley, for example, argued that Locke's distinction between "primary" and "secondary" was a very dubious and tenuous one; neither of these qualities had any existence apart from the perceiver's mind. This was tantamount to saying that matter does not exist—or at least that there was no way of proving the existence of matter. Indeed, Berkeley insisted that only spirit exists and that this spirit is God. Thus spirit, the subject of religion, was defended by attacking matter, the subject of science. A further step was taken by David Hume: the mind could know nothing outside itself; all human knowledge of the external world is therefore impossible. Hume's work will be discussed in a later context since it was at this point that Immanuel Kant began his own philosophical system.

Among many French philosophers, in contrast, Locke's ideas were translated into scientific materialism—a development probably related to the rigid and capricious absolutism in France and its support of the Church. Materialism appeared as an effective ideological weapon against Church dogma. Condillac expounded and elaborated Locke's theory of the origin of knowledge. The most thoroughgoing in this respect was Holbach who rejected all spiritual causes and reduced consciousness and thought to the movement of molecules within the material body. While Helvetius, Holbach, and La Mettrie became exponents of materialism, Condillac, though accepting Locke's theory in most of its essentials, introduced important modifications whose implications Kant was later to develop even further. Describing Condillac's view, Cassirer writes that from the simplest sense data which the mind receives, it "gradually acquires the capacity to focus its attention on them, to compare and distinguish, to separate and combine them." (p. 18.) Condillac thus attributes something of a creative and active role to the mind; knowledge is somewhat mediated by the mind and its reasoning powers. If Locke's theory implied a passive role on the part of the observer—merely receiving sensory impressions, with the mind not playing any active role in their organization—Condillac now argues that once the power of thought and reasoning is awakened in man, he is no longer passive, and no longer merely adapts himself to the existing order. Now thought is able to advance even against social reality "summoning it before the tribunal of thought and challenging its legal titles to truth and validity. And society must submit to being treated like physical reality under investigation." (p. 18.) Sociology is to become a science whose method, states Condillac in his *Treatise on Sensation*, "consists in teaching us to recognize in society an 'artificial body' composed of parts exerting a reciprocal influence on one another." Condillac thus assigned a decisive role to judgment and reason even in the simplest act of perception; and this was true whether one was perceiving the natural world or the social world. The senses in themselves could never produce the world as we know it in our consciousness; the cooperation of the mind is an absolute necessity.

It should be clear, then, why the Enlightenment is a most logical point of departure if one is interested in the origins of sociological theory. It is in that period that one may see more consistently than before the emergence of the scientific method. Reason in itself will not yield a knowledge of reality; neither will observation and experimentation alone yield such knowledge. Knowledge of reality, whether natural or social, depends on the unity of reason and observation in the scientific method. The Enlightenment thinkers were as interested in society and history as they were in nature, and these were treated as an indivisible unity. By studying nature—including the nature of man—one could learn not only about what *is*, but about what is *possible;* likewise, by studying society and history one could learn not only about the workings of the existing factual order, but about its inherent possibilities. These thinkers were "negative" in that they were always critical of the existing order which, in their view, stifled man's potential and did not allow the possible to emerge from the "is." The existing factual order was studied scientifically by these men in order to learn how to transcend it. These premises, as will be seen, were either accepted, modified, or rejected in the subsequent development of *sociological* thought. In these terms, much of Western sociology developed as a reaction to the Enlightenment. But before examining this reaction, it would be well to consider two *Philosophes,* Montesquieu and Rousseau, who may be regarded as the forerunners of sociological theory.

2

Montesquieu

(1689–1755)

With the exception of Giovanni Vico, who exerted no influence
on the Enlightenment (and who remained relatively unknown
outside Italy until his name was discovered by Jules Michelet in
1824), it was Montesquieu who made the first attempt in modern
times at constructing a philosophy of society and history. Vico
had read Francis Bacon and simultaneously with the *Philosophes,*
and apparently independently of them, had decided it ought to
be possible to apply to the study of human society and history
the method advocated by Bacon for the study of the natural
world. In 1725, Vico wrote and published a work informed by
this point of view: *Principles of a New Science Dealing with the
Nature of Nations, Through Which Are Shown Also New Principles of the Natural Law of Peoples.* "The nature of things,"
wrote Vico, "is nothing other than that they come into being
at certain times and in certain ways. Wherever the same circumstances are present, the same phenomena arise and no others."[1]
Thus Vico perceived order, regularity, and perhaps even causation in the natural world; and this, he believed, was equally true
of the social realm: *"the social world is certainly the work of
men;* and it follows that one can and should find its principles
in the modifications of the human intelligence itself. Governments

[1] Edmund Wilson, *To The Finland Station* (Garden City, New York:
Doubleday and Company, Inc., 1940), p. 3.

must be conformable to the nature of the governed; governments are even a result of that nature."[2] Nonetheless, human progress and the perfectibility of man in the secular realm, the central ideas of the Enlightenment, are nowhere expressed in Vico's writings. He remained essentially medieval and theological in his outlook and viewed improvement and salvation as dependent on the grace of God. Though he saw successive phases of development, these were cyclical and repetitive rather than progressive in the Enlightenment sense.

Montesquieu, on the other hand, was a true son of his age, for he had thoroughly emancipated himself from the medieval heritage.[3] His concern with regularities was more in keeping with the modern conception; he sought the *laws* of social and historical development and this was his main purpose in studying the social facts. Facts are studied not for their own sake but for the laws which become manifest through them. In his preface to his *Spirit of the Laws,* Montesquieu wrote: "I began to examine men and I believed that in the infinite variety of their laws and customs they were not guided solely by their whims. I formulated principles, and then I saw individual cases fitting these principles as if of themselves, the history of all nations being only the consequence of these principles and every special law bound to another law, or depending on another more general law." Particular facts become the medium through which he hopes to gain an understanding of general forms and tendencies. In putting forward his conception of these forms, he becomes the first thinker to utilize consistently in his analysis of society and history the construct we today call "ideal-types." His major work, *Spirit of the Laws,* and all his other writings to a somewhat lesser extent, is an analysis based on political and sociological types. This was an indispensable intellectual tool by means of which one could make sense out of an otherwise incomprehensible welter of facts.

There are forms of government called republic, aristocracy, monarchy, and despotism; these are not aggregates of accidentally acquired properties. Rather, they express certain underlying social structures. These structures remain hidden so long as we merely observe political and social phenomena, so long as we merely observe the facts. These seem so complex and varied that they appear to defy understanding. Yet, understanding becomes possible, writes Cassirer describing Montesquieu's conception, "as soon as we learn to go back from appearances to principle, from the diversity of empirical shapes to the forming forces. Now we recognize among many instances of republics the *type* of republic, and among the countless monarchies of history we find

2 *Ibid.,* p. 3.

3 In the present discussion I rely, in addition to primary sources, on Cassirer's work cited earlier and the following: John Plamenatz, *Man and Society* (London: Longmans, Green and Co., Ltd., 1963) ; Emile Durkheim, *Montesquieu and Rousseau* (Ann Arbor: The University of Michigan Press, 1960) ; Werner Stark, *Montesquieu: Pioneer of the Sociology of Knowledge* (London: Routledge and Kegan Paul Ltd., 1960) .

the type of the monarchy."[4] What are the principles underlying the types? The republic rests on civic virtue; monarchy depends on honor, and despotism on fear. Again this is proposed in an ideal-typical sense. No actual political form will conform precisely to its ideal qualities; but possibly these qualities enable us to study the actual forms.

Montesquieu views all the institutions making up a society as having an interdependent and correlative relationship to one another and as depending on the form of the whole. Education and justice, forms of marriage and the family, and political institutions have not only a reciprocal influence but depend on the basic form of the state; and the character of the state in turn rests upon these aspects of society. While Montesquieu's ideal-types are static forms employed in the study of social structures, he has no doubt of their usefulness for the study of process. If the study of a society discloses a certain interdependence among its elements, and if a number of societies have so much in common that they may be classed under the same type, then the functioning processes of these societies may also reveal certain similar, characteristic tendencies. These processes and the fate of peoples are not determined by accidents. In his study of Roman civilization, for example, he proposed to show that there are cultural as well as physical causes that bring about the rise, maintenance, and fall of systems of power and even civilizations. Although much has been made of Montesquieu's attention to physical conditions like climate, soil, etc., he sees these as primarily limiting factors and assigns to them much less importance than socio-cultural variables in determining the forms of government, laws, and other institutions.

Montesquieu was perhaps the most objective of all the *Philosophes*. He was so interested in the "facts" that Condorcet once remarked that Montesquieu would have done better if he had not been "more occupied with finding the reasons for that which is than with seeking that which ought to be."[5] Having made a rather careful and empirical study of past and contemporary societies to determine the causes of the variety of institutions, he concluded that there is no single government which is universally suitable. Political institutions must conform to the peculiarities of the society for which they are intended. If he differed from his contemporaries it was in the moderation so evident in his work and in his insistence that one cannot legislate for all men and all places on the assumption of universally applicable laws. He did not hesitate to point out virtues as well as faults in all forms of government. His conspicuous moderation and objectivity provided all parties on the political spectrum with arguments supporting their respective positions.

Though he may have been somewhat less critical than his contemporaries, he nonetheless shared their ideal of human freedom. However, here too he

---

[4] Ernst Cassirer, *The Philosophy of the Enlightenment* (Princeton: Princeton University Press, 1951), pp. 210–11.

[5] Carl Becker, *The Heavenly City of the Eighteenth-Century Philosophers* (New Haven: Yale University Press, 1932), p. 101.

deviates somewhat in his approach. One of his major concerns was power and its relation to freedom. Power should be distributed among the individuals and groups of a society so as to ensure maximal freedom. Men are not free because they have natural rights, or because they revolt if oppression becomes unbearable; they are free to the extent that power is distributed and organized so as to prevent, or at least minimize, its abuse. Liberty is best preserved where interest groups or organized publics check one another as well as the government, and where laws provide for such checks.

Throughout his life, he retained an insatiable curiosity about other countries and cultures; and his comparative approach to society and culture was in a large part based upon his own travels as well as those recounted by others.[6] When he was not actually traveling he fancied himself to be. For example, when he wrote and published his *Persian Letters* in 1721, it was for comparative methodological reasons. Two traveling Persians were writing to their friend at home and giving their impressions of France as a foreign culture. In this way, Montesquieu could at least in his imagination adopt another perspective and view French institutions through foreigners' eyes. This was a way of illustrating the variety and relativity of man's institutions. Though he had never actually traveled outside of Europe, he did visit in 1728–29, Germany, Austria, Italy, Holland, and, finally, England where he stayed about two years. His English experience was to influence him profoundly, for he remained throughout his life quite impressed with the English political system, particularly the constitutional separation of powers. When he returned to France, he prepared his chief work, *The Spirit of the Laws,* and then a second one, *Considerations on the Greatness and Decadence of the Romans,* published in 1734. When his *Spirit of the Laws* finally appeared in 1748 it met with immediate and almost universal enthusiasm in European intellectual circles. The new questions he asked and the new assumptions he employed, together with his obvious attempt at maintaining objectivity, earned him a reputation of originality. This latter quality had already become evident in his first work, the *Persian Letters,* where for the first time, perhaps, many institutions of a European society were examined from the standpoint of an outsider.

His book on the Romans was also quite innovative, since he studied Roman society and institutions not merely to describe them but in order to put forward a theory that might account for the rise, development, and decay of Roman civilization. Roman institutions are treated as functionally interdependent and interrelated elements of a complex system. Rome's victories and conquests are explained as the effects of specific social and political conditions. Her success, which required changes in the political structure, led inevitably to decline and, finally, to collapse. The final collapse is viewed as a

6 For these and other biographical details, see John Plamenatz, *op. cit.,* p. 253 *ff.*

consequence of the initial success which so transformed the whole structure of society as to destroy the very conditions which made for success.

Montesquieu viewed the social institutions of a society as intimately connected; even forms of thought were considered in their relation to those institutions. Since he was among the first to take this approach, he may be regarded as a founder of the subdiscipline called the sociology of knowledge.[7] He looked at a people not as a multitude of individuals but as a society which could be distinguished from others by its customs and institutions, variables so intricately connected that a significant change in one is bound to affect the others. Political, economic, and other institutions are viewed as aspects of a people's life related to still other aspects. And the focus is most often on the social rather than the nonsocial. Some traditional interpretations notwithstanding, Montesquieu was not a climatic or geographical determinist. Climate and geography, which he did indeed take into account, are treated as extra-social conditions which impose certain limits, at least temporarily, on a given society. The limiting effect of these conditions is regarded as temporary and variable because the further a particular people is from nature, that is, the more developed its institutions and technology, the less is the influence of these nonsocial conditions.

"Spirit" for Montesquieu refers to the distinctive character of a system of laws. The way these are related to one another and to other aspects of a people's life distinguishes one society from another. Although he is interested in the origins of institutions, this is less important than their functions or consequences, as is evident in his thesis about the rise and fall of the Romans.

His sociology of knowledge, however rudimentary, anticipates many, if not all, of the major postulates about a society and its consciousness. There is an intimate relationship between these aspects of a people's life, between thinking and doing. How one views the customs and ideas of a society depends on the social position one occupies and hence on the cultural perspective one adopts. That Montesquieu understands this is clear from the reactions of his Persian travelers. They begin to doubt their own customs and ideology as soon as they leave their own society; and the longer they are in Europe, the less strange do the new customs appear. He posited the social genesis of ideas, and the functional interdependence of social action and ideas; and while, at times, he invokes physical causes, too, these are generally subordinate to sociocultural conditions. He was more aware than most of his contemporaries of the human "cultural variety."

He posited a constant, ubiquitous nature in man which is modified by the specific culture; and within a given society and culture, the position one occupies in the division of labor—occupations and professions—tends to determine one's character as well as one's outlook on life. As will be seen in a later discussion, however, Montesquieu is not always consistent; for he

---

7 See Werner Stark, *op. cit.,*

occasionally speaks of laws of nature which he regards as eternal and universal. Men must try to discover these laws and truths and bring their society into harmony with them. This is an ideal which can be approached but never attained. For man, even with the sharpest of reasoning powers, cannot know these truths because of error and ignorance. Man's limited perspectives—the particular position from which he views the world—and his special interests make error and ignorance unavoidable. Much later, as we shall see, Mannheim was to suggest some possible ways in which the limited perspectives could be enlarged and transcended; certain groups in society were potentially capable of overcoming, at least partially, the limitations of their standpoint.

Montesquieu, then, may definitely be regarded as a forerunner of sociological theory and method. His consistent concern with laws of development and his utilization of the ideal-type construct were something of an innovation in his time in comparison with the methods of his predecessors and contemporaries. If he is therefore regarded as an important forerunner, this is meant in the sense of his having delineated the subject matter of sociology and of having pioneered in the sketching out of a method. This is the sense in which Émile Durkheim referred to Montesquieu as a *précurseur*.[8] A closer look at Montesquieu's work is necessary in order to see that the attention given him is altogether warranted.

The study of "reality," Montesquieu understood, is an enormously complicated enterprise involving many difficult problems. One of the tasks of science is to describe the realities with which it deals; but if these realities differ among themselves to such a degree that they cannot be classified or subsumed under types, then they truly defy rational comprehension. If there were nothing generally discernible about these realities, they would have to be considered one by one and independently of one another; but since each individual phenomenon involves an infinite number of properties, this would be a hopeless and impossible task. In short, without classification and without typologies, science is impossible and, of course, so is a science of human phenomena.

Was this not understood before Montesquieu? Yes, indeed, but to a very limited extent. Aristotle, for example, did indeed employ the concept of type but confined it to political states. Moreover, even if two societies differed greatly but both were ruled by kings, he was satisfied to classify them as monarchies. His types therefore tell us little about the nature of a specific *society* and its system of government. Aristotle established a tradition in this respect and was followed by a great number of philosophers who adopted his classification and made no attempt to modify it or provide another. As Durkheim had observed, these philosophers "thought it impossible to compare

---

[8] Émile Durkheim, *Montesquieu and Rousseau* (Ann Arbor: The University of Michigan Press, 1960).

human societies in any respect other than the form of the state. The other factors, morality, religion, economic life, the family, etc., . . . seemed so fortuitous and variable that no one thought of reducing them to types. Yet these factors have a strong bearing upon the nature of societies; they are the actual stuff of life and consequently the subject matter of social science."[9] Precisely because Montesquieu did give attention to the "actual stuff of life," and employ the ideal-type method to comprehend it, his work may be regarded as innovative to a significant and conspicuous degree.

Science, however, requires more than description and classification; it involves interpretation and explanation. These processes presuppose a determinate order in phenomena, such as causal relationships. What is perceived as happening is neither arbitrary nor fortuitous; neither is interpretation the imposition of a wholly subjective order—an order existing only in the mind— upon a reality essentially chaotic and erratic—in short, orderless. This, too, was a basic assumption which guided Montesquieu in his social analysis. In his major work, *Spirit of the Laws*, he not only describes the laws, customs, and other diverse practices of a number of peoples, but attempts also to uncover the origins and causes for being of specific institutions. He does not primarily evaluate but rather tries to understand; thus he suggests the conditions which made possible polygamy, "false religions" and slavery. These may even have been necessary, he believes, under the conditions he observed. Though he tries to be objective, he is also anxious to make recommendations which appear to flow from his analysis. Democracy, he observes, is suited only to small states; therefore, he adds, a democracy should refrain from overextending its frontiers.

Montesquieu's use of the ideal-type differs in still another respect from that of his predecessors. His types make no pretense of transcending time and place. He recognized that the customs, laws, and other institutions of societies vary with other conditions of their existence. He saw certain general types, *e.g.*, monarchy, but saw, too, that specific monarchies vary according to time and place. Therefore, rules could never be valid for all societies or for all peoples. He was as mindful of the constants as of the variables. Regardless of the particular form of a society, the nature of man requires that certain basic needs be met.

Montesquieu's Classification of Societies

When Montesquieu speaks of a republic (including aristocracy and democracy), a monarchy, or a despotism, these terms refer to whole societies, not just to political systems as is the case with Aristotle. Also, these types are not derived from an a priori principle but are founded on observation. His study

9 *Ibid.,* p. 9.

of a large number of societies, his study of history and travelers' accounts, and his own travels, all serve as comparative empirical material for his classification and the conclusions he draws. When he talks for instance about "republic" he has in mind the Greek and Italian city-states—Athens, Sparta, and Rome. Mainly, he is trying to show that there is a definite relationship between political systems and other social and nonsocial conditions. Monarchy is suited to the conditions of the large nations of modern Europe. The peoples of antiquity also had "kings"; the Greeks, the Germans, and the Latins, for example. But these impressed him as quite different from the absolute monarch of modern Europe upon which he based his ideal-type. Forms of despotism have also been known to exist in various places and periods, often resulting from corruption of other political forms. Nonetheless, despotism had its "natural" or "perfect" existence only in the Orient. Thus when he puts forward his types, he is intent upon showing that these are to be distinguished from one another not only as different systems of government but because these systems are functionally interrelated with other conditions. Among the latter, he includes for example, the population size of a society, the distribution of the people in a society, and its structure.

The republican form, he argues, has been found in towns and cities and is best suited to a small population. When numbers grow beyond a certain point, the republican form breaks down. The despotic state, on the other hand, is found in large societies and is spread over vast areas, especially in Asia. And the monarchical state stands in between: it is of medium size, having a population larger than that of the republic but smaller than that of the despotic state. More importantly, however, these are distinguished with regard to their respective social structures. All citizens are equal, and even alike, in a republic; and this is particularly true of a democracy. A kind of social homogeneity, and hence order is evident. There are definite restrictions on excessive accumulation of wealth and power which, it is suspected, might undermine the solidarity and the very existence of the republic. Thus democracy can become debased by transforming itself into an aristocracy, and the more democratic the republic, the more "perfect" it is. In a democracy, the common welfare of all is emphasized. A democratic republic, then, is relatively small, equalitarian, and homogeneous and is characterized by solidarity.

In a monarchy social classes have emerged. Farming, trade, and industry, and an increasingly complex division of labor in general make for a complex system of stratification which was absent from the republic but now reaches its maximal development in the monarchy. Yet, it is here and not in the democracy that Montesquieu envisions maximal political freedom. Classes check and limit not only the power of the monarch but one another as well. Each prevents the other from becoming too powerful and is thus free to pursue its special interests, but in moderation. Since the monarchy is structurally complex, composed of classes and groups with varying degrees of wealth, power, and prestige, personal interest, envy, rivalry, and class interest as well emerge as strong forces. Individuals and groups now tend to disregard the general welfare of society in favor of personal and class interests. In this way Montesquieu anticipates the utilitarian doctrine, for he argues that class and personal rivalry lead the members of society to perform their respective functions as well as possible and that this conduces ultimately to the common good. Honor, too, becomes a major incentive in the public life of a monarchy as men seek to raise their status as high as possible.

Finally there is the third type, despotism. Either all orders of the society have become so weakened that they can offer no organized resistance to the despot, or the regime becomes a "democracy" in which all but the ruler are equal in their condition of servitude. If *virtue* is the basis for participation in the republic, and *honor* is such a basis in a monarchy, then *fear* is the basis for submission to a despot.

Thus Montesquieu distinguished different types of *society,* differing in many important aspects. He gave as much attention to the differences among societies as to their similarities. The reasoning underlying his classification is still cogent today. He understood that the growth in complexity of the economic and social structures, the growth of differentials in wealth, the emergence of strata, etc. forced changes in the political structure. He grasped the fact that a republic like ancient Athens or Rome, where private property was little developed, would logically exhibit the high degree of social solidarity found there; and that a modern society, characterized by a complex division of labor, classes, and special interest groups, would exhibit less. Each now draws a sharper distinction between himself and his special interest group on the one hand and society on the other. Social solidarity to the extent that it exists in the modern society springs from a different source. It no longer depends on equality and sameness, but precisely upon the division of labor which makes individuals and groups mutually interdependent. Later, Durkheim borrows this idea from Saint-Simon (who in turn borrowed it from Montesquieu) and develops his own classification of types of society and their corresponding types of solidarity.

Before concluding the discussion of Montesquieu's classification of societies, attention should be drawn to a fourth type he presented. There are societies that live by hunting or cattle raising. Typically, these have small populations and hold the land in common. Conduct is regulated by custom, not laws. The elders have supreme authority but they are so jealous of their freedom that they tolerate no lasting power. This is further divided by Montesquieu into two subtypes: savages and barbarians. Savages are generally hunters living in small, relatively nonsedentary societies, while barbarians raise cattle, live in larger societies, and are relatively sedentary. These distinctions are still tenable and useful today in studying nonliterate and traditional societies. This fourth type, in particular, shows clearly that Montesquieu did not merely take over Aristotle's classification but produced an original system.

Montesquieu's Conception of Laws

As was stated at the outset, Montesquieu's originality with respect to sociology lies basically in two areas: his classification of societies into types, which enabled him to compare them in all their important aspects; and his concern with "laws," that is, the necessary relations arising from the nature of things. Laws do not apply only to nature but also to human societies. In the social realm, laws depend on the form of a society; thus the laws of a republic differ from those of a monarchy. Forms of society in turn depend on certain conditions—a major one being the "volume of society."[10] The republic, as we have seen, has a small population and is confined to relatively narrow limits. The affairs of the community are known to every citizen. Since differentials in wealth are small or nonexistent, conditions are approximately the same for all citizens. Even the leaders of the community have very limited authority and are viewed as first among equals. But if the volume of the society increases—population grows and the geographical limits are widened—all aspects of the society will change accordingly. The individual can no longer perceive the whole society; he tends to see only the interests of his special interest group or class. Increasing stratification gives rise to divergent viewpoints and objectives; and great differentials in private property give rise to great inequality in political power. The leader is now a sovereign who stands far above everyone else. As these changes have occurred, the society has inevitably evolved from a republican to a monarchical form of government. If these developments continue in the same direction, monarchy will yield to despotism which is now necessary to control the masses.

Montesquieu thus sees the structure of and any changes in a society determined by demographic and social variables. The growth in population of a society and the expansion of its geographical limits, a key variable, will force changes in all its other aspects. Although the growing division of labor and the growth of private property (and the resultant greater differentials in wealth) accompany the transition from the republican to the monarchical type of society and seem to be functionally interdependent, the volume of a society appears to Montesquieu as the chief cause of these changes. This is an emphasis which Durkheim later adopts as his own.

Traditional interpretations of Montesquieu's theory have neglected his recognition of the social variables and have drawn attention instead to others: geography, topography, fertility of the soil, climate, proximity to (or remoteness from) the sea, and the like. Montesquieu recognized all these factors as limiting influences upon the structure of a society; they are the differing "constants" that by their presence or absence orient a society in a particular direction. But these factors remained less important in Montesquieu's mind than the social variables.

10 This concept, and others to be discussed later in the chapter on Durkheim, show just how great was his intellectual debt to Montesquieu.

A "sociological" approach is taken toward all the institutions of a society and is applied to an analysis of custom and law. Custom has certain definite social correlates which are different from those of law. Customs emerge spontaneously from social existence; laws, on the other hand, are established by a lawgiver in a formal and explicit fashion. In the latter case, the "law" emerges spontaneously, too. The more complex social structure seems to require certain definite laws most appropriate to that structure. But these would remain hidden and implicit, Montesquieu believed, if some lawgiver had not discerned them and formulated them explicitly. These laws may nevertheless be at variance with the requirements of a certain society because what the nature of a society requires is a matter of judgment. Men have the ability to deviate from that nature because their judgments are subject to ignorance and error. An element of contingency is thus introduced. A society would be what its nature prescribes were it not for the ignorance and errors of those interpreting what these prescriptions are.

Montesquieu's conception of law as expressing the necessary relation among things retains ambiguous elements. He seems to believe that by studying a society one can discover its laws (what its nature requires) and therefore create legal forms and other institutions which best suit that nature. The creation of these institutions involves interpretation of what a society's true nature is, and therefore is subject to error. In the absence of this element of contingency—ignorance and/or error—man would devise laws in perfect accord with society's nature and, apparently, this would be good. Man's life in society would be wholly determined, and the elements of society would be perfectly articulated and integrated. The elements of contingency which Montesquieu introduces seem to imply that man can never achieve such perfect articulation. Moreover, these elements lead to no small deviations from the natural laws. For example, though the institution of slavery was present in all the ancient Greek and Italian republics, Montesquieu insists that this institution is repugnant to the nature of republics. If men had not made mistakes in interpreting this nature, slavery would not have emerged. In a republic, slavery is not natural and therefore not necessary. On what does Montesquieu base his judgment? Apparently upon the ideal republic he had in his head. Slavery may be the necessary result of certain social conditions but one of these conditions is the misinterpretation by man of the true nature and requirements of a republic. This true nature, which expresses not what is but what ought to be, has remained hidden from the view of society's members. Montesquieu's social laws, then, sometimes are, and sometimes are not, like other laws of nature, inherent in phenomena. Laws in the social realm are sometimes *above* the phenomena, where they remain unrecognized and therefore inoperative.

The ambiguity in Montesquieu's conception of "laws" seems to flow from his recognition of certain degrees of freedom in man. Men are not mindless creatures adapting themselves passively and automatically to existing conditions. Montesquieu seemed to understand at least intuitively that men also act upon the conditions of their environment and change them. This action involves an interpretation of what those conditions are and therefore, being subject to ignorance and error, men very often bring about conditions which are contrary to their nature. However, the degrees of freedom which enabled men to institute slavery—which is contrary to the true nature of a republic—also enable them, once having recognized their mistake, to eliminate it.

To summarize, Montesquieu appears to have seen two kinds of laws—both "natural"—one of the physical world and the other of human life. The first works itself out automatically, "naturally." The second refers to the "laws of nature of human life" which ought to regulate the affairs of men. But acting in accordance with these laws is virtually impossible due to the unavoidably limited perspectives of men in their respective social positions, and due, also, to the fact that men's acts are not totally determined. Montesquieu postulates a few small degrees of freedom: it is in the nature of men to act of themselves.[11]

Experience and observation are important for Montesquieu; and more than any of his contemporaries he subordinates deduction to these processes. Yet, as outstanding as he was in anticipating the method of social science, he more often than not sets down the facts briefly and summarily without taking pains to verify them even when they are controversial. He was too credulous, for example, of travelers' reports which were extremely unreliable. Moreover, as Durkheim observed, when " . . . he asserts that there is a causal relation between two facts, he does not trouble to show that in all or at least most cases they appear simultaneously, disappear simultaneously, or vary in the same way."[12] Sometimes his types are defined by a single characteristic observed in one society. For instance, being a great admirer of the English constitution, he treats the separation of powers, found in England alone, as essential to a monarchy. English liberty, he believed, was a result of the constitutional separation of executive, legislative, and judicial authority. Apparently he did not see the role of the revolutions of the seventeenth century in establishing the supremacy of Parliament over the executive and the judiciary.

It is, no doubt, always a mistake to trace the birth of certain ideas to a particular thinker. Nevertheless, because he used the concepts of ideal-type and laws with more consistency than any of his antecedents or contemporaries, because he understood the need for comparative studies, and because he advanced the assumption that the elements of a society are functionally interdependent, Montesquieu may be regarded as an important forerunner of sociological thinking.

11 See Werner Stark, *op. cit.*, p. 210.
12 Durkheim, *op. cit.*, p. 53.

3

Rousseau

(1712–1778)

Rousseau was very much of an Enlightenment thinker and shared with his contemporaries several pre-Revolutionary premises and ideals. It would be wrong to interpret Rousseau's concern with the "state of nature" as evidence of a yearning for that lost condition to which men must return in order to regain their freedom and happiness. For Rousseau, man's freedom remained a fundamental ideal but one which was not to be attained by shaking off all society and civilization or by reverting to a so-called natural state. The perfectibility of man, his freedom and his happiness, and the increasing mastery of his own fate, all depended on a clear understanding of the laws of nature. In common with the other *Philosophes,* Rousseau believed that nature and society worked according to such laws; and like Montesquieu, he believed that society could depart from the requirements of its natural laws. Men act of themselves; it is they who must interpret these laws. Because of limited perspectives and insufficient knowledge, they err—*i.e.,* they act contrary to their nature by establishing a social order that violates their basic nature. Rousseau's chief objective, therefore, was to find a social order whose laws were in greatest harmony with the fundamental laws of nature. He sought an alternative to the prevailing order which, to his mind, precluded man's perfectibility and even deformed and violated his nature.

, then, there were two conditions, the natural and the social; chasm between them was already very great, they could be reconciled. To accomplish this, one must always keep al aspects of man. In order to assert that the social order ith man's nature, one must know something about that ____. how can one speak of social man doing violence to natural man unless one really knows something about natural man? And how can one know "natural man" when men nowhere live outside of society? It was precisely with the purpose of addressing himself to these questions that Rousseau postulated man in a "state of nature." This was a hypothetical construct, a heuristic device, by which man would be theoretically divested of his social and cultural aspects. This would yield a concept of natural man which could serve as a kind of yardstick by which to measure the degree of repression imposed by a specific society. Or, what amounts to the same thing, it could serve as a relatively objective, nonideological means by which to measure the degree of perfection and freedom offered by a specific "civil state." If one could determine how men departed from their natural condition and how they imposed upon themselves a social order at variance with that condition, then, perhaps, one could know better how to change that order and replace it with a better one.

The State of Nature

In the development of this concept, Rousseau is engaged in a very imaginative thinking experiment; but the concept also rests, as will be seen, on an experiential basis. He knew that there was no such state in which men lived before and outside society; in their "pre-social" state men were not men. He says clearly that it is a state "which no longer exists, which perhaps never did exist, and probably never will exist; and of which it is, nevertheless necessary to have true ideas in order to form a proper judgment of our present state."[1] "Natural man" is simply man divested of what he has acquired in society. Think away all his social qualities and the residue is bio-psychological man, or man reduced to what he might have been if he had actually lived in isolation. That this idea is being used in a strictly heuristic sense becomes clear when he insists that his description of natural man should not be taken as historical truth but as a hypothetical condition. Speculation about the primitive state may throw some light on the basic nature of man.

Even savages yield a very inaccurate picture of the state of nature, for despite their primitive condition they are quite remote from that state. Therefore, Rousseau argues, those who have imputed to natural man cruel and warlike tendencies are wrong: they have attributed to natural man character-

[1] Jean Jacques Rousseau, *The Social Contract and Discourses,* translated with an introduction by G. D. H. Cole (New York: E. P. Dutton and Company, Inc., 1950) , p. 191.

istics acquired in society. How then does one acquire an adequate conception of the hypothetical state? Fully realizing how complex a problem this was, he asked: *"What experiments would have to be made to discover the natural man? And how are those experiments to be made in a state of society?"*[2]

Such experiments would be extremely difficult if not impossible. Therefore he suggests some alternative techniques with which to approach the problem. One can observe animals in their natural habitat to gain insight into natural behavior uninfluenced by society. Secondly, one can study primitive peoples— savages—keeping in mind that they have acquired considerable socio-cultural baggage. Finally, one could deduce all the factors implied by man's subsequent social development, such as language, and think them away. Rousseau thus sought an objective, nonideological yardstick by which to evaluate society.

If we know something about man's real nature, he reasoned, we can ask whether or not certain historical societies have been suited to this nature. If it is concluded that a particular social order is unsuited, and we therefore decide to change or replace it, an analysis of natural man must provide the principles by which to guide the process of change. In order that these principles be as free from ideology as possible, we must arrive at this "natural man" by putting aside all those elements which have been implanted in man as a result of his social existence. Otherwise, our judgments would be purely ideological, *i.e.*, we would simply be justifying what we desire and condemning what we do not, and in both cases the judgment would be based on the special position and interests we have in the society. In such a case one would be demonstrating one prejudice by another—an error Rousseau observed in others and wanted to avoid. Hobbes, for example, had, in Rousseau's view, invested his "natural men" with very social qualities indeed.

Rousseau's method therefore required that one subtract all the qualities of socio-cultural origin until only the "natural foundation" remained. In his "state of nature," then, Rousseau was not describing a lost golden age; rather, he was proposing a methodological device by which one might lay bare the components of man's basic psychological makeup. In more recent times, too, similar approaches have been taken: Freud, for example, having employed some premises about man's basic nature, concluded that there is an irremediable antagonism between natural man and civilized man. Marx, on the other hand, as we shall see, also based his theory on a conception of natural man. "Species-being," an idea derived from Feuerbach, resembles in some ways Rousseau's notion that there is a natural man and that the best social system is that which enables him to realize his potentialities to the fullest. Man is perfectible and social systems should be judged by the degree to which they facilitate his perfection. Clearly, if such evaluative judgments are to be made about particular societies most objectively and least ideologi-

2 *Ibid.,* p. 191.

cally, then some relatively precise conception of natural man is required. This is the task that Rousseau set himself when he advanced his ideal construct, the "state of nature."

How does Rousseau conceive of this ideal state which is to provide insight into man's basic psychological nature? It is a perfect balance between man's needs and the resources at his disposal. He desires and needs only what is to be found in his immediate physical environment. Like other animals, he has only sensations, but no knowledge and no language. Accepting Condillac's theory that general, abstract knowledge is impossible without language, Rousseau postulates that since language is the product of society, one can safely conclude that man in nature has neither language nor knowledge. His needs are extremely simple and purely physical—food, a mate, and rest; he cannot conceive of the future and is oriented exclusively to the present. Harmony is achieved between his internal nature and external nature through satisfaction of all his needs; conditions for discord are wholly lacking. Then what, if any, is the relation among humans? Certainly not a state of war. He rejects the Hobbesian notion of the natural state as a "war of each against all." In part one of his *Discourse on the Origin of Inequality*,[3] Rousseau develops his own view in opposition to Hobbes.

In the primitive, natural state men are isolated from, and indifferent to, one another. The incentive to war, arising from unmet needs, is lacking. If he has what he needs, why should man attack others? Men have no moral or senti- mental bonds, no sense of duty or feeling of sympathy; each man lives for himself and strives for self-preservation. Rousseau agrees with Hobbes that natural man is egoistic, solitary, and perhaps even brutish; but he disagrees that this results in war. Hobbes had not succeeded in divesting natural man of all the elements he acquired in society. War is a social institution and men learn to make war, Rousseau argued, only in society. Robbery, domination, and violence, are unknown to natural man; not violent subjection of others, but indifference to them, is the rule. Man is withdrawn and tends to live separately. He is, however, capable of sympathy, which is not rooted in his instincts but rather a product of his imagination. Even without knowledge and without language, man has the ability to place himself in the position of another and to sense his feelings; he can empathize with others and to a certain degree feel their sorrows. Not being a wolf to his fellows, however, does not mean that he is inclined to join with them to form a society. He has neither the means nor the need to do so. In the state of nature, then, men are in many respects like other animals: They are neither good nor evil, neither quarrelsome nor domineering. In this state, there is no education, no progress, and no speech; generations follow one another, but sons are no different from their fathers. In short, men do not live in society and have no culture.

3 *Ibid.*, p. 222 *ff.*

At this state a perfect balance exists between man and his physical environment. But changes occur and the balance is upset. This is not bad in Rousseau's view, for it reveals certain previously hidden potentialities in man. It is not society in general which stands opposed to man's nature but a certain kind of society which divides man against himself.

The Origin of Society

The harmonious balance would have prevailed if something in the physical environment had not upset it. Man would never have voluntarily surrendered a perpetual springtime on earth, a paradise of plenty and sunshine. Probably, two developments eventually forced men to come together in society: "In proportion as the human race grew more numerous, men's cares increased. . . ." And "Barren years, long and sharp winters, scorching summers which parched the fruits of the earth, must have demanded a new industry."[4]

Now men had to unite and coordinate their efforts and they could do so because they had the potential for society. They were intelligent and resourceful enough to respond to the challenge; they discovered that they could not only adapt to the changed natural conditions but could also, to an increasing degree, bend these conditions to their own collective will. First families formed and then they banded together to form societies; as they learned to act together they learned to speak, and with speech they acquired the ability to accumulate knowledge and pass it on to their children. Man had invented culture. At this stage there was as yet no social inequality. Such inequalities as did exist were within families and not among them; children were dependent for survival upon parents. This was not a harmful dependence because it was natural and temporary. This was the happiest period for man, for though now capable of vanity and envy, he was also capable of love, loyalty, and the desire to please. For these reasons Rousseau prefers this period to the natural state in which lonely and natural man never experienced such feelings; he prefers it also because men have not yet become masters and slaves.

The cultivation of plants, the domestication of animals, and the division of labor generally, opened the way to all kinds of social inequalities which now appeared for the first time. Some men begin to prosper more than others, accumulate wealth, and pass it on to their children. Once inequalities come into being, they create greater opportunities for the rich than the poor; the rich increasingly dominate the poor who become correspondingly resentful and envious. Strata and classes emerge; society is now for the first time divided against itself. Some of the poor acquiesce in their condition of servitude while others prefer to live by plundering the rich. Insecurity and violence—from which everyone stands to lose, but the rich more than the

---

4 *Ibid.*, p. 236.

poor—are now felt and feared. Under these circumstances, the rich think of a device from which all can benefit, but the rich more than the poor. Laws are instituted and political society comes into being.

Like Locke, then, Rousseau believed that government originated to protect property—ultimately to protect the rich. Rights, obligations, and rules of property, are therefore products of society, as for the first time man learns to act against another, to attack him. War, therefore, is not a conflict of individual men in a state of nature; it is a social phenomenon. Hobbes is wrong, Rousseau argues, to assume that men made society and submitted to a strong central power to escape the war in nature. On the contrary, man makes war as a member of an organized community—his own community against another. He becomes a warrior only after he has become a citizen.

However, aggression and war also emerge within society and this—what later thinkers called class and civil conflict—is the result of social inequalities. Social relations among men, in which some are rich and some poor, in which some dominate and some serve, also give rise to hostility and conflicts among them. It is for the purpose of controlling this war that the civil state is established. This is quite the reverse of Hobbes' view, in which war in the natural state led men to establish a civil state for their mutual security and protection. For Rousseau, in contrast, tranquillity and peace reigned in the natural state, where plenty, not scarcity, was the rule and thus allowed for a perfect equilibrium between man and his environment. It was only after this equilibrium was disturbed and finally upset that men created society. The social condition led to inequality, inequality to war, and war to the civil state.

For Rousseau, man is perfectible, and this distinguishes him from other animals. Perfectibility is possible only through society, but man has this potential already in a state of nature. With society, inequalities come about and the civil state arises. This state is incompatible with natural man because far from allowing for self-fulfillment it repressed and deformed him. Man was prevented from becoming what he "could be" under different *social* conditions.

Rousseau conceives of society at this stage as a new kind of entity. It is a single, definite body distinct from the individuals who compose it; but since only the individual is real and natural, the society is not; it is a product of interaction and interdependence. Since individuals compose it, are its matter and substance so to speak, society can never attain the unity of a natural organism. "It is impossible," says Rousseau, "to prevent each one from having an individual and separate existence and attending to his own needs."[5] Whatever unity society has is a function of mutual need, coercion, and—least often—reason. In the society of unequals which has now arisen, this "mutual need" is highly asymmetrical, even spurious. Rousseau writes: "You need me,

---

[5] Quoted in Durkheim, *Montesquieu and Rousseau* (Ann Arbor: The University of Michigan Press, 1960) , p. 84.

for I am rich and you are poor. Let us therefore make a contract with one another. I will do you the honor to permit you to serve me under the condition that you give me what little you still have left for the trouble I shall take in commanding you."[6]

Since such a relationship involves elements of coercion, Rousseau replies to Hobbes that this "contract" is absurd and unreasonable. Instead of inwardly uniting their individual wills, members are compelled to unite in a society which is inherently unstable and devoid of an ethical foundation.

For authority to have moral value the individual will must freely submit to the general will. Social unity must be founded on liberty; and liberty includes the active submission of the individual to the *general* will—not to another individual or group. But this is far from being the case, Rousseau argues, in society as it is today. Men are not united by reason in liberty; they are divided by artificial inequalities and held together by force. Such a society is contrary to man's nature and hence unreasonable. The prevailing social inequalities have no direct relationship to natural differences—differences of age, health, physical strength, and mental abilities. In society some men enjoy privileges to the detriment of others, some are richer, more respected, and more powerful than others; these differences are not natural. Social institutions and conventions invest certain individuals and groups with a "superiority"; these same individuals and groups, in a state of nature, would not be superior and might even have been inferior. In Rousseau's words, "it is plainly contrary to the law of nature, however defined, that children should command old men, fools, wise men, and that the privileged few should gorge themselves with superfluities, while the starving multitude are in want of the bare necessities of life."[7] The unnatural inequalities, perpetuated by the social institution known as inheritance, soon acquire stability and legitimacy. So man, who began independent and free, now becomes the tool and victim of another. "Man is born free; and everywhere he is in chains."[8]

But if society as it is now constituted violates man's nature, will this be true of every society regardless of its form? Is this inherent in all social organization, in civilization in general? Is there some irremediable antagonism between man's nature and life in society, or can they be reconciled? For Rousseau, the suffering caused by civilization seemed far to outweigh its "grandeur." Since, however, man is reasonable, perhaps the present evils could be eliminated thus leading to a new level of perfection superior even to his original state. The prevailing condition was neither inevitable nor necessary. Rousseau proposed, therefore, to emancipate the individual not by releasing him from society altogether, which he recognized as quite impos-

---

[6] From Rousseau's article, "Économie Politique," *Encyclopédie* (Paris, 1755, vol. v, p. 347). Quoted in Cassirer, *The Philosophy of the Enlightenment* (Princeton: Princeton University Press, 1951), p. 260.

[7] Rousseau, *op. cit.*, p. 272.

[8] *Ibid.*, p. 3.

sible, but by releasing him from a particular form of society. The problem was to find a form of society in which every member would be protected by the united power of the entire political organization and in which each individual, though uniting with others, remains free and equal, obeying nobody but himself. In short, "each man, in giving himself to all, gives himself to nobody; and as there is no associate over which he does not acquire the same right as he yields others over himself, he gains an equivalent for everything he loses, and an increase of force for the preservation of what he has."[9] This is the ideal solution Rousseau proposes in his *Social Contract*.

The Social Contract

The new society, or social contract, enables the individual to be absorbed into the common, general will without losing his own will, because in giving himself to this common will he gives himself to an impersonal force—almost indeed a natural force. When a man submits to it, no immoral dependency results. He loses little or nothing and gains in return the assurance that he will be protected by the full force of society against the encroachment of individuals and groups. He is now a member of a society of equals and has regained an equality not unlike the one he enjoyed in nature—but in a new form and on a higher level. Freedom and equality are now not only preserved but are more perfect than in the state of nature. There is a vast moral difference, Rousseau believed, between subjection to an individual and subjection to the whole community. The general interest is expressed in the fact that all desire the happiness of each. Yet, when Rousseau set about examining the prerequisites of such a society he made many compromises.

In the new society, Rousseau had argued, sovereignty is inalienable and indivisible. In practice, however, he recognized that it was impossible outside a very small community to have democracy without representatives and without the delegation of powers. He understood that the force of government, though it called itself a public force and though it professed to represent the general will, could usurp power and act against the common good. Government is a constant threat to man's freedom and yet it is indispensable; government is the corrupting element in society and threatens continually to undermine the sovereignty of the people. Thus Rousseau's judgments about realizing his good society were not altogether confident and optimistic. If democracy is open to constant threat from the very government it requires, then "aristocracy" may be the best form of government. This seemed to be the best compromise between democracy and monarchy. Aristocracy was to be a government composed of a minority chosen on the basis of age and experience. But even then, those who govern will have to be guided by divine wisdom and patience.

9 *Ibid.,* p. 14.

Even the wisest, most patient, and best of legislators, however, are doomed to failure in the absence of certain preconditions. If legislation is to facilitate the desired profound transformation, then the people for whom it is intended must be neither too young nor too old. In the latter case they are set in their ways and immune to change; and if they are too young, they are not ready for the efforts and discipline required. Then, too, the nation must not be so large that it will lack homogeneity; for where this is lacking, a general will is impossible. Neither must it be so small that it cannot maintain itself. The critical moment must be seized before it passes. "The whole *Social Contract* favors the establishment of a small society on the model of the ancient city-state or the Geneva Republic."[10] Finally, peace and plenty must prevail. Although the role of the legislator is a very important one, his success depends on certain conditions which are at best problematical. Rousseau appears to have believed that the new society will have to wait for some charismatic figure who would emerge in an unpredictable way, quite by accident. If and when this occurred, and if the other objectively necessary conditions were present, success might be possible. On balance, however, he was somewhat pessimistic.

Late in life, when he was asked for some practical advice by the government of Poland and thus had to address himself quite concretely to the question of transforming a society, Rousseau advocated slow change and suggested the institution of several formal democratic mechanisms. Emancipate the serfs, he counsels, only when they prove their fitness for liberty, because men who have been servile cannot become citizens overnight. Do not get rid of the "old" hastily, but change it slowly. The national assembly is to be elected by provincial assemblies; the executive is to be appointed by the legislative; and the king is to have great honor but little power. Finally, those elected are to be closely bound by instructions. In sum, Rousseau sees social change as a deliberate and slow process.[11]

Later, when the French revolutionaries were to turn their attention to Rousseau, they ignored this part of his teachings; and it was only after the Revolution that his emphasis on "organic" change was discovered and elaborated by the Romantic-Conservative Reaction to the Enlightenment and the Revolution.

In conclusion, there are several reasons why Rousseau may be regarded as a forerunner of sociology. As a result of his attention to "natural man" and the methodological device he employed to deduce him, he had an accurate conception of culture—or what man acquires in, through, and from society. Also, he was among the first to address himself in a relatively systematic manner to the origins, forms, and consequences of inequality in society. He saw clearly that the existence of classes and class conflict affected all aspects

10 Durkheim, *op. cit.,* p. 120

11 See John Plamenatz, *Man and Society* (London: Longmans, Green and Co. Ltd., 1963) , pp. 387–88.

of men's lives. Inequality had definite inhuman consequences and led to strife and war within and among societies. Finally, he saw the possibilities of change. There should be a way, he believed, to change or remake the society which man's own action has produced but in which he is not his own master.

PART II

POST
REVOLUTIONARY
THOUGHT

4

The
Romantic-Conservative
Reaction

The philosophy of the Enlightenment, as we have seen, was rooted in the thought of the seventeenth century. The two main philosophical currents of that century—rationalism and empiricism—were synthesized rather successfully by the *Philosophes*, who expressed great confidence in reason and observation as means of solving men's problems. The universe was governed by immutable laws, and man and society could be made better by ordering the social and political environment according to these discoverable laws. These ideas became the foundation of the intellectual movements of the nineteenth century as well but they were modified considerably by romantic and conservative thinkers. They turned away from what they considered to be the naïve optimism and rationalism of the eighteenth century; they did so not only by recognizing the irrational factors in human conduct but by assigning them positive value. Tradition, imagination, feeling, and religion were now regarded as natural and positive. Generally deploring the disorganizing consequences for Europe of the French Revolution, the Romantic and conservative thinkers attributed these consequences to the folly of the revolutionaries, who had uncritically accepted Enlightenment assumptions and had attempted to reorder society according to rational principles alone. In reaction to the eighteenth-century exaltation of reason, then, the nineteenth century extolled instead emotion and imagination, leading to a great revival of religion, poetry, and art. In addition, *the group, the community,* and *the nation* now became important concepts. Historic memories and loyalties were viewed as binding the individual to his nation, a category now elevated to a position of supreme importance. Gone was the cosmopolitanism of the Enlightenment. Increasingly, the nineteenth century turned to the investigation of the origins of existing institutions rather than to their transformation according to rational principles. An historical attitude emerged in which more than ever before institutions were regarded as the product of slow organic development and not of deliberate rational, calculated action.[1]

Although the Romantic movement was in evidence throughout Europe, its form varied from one country to another. In England, and especially in Germany, this movement reflected a strong national reaction to the radicalism of the Enlightenment as expressed in the Revolution and against Napoleonic expansionism. In general, the Enlightenment conception of a rational, mechanistic universe was now rejected. In every field—literature, art, music, philosophy, and religion—an effort was made to free the emotions and the imagination from the austere rules and conventions imposed during the eighteenth century. In religion, the importance of inner experience was restored; and in philosophy, the individual mind was assigned a creative role in shaping the world. It is the philosophical movement, in particular, which is most directly pertinent to our discussion of social theory.

This movement, which began with the work of Rousseau and Hume and was further developed in the philosophy of Immanuel Kant, expressed a shift in emphasis from the mechanistic universe of Newton to the creative character of the personality, and had as its intention the liberation of the mind from purely rationalistic and empirical thinking. Rousseau, as we have seen, though an Enlightenment thinker, departed somewhat from the "typical" standpoint; he was less inclined than his contemporaries to counsel the reconstruction of society according to abstract rational principles alone. Inner moral will, conscience, and convictions are also important if man is to free himself.

The most dramatic break with the Enlightenment, however, was expressed in the work of David Hume.[2] His critical examination of its leading assumptions served to undermine the prevailing faith in the universe as a network of cause-effect relationships. These are far from being immanent in the universe;

---

[1] The present general discussion has been distilled from a variety of sources the most important of which are: C. J. H. Hayes, *Historical Evolution of Modern Nationalism* (Smith, 1931) ; J. H. Randall, *The Making of the Modern Mind* (Houghton Mifflin, 1926) , Chapter 16; G. H. Sabine, *A History of Political Theory* (Holt, 1937) , Chapters 28–30; R. Aris, *History of Political Thought in Germany from 1789–1815* (Macmillan, 1936) ; F. B. Artz, *Reaction and Revolution, 1814–1832* (Harper, 1934) ; and H. H. Clement, *Romanticism in France* (Modern Language Association, 1939) .

[2] See Gladys Bryson, *Man and Society: The Scottish Inquiry of the Eighteenth Century* (Princeton: Princeton University Press, 1945) .

instead, he argued, "causality" is simply an idea, a customary way of thinking. Since phenomenon B follows A, one assumes that B is the effect of A. Hume thus assigned a creative role to the mind by insisting that the mechanistic conception is merely a way of thinking whose relationship to the real world is an open question. In this way, Hume along with other thinkers, notably Leibniz—who accepted the Newtonian conception but saw in it personal, idealistic, and teleological elements—laid the groundwork for Kant's epoch-making philosophy.

With Kant, explicit, consistent, and careful attention was for the first time given to an epistemological question which has continued to occupy philosophers since that time: the role of the mind in the determination of knowledge.[3] Kant insisted that one cannot know the world as it actually is in itself. There are certain patterns like space, time, and causality, which are inherent in the mind; and science describes the universe in terms of these a priori categories. If, therefore, Newton had viewed the universe as a mechanism, it was not because it actually was a machine but because the logical categories of his mind had conduced to such a view. In contrast to Locke, who attributed to the mind an essentially passive function, Kant assigned it a creative and dynamic role: it actively shaped and organized the data of the senses into a particular conception of the phenomenon in question. In this way Kant tried to free the mind from its dependence on solely external sources for knowledge and to give a renewed validity to truth derived from the spiritual realm—religion, morality, and art.[4] The *Philosophes* had regarded "knowledge" derived from these realms as inferior to that provided by science; only science could provide a true conception of nature and society, that is, a conception of the world as it actually is. For Kant, the knowledge derived from both realms, the spiritual as well as the scientific, had the same validity. If the concepts "causality" and "necessity" are also the product of the creative activity of the mind, why should scientific knowledge have greater validity than nonscientific knowledge? By demonstrating the limitations of scientific knowledge, Kant intended to restore the validity of faith and intuition. And, indeed, in sharp contrast to the Enlightenment, the Romantic thinkers regarded faith and intuition as essential for an understanding of nature and society.

If it was Kant who challenged the general methodological assumptions of the *Philosophes,* it was Edmund Burke who criticized their sociological assumptions.[5] He expressed the growing national and conservative reaction to both the principles of the Enlightenment and the French Revolution. Burke's

---

[3] See Ernst Cassirer, *The Philosophy of the Enlightenment,* (Princeton: Princeton University Press, 1951) , pp. 93–133.

[4] William J. Bossenbrook, *The German Mind* (Detroit: Wayne State University Press, 1961) , p. 227 *ff.*

[5] George H. Sabine, *A History of Political Theory* (New York: Holt, Rhinehart and Winston, 1961) , p. 597 *ff.*

views, as well as those of Hegel, provide an important background for an understanding of the intellectual and historical context in which the founders of sociology, Saint-Simon and Comte, developed their own ideas. Burke's critical reflections contributed greatly, not only in England but also on the Continent, to the formation of a conservative political and social philosophy. While he criticized and condemned the French revolutionary leaders, he had a different view of the American Revolution. The American colonists were attempting to preserve the organic character of society by struggling to retain their ancient rights and privileges; and, in effect, it was George III who was undermining this organic character by attempting to deprive them of these privileges. Society is an "organism," but its separate organs are not necessarily perfectly coordinated as they are in a natural organism. In the social organism some parts may change more rapidly than others. And when this occurs reforms are necessary to bring the parts into harmony again. Reforms, not revolution. That he favored reforms is clear from his stand with respect to British rule in India and Ireland. Reforms were necessary to bring the state into harmony with the other social conditions. But there should be no sudden breaks with the past as had been the case in France.

In advancing his *organic* conception of society, Burke was explicitly repudiating the abstract rational conception of the *Philosophes,* namely, that there were general natural laws and natural rights which could be discovered by the mind; and that the laws men make should conform with the ideal principles as nearly as possible. In their application of this doctrine, Burke argued, the revolutionaries had treated society as a machine, thinking they could simply pluck out the obsolete parts and replace them with new ones. They therefore discarded old and established institutions, which had developed through time and which were integral parts of the social order and tried to replace those institutions on the basis of some abstract formula. The individual was proclaimed more important than the nation or state, the element more important than the whole; and the state, far from being conceived as organically related to the rest of the social order, was treated as a mere contractual relationship. The implications were clear: if the state is a mere contract, then it can, and indeed should, be dissolved as soon as the contracting parties decide that it no longer satisfies their interests.

In his *Reflections on the Revolution in France,* Burke presents a point-for-point rebuttal of the rationalistic position.[6] The individual has no abstract rights. On the contrary, he has only those rights and privileges which prevail in a given community and which he acquires by virtue of having been born there. Rights and privileges develop slowly and organically; they are historical in character not abstract. A community does not exist merely in the present; it is an endless chain of generations, each one inheriting from its predecessors and each individual being but one link. The generation of the

---

[6] Edmund Burke, *Reflections on the Revolution in France* (New York: Dutton), 1960.

Revolution therefore had no right to destroy customs and institutions which belonged not solely to them but to past generations and even future generations. Twenty-six million Frenchmen had no right to regard themselves as having sovereign authority over what belonged equally to the past and the future. Each generation should merely add to what the dead have achieved and left behind, and pass on the total to its heirs.

As for the state, it is no mere contract made by individuals for the attainment of limited ends and therefore to be dissolved when the ends are attained or the agreement breached. Quite the contrary, the state is a higher organic unity, an integral part of the national community. The state, Burke wrote, "is a partnership in all science; a partnership in all art; a partnership in every virtue, and in all perfection. As the ends of such a partnership cannot be obtained in many generations, it becomes a partnership not only between those who are living, but between those who are dead and those who are to be born."[7] The state and the nation are organisms and hence the product of a long process of growth; they are not deliberate calculated inventions out of whole cloth. Moreover, it is not calculated interest nor rational convictions which hold nations and societies together, but certain nonrational factors. Not only material interests but spiritual ties and sentiments bind the members of a community together. These ties may be "light as air" but they are "as strong as links of iron."[8] Burke had thus formulated his conservative reflections on the Revolution. As an Englishman, and a privileged one at that, he cherished the liberties he had inherited from his forefathers. It is therefore no wonder that he desired to conserve them and that when he looked at France from his perspective he could see only the "reign of terror" of his time, not the thousand-year reign of terror that preceded it and led to the upheaval he so abhorred.

The ideology he developed, however, also embodied within it a relatively new conception of society, which now alerted social thinkers to a variety of factors the Enlightenment had relatively ignored. Burke had advanced a historical, developmental, organic view of society and together with his emphasis on the nonrational elements in human conduct, presented an important perspective from which to view the structure of a society and the process by which it changed. Burke's historical and conservative conception of the state and nation was given a more explicitly philosophical foundation by the German philosopher, Georg Wilhelm Friedrich Hegel.

Hegel's Historical Synthesis

For Hegel, the Romantic-Conservative conception of "historical development" and the Enlightenment emphasis on reason were each in their own way very important ideas. He therefore attempted to bring them together in one

7 *Ibid.,* p. 117.
8 *Ibid.,* p. 219.

philosophical synthesis. Reason, he argued, is not merely a faculty existing in the individual by which he might measure customs and institutions; reason is inherent in the process of development itself. This is the meaning of his celebrated notion that "what is rational is real" and "what is real is rational." Reason is not, as the *Philosophes* had regarded it, a mere abstraction from the real; it is an immanent force which determines the structure and development of the universe. In this way Hegel transforms reason into a great cosmic force which he variously calls the Idea, the Spirit, the Absolute, or, finally, God. This is not an unchanging essence, but is continually developing and becoming. Moreover, it is an impersonal, logical, and cosmic process which unites the social as well as the natural realm; all customs, habits, institutions, and conceptions are united into one dynamic and organic whole.

The historical process is the manifestation of the progressive unfolding of Reason in the various social and cultural institutions; and this development follows a form not unsimilar to the way human thought develops. The cosmic reason objectifies itself in institutions by the process of fusion of contradictions; this fusion produces new contradictions, which in turn are brought together in a new synthesis, and so on to infinity. In other words, each thesis engenders its own antithesis; both are then resolved in a synthesis, which in turn becomes a new thesis. If the cosmic reason is to be distinguished in any way from individual reason it is by the greater or more complete unfolding of the former's inherent potentialities. The individual mind can comprehend only aspects of reality; the acorn, however, becomes what it can become; it unfolds into an oak tree.

In the human realm, the nation stands higher than all other institutions, for it is the vehicle through which the cosmic reason realizes its destiny. This becomes clear from Hegel's philosophy of history in which he divides history into a series of succeeding epochs each of which expresses a particular phase in the development of the World Spirit. When a nation is still in its ascending phase, it embodies not the whole of cosmic reason, but only a particular phase of its ultimate fulfillment. A nation is an individualized expression of the World Spirit and is therefore the medium through which the spirit achieves self-consciousness. In his *Philosophy of History,* one learns, much to one's astonishment, that Hegel concludes the process with the Spirit ultimately having reified itself in the Prussian state, the highest expression of the Cosmic Reason on earth. A surprising conclusion indeed! One can see, then, two distinct and opposing tendencies in Hegel's thought. On the one hand, it led explicitly to the ideological defense of the Prussian state and of German society at the time; many concluded that what is, is rational and therefore necessary and unavoidable. So in these terms Hegel's philosophy became definitely conservative in its influence. But on the other hand, there was the emphasis on constant change, a dynamic and dialectical development which would continue ceaselessly and inexorably.

To perceive more clearly the two tendencies in Hegel's thought it will be instructive to examine more closely his conception of dialectical development.[9] On the one side, one can see the emphasis on slow, organic growth determined by immanent rational laws. Between phases, however, as in the transition from the acorn to the oak tree, there is a kind of "dialectical leap" from one quality (acorn) to another (oak tree). This takes place when the quantitative accumulation of slow organic change reaches a nodal point at which the addition of a quantum produces a *qualitative* change. This process may also be described as the "negation of the negation." The acorn in this example was itself a negation of the previous form (the seed), in which the acorn was inherent. With the continuation of the quantitative changes it, too, is negated by the new and potential form within it—the oak tree. Contained already within the seed is the chain of opposing forces which, if the seed is to develop, must continue to negate one another until its full potential is actualized. Each thing or form contains its own negation, and each is a unity of opposites. When a particular thing is "negated," it is superseded by a new force which continues to develop until it, too, engenders its own negation. This is precisely what "development" means—changing according to the immanent pattern of a given thing. Negation, then, is not synonymous with outright destruction. The seed, or acorn, or even the tree, is not *negated* when it is destroyed—*e.g.*, by crushing the seed. Negation occurs only when the initial form is transcended by new qualities inherent in the first, and when the new qualities in their subsequent development actualize the full potential of the initial form.

Things strive to attain *actually* what they always were *potentially*, Hegel is saying, in his own formulation of an essentially Aristotelian notion. In natural organisms, this takes place in a "direct, unopposed, unhindered manner." Why? Because between "the Idea and its realization—the essential constitution of the original germ and the conformity to it of the existence derived from it—no disturbing influence can intrude."[10] In nature, typically, essence is actualized in existence as an undisturbed process, harmoniously. The opposite, however, is true in relation to Spirit, or the human, socio-cultural realm: " . . . the realization of *its* Ideal is mediated by consciousness and will. . . . Thus Spirit is at war with itself; it has to overcome itself as its most formidable obstacle. That development which in the sphere of Nature is a peaceful growth, is in that of Spirit, a severe, a mighty conflict with itself. What Spirit really strives for is the realization of its Ideal being; but in doing so, it hides that goal from its own vision, and is proud and well satisfied in this alienation from it." The development of the socio-cultural sphere,

---

[9] See Hegel, *Science of Logic,* translated by W. H. Johnston and L. G. Struthers (New York: The Macmillan Company, 1951), Vol. I, p. 147 *ff.*
[10] G. W. F. Hegel, *The Philosophy of History* (New York: Dover Publications, Inc., 1956), p. 55.

therefore, " . . . does not present the harmless tranquillity of mere growth, as does that of organic life, but a stern reluctant working against itself."[11]

In rather obscure metaphysical terms Hegel is saying that the dialectical development in the social realm is a process characterized by conflict; if development means that each succeeding phase is a step forward or "higher" than the preceding phase, then this progressive development is a conflictive one. It is easy to see some of the radical implications of this philosophy, particularly those which Marx later found so appealing. For in the cultural realm Hegel had emphasized that development toward freedom, far from being a natural and mindless process, was contingent upon consciousness and will. "Universal history . . . shows the development of the consciousness of Freedom on the part of the Spirit, and the consequent realization of that Freedom. This development implies a gradation—a series of increasingly adequate expressions or manifestations of Freedom, which result from its Idea."[12]

Yet, this philosophy, as we have seen, had its conspicuously conservative side. Much like Burke, Hegel argued that it is not the individual, not even the family, but the State that is the embodiment of Law. The State is the highest order to which all others must subordinate themselves. Real World History, for Hegel, begins with the State; and its Right and Law supersede all prehistorical forms—family, community, etc.—with their right and law. But in the final analysis, it is not just any state or nation, but the German state which embodies the true, the eternal wisdom of the Spirit—of God. Thus Hegel concludes: "We have now arrived at the third period of the German World, and thus enter upon the period of Spirit conscious that it is free, inasmuch as it wills the True, the Eternal—that which is in and for itself Universal."[13] Hegel believed that he was living in the final and most perfect state of world history.

As will be seen later in a discussion of Marx's intellectual origins, he adopted some of the negative-critical or radical aspects of Hegel's thought but rejected the others. Marx's theory is of a completely different order and cannot be adequately comprehended as an extension of any of Hegel's themes. But before this can be taken up, other aspects of the Conservative Reaction to the Enlightenment and the Revolution must be explored.

11 *Ibid.,* p. 55.
12 *Ibid.,* p. 63.
13 *Ibid.,* p. 412.

5

Bonald and Maistre

The Conservative Reaction to the Enlightenment and particularly to the Revolution was felt throughout Europe. While outside France, especially among German thinkers, the movement took on a strong nationalistic character as a reaction against Napoleonic imperialism; among French thinkers the movement assumed both a religious and reactionary character. The French conservatives who reflected on the Revolution and its aftermath regarded the period after 1789 as a terrible ordeal and generally abhorred its events and consequences. Two thinkers in particular, Bonald and Maistre, developed the Catholic counterrevolutionary philosophy, which not only provided an ideological defense of the post-Revolutionary order—the Restoration—but called for additional regression to the order of the old regime. These men were traditionalists who idealized the lost medieval order and who yearned for its providentially arranged harmony. Contradicting the ideas of the Enlightenment, they posited the inferiority of individual reason as compared with revealed and traditional truth. They put forward a religious and philosophical doctrine in which man acquired knowledge not by means of his individual reason, but rather as a social being through tradition, that is, by growing up in a cultural community. However, unlike the secularists whose conceptions of this process only emerged later, Bonald and Maistre viewed tradition as beginning with an original revelation, afterwards transmitted and supported by the Church and other fundamental institutions. This was a reaction against the optimistic faith of the eighteenth century in the power of individual reason to fashion and refashion social systems. The traditionalists rejected this major premise of the Enlightenment thinkers; instead they revived all the dead elements of a transcendental philosophy of history—Divine Providence, original sin, final causes, and an infallible Church. Thus Bonald and Maistre rejected the *immediate* past by defending Providence against the naturalism of the *Philosophes*. Resisting the secularization of thought and society by insisting that Providence worked through historical and social laws, Bonald and Maistre furthered the tendency toward historicism begun by the Romantics. Ironically, however, they thus unknowingly provided the major concepts which ultimately were to become the elements of a secular social science. The philosophy of Bonald and Maistre merits consideration, then, in the light of the proposition that philosophical conservatism is the source, historically, of major sociological concepts and ideas.

Louis de Bonald (1754–1850)[1]

Bonald's first and best known work, *Théorie du Pouvoir*, was a polemic against Rousseau's *Social Contract* and Montesquieu's *Spirit of the Laws*. In his *Théorie*, Bonald treats all forms of "knowledge," such as art and literature, as products and expressions of the society which produces them. Literature, for example, is a manifestation of the moral aspect of society, of its constitution, which is the soul, the spirit, and the character of a society. Bonald thus denies the efficacy of individual action or creativity by treating literature and other arts as social products. Every art is a collective effort and therefore the individual is simply the tool rather than the creator of an art work. Not only are the positive achievements of an artist viewed as the achievements of society, but his errors as well are viewed as the fault of an age not of the man. In this as in all his subsequent work, Bonald is intent upon proving the errors of individualism and the validity of traditional ideas. His "sociology" is thus developed in the course of a sustained polemic against the Enlightenment: Liberty, equality, and other such ideas, are not general abstractions nor are they the results of natural law as the *Philosophes* understood it. Quite the contrary, rights exist only in definite and concrete social relationships.

1 The following discussion is based on Bonald's *Oeuvres,* and particularly on his *Démonstration Philosophique du Principe Constitutif de la Société* (Paris: Libraire D'Adrien Le Clere et C, 1840). This work, Volume 12 of his *Oeuvres,* which he wrote in 1829, is a general summary of his social philosophy. In addition, I have consulted the following secondary sources: Émile Faguet, *Politiques et Moralistes du Dix-Neuvième Siècle* (Paris: Société Francaise D'Imprimerie et de Librairie, 1890); and George Brandes, *Main Currents in Nineteenth-Century Literature* (New York: The Macmillan Company, 1906).

The term *"natural"* as it was used by Rousseau and his contemporaries implied to Bonald simply the existence of natural man anterior to society. Men's rights, thus understood, were natural and did not result from social organization. This conception of natural man was a meaningless abstraction for Bonald. There is no natural man, he argues, only social man; there are no natural rights only social rights, and these are relative to a particular social order. The men of the Enlightenment had wrenched words out of their social context and had transformed them into weapons for criticism and revolution. Bonald also attacked Condillac's view of ideas and language, namely, that ideas were the result of sensory experience and that men invented language by transforming their gestures and natural signs into spoken words. Bonald rejected this theory because of its secular and revolutionary implications. If men could invent language and language in turn was necessary for social existence, then men could create and recreate society according to their desires. It reinforced the view that man was not always a social being but evolved into a social state from a natural one. Condillac's view was offensive, because it denied revelation and affirmed that man *not God* made society, that man could make, change, and destroy its forms. In opposition to this view, Bonald wanted to demonstrate logically the divine origin of society, the organic links between the present and the past, the unbroken chain of tradition, the divine basis of authority, the superiority of society over the individual, the general over the particular, and duties over rights. In short, his work was an attempt to undermine every major assumption of the Enlightenment.

Ideas, for Bonald, were innate, but not, in the Cartesian sense, in the individual man. Knowledge of moral truth is innate in society, and is transmitted to the individual through speech. Thus "the word" is the principal instrument of Truth. Man did not invent language—it had a divine origin as the Old Testament had shown. Language did not arise out of social interaction; the opposite is true: knowledge and language preceded society. In the beginning there was the word. The word was given by revelation which imparted general truth, and society became the context for language and truth. The family, the Church, and the State derived their respective aspects of the truth from the general Truth. Man is born into society and becomes a part of it by acquiring language and the social truth. He learns aspects of this truth within the respective social institutions. In this way, Bonald sought to restore revelation, tradition, and authority as the bases of Truth. Man receives the word from God and tradition is preserved in the continuity of the family, the Church, and the state authority, the last of these being the main defender of tradition. The individual should therefore obey God's will by subordinating himself to the domestic, religious, and political traditions and institutions of society.

Clearly, Bonald was developing a point-for-point rebuttal of the Enlightenment ideas whose consequences he decried and whose implications he still feared. The assumption that language was a human product he found particularly abhorrent. If men invented language, then the meaning of words was arbitrary and conventional; these meanings could be changed. "The Church," contrary to the meaning it had in its original context, could be construed as the guardian of superstition; and "the State" could be conceived as a despotism and therefore criticized and undermined with all the fearful results of the French Revolution. On the other hand, if language were a divine gift, a tool of Providence, and the word acquired its meaning from the traditional social complex, then the individual by his own reason could not know meanings and could learn them only in particular social relationships. In this way, Bonald reasoned, God's order could be protected from individual reason and criticism. God imposed language, society, and authority, and individual men had no right to tamper with them. Apparently, Bonald did not see how quite opposite conclusions could be drawn from his theory, as in fact they later were. If meaning was dependent on definite social relationships, then by rejecting his first premise of divine revelation one could argue that knowledge is a function of social conditions. In these terms one could argue, as indeed a sociologist would, that both the ideas of the Enlightenment and of Bonald—indeed all ideas—were a function of the socio-historical conditions in which they were conceived and formulated. And this, of course, eventually became a major postulate of Marx's theory of ideology and later of the sociology of knowledge—both eminently *secular* theories.

For Bonald, authority, like language, was divinely established and fit into the providential scheme. His fondness for the number "three," no doubt inspired by the Catholic conception of the Trinity, led him to posit three functions which expressed the divine: "A general will, a general love, (and) a general force achieve the aim which is the conservation of social beings."[2] Authority is a unity which must be both general and perpetual in order to avoid social divisiveness and strife. The father guarantees the perpetuity of domestic authority and the Church, as the expression of Christ, guarantees religious authority. If, however, unity and perpetuity in these realms are not guaranteed in the political realm, the society will be wracked by conflict and revolution. The continual authority of the State must therefore be assured, and this is best accomplished by a hereditary monarchy.

The family, the Church, and the State must assure general social stability and cohesion. These institutions are based on fundamental laws, for the structure of society has been decreed by God, nature, and history as a unity. Society's structure is an ensemble of laws or necessary relationships that exist between the beings who compose them. These laws and relationships are based on the nature of man—a God-given nature. Social laws express the will of God, the ultimate author of the underlying social relationships. And the

2 Louis de Bonald, *Oeuvres,* I (Paris: Librairie D'Adrien Le Clere et C, 1840), p. 146.

purpose of society is the conservation of being which is desired by the general will. This will, unlike Rousseau's, is not the sum of particular wills, but an expression of the divine, natural order, the will of God.

Bonald also rejected, as did Burke, the Enlightenment idea of the *Social Contract*. There was no evidence of such a contract in any social relationship —between God and man, father and son, monarch and subject. Society was not, as implied in the contract notion, dependent on the will of man. There was no contract, but natural (divine) and necessary relationships. Society must have three elements. These are monarchy, nobility, and subjects, the best and most natural elements. A single hereditary monarch must reign supreme in a given society, best administered by a hereditary nobility serving both monarch and subjects and acting as a buffer between them. In order to do so, the nobility must remain an independent class—*i.e.,* propertied and thus financially independent. The best form of society is one guided by a paternalistic monarchy and nobility; all other forms, including of course democracy and aristocracy, are inherently unstable because they lack a definite center of authority and are therefore destined to suffer from chronic conflict and disorder. Against the Enlightenment, Bonald thus argued that anything which undermined the patriarchal, monogamous family, the Catholic Church, and the monarchical state would result in anarchy. For this reason he inveighs against divorce, which had been legalized in 1792.

It is clear, then, that Bonald's theory was an idealization of the *status quo ante,* the medieval order, which for him symbolized perfection. This was his model for the reconstruction of post-Revolutionary society; in fact he supported the Restoration as an attempt to reestablish such a society. Subjects must obey authority which represents the general will of society and which in turn is a manifestation of the will of God. Anything which contradicts this order—popular sovereignty, representative government, separation of powers —he abhors. Naturally, most of all he detests the two historical events that contributed most to the downfall of the old order—the Reformation and the French Revolution. The first had destroyed the unity of the Church and the second, the feudal social system.

If Bonald admired the feudal order, it followed that he would despise what the bourgeoisie stood for, *i.e.,* commerce and industry. It was the very same principles of the *Philosophes,* he noted with irony, which held up natural man as a standard for measuring existing societies and for condemning their crippling and deforming tendencies, that led to the Industrial Revolution—a far cry from the original image and ideal. Bonald's work thus became in part a severe critique of bourgeois society, a critique which anticipated in many respects later socialist thinking, but from a different standpoint.

Bonald longed for the "good old days" of the pre-bourgeois era, while the socialists looked forward to a future condition which would transcend and supersede bourgeois civilization. Bonald scoffed at those who now saw industry as providing for man's needs and pleasures, at those who wished

" . . . to see us all in palaces, spinning cloth of gold and silk. . . . Everything is resolved for man in society to produce in order to consume and to consume in order to produce; and to their eyes all of society is divided into two classes, producers and consumers. . . ."[3] He derided them for seeing industry as an independent force which guarantees peace and liberty, while, in fact, it was agricultural society that was in all respects superior to industrial society. The agricultural family can feed and nourish itself; it is not dependent on other men and other social events to assure its continued existence. The industrial family, on the other hand, produces children whom it cannot be sure of supporting, dependent as it is on the vicissitudes of the market. In the agricultural family, moreover, the natural and divine order is respected because the father is the authority. Which is not at all the case in the industrial system where the father, mother, and children are isolated, and family unity is disturbed. The industrial system thus undermines the most natural and sacred of social units. It imposes harsh labor on children thereby preventing their education and destroying their health in an artificial and foul environment. And while it cripples the young, it also discards the old and weak who cannot work.[4] Agriculture, therefore, unifies society while industry tends to divide it into hostile classes and factions. Bonald's critique of bourgeois-industrial society, though made from a conservative standpoint, did anticipate some of the criticisms of later socialists. For example, Saint-Simon, as we shall see, acknowledged Bonald's influence and expressed admiration for his ideas.

Ultimately, Bonald justified his conception of things by arguing that society must express the fundamental laws of God or suffer from crisis and anarchy. God's laws gave order to society and guaranteed the conservation of being. The individual learns these laws only through his social existence, *i.e.*, within social institutions which are the depositories of tradition and which thus impart truth to man. Knowledge (culture) is transmitted by tradition, historical development, and revelation. The individual, an integral part of society, may in no instance place his individual will above the general will. Man must not arrogate to himself the right of judging, changing, or rebelling against general society, for then he is dethroning the general, providential reason and wisdom, historically arrived at, and putting in its place individual reason.

In Bonald's scheme, then, the words "nature" and "natural laws" have a meaning quite different from that of the *Philosophes*. For Bonald, God was beyond nature, not in it nor of it. He was the great conserver of being who employed toward this end nature, history, and men. Yet, in one ambiguous formulation he comes close to compromising this view and thus opens the way for the secularization of his theory; and, indeed, later thinkers were to note that, divested of its metaphysical assumptions and aspects, Bonald's theory

---

3 *Ibid.*, II, p. 237.
4 *Ibid.*, II, p. 239.

could be transformed into a secular sociological one. "The general will of society," Bonald writes, "of the social body, of social man, the nature of social beings or of society, the social will, the will of God are synonymous expressions in this work."[5]

One sees how easily this could lead to a proposition quite the reverse of Bonald's, *viz.*, that "God" is an expression of society—as Durkheim later formulated it. Stripped, then, of its theological assumptions and aspects, Bonald's work becomes the source of major sociological concepts and ideas. Society is an historically evolved, organic unity of institutions. Common values and traditions constitute its major binding force. Language and culture, though not viewed as products of social interaction by Bonald, are nonetheless seen as embedded in the social context and inseparable from that context. And it is the "individual," not society, which is an abstraction; for outside society an individual is nonexistent—an impossibility. Furthermore, Bonald saw clearly the historical forces and trends which had led to the dissolution of the medieval unity; he saw and feared the growing secularization that had accompanied the Reformation, the Enlightenment, and the Revolution and thus anticipated the various theorists who later centered attention on the historical shift in Europe from the *Gemeinschaft* of the Middle Ages to the increasingly *gesellschaftliche* character of the modern era. Finally, he saw clearly some of the repressive and alienating consequences of industrial civilization.

Bonald had written his *Théorie du Pouvoir* as an emigré in Heidelberg. Although the police of the Directory had destroyed almost the entire edition of the book, a copy sent to Napoleon impressed him so favorably that he had the author's name removed from the list of the exiled. And little wonder that Bonaparte was so impressed. In Bonald's view, history expressed the tension between the divine will to order society according to a larger providential design and man's ability either to sabotage that design or to cooperate in bringing it about. Being a free agent but tainted with original sin, man does in fact, at least periodically, obstruct and even destroy that design. Whenever this happens there is little doubt that Providence will sooner or later prevail. The obstruction of the design and the consequent social chaos is always temporary, because it cannot long oppose the nature of being. In these terms, even that most violent of upheavals, the French Revolution was a "salutary crisis." The revolutionaries were instruments of providence, and the obstructions they had erected before the providential design were eventually turned against the revolutionaries themselves.

The Revolution, therefore, even for Bonald, was not purely negative and destructive. It was a kind of chastisement of man by Providence which, despite its temporary catastrophic results, was bound, like all other crises, ultimately to have salutary effects; for it cleared the way for the reestablish-

[5] Bonald, *Théorie du Pouvoir, Oeuvres*, I, p. 133.

ment of order. Napoleon could not fail to be impressed, then, when Bonald taught that revolutions begin with the subjects but end with the ruler; that they break out because the authorities have become weak and have yielded, but subside when authority has been restored and strengthened. Every disturbance will ultimately serve only to strengthen authority. Bonald had prophesied that the revolution which had begun with the declaration of the rights of man would culminate in the declaration of the rights of God; and since these were the very rights Bonaparte was now proclaiming, Bonald's position was very secure indeed.[6]

Before turning to a more detailed examination of Bonald's sociological concepts, it will be instructive, first, to consider briefly the ideas of another conservative thinker, Bonald's contemporary and "partner in arms," Joseph de Maistre.

Joseph de Maistre (1754–1821)

Joseph de Maistre was born in the same year as was Bonald; and although the two men had never met personally, they agreed on all the fundamentals of their respective theories and expressed great admiration for each other. Bonald tells of a letter he received from Maistre not long before he died: "Je n'ai rien pensé que vous ne l'ayez écrit; je n'ai rien écrit que vous ne l'ayez pensé."[7]

Maistre's work, like that of Bonald, may be read as a sustained polemic against the philosophy of the Enlightenment. He also devoted his life to discrediting those principles which had led to the Revolution and to defending those of the counterrevolution.

Maistre found particularly offensive the Enlightenment conception of the origin of society. He had read Rousseau's discourses less as an attempt to fashion a device by which natural man could be "separated out" by stripping him of his socio-cultural attributes, than as an assertion that there was in fact a pre-social state of man. Thus understood, Rousseau's conception offended Maistre because it implied that human society had a beginning without the intervention of the Divine and that there had existed somewhere in the remote past a pre- or nonsocial condition of man. This assumption Maistre rejected altogether. Man is unthinkable, an impossibility, before, or outside, society; and if such creatures did exist, whatever they were they were not men. He insists that the opposite possibility be entertained—that society had no beginning in a temporal or historical sense, and, therefore, that it may very well be an aspect of human nature by definition.[8]

This approach is on firmer ground than the other, Maistre argues, since it

---

6 See George Brandes, *op. cit.*, p. 113.

7 Bonald, *op. cit.*, XII, pp. 198–199.

8 Joseph de Maistre, *Oeuvres Complètes* I, (Lyon: Vitte et Perrussel, 1884–86), p. 315. Translated selections may be found in Joseph de Maistre, *Works*, selected, translated and introduced by Jack Lively (New York: Macmillan, 1965).

coincides with our experience and our historical knowledge. He misreads Rousseau as having posited an antithesis between nature and society, between natural and social man, and ignores the fact that Rousseau posited such an antithesis only between "natural man" and *certain definite forms* of society—not society in general. Rousseau was not, as Maistre assumed he was, positing the superiority of the state of nature ("man is born free") to all society ("and everywhere he is in chains"). But having understood it in this way, he resented the implication that society was inferior to the state of nature. Apparently, he conveniently ignored the proposition that Rousseau insisted upon, namely, that certain social states were unquestionably superior to the so-called natural state (which he admitted probably never existed), because they allowed for man's perfectibility, a goal he cherished and considered impossible outside of society.

Maistre really understood that Rousseau was to a large degree exercising his imagination when talking about the "state of nature," and that he had advanced this concept for heuristic purposes. Even so, he found himself indignant at the way in which Rousseau had raised and resolved the issue in question: Is man essentially a natural being or a social being? Rousseau had suggested that man in the "natural state," though he had the potential for society and thus for perfection, lived out his life as a nonsocial being. And what bothered Maistre most about this image was both the amoral character of man's natural life as Rousseau had depicted it, and the fact that when he spoke of man acquiring "conventions" he treated them negatively and thus tended to stigmatize basic moral conceptions of Western and Christian civilization.

When Rousseau had said that in the state of nature, man gets together with woman for physical love only, and that immediately with the mutual satisfaction of their needs they parted and became independent again; when he said that children remained with parents only so long as it was necessary for their survival and then cut off the natural relation, after which neither father nor children had any mutual obligations; when he argued, in short, that the family as a moral unit did not exist in the natural state, this offended Maistre's religious sensibilities. For in this description Rousseau was not only being cavalier about historical and anthropological fact, he was questioning the sacred character of one of the most fundamental institutions of Western Christendom: the monogamous family.

First, on the anthropological level, Maistre criticizes Rousseau for his inconsistencies. He observes that Rousseau himself had noted the brutality of savages and had tried to save himself from a contradiction by asserting that even the most primitive savage was far removed from the state of nature. Maistre attacks Rousseau for his ambiguity and, for all practical purposes, dismisses his views as nonsense. The brutality of the savage does pose a problem, Maistre admits: This is not a *later* stage than the tranquil *first* state, as Rousseau had suggested, but a degraded state, an objectification of original sin. The savage state follows the civilized state, and, wherever it is in evidence, it represents the degeneration of a civilized people. Maistre thus reversed Rousseau's picture in keeping with Christian mythology. Savagery is not an original condition of mankind but a terminal state in which man has completely lost his original and natural perfection.

Maistre insists that history is the full account of man's stay and development on earth; and that if we address ourselves to history, we shall see the incontrovertible fact that man is and always has been a *social* being.[9] And if anyone believes differently, the onus is upon him to prove it. But since in fact such proof is impossible, Maistre believes that history and anthropology have demonstrated beyond any doubt that man has always dwelt in society and that he is social by nature. Was there, however, an historical origin to society? Treating the Old Testament as an historical document, Maistre builds upon the story in Genesis.

The family is prototypical of society. Sexual differentiation was constituted with the divine purpose of peopling the earth. It was a kind of secondary causal force by which Providence intended to carry out its purpose. The end, the total human society, or series of societies, was posited in the first sexual pair and their offspring. The first pair was physically mature. When blood line no longer suffices to unite a group, when the genitor can no longer be the sole source of authority due to multiplication, death, etc., then a "lawgiver" like Moses must arise to substitute a moral for a physical bond of unity. The "nation" emerges. Here Maistre views all aspects of culture—morals, religion, government, art—as fulfilling essential social functions: the conservation of being through society.

A nation has a common consciousness, a common soul, a common language; it is a cultural unity. A society's continuity requires as much moral unity, even unanimity, as possible; and for Maistre, as for Bonald, the ideal form of this unity was approximated in the Middle Ages. Unlike Burke, however, who saw the necessity and desirability of reforms, Maistre regarded reforms as dangerous. Reforms will inevitably lead to unforeseen consequences, worse than the original, alleged wrongs that one wants to correct. Reforms are dangerous because man has incomplete knowledge. In order to reform, man would have to possess a thorough knowledge of the course and trend of the historical process, a complete survey of its elements. This is impossible. Therefore, it is in the best interest of man to leave the entire matter in the hands of Providence, the sole force capable of perfecting social forms.

Both Maistre and Bonald, then, maintained that man by his very nature is a social, moral, and cultural being. Man had never had an existence before or outside society, and to the extent that Rousseau or his followers believed otherwise, their speculations were immoral as well as absurd. If Rousseau had wanted to use the concept of "natural man" as a criterion for evaluating

9 *Ibid.*, VII, p. 541.

specific social systems, and thus for providing man with some guidance in changing society to facilitate his perfection, Bonald and Maistre now insisted that man is and always has been social and that the historical development of society is guided by an omniscient Providence. Man, being less than omniscient, must not tamper with society nor attempt to reform it, because the cure will always be worse than the alleged disease. In developing their ideological standpoint, however, Bonald, Maistre, and other representatives of the Conservative Reaction advanced a number of ideas which have since been incorporated into sociology as important working concepts and assumptions.

Conservative Philosophy and Sociology, A Summary

We have seen how the principles of the Enlightenment, as they became manifest in the Revolution, engendered a conservative philosophical reaction. This reaction, in turn, engendered a new interest in *social order* and various related problems and concepts.

Conservatives, like Burke, Hegel, Bonald, and Maistre, are so called because they desired quite literally to conserve and maintain the prevailing order. Moreover, some of them, as we have seen, sought not so much to conserve the existing order as to regress to a *status quo ante*. The disorder, anarchy, and radical changes which these thinkers observed after the Revolution led them in their philosophy to generate concepts which relate to aspects of order and stability: tradition, authority, status, cohesion, adjustment, function, norm, symbol, ritual. As compared with the eighteenth century, this constituted a definite shift of interest from the individual to the group, from criticism of the existing order to its defense, and from social change to social stability.[10]

From the conservative standpoint, the social changes following in the wake of the Revolution had undermined and destroyed fundamental social institutions and had resulted in the loss of political stability. The conservatives traced these results to certain preceding events and processes in European history that had led, they believed, to the progressive weakening of the medieval order and hence to the upheaval of the Revolution. Quite precisely, they singled out Protestantism, capitalism, and science as the major forces. These processes, furthermore, which were hailed as progressive by their liberal and radical contemporaries, were leading even now to an increasing atomization of peoples. Large "masses" now appeared, presumably unanchored in any stable social groups; widespread insecurity, frustration, and alienation became evident; and, finally, a monolithic secular power had emerged which was dependent for its existence on the mass of rootless individuals.

[10] In the present discussion I have drawn upon a number of points made by Robert A. Nisbet in his article entitled "Conservatism and Sociology," *American Journal of Sociology* (September, 1952) .

The conservatives had idealized the medieval order, and from this stand-point the modern era was very wanting indeed. As an antidote to the principles of the *Philosophes,* and as a critique of the post-Revolutionary *"disorder,"* the conservatives advanced a number of propositions about society:

1. It is an organic unity with internal laws of development and deep roots in the past, not simply a mechanical aggregate of individual elements. The conservatives were "social realists" in the sense that they firmly believed in society as a reality greater than the individuals who comprise it. This was in direct opposition to the social nominalism of the Enlightenment, the view that only individuals exist and that society is simply the name one gives to these individuals in their interrelationships.

2. Society antedates the individual and is ethically superior to him. Man has no existence outside of a social group or context, and he becomes human only by participating in society. Far from individuals constituting society, it is society which creates the individual by means of moral education, to employ Durkheim's term.

3. The individual is an abstraction and not the basic element of a society. Society is composed of relationships and institutions; and individuals are simply members of society who fulfill certain statuses and roles—father, son, priest, etc.

4. The parts of a society are interdependent and interrelated. Customs, beliefs, and institutions are organically intertwined so that changing or remaking one part will undermine the complex relationships maintaining the stability of society as a whole.

5. Man has constant and unalterable needs, which every society and each of its institutions serve to fulfill. Institutions are thus positive agencies by which basic human needs are met. If these agencies are disturbed or dis-rupted, suffering and disorder will result.

6. The various customs and institutions of a society are positively func-tional; they either fulfill human needs directly or indirectly by serving other indispensable institutions. Even prejudice is viewed in these terms; it tends to unify certain groups and also increases their sense of security.

7. The existence and maintenance of small groups is essential to society. The family, neighborhood, province, religious groups, occupational groups, these are the basic units of a society, the basic supports of men's lives.

8. The conservatives also conceived of "social organization." The Revolu-tion, as they saw it, had led not to a higher form of organization, but to social and moral disintegration. They wanted to preserve the older religious forms, Catholicism not Protestantism, and sought to restore the religious unity of medieval Europe. Protestantism, in teaching the importance of individual faith, had undermined the spiritual unity of society. And as we have seen in the case of Bonald, the disorganizing consequences of urbanism, industry, and commerce were recognized.

9. The conservatives insisted, in addition, on the essential importance and positive value of the nonrational aspects of human existence. Man needs ritual, ceremony, and worship. The *Philosophes,* in their merciless criticism of these activities as irrational vestiges of the past, had weakened the sacred supports of society.

10. Status and hierarchy were also treated as essential to society. The conservatives feared that equality would destroy the "natural" and time-honored agencies by which values were passed on from one generation to another. Hierarchy was necessary in the family, the Church, and the State, without which social stability was impossible.

These are some of the major sociological tenets of the conservative legacy—a legacy which greatly influenced such thinkers as Saint-Simon, Comte, and, later, Durkheim. These and other thinkers attempted to take conservative ideas and concepts out of their theological-reactionary context and to make them part and parcel of a scientific sociology. To see the beginnings of this attempt, the work of Saint-Simon and Comte, the founders of modern sociology, has to be considered.

6

Saint-Simon

(1760–1825)

The conservatism of Louis de Bonald and Joseph de Maistre, as we have seen, took the form of a reactionary response to the Revolution and to the principles of the Enlightenment. They called for a post-Revolutionary society similar to that of medieval times. In advancing their philosophy they centered attention on a number of problems and aspects of society which later became a major source of sociological concepts and ideas. In fact, both Saint-Simon and Comte, the official founders of sociology, were directly influenced by Bonald and accepted some of his basic assumptions even while reinterpreting them and placing them in a different theoretical context.

From an ideological standpoint, Comte was conservative in a different sense from Bonald and Maistre. Comte wanted to conserve not the *status quo ante* but the status quo, that is, middle-class society then in the process of emerging and consolidating itself. Comte's so-called *positive philosophy* was an explicit repudiation of the "negative" philosophy of the Enlightenment and Revolution. Comte wanted to preserve the "is." Each stage in the evolutionary development of society as he saw it was necessary and perfect. He had great respect for the existing factual order, which was not to be transcended or negated under any circumstances.

The philosophy of Saint-Simon, on the other hand, in which

virtually all of Comte's ideas originated and which he so ungraciously pla-
giarized, was at least in some limited respects a critique of the status quo.
It is for this reason that Saint-Simon has sometimes been regarded as a founder
of socialism. Yet, this opinion, as we shall see, is by no means unanimous.
Some students of his work deny any socialistic tendency in his theories.
Others, like Karl Marx, dubbed him a "utopian socialist"—meaning by that
term that Saint-Simon lived and wrote before industrial development had
reached the critical point at which the "contradictions" of capitalism had
become clear—*i.e.*, before class conflict between bourgeoisie and proletariat
had become a normal phenomenon. In Marx's view, then, Saint-Simon apparently could not, or did not, see the conflict of interests between these major
classes of the industrial system and therefore not only treated them as one
class with common interests, but left bourgeois property institutions intact in
his blueprint for the future society.

Still other students of Saint-Simon's thought have argued that there is no
appreciable difference from an ideological point of view between the ideas of
Saint-Simon and Comte and that both thinkers advanced a sociological theory
which is little more than a "scientific" rationale for a totalitarian type of
society.[1]

In comparison with his students, particularly Thierry and Comte, and
despite his aristocratic background, Saint-Simon's education was relatively
unsystematic. For the most part he was self-educated except for the help of
some private tutors, the best known being d'Alembert, the Encyclopedist.[2]
Since, in addition, he had once visited Rousseau, it is clear that he had some
firsthand contact with the Enlightenment thinkers. The versatility of his
interests and activities is demonstrated by the fact that among other things he
had fought with distinction in the American Revolution and had been among
the first to advance a scheme for a canal to join the Atlantic with the Pacific.
As for the French Revolution, he was ambivalent toward that momentous
event and indicated this in his autobiography of 1808: "I did not wish to take
part in it, because, on the one hand, I was convinced that the *Ancien Regime*
could not be prolonged, and, on the other, I had an aversion to destruction."[3]
Records from the revolutionary period reveal, however, that he had been
much more enthusiastic a follower of the Revolution than he afterwards

[1] This view may be found in Albert Salomon, *The Tyranny of Progress* (The
Noonday Press, 1955).

[2] These and other biographical details may be found in F. M. H. Markham's
excellent introduction to the selected writings of *Henri Comte de Saint-Simon*
(Oxford: Basil Blackwell, 1952). To the best of my knowledge, the most
thorough study of Saint-Simon and his work is Frank E. Manuel's *The New
World of Henri Saint-Simon* (Cambridge, Mass: Harvard University Press, 1956).
Another important source, of course, is Émile Durkheim's *Socialism and Saint-
Simon* (London: Routledge and Kegan Paul Ltd., 1958).

[3] Claude Henri Saint-Simon, *Oeuvres Complètes de Saint-Simon et Enfantin,
1865–76*, XV, Paris, 1865–76, p. 66.

admitted. He had, for instance, given up his aristocratic title, prepared the *cahier* of his local canton for the Estates-General, and presided at the first meeting of his commune. In addition, he was awarded in 1793 two certificates of *civisme* (good citizenship) and in the autumn of the same year was active in *Hébertist* and other radical circles in Paris. Saint-Simon's ideas retained to the end elements of Enlightenment and Revolutionary thought; but these, as we shall see, were fused with Romantic and conservative elements.

Scholars have now firmly established that Saint-Simon developed before 1814 all the major ideas which Thierry and Comte later claimed as their own. These ideas—positivism, industrialism, internationalism, a "new religion"—and the originality with which he approached them make Saint-Simon one of the most important social thinkers of the nineteenth century.

Like Bonald before him, Saint-Simon attributed the great stability of medieval civilization to its universally accepted religion; and like Marx after him, Saint-Simon viewed the historical transformation of European society as the result of forces which had been maturing in the womb of the old order. The growth of science, the emergence of an industrial and commercial bourgeoisie, the Protestant Reformation, and, finally, the negative-critical philosophical movement of the Enlightenment, all served to undermine the Catholic Church and hence the unity of medieval society. The *Philosophes*, Saint-Simon argued, with their insistence on the principles of equality and natural rights had contributed to the disintegration of the old order. Their principles were destructive of the old society and led ultimately to that great revolutionary crisis of his time. Yet, these same principles gave little or no guidance for the successful reconstruction of society. Saint-Simon therefore saw it as his task and the task of his contemporaries to create a new and organic social order based upon the new principles and forces that had come into view. Thus he wrote that "The philosophy of the eighteenth century has been critical and revolutionary; that of the nineteenth century will be inventive and constructive."[4]

If Saint-Simon admired the social unity of the medieval order quite as much as Bonald, he also recognized that there was no going back to that order, thus parting ways with the theorists of the Catholic revival. The new social unity must rest on a new unity in the realm of thought, of intellectual principles. Human knowledge has passed through three stages in its development; from the theological to the metaphysical and finally to the scientific. The study of human conduct, which Saint-Simon called "social physiology" must become a positive science in much the same way as the study of physical phenomena had become scientific. Scientific knowledge will thus take the place of religious dogma, and scientists and industrialists will emerge as the new "natural" élite to replace the leaders of medieval society, the clergy and nobility. Again, like Bonald, Saint-Simon admired the educated international

4 *Ibid.*, p. 92.

élite of the old order and believed that such an élite would also be necessary in the new society. The older cultivated and educated élite of the Middle Ages would be replaced by a new international, scientific-industrial élite. Science in the new order must fulfill the function of religion in the old. How? By means of positivism, or the application of scientific principles to all natural and human phenomena.

Positivism in this sense was evident, if not in name then in spirit, in the seventeenth and eighteenth centuries. Saint-Simon drew his inspiration from the scientific work of his predecessors and modeled his approach after theirs. He hoped that the human sciences would attain the unity and elegance of the natural sciences and was particularly impressed with Newton's law of gravitation. He realized that he was not a scientist and admitted that he lacked the training to carry out the program of making the social studies positive. Although he eventually abandoned the idea of unifying the sciences, he held on to his conception of science as a body of verified and established beliefs which could take the place of religion as the binding force of society. Religion, whose essential function had been to provide a coherent view of the universe and of human existence, and thus to unite people on the basis of common truths, would now be replaced by science. For those who are unable to grasp scientific truth intellectually, knowledge will be imparted by means of rituals, cults, and mystical processes. The educated élite, on the other hand, will learn the ideas directly as scientific principles.

A spiritual as well as a temporal élite remain essential in Saint-Simon's picture of the future society; the former is made up of scientists and the latter of industrialists and other "productive" property owners. It is an authoritarian society in which a scientific-technological élite will rule together with the property owners. This vision of the structure of the new society holds throughout his work. For example, in his *Letters from an Inhabitant of Geneva,* one of his earlier works, he views the old society as divided into three classes. The first is made up of the scientists, artists, and men of liberal ideas; the second, the property owners, resists change and wants to preserve the old order; the third class, "which rallies to the word 'equality,' comprises the rest of humanity." The class structure, in short, consists of the intellectuals, the "haves," and the "have-nots." As the class conflict between the haves and have-nots increased in intensity, and as the insurrection of the latter began to succeed, the intellectuals joined their movement as its leaders. The Revolution occurred because the haves could no longer contain this movement, could no longer control the have-nots. The reason for this was the loss of cultural and intellectual superiority on the part of the old élite consisting of monarch, priests, and nobles.

For the post-Revolutionary society to regain its unity, a new scientific élite, a council of Newton, must replace the spiritual authority of the Church by providing a unified scientific doctrine centered on Newton's law of gravitation. Thus the structure of the new society remains essentially the same:

Science replaces religion as the main force holding society together and each élite of the old system is superseded by a new one—priests by scientists, and feudal lords by industrialists. The conflict between the new haves and have-nots will continue, but the former may now regain control over the latter. In effect, Saint-Simon is imploring the propertied classes to align themselves with the most enlightened group in society, the intellectuals. Such an alignment will bring about a stable social order in which control over the have-nots is regained and revolution is thereby forestalled. Speaking to his imaginary audience of property owners, he asks them to do with good grace "what the scientists, artists, and men of liberal ideas, allied with the have-nots, will sooner or later compel them to do."

It is easy to see, then, the extent to which Saint-Simon's view of society was inspired by his conception of the social order of the medieval period. This, for him, was not a totally dark age as it had been for the Enlightenment thinkers. After all, the modern era had had its beginnings in that period; and science, too, stimulated by the Arabs in Europe, had emerged in the Middle Ages. He admired the alleged spiritual and social unity of medieval society and the alliance between the spiritual and temporal élites which had maintained that unity. He differed with Bonald and Maistre, however, about the possibility of restoring that unity on the basis of Catholic theology. Science has made this impossible once and for all. The dualism of mind and matter which emerged as an attempt at compromise between spiritual and temporal powers must be eliminated. Mind and matter must again be viewed as aspects of one and the same unity—*but* this is not to be accomplished by an outmoded theology but rather by means of scientific laws.

Changes in history are thus related to changes in religious ideas, and these in turn represent the state of beliefs and knowledge in a given period. History has passed through polytheism and theism, and now with physicism has left the conjectural stages to arrive at a positive stage in which all knowledge will be unified on a scientific positive basis. The conclusion is therefore inescapable that Saint-Simon conceived both the name and the essentials of positive philosophy. Émile Durkheim was among the first to realize this and he sought tirelessly to demonstrate the fact: " . . . the idea, the word, and even the outline of positivist philosophy are all found in Saint-Simon. He was the first to conceive that between the formal generalities of metaphysical philosophy and the narrow specialization of the particular sciences, there was a place for a new enterprise, whose pattern he supplied and himself attempted. Therefore, it is to him that one must, in full justice, award the honor currently given Comte."[5] Durkheim goes on to show that the credit for founding positive sociology also belongs to Saint-Simon and not to Comte. Contemporary students of the problem agree with Durkheim; the judgment of F. M. H. Markham is typical in this regard: "The 'Law of the Three Stages,' pomp-

5 Durkheim, *op. cit.*, p. 104.

ously announced by Comte as an original discovery, is merely a precise formulation of Saint-Simon's argument, which goes back to the *Letters from an Inhabitant of Geneva.*"[6]

That the medieval order is always the model for Saint-Simon's conception of society is also borne out by his approach to the *Reorganization of European Society*. In this work the influence of the theorists of the Catholic revival is again evident; for Saint-Simon viewed medieval civilization as an international order, resting on an international organization—the Church. Since there is no going back, one must go forward and establish a new international organization on the basis of new international principles. And are there any principles more international than scientific ones? Science and positive philosophy must bind the nations of Europe into one international community, for without international order there can be no order or stability in the individual societies of Europe.

In his later as well as his earlier works, the structure of each national society is the same: there are "producers" and there are "idlers." In the "productive" class Saint-Simon lumped together bankers, industrialists, scientists, managers, *and* manual workers, assuming that they all share common interests. This was later to strike Marx as a very naïve view of the class structure of industrial society and perhaps the weakest part of Saint-Simon's system. Moreover, in his projection of the "new" society, Saint-Simon leaves the class structure and, hence, the institution of private property intact; the only change he advocates is the compensation of tenants for improving the land they worked. Equality, he believed, is a foreign idea having no place in European civilization.

In the earlier years of his intellectual labors (1815–21), Saint-Simon's views toward economics are clearly *laissez-faire*. But he differs with the Classical Economists in several important respects. He sees production not as an end in itself but as a means of improving the conditions of life; and this becomes possible in his hierarchical and organic society only by means of rational planning of production. In his work, *Organisateur,* he outlines a plan for an industrial parliament, or planning body, composed of three chambers: invention, examination, and execution. The first consists of the scientists, artists, and engineers who are to plan the various public projects; the second, of the scientists who are to supervise the projects and control education; and the third, of industrialists, who are to carry out the plans and control the budget. He also disagrees with the assumption of the Classical Economists that the pursuit of individual well-being will lead automatically to the general good. The unbridled egoism of the rich as well as the uncurbed rebelliousness of the poor will have disorganizing consequences in the absence of a worldly ethic of some kind; the new society will therefore require a secular equivalent of religion. Saint-Simon had been influenced by Sismondi's *Nouveaux Prin-*

[6] F. M. H. Markham, *op. cit.,* p. xxv n.

cipes d'Economie Politique (1819) in which he had shown that the poor suffer most from economic crises and depression, and therefore that the utilitarians and Classical Economists were wrong. Saint-Simon begins to emphasize in his *Système Industriel* the necessity of improving the condition of the poorest classes and of founding the industrial system on the principle of brotherly love. The artists must contribute to the moral unity of society by shaping beliefs, opinions, and sentiments.

Thus as Saint-Simon viewed the historical transformation of European society, the supersession of the feudal nobility by the industrial bourgeoisie was inevitable; but as F. M. H. Markham has observed, for him to go on to predict, as Marx later did, that the bourgeoisie would in turn be superseded by the proletariat was unthinkable. Always keeping in mind as an ideal the spiritual élite of the Middle Ages, he could not conceive of a society governed by anyone but an educated élite. The scientists and industrialists were therefore to his mind the "natural" leaders of the working class. He did foresee conflict between owners and non-owners, between capitalists and workers, and between rich and poor generally, but he believed that this conflict could and should be averted in a truly organic society. Further, he argues that the main purpose of politics is to preserve property and that "the only barrier which the property owners can put up against the proletariat is a system of ethics."[7] Comte, as we shall see, becomes quite fascinated with this idea and his ideological defense of the bourgeoisie becomes much more blatant. Later, the unresolved problems raised by Saint-Simon and Comte were to intrigue Durkheim, much of whose work can be read as an attempt to reconcile the structured inequality of modern society with the requirements of social solidarity.

From the foregoing discussion, one can truly wonder why the term "social-ist" was ever applied to Saint-Simon's doctrine, particularly if this term is taken to mean the abolition of private property and the maximal equalization of life chances. Saint-Simon's doctrine is quite remote from the Marxian conception of the future society, in which class conflict and the classes themselves would be abolished. What remains, then, as the sole "socialist" element in Saint-Simon's new society is centralized planning of the economic system. More than Saint-Simon himself, it was his followers—Bazard, Enfantin, and others—who somewhat radicalized his critique of the "idlers" in society and who attacked the institution of inheritance and combined this with the advocacy of a planned economy. But their "socialism," too, was short-lived.

To summarize—knowledge, for Saint-Simon, is the underlying and sustaining factor of society; a social system is the application of a system of ideas. The historical growth of knowledge, or science, was a major cause of the transformation of European society. Knowledge, therefore, is both the moving

---

[7] Saint-Simon, *Oeuvres Complètes,* XVIII, p. 221.

power of progress and the binding force of society, which is in fact a *community of ideas*. Given the importance of ideas, Saint-Simon saw it as his task to determine which ideas were best suited to the condition of European society at the beginning of the nineteenth century. What unites people is their common way of thinking and of picturing the world; but this way of thinking among the people as a whole lags behind the progress of scientific knowledge, behind positive fact. Therefore, by systematizing scientific knowledge one could define what the consciousness of a people should be at a given time. Inasmuch as a social system is the application of ideas, it will be impossible to build the new society until positive philosophy, which is to be its basis, has developed. While there already exist many sciences, the most important one is missing: a science of man. This is the only science which can *reconcile the interests of classes* and thus serve as the foundation of a unified organic society. The human science should be modeled after the other natural sciences because man is, after all, a part of nature.

Saint-Simon thus looked forward to a time when politics would be a science and political questions would be handled in much the same way that other phenomena are treated by science. The main task of science is to discover the laws of social development, evolution, and progress; these are inevitable and absolute. All that man can do is submit. Progress takes place in stages and each stage is necessary and contributes something to the further progress of mankind. (As we have seen, medieval civilization was not all dark, since the elements of modern civilization had their origin here.) Once man has discovered the laws of social development, they will indicate the direction progress must follow. Thus the future can be deduced from the past and the present. The scientific élite will discover the principles or laws most appropriate to the new society and will appeal to the haves to cooperate in bringing that society about. Failing such cooperation, the haves are warned, the have-nots may again, as in the case of the French Revolution, win over the disaffected intellectuals, who will become the leaders of a new insurrection. Individual freedom has no place in this scheme and appears not to have concerned Saint-Simon. All considerations are subordinated to the establishment and maintenance of a hierarchical but "organically unified" society.

Saint-Simon's Developmental View of History

Simultaneously with Hegel, but independently of him, Saint-Simon advanced a remarkably similar conception of historical development. Hegel viewed the historical development of society as the increasing realization of reason; Saint-Simon placed scientific knowledge in this role. Both thinkers conceived of historical development advancing in stages; for Saint-Simon as for Hegel each stage embodied some degree of rationality, and therefore some necessity. Both thinkers regarded development and progress as the struggle of opposing forces. Keeping Hegel's conception in mind, we can sketch Saint-

Simon's conception of European history, as found in his *Organisateur,* and note the similarities underlying the general outlook of both thinkers.

As a social system comes into being it enters its ascending phase, which continues until it reaches maturity; with maturity the system begins to decline. The feudal system, for example, reached maturity according to Saint-Simon during the tenth century or thereabouts and from that time to the eve of the Revolution showed an uninterrupted decline. During this period of decline, the industrial and scientific forces, which had formed in the midst of the old system, manifested themselves not only by their tendency to undermine and ultimately to destroy the old order, but also by giving rise to the new one. The new forces, while detaching consciences and wills from the old centers, which until then had provided direction and unity to the system, gathered momentum and increasingly became themselves new foci of common action and centers of organization. A new social system was emerging in the bosom of the old, which was now powerless to arrest the process and was thus moving inevitably to its demise. Émile Durkheim described Saint-Simon's general conception of these processes in the following terms: "In the measure that the ancient social system gave way, another was formed in the very bosom of the first. The old society contained within itself a new society, in process of formation and every day acquiring more strength and consistency. But these two organizations are necessarily antagonistic to each other. They result from opposing forces and aim at contradictory ends. One is essentially aggressive, warlike, the other essentially pacifist. The one sees in other peoples enemies to destroy; the other tends to view them as collaborators in a common undertaking. One has conquest for its aim, the other, production. Similarly in spiritual affairs the first calls on faith and imposes beliefs which it puts beyond discussion. The second calls on reason and even trust—it requires a type of intellectual subordination which is essential to rationality, a commitment to further exploration and testing. Thus these two societies could not coexist without contradicting each other."[8] In this formulation, Saint-Simon's organic and conflictive view of historical development becomes quite evident; as we shall see, this conception of the historical change which European society had undergone profoundly influenced Marx's theory of social change.

In his *Système Industriel,* Saint-Simon shows that this process eventually led to the French Revolution. "This tremendous crisis did not at all have its origin in this or that isolated fact. . . . It operated as an overturning of the political system for the simple reason that the state of society to which the ancient order corresponded had totally changed in nature. A civil and moral revolution which had gradually developed for more than six centuries engendered and necessitated a political revolution. . . . If one insists on

---

8 Durkheim, *op. cit.,* pp. 118–19.

attributing the French Revolution to one source, it must be dated from the day the liberation of the communes and the cultivation of exact sciences in western Europe began."[9] Thus Marx's theory of revolution, at least in its very general aspects, is anticipated.

For Saint-Simon, the Revolution was necessary and inevitable; nevertheless, he criticizes the revolutionaries: it was rash to overthrow the old institutions without determining what to put in their place. He objects not to the Revolution but to its not having become what it might have; the Revolution stopped midway in its course and did not culminate positively. The critical, destructive, and negative work of the metaphysicians and revolutionaries was necessary to clear the way for the new order; but they never went beyond their negative, rigid, abstract principles to form a positive philosophical basis for the new order. The new organic society must be built exclusively on positive principles. Had it not become clear that societies based on conflicting tendencies and principles are doomed to instability, crisis, and revolution? Like Hegel, then, who brought his dialectical process to an abrupt stop with the Prussian state, the highest expression of reason, Saint-Simon, too, now wanted to eliminate all conflictive elements from the new organic system.

Saint-Simon perhaps meant well when he advocated the rule of the scientists and industrialists. He wanted not the strongest to rule but the most capable and knowledgeable in science and industry. The scientific-industrial élite was not to dictate orders but only to declare what conforms to the nature of things. "In the old system," he wrote, "society is governed essentially by men; in the new it is governed only by principles."[10] In the new society there was to be scientific administration, but no politics properly speaking. Those who direct and administer would not be "above," they would merely fulfill a different function. How would this be reconciled with the preservation of private property? Would not the ownership of productive resources on the part of the industrialists lead to the concentration of power in their hands? Perhaps, but more important is that property should not run counter to the general need; it must not be separated from so-called intelligence and capacity.

The check on egoism in the new society is to be Christian brotherly love. "Love one another," is the motto Saint-Simon inscribed on the first page of his *Système Industriel*. The fate of the proletariat is to be improved as much as possible, not so much for their sake as for that of the élite. There are two ways of keeping this class in check: either use force to impose the social order, or make them love it. The latter is by far the more rational for the propertied and scientific élite and will ensure the social peace more effectively than repressive measures.

9 Quoted in Durkheim, *Ibid.,* p. 120.
10 Saint-Simon, *op. cit.,* IV, p. 197.

Saint-Simon's "new society" will no doubt strike many as a rather transparent ideological rationale for the emerging élites of his time. And when one considers the various approximations of his "new society" in the twentieth century, its grotesque quality, which he apparently never saw, becomes very obvious indeed. Individual freedom counted for nothing in his new order, a fact that has prompted Albert Salomon, among others, to regard Saint-Simon as one of the founders of totalitarian ideology. This will be further explored in our discussion of Comte in whom this tendency is even more pronounced. But first we must consider a final aspect of Saint-Simon's doctrine: the role of internationalism and religion in the new society.

Internationalism and Religion

The transition to the new society cannot take place in a single country, independently of the developments in others. The European societies are not isolated from one another; rather, there are definite bonds which unite them. Therefore they must become a community of nations where despotism is eliminated from each and every one. "The great moral movement," Saint-Simon wrote, "which should make society pass from the modified despotic regime to one most advantageous to the majority of society, cannot be effected except by being common to the most enlightened peoples."[11] Why does this interdependence exist among the societies of Europe? They are neighbors who share a similar social, economic, and religious history. They were all at one time subjected to feudal regimes and shared a common religion and clergy, whose head, the Pope, was independent of all individual governments. Any important change in one European nation is bound to have repercussions in another, as was proved by both the revolution and the counterrevolution. Europe must be unified in peace. But how can one nation disarm and become peaceful while the rest remain armed and warlike? Peace would in fact be impossible, Saint-Simon argues, were it not for the newly emergent industrial forces and spirit which now render the military spirit quite obsolete. National rivalries and hatreds as expressed in international military conflicts can only hinder the development of the industrial civilization on which the future well-being of all Europe rests. The industrial spirit will bind peoples instead of dividing them; for all the countries of Europe will now have the same interests of furthering production and this will increasingly be the case. All the societies of Europe will now be united by the common need for security in production and liberty in exchange. "The producers of all lands are therefore essentially friends." Thus it is not only nationally but internationally as well that all "producers" have common interests conducing to social solidarity.

In addressing himself to the possibility of a peaceful and united European

---

[11] Quoted in Durkheim, *op. cit.*, p. 170.

community, Saint-Simon did not adequately take into account the survival of feudal elements in each society. Nor did he foresee the new nationalism in Europe, which became manifest later in the century as a distinctly economic rivalry among nations and which led to ever more bitter and extensive military conflicts. The so-called common industrial spirit did not prove itself to be the internationally unifying factor Saint-Simon had assumed it would be.

Saint-Simon also regarded science as an antidote to nationalism. An international community of scholars and scientists—a new international spiritual élite to replace the old—would emerge as a unifying force. Although national rivalries would remain for a time, they would merely be vestiges of a transitional phase. Saint-Simon saw some kind of professional and occupational solidarity emerging, capable presumably of corroding the irrational nationalistic sentiments. The universalistic interests of the industrial professions and occupations would undermine and supersede all the particularisms of the old order. Eventually the industrial system would embrace all of Europe and, perhaps, even all of humanity. Nations would not disappear entirely; they would retain some degree of cultural distinctiveness and political autonomy, but not the moral importance they historically have had.

Nationalism is a form of egoism which must be drastically reduced, if not eliminated, in the new society. Patriotism, he writes, ". . . is nothing but national egoism; and this egoism causes the same injustices to be committed by nation to nation as personal egoism does among individuals."[12] Saint-Simon did not expect this international community to develop in an altogether spontaneous fashion. Common institutions and organization will be necessary —otherwise everyone will continue to resort to force. Supranational forms of organization based on the common industrial spirit will bring about a revolution in international relations. However, these conditions, conducing to an international, temporal bond, are insufficient for real international peace and unity. In addition, a spiritual bond will be necessary—a common body of doctrines and beliefs affording moral unity to all European societies. And again, as in the Middle Ages, this will take the form of a common religion, for it is conflicting beliefs which lead inevitably to war. The spiritual and moral unity of men and nations would be based on the New Christianity.

Although *Le Nouveau Christianisme* did not constitute an about-face, it did represent a discernible change in his outlook. In his earliest writings, the emphasis is on the purely scientific. But in his *Système Industriel* and especially in this final work, the idea of God comes to the fore. Increasingly Saint-Simon was led to the conclusion that interests and organizations were not sufficient to guarantee peace and unity, either within societies or among them. *Moral sentiments* were now assigned an important role. Thus he differs from the utilitarians who relied on self-interest to ensure the well-being of

12 *Ibid.*, p. 175.

society. Saint-Simon, more emphatically and systematically than they, begins in his later works to stress the need for moral unity as an additional and equally essential basis of social order and unity. Charity, mutual obligation, and philanthropy are essential; and while the new religion will have its creed and dogma, morality will be its central core. (Later, it will be seen how Durkheim employs Saint-Simonian ideas in his attempt to reconcile the disorganizing effects of industrial development with the requirements of social order and unity.)

Saint-Simon's God is impersonal and immanent in all nature. His final doctrine is a form of pantheism in which spirit and matter are once again unified. For Saint-Simon, morality is basically secular having no end beyond the temporal. It is only by procuring for mankind "the greatest degree of happiness it can achieve during its worldly life that you will succeed in establishing Christianity."[13] His final word on the subject, then, is that the new world will require religion as well as science. Positive philosophy and science, which were to supersede once and for all the theological and metaphysical stages, become a somewhat secularized religion. Eventually, as we shall see, things go so far in this direction that Comte, in his later work, *Politique Positive*, proclaims himself the pope of the new positive religion.

Looking back over Saint-Simon's doctrine as a whole, one sees clearly the two main intellectual currents which shaped it. He lived and wrote at the turn of the century, when the Romantic, conservative, and Catholic movements were challenging every single premise bequeathed by the Enlightenment. Like the *Philosophes*, Saint-Simon had great faith in the power of reason to change the world; he was optimistic and cosmopolitan in his outlook. As for the Revolution he did not condemn it. It had simply not gone far enough, and this was mainly due to the negative-critical principles of the *Philosophes*. Where he parts company with the Enlightenment thinkers is in their evaluation of the Middle Ages. He rejects their total repudiation of that period as an age of superstition and ignorance. Here the influence of the reaction is clear. For like the conservatives and the theorists of the Catholic revival, he admired the "medieval unity" so much that he adopted it as the model for his new world. The medieval world, he believed, was for a time an intellectual and social unity; it was international, organic, hierarchical, and stable, and it was ruled by both a spiritual and a temporal élite. But such social orders do not flower twice in history. Science and industry, from the moment they appeared in the bosom of the old order, sounded its death knell. And this is where he departs from Bonald and Maistre. Science and industry have not only led once and for all to the demise of the old order, they have become the essential positive principles of the new one. The emergence of conflicting principles and forces within the old system inevitably led to the Revolution and to the destruction of the medieval order. The new society,

---

13 Saint-Simon, *op cit.*, VII, p. 154.

therefore, must not be based on conflicting principles if it is to escape the fate of its predecessor. It, too, must be international, organic, hierarchical, and stable, ruled by a spiritual and a temporal élite, and, finally, unified by an international religion. In this way Saint-Simon absorbs and reflects the influence of both the Enlightenment and the counterrevolution. On balance, however, his synthesis represents, ideologically, the bourgeoisie and the related professional and scientific élites who were struggling to consolidate and advance the position of power they had gained during the Revolution and the Empire. When the bourgeoisie finally repudiated him, it was not for his "socialism" but for his theological tendencies.

Saint-Simon viewed the new elements of his age not as conflicting forces but potentially as parts of an organic whole. In a larger context, his thought patterns merely reflect the conditions of *early* nineteenth-century Europe: nationalism was offset by a semblance of European unity; Catholicism seemed to be making its peace with liberal democracy; and large-scale industry with its accompanying proletariat had not yet appeared on the Continent. Therefore the intense class struggles of the latter part of the century were still unknown phenomena in Saint-Simon's time. The peoples of the nineteenth century failed to achieve an integrated industrial civilization, and those of the twentieth experienced directly a type of "technocratic utopia" not unlike the one Saint-Simon had advocated. He had ignored the problem of freedom and had looked forward to an essentially rigid, caste society.

Auguste Comte, though he denied it, appropriated virtually all of Saint-Simon's ideas, as we shall presently see.

7

Auguste Comte

(1798–1857)

The term "positive," as Comte employed it in his positive philosophy, was explicitly polemical and intended as an ideological
weapon with which to combat the philosophical legacy of the
Enlightenment and the Revolution. The critical and destructive
principles of *negative* philosophy were to be discredited and repudiated so that they could be replaced by the affirmative and
constructive principles of *positive* philosophy. Actually, this
counterattack also took place in Germany, where positivists attempted to challenge the radical tendency in Hegel's thought.
Their most fundamental objection to Hegel's negative philosophy
was that it ". . . 'negates' things as they are. The matters of fact
that make up the given state of affairs, when viewed in the light
of reason, become negative, limited, transitory—they become
perishing forms within a comprehensive process that leads beyond
them. The Hegelian dialectic was seen as the prototype of all
destructive negations of the given, for in it every immediately
given form passes into its opposite and attains its true content
only by so doing. This kind of philosophy, the critics said, denies
to the given the dignity of the real; it contains the principle of
revolution."[1] In the present discussion, attention will be confined
to France where Comte fought against the heritage of the *Philosophes* and in the process formed his own philosophy.

[1] Herbert Marcuse, *Reason and Revolution* (Boston: Beacon Press,
1960), p. 325. For a full discussion of the positive reaction, see pp. 323–
74.

Comte saw a "deplorable state of anarchy" in his time, and he believed that his "social physics," bearing directly upon the "principal needs and grievances of society," would help bring order out of chaos.[2] He hoped to call this "science" to the attention of statesmen who "profess to devote themselves to the task of resolving the alarming revolutionary constitution of modern societies." Social and moral anarchy are the result of intellectual anarchy, itself a consequence of the fact that, on the one hand, theologico-metaphysical philosophy has declined and, on the other, positive philosophy has not yet reached the point where it can provide an intellectual basis for a new organization and thus deliver society from the peril of dissolution.

Order and progress, which the ancients thought irreconcilable, must be united once and for all. Comte considered it the great misfortune of his time that the two principles were regarded as contradictory and were represented by opposing political parties. What he called the retrograde party was for order, while the anarchical party was for progress. The principle of order was derived from the Catholic-feudal, or theological, state of social philosophy, whose exponents were Bonald, Maistre, et al. The principle of progress, on the other hand, was derived from the critical tendencies of the Reformation and the Enlightenment. Existing social classes, much to Comte's chagrin, tended to polarize and to support either one or the other. Hence, class conflict, disorder, and anarchy. In every crisis, the retrograde party argued that the problem was due to the destruction of the old order and therefore demanded its complete restoration; the anarchical party, in contrast, argued that the trouble stemmed from the fact that the destruction of the old order was incomplete, and, therefore, that the revolution must continue.

Comte, like Saint-Simon, appreciated certain aspects of the feudal-theologi-cal order and did not reject it altogether. True, it had become "pernicious" by outliving its usefulness, but it had facilitated the development of modern society. Since, however, it can no longer hold its own before the natural progress of scientific intelligence and other social changes, the theological polity can never again become the basis of social order. Thus Comte, unlike Bonald, believed it was impossible to restore the old order. The decline of the old is not temporary; neither is it the work of Providence. Somehow, Comte argues, a synthesis of the opposing ideas, order and progress, must be achieved, because only through intellectual unity and harmony can social unity be restored.

Science and industry were the main causes of the decline of the feudal-theological order, and the rise of the scientific spirit now precludes the

---

[2] The present discussion of Comte is based on the second volume of Harriet Martineau's translation and condensation of his Cours de Philosophie Positive. It appeared in English as The Positive Philosophy, 2 Volumes (London: Kegan Paul, 1893). Her rendition so impressed Comte that he recommended it over the original and as a result her version was retranslated into French. (The following references to this work will merely cite the page numbers in parentheses after the passage.)

restoration of that order; likewise with the industrial spirit, which now prevents the recurrence of the feudal-military spirit. Moreover, the new spirit is so strong that the spokesmen for the theological school are themselves infected with it. De Maistre, for example, tried to justify the restoration on the grounds of *reason* rather than divine right, thereby showing he was a child of his times. Also, the spokesmen for this school are not unified; torn as they are by sects, they have even accepted many basic principles which are antagonistic to their theological spirit, *e.g.*, subordinating the spiritual to the temporal authority. If, finally, they could succeed even temporarily in restoring the old order, the crisis would break out all over again—but even more violently than before because the same disintegrating forces would constantly be at work within it. So much for the theological stage and any hopes for restoring it: What about the metaphysical?

The principles of the "metaphysicians," Comte's term for the Enlightenment thinkers, were essentially critical and revolutionary. They contributed to progress but only in a negative sense. The metaphysical stage was necessary because it broke up the old system and paved the way for the next stage— the positive one which will put an end to the revolutionary period by the formation of a social order uniting the principles of order *and* progress. The metaphysical stage, necessary but provisional, "must be dangerously active till the new political organization which is to succeed it is ready to put an end to its agitation." (p. 9.) The metaphysical spirit was necessary to direct the struggle and organize the maximum energy for the overthrow of the great ancient system. But, it, too, has outlived its usefulness and has become obstructive. Comte is especially indignant at the metaphysical view that represents "all government as being the enemy of society, and the duty of society to be to keep up a perpetual suspicion and vigilance, restricting the activity of government more and more, in order to guard against its encroachments. . . ." (p. 11.) Liberty of conscience is a dogma which *had* value as a weapon against theological dogmatism but is no longer useful because it can never be a positive organic principle, *i.e.*, the basis for the reorganization of society. The various demands for liberty are strictly "negative" principles. Just as astronomers, physicists, and chemists would not allow laymen to question or interfere with their operations, so in social physics (the term "sociology" does not yet appear at this stage of his discussion) the scientific experts should not yield to the incompetent. Social reorganization requires intellectual reorganization, and this is impossible so long as individuals have the right of inquiry on subjects above their qualifications. Comte insists that unity and unanimity will be essential in the new organic society. Social order, he writes, " . . . must ever be incompatible with a perpetual discussion of the foundations of society." (p. 13.)

Equality is another dogma: it had limited historical value as a weapon, but must not be turned into an absolute. It is an anarchic principle and hostile to order, as is the dogma of the "sovereignty of the people," which condemns the superior to dependence on the masses and opposes reorganization on different principles.

Comte also finds particularly objectionable Rousseau's "metaphysical notion of a supposed state of nature" and his representation of "civilization as an ever growing degeneracy from the primitive ideal type." Rousseau's presupposition that one can ask questions about the suitability of social systems for the nature of individuals was for Comte presumptuous and dangerous. He therefore dismisses Rousseau's conception as nothing more than the "metaphysical form of the theological dogma of the degradation of the human race by original sin." (p. 16.) The disciples of the metaphysical school are also inconsistent if not hypocritical; for once in power they change their conduct and adopt many retrograde principles: war, centralization, natural religion, etc.

Social crisis will continue so long as the two conflicting doctrines, the theological and the metaphysical, prevail. No order is possible until both are superseded by the positive stage, which will be more *organic* than the theological and more *progressive* than the metaphysical. But one must not rush to bring about the new order. Rather, the people must wait patiently for the new system to emerge, and when the right conditions arise society will submit to the rules which will assure its preservation. The new society will not arise so long as the theological and metaphysical spirits prevail, for they are mutually contradictory and cannot survive together indefinitely in one system. All contradictions must be banished from the new order. England's constitutional monarchy is based on contradictory principles and therefore, predicts Comte, its "inevitable end cannot be very far off." (p. 22.)

Comte despised intellectual anarchy and regarded it as the main cause of moral disunity. He had disdain for those laymen who expressed themselves about complex social and political issues as if these were not dependent on education and training. True moral order, Comte believed, "is incompatible with the existing vagabond liberty of individual minds if such license were to last; for the great social rules which should become customary cannot be abandoned to the blind and arbitrary decision of an incompetent public without losing all their efficacy." (p. 25.) Comte feared and disliked social criticism and its disorganizing results. Criticism of the traditional patriarchal family, for example, had led to the legalization of divorce, and hence to personal and domestic disorder. Questioning and criticizing time-honored institutions is destructive and threatens to undermine all social life. No important social duties should be questioned or discussed until such time as the discussion is directed by "true" positive principles. Such principles will provide a basis for intellectual unity; lacking this unity, society also lacks a moral authority and degenerates into a state of terror, anarchy, and corruption.

Comte also feared the contemporary emphasis on "material" considerations and regarded it as fatal to progress. This emphasis had revolutionary implications, dangerously annulling the resignation and submissiveness of the lower classes which he so strongly desired. The source of social evils is not to be sought in basic economic and political institutions but in ideas and manners. "When all political evils," he writes, "are imputed to institutions instead of to ideas and social manners, which are now the real seat of the mischief; the remedy is vainly sought in changes, each more serious than the last, in institutions and existing powers." (p. 31.) Private property, to be sure, brings with it certain evils but "it is equally evident that the remedy must arise from opinions, customs, and manners, and that political regulations can have no radical efficacy." (p. 32.) The point, then, is not to tamper with, or change, existing institutions but rather to bring about a moral reorganization—a euphemism for the acquiescence of the lower classes to their social condition. There will be neither order nor progress so long as men fail to recognize that their suffering is not of a physical but "of a moral nature."

The Advent of Positive Philosophy

Comte had great confidence in the ascendancy of the positive doctrine. Its "perfect logical coherence" and its social function assured this. For this doctrine "will impart a homogeneous and rational character to the desultory politics of our day, and it will . . . establish a general harmony in the entire system of social ideas. . . ." (p. 35.) Positive philosophy, he believed, is undoubtedly superior to its predecessors. For while the metaphysical school condemned all periods prior to the Revolution, and the retrograde school disparaged the whole of the modern era, only the positive principle is able to recognize "the fundamental law of continuous human development, representing the existing evolution as the necessary result of the gradual series of former transformations, by simply extending to social phenomena the spirit which governs the treatment of all other natural phenomena." (p. 36.) And toward what end is this positive science to be developed? "It is plain that true science has no other aim than the establishment of intellectual order, which is the basis of every other order." (p. 36.)

We must let Comte speak for himself to demonstrate the degree to which he advanced his positive doctrine with one purpose in mind—to avert revolution and to achieve the resignation of the "multitude" to the conditions of the existing order. He explicitly pushes to the extreme some of the conclusions which were only implicit in Saint-Simon's work and purges from that work every last critical element that might have remained. "It is only by the positive polity that the revolutionary spirit can be restrained, because by it alone can the influence of the critical doctrine be justly estimated and circumscribed. . . . Under the rule of the positive spirit, again, all the difficult and delicate questions which now keep up a perpetual irritation in the bosom of society, and which can never be settled while mere political solutions are proposed, will be scientifically estimated, to the great furtherance of social peace. . . . At the same time, it [the positive polity] will be teaching society that, in the present state of their ideas, no political change can be of supreme importance, while the perturbation attending change is supremely mischievous, in the way both of immediate hindrance, and of diverting attention from the true need and procedure. . . . Again, the positive spirit tends to consolidate order, by the rational development of a wise resignation to incurable political evils. . . . A true resignation—that is, a permanent disposition to endure, steadily, and without hope of compensation, all inevitable evils, can proceed only from a deep sense of the connection of all kinds of natural phenomena with invariable laws. If there are (as I doubt not there are) political evils which, like some personal sufferings, cannot be remedied by science, science at least proves to us that they are incurable, so as to calm our restlessness under pain by the conviction that it is by natural laws that they are rendered insurmountable. Human nature suffers in its relations with the astronomical world, and the physical, chemical, and biological, as well as the political. How is it that we turbulently resist in the last case, while, in the others, we are calm and resigned. . . ? Finally, the positive philosophy befriends public order by bringing back men's understanding to a normal state through the influence of its method alone, before it has had time to establish any social theory. It dissipates disorder at once by imposing a series of indisputable scientific conditions on the study of political questions. By including social science in the scientific hierarchy, the positive spirit admits to success in this study only well-prepared and disciplined minds, so trained in the preceding departments of knowledge as to be fit for the complex problems of the last. The long and difficult preliminary elaboration must disgust and deter vulgar and ill-prepared minds, and subdue the most rebellious." (pp. 37–38.)

The positive conception of progress is superior to all others, and especially superior to the revolutionary view in which progress consists of the continuous extension of freedom, and the "gradual expansion of human powers. Now, even in the restricted and negative sense in which this is true—that of the perpetual diminution of obstacles—the positive philosophy is incontestably superior: for true liberty is nothing else than a rational submission to the preponderance of the laws of nature. . . ." (p. 39.) The scientific élite will be the final authority of what these laws are and will indicate the degree to which the lot of the lower classes may be slowly improved. In this way the positive doctrine will provide a so-called constructive alternative to the insurrectionary solution advocated by the revolutionary school. Basic economic and political institutions are not to be changed, for history has shown that such change avails nothing. The class structure should remain as it is; and class conflict presumably will be reduced, even eliminated, through the moral reconciliation of the classes. This will be facilitated by imposing a moral authority between the working classes and the leaders of society.

Those who identify with the theological-retrograde school probably will not support the positive doctrine because they are not interested in just any order but in their unique one. The "stationary school," the defenders of the status quo, on the other hand, may be won over when they recognize that it will further their interests. But Comte's real target is the revolutionary school whose "doctrines will be absorbed by the new philosophy, while all its anarchical tendencies will be extinguished." The present generation of scientists, however, is too much infected with revolutionary principles to adopt the positive view. Therefore the chance of winning over the scientists will depend on the younger generation who will be given a really thorough positive education. In all cases, "progress" will depend on "an intellectual, and then a moral reorganization [which] must precede and direct the political." (p. 42.)

The Positive Method in its Application to Social Phenomena

For Comte, what distinguishes the scientific spirit is its steady subordination of imagination to observation, of reason to "facts." This is quite different from the eighteenth-century conception in which reasoning and observing are coordinate functions of the scientific method. In Comte's view, prediction, or "prevision" as he calls it, will facilitate social control, a primary and even exclusive aim of his positive doctrine. In these terms, "to predict in order to control," becomes a totalitarian slogan in his hands. This becomes even clearer in his "scientific" conception of society.

Order and progress are the static and dynamic aspects of a society. Order refers to the harmony which prevails among the various conditions of existence, while progress refers to the society's orderly development according to natural social laws. Thus the two principles, previously mutually antagonistic, are reconciled. It is natural and normal for the elements of the social system, the institutions of society, to be interdependent and interrelated. Therefore, even for analytical purposes social elements should not be contemplated separately as if they had an independent existence. All the parts of the system make up an harmonious whole, which, by definition, is divested of all conflictive, contradictory, and antagonistic elements. He enunciates as a scientific principle "that there must always be a spontaneous harmony between the whole and the parts of the social system," and he insists that harmony will establish itself through radical consensus, the only condition proper to the social organism. Emphasis is always on adjustment to the "natural" social laws, quite deliberately opposed to Enlightenment principles where the emphasis is on changing the social system to allow for the infinite perfection of man. Again and again Comte stresses that the scientific method requires that society be studied as a whole and not separated into its component parts. It is as if he fears that the logical analysis of a society's institutions will inevitably lead to its actual dissolution; an analytical view of society, in which essential relationships are critically scrutinized, will revive the very same critical, negative, and revolutionary philosophy that positivism was to replace once and for all.

Social dynamics refers to the study of the patterns of evolutionary progress in which the sequences of development are necessary and inevitable. Social dynamics, then, is really "dynamic order" proceeding according to natural, orderly, and necessary laws. For "unless the movement was determined by those laws, it would occasion the entire destruction of the social system." (p. 72.) Amelioration accompanies development but it is not unlimited. "The chimerical notion of unlimited perfectibility is thus at once excluded." (p. 73.) The tendency toward improvement is spontaneous, and therefore does not require any special political action directed toward change. The latter is in effect "superfluous," because each stage is as perfect as it can be. Not only political action but human action in general is very limited in its effects and subject to the constriction of natural laws. Can these laws nevertheless be modified in any way? The human race could perhaps accelerate or retard certain tendencies but never change the nature of those tendencies. It certainly cannot reverse certain orders of development nor can it skip stages. The importance of human action, in general, and political action, in particular, has been greatly exaggerated.

As for other aspects of Comte's method, he emphasized such techniques as observation, experiment, and comparison. And in spite of the transparent ideological elements of his methodology, he does manage to grasp some of the principles of scientific method—which always remains subordinated, however, to the construction of his hierarchical, organic, authoritarian society. Observation is impossible without theory, first to direct it and then to interpret what is observed. Facts cannot speak for themselves, for "though we are steeped to the lips in them, we can make no use of them, nor even be aware of them, for want of speculative guidance in examining them." (p. 81.) Facts must be attached at least by a tentative hypothesis to the laws of social development. But for Comte, as we have seen, these laws as well as all his other assumptions and concepts about society were in the first instance inspired by their ideological function. The whole apparatus of his positive doctrine is ideological in the strictest sense of that term, and science never achieves very much autonomy in his doctrinaire and totalitarian system. He remained blind throughout his work to the ideal of freedom even as it related to science and apparently failed to see how many aspects of society he had dogmatically closed off from the view of science by means of his doctrinaire pronouncements.

As Comte proceeds in his exposition of social statics, he considers the individual, the family, and society, "the last comprehending in a scientific sense, the whole of the human species, and chiefly, the *whole of the white race*." (p. 105, italics added.) Not the individual but the family is the true social unit; for the family is the school of social life. Man is a social being whose social nature is formed in the family context. But these assertions and the like are always made with a specific ideological intention in mind. The subordination of woman is natural and will continue in the "new" society: The female sex is in a state of perpetual infancy. "Sociology will prove that the equality of the sexes, of which so much is said, is incompatible with all social existence. . . ." (p. 112.) Thus Comte argues the organic inferiority of woman and attempts to provide a "scientific" rationale for the same state of affairs that the theological school regarded as determined by Providence.

Generally, "providential wisdom," though in a secularized form, dominates Comte's conception of society and its development. The changes brought about by the inherent wisdom of the spontaneous evolutionary process are always "superior to any that the most eminent reformers would have ventured to conceive of before hand." (p. 114.) Nevertheless, there are developments which, though natural, can threaten the very existence of society—particularly its consensus and solidarity. Comte views the division of labor, growing increasingly complex, in this light. It seems to be an inexorable process, the very principle of society's development; but at the same time as the division of labor is extended, it seems to decompose and fragment society. Thus government is assigned the role "to guard against and restrain the fundamental dispersion of ideas, sentiments, and ideals, which is the inevitable result of the very principle of human development, and which, if left to itself, would put a stop to social progression in all important respects." (p. 119.) Every element and institution of the society, including government, must serve to further stability, solidarity, and order. Society is everything in Comte's scheme—the individual, nothing. Each must subordinate himself, but this has its rewards because "there can be no one who, in his secret mind, has not often felt, more or less vividly, how sweet it is to obey when he can have the rare privilege of consigning the burdensome responsibility of his general self-conduct to wise and trustworthy guidance. . . ." (p. 122.)

This review of Comte's work should suffice to show how much of it was explicitly justificatory and apologetic of his "best of all possible worlds." Despite the lip service he paid to "science," virtually every assertion he makes is based not on experience and observation but on values and sentiments. And these are primarily the values, sentiments, and interests of the bourgeoisie. He did not see, or did not want to see, that the principles of organization he enunciated—his a prioris—were rooted in a specific socio-historical context. He refused to see that man is not merely an object but an active subject; that he *determines* and is not merely determined; that he can change society according to goals, ". . . something which positivism must deny, for goals, in their very nature, are something that have not as yet been experienced." [3] He rejected, as extremely dangerous, the idea that man can transcend the immediate factual order to comprehend and organize social

---

[3] See Frank Hartung, "The Social Functions of Positivism," *Philosophy of Science*, Vol. 12, April 1945, no. 2.

reality and thus free himself from so-called "inexorable" forces and conditions.

In his later work, *Politique Positive* (1851–54), the religious and sentimental factor finally prevailed and Comte unabashedly proclaimed himself pope of the new positive religion—an ironic turn of events for the ardent defender of positive science. Little wonder, then, that J. S. Mill described Comte's later views as "the most complete system of spiritual and temporal despotism that ever issued from the brain of any human being—except, perhaps, Ignatius Loyola."[4]

Despite Comte's philosophic efforts, the peoples of Europe failed to achieve an organic, integrated, conflict-free civilization. And it was Karl Marx who was to draw the most radical conclusions from this failure.

[4] Quoted in F. M. H. Markham, *Henri Comte de Saint-Simon,* Oxford: Basil Blackwell, 1952, p. xlviii.

PART III

THE
MARXIAN
WATERSHED

8

Philosophical
Orientations

Comte's positive philosophy, as we have seen, was a conscious attempt to discredit and repudiate what he and other positivists had termed "negative" philosophy. The negative-critical philosophy which emerged and took shape with the Enlightenment had proved itself a formidable weapon in the hands of the rising bourgeoisie in its struggle against the older classes of the theological-feudal order. Ultimately, this struggle resulted in the French Revolution and the dissolution of the old order. In these terms, negative philosophy, even for Comte, had fulfilled a useful historical function. Now, however, with the establishment of the bourgeois order, Comte believed negative philosophy, the legacy of the Enlightenment, had outlived its usefulness. Now, when the major task had become consolidation of the new bourgeois-industrial order and creation of a truly organic and integrated society, negative philosophy led only to divisiveness, conflict, and disorder. It stirred the imagination and hopes of the proletariat and encouraged class conflict. The proletarians, instead of finding their place in the new organic society and adjusting peacefully to it as Comte desired, were being agitated to struggle for the transformation of the existing society. Not that Comte did not see the need for improving the condition of this class; but the emphasis for him was always on *improvement* and precisely that.

Each stage in the evolution of the new organic society was

viewed by him as a necessary one; therefore, the working class must adjust to the present stage. Improvement would come about organically as the society progressed harmoniously from stage to stage. Revolution—*i.e.*, a total transformation of the social system—was out of the question. Revolution could have only negative consequences; it would only shatter the existing order without bringing in its wake any fundamental change in the condition of the vast majority of the people. Progress was best assured not by criticism, class conflict, and revolutionary activity but by reconciling the conflicting tendencies and classes; by educating all classes of society—and especially the lower classes—to take their proper place in the new, hierarchically organized society and to resign themselves to their condition. This is what the new positive science taught and this was to be its chief function: to achieve an organic and conflict-free social order.

If with Comte, then, there is a complete renunciation of the legacy of the Enlightenment (and the French Revolution), with Marx we return full circle to a whole-hearted reaffirmation of that legacy. Marx restores, and skillfully employs, the very philosophical premises Comte so intensely detested.

First among these premises was the perfectibility of man. Marx had a conception of "natural man"—the individual human being, his needs, and his potential for development—not unlike that of Rousseau and, more generally, of the Enlightenment thinkers. Although this conception is expressed most explicitly in his early writings, it remains throughout his life the basis of his analysis and criticism of the capitalist system, and of his hopes for the attainment of a truly *human* society.

Man, Marx believed, as did the *Philosophes* before him, is infinitely perfectible. Man's *essential* powers—his latent and potential human powers—are unlimited in their capacity for development. If man is now no more than a laboring beast, he need not remain in this condition; he can attain the highest forms of creativity, thought and action. This is the underlying conception by which Marx assessed and evaluated social systems. Man's latent creative powers were stifled and repressed under the social conditions of all class societies. The existing system, capitalism, was not only preventing the fulfillment of his potential as man, it was even depriving him of his animal needs—fresh air, food, sex, etc. Hunger, for example, was not felt as a result of external, natural conditions nor was it experienced simply as a phase in the recurrent and inevitable rhythm of man's metabolism. Quite the contrary: hunger was a condition of deprivation imposed by other men. Marx thus condemned the capitalist system for its effect on individual human beings. This view finds its clearest and most consistent expression in one of Marx's early philosophical works, *The Economic and Philosophic Manuscripts of 1844,* to which we now turn.

It offended Marx's conception of man that the capitalist-industrial system had reduced him to an *animal laborans,* "a beast reduced to the strictest bodily needs."[1] The workers' "needs" were now at the "barest and most miserable level of physical subsistence" and their activity for the better part of their waking day was a tedious and repetitive mechanical movement. The lowest possible level of life and activity had become the general standard— one in which men were deprived not only of their human needs but of their animal needs as well.

Even the need for fresh air ceases for the worker. Man returns to living in a cave, which is now, however, contaminated with the mephitic breath of plague given off by civilization, and which he continues to occupy only *precariously,* it being for him an alien habitation which can be withdrawn from him any day—a place from which, if he does not pay, he can be thrown out any day. For this mortuary he has to *pay.* A dwelling in the *light,* which Prometheus in Aeschylus designated as one of the greatest boons, by means of which he made the savage into a human being, ceases to exist for the worker. Light, air, etc.—the simplest *animal* cleanliness— ceases to be a need for man. *Dirt*—this stagnation and putrefaction of man —the *sewage* of civilization (speaking quite literally) —comes to be the *element of life* for him. Utter, unnatural neglect, putrefied nature, comes to be his *life-element.* None of his senses exist any longer, and not only in his human fashion, but in an *inhuman* fashion, and therefore, not even in an animal fashion." (p. 117.)

Clearly Marx had an image of man as he could be and hence ought to be, and what he saw and described was a far cry from that image. Far from developing his essential human powers, man was being debased and deformed and thus becoming something less than an animal.

In these philosophical writings, the dehumanization of man was viewed by Marx as a consequence of *alienation.* This idea, though Hegelian in origin, was fundamentally transformed in the hands of Marx. Alienation for Hegel, like his other constructs, was exclusively a phenomenon of the mind. With the Left-Hegelians the concept was significantly altered but remained primarily a philosophical notion, *viz.,* a condition in which man's own powers appear as independent forces or entities controlling his actions. Feuerbach, for instance, had used the concept of alienation in his explanation of religious phenomena and viewed extramundane beings as man's own invention: The higher beings which man's religious fantasies created were, unbeknownst to him, the fantastic reflections of his own essence. Marx, going beyond Feuerbach, no longer treated alienation as a strictly philosophico-psychological phenomenon. Rather, alienation was now analyzed as an explicitly social phenomenon in the context of specific social relationships and in a specific socio-historical system. (As we shall see, Marx never abandons his interest in the problem of alienation, though his express mention of the term becomes less frequent in his

1 Karl Marx, *Economic and Philosophic Manuscripts of 1844* (Moscow: Foreign Languages Publishing House, 1961), p. 30. (Subsequent references to this work will be cited in parentheses after the particular extract.)

later writings.) Moreover, already in these early writings he is moving from predominantly philosophical concepts to those of political economy. He is intent upon assuring his reader that his conclusions have been reached "by means of a wholly empirical analysis based on a conscientious critical study of political economy." (p. 15.) His analysis proceeds from actual economic facts—not, as we shall see, in order to resign himself to those facts, but precisely in order to change them.

There are a number of senses in which Marx employed the term "alienation"; and the meanings which he assigned to the concept may best be grasped from the two German words he used most frequently to describe the phenomenon he had in mind: (a) *entäussern* (verb) or, in its noun form, *Entäusserung;* and (b) *entfremden* (verb) and *Entfremdung* (noun). The first of these means "to part with," "to give up," "to deprive one's self of," "to divest one's self of," and, as noted by the translator of these manuscripts, it also implies "making external to one's self." The noun *Entäusserung* is also explicitly defined as alienation (of property). The second German word, also rendered in English as "to alienate," connotes primarily two people becoming estranged from each other. Thus, the term "alienation" refers to a complex process with several aspects. As will be seen in a later discussion of *Capital,* Marx described this process and its consequences in great detail. Here it may be summarized in general terms.

The process begins with the separation of men from their means of production and subsistence (as was the case in England when the yeomen were driven from their land following passage of the various Enclosure Acts). Men are alienated from their property and therefore compelled, if they are to avoid starving and becoming vagabonds, to sell their labor power to the capitalist entrepreneurs awaiting them. The two parties, capitalist as well as laborer, thus enter into an essentially instrumental relationship with each other. Forming this relationship is and remains an act of expediency, and the two parties remain estranged from each other because the relationship is based on conflicting interests and fundamentally different conditions of life.

Immediately upon entering this relationship, the worker begins to consume his energies in the production of things; his labor power becomes objectified in commodities over which he has no control. In this sense the more he produces, the poorer he becomes.

> All these consequences are contained in the definition that the worker is related to the *product of his labor* as an *alien* object. For on this premise it is clear that the more the worker spends himself, the more powerful the alien objective world becomes which he creates over against himself, the poorer he himself—his inner world—becomes, the less belongs to him as his own. . . . The worker puts his life into the object; but now his life no longer belongs to him but to the object. Hence, the greater this activity, the greater is the worker's lack of objects. Whatever the product of his labor is, he is not. Therefore the greater this product, the less is he himself. The *alienation* of the worker from his product means not only that

his labor becomes an object, an *external* existence, but that it exists *outside him,* independently, as something alien to him, and that it becomes a power on its own confronting him; it means that the life which he has conferred on the object confronts him as something hostile and alien. (p. 70.)

The worker has no control over the process of production or its results; his labor is an alienating activity, not only because he loses the product in which he has reified a part of himself, but because the whole productive process is external to him and his human needs. In "his work, therefore, he does not affirm himself but denies himself, does not feel content but unhappy, does not develop freely his physical and mental energy but mortifies his body and ruins his mind. The worker therefore only feels himself outside his work, and in his work feels outside himself. He is at home when he is not working, and when he is working he is not at home. His labor is therefore not voluntary, but coerced; it is *forced labor.* It is therefore not the satisfaction of a need; it is merely a *means* to satisfy needs external to it. Its alien character emerges clearly in the fact that as soon as no physical or other compulsion exists, labor is shunned like the plague." (p. 72.) Consequently, he experiences the process of production as an oppressive activity, as a loss of freedom. He

no longer feels himself to be freely active in any but his animal functions—eating, drinking, procreating. . . . And in his human functions he no longer feels himself to be anything but an animal. . . . Certainly eating, drinking, procreating, etc., are also genuinely human functions. But in the abstraction which separates them from the sphere of all other human activity and turns them into sole and ultimate ends, they are animal. (p. 73.)

Man, as worker, has become something less than human for he is separated from his potential human qualities. The animal, Marx says, is immediately identical with its life activity; man, on the other hand, has the ability to make his life activity the object of his will and consciousness. This is what makes it possible for man to attain ever greater degrees of freedom. The animal produces only when dominated by his immediate physical needs; man, however, can produce "even when he is free from physical need and only truly produces in freedom therefrom." (p. 75.) This is reversed under conditions of alienated labor where man's whole conscious being and life activity, "his essential being [becomes] a mere means to his existence."

Thus we have an initial alienation from his means of production which forces a man (the worker) to form an estranged relationship with another man (the employer). The activity itself, which he now performs for the means of his existence, is an alienating activity, for the product remains alien to the worker and the process of production itself remains external to his consciousness and to his human needs and desires. Man becomes increasingly alienated from himself, a fact that expresses itself in his estrangement from others. One can then see why Marx remained unimpressed with the "forcing-up of wages" and other such ameliorative measures that would not alter the basic relationships underlying the conditions of alienation and "would therefore be nothing but *better payment for the slave,* and would not conquer either for the worker or for labor their human status and dignity." (p. 81.)

It is not the worker alone, however, but the nonworker as well (albeit in a different form and in differing degrees) who is subject to the condition of alienation. Everything " . . . which appears in the worker as an *activity of alienation, of estrangement,* appears in the nonworker as a *state of alienation, of estrangement.*" (p. 83.) The capitalist who regards as luxury everything the worker desires above his barest physical needs is himself subject, though to a lesser extent than the worker, to denial and want. For political economy, denial and want, or thrift and saving, were major virtues of both the capitalist and the worker. "This science of marvelous industry is simultaneously the science of *asceticism,* and its true ideal is the *ascetic* but *extortionate* miser and the ascetic but *productive* slave. . . . Thus political economy—despite its worldly and wanton appearance—is a true moral science, the most moral of all the sciences. Self-denial, the denial of life and of all human needs, is its cardinal doctrine. The less you eat, drink, and read books; the less you go to the theatre, the dance hall, the public house; the less you think, love, theorize, sing, paint, fence, etc., the more you *save*—the *greater* becomes your treasure which neither moths nor dust will devour—your *capital.* The less you *are,* the more you *have;* the less you express your own life, the greater is your *alienated* life—the greater is the store of your estranged being." (p. 119.)

This general condition, then, a consequence of specific social relationships and processes, was one that had to be abolished if men were to elevate themselves to a truly *human* status. For Marx, this was possible only *"in a practical way,* by virtue of the practical energy of men." (p. 109.) If men were to develop their essential human powers, if they were to perfect themselves, they had first of all to abolish the conditions of their present malaise. This was to be a process, a movement. Therefore, the establishment of what Marx called "communism" was not an end but a means to man's greater freedom and hence to man's greater humanity. "Communism," wrote Marx in another early work, *German Ideology,* "is for us not a stable state which is to be established, an *ideal* to which reality will have to adjust itself. We call communism the *real* movement which abolishes the present state of things. The conditions of this movement result from the premises now in existence."[2] Communism is no static utopia toward which men should strive but a critical and revolutionary movement. "Communism . . . is the *actual* phase necessary for the next stage of historical development in the process of human emancipation and recovery."[3]

It is clear, then, that Marx had a conception of the human individual as he

---

[2] Karl Marx and Frederick Engels, *The German Ideology* (New York: International Publishers, 1960), p. 26.
[3] Karl Marx, *op. cit.,* p. 114.

could be and that this was his measure of the existing social system. Man's creative powers, his capacity for self-perfection and self-realization, are practically unlimited—given the abolition of those relationships and conditions which until now have so drastically impeded this development. Man is a creature of the very social conditions he himself has created, but *he need not remain a prisoner of those conditions.* To understand how, in Marx's view, men could make their history more consciously than ever before, we must examine another aspect of the Enlightenment legacy—negative-critical thinking—the dialectical form of which Marx learned directly from Hegel but fundamentally transformed.

Style of Thinking

For Hegel, it will be recalled, reason embraced the total universe; all of its realms, the inorganic as well as the organic, nature as well as society, were governed by the Idea and its dialectical logic. Reason was an immanent force that expressed itself in the unfolding of reality. In the natural realm, development and change—things becoming actually what they always were potentially—took place in "a direct, unopposed, unhindered manner." It was both a peaceful process and one of blind necessity. Not so in the human realm, where history had shown that development was a conflictive process dependent on human consciousness and will. The rational structure of being could be comprehended by the human mind and this was a necessary condition of freedom: the actualization of the potentialities inherent in reality. "Truth" was not strictly a function of formal propositions; the criterion of truth was reality in process. Herbert Marcuse has explained Hegel's view rather well: "Something is true if it is what it can be, fulfilling all its objective possibilities."[4] If, for instance, a man is a slave, he nevertheless retains some freedom to change his condition. One must always see the possibility of negating the relationship implicit in the statement, "A man is a slave."

For Hegel, the form in which a thing immediately appears is not yet its true form. What one sees at first is a negative condition, not the real potentialities of a thing. Something becomes true "only in the process of overcoming this negativity, so that the birth of the truth requires the death of the given state of being. . . . All forms are seized by the dissolving movement of reason which cancels and alters them until they are adequate to their notion."[5] In these terms, there is a revolutionary side to Hegel's philosophy. The given facts as they appear can never be more than a temporary and partial truth. For they represent only one negative phase in the unfolding of truth which reveals itself precisely by the destruction and supersession of that phase.

[4] Herbert Marcuse, *Reason and Revolution,* 2nd ed. (Boston: Beacon Press, 1954), p. 25.
[5] *Ibid.,* p. 26.

This dialectical conception of reality which can be traced to Aristotle and even to certain pre-Socratic philosophers profoundly influenced Marx's thinking about social phenomena.[6] The realm of the "is" must always be criticized and challenged to reveal the possibilities within it. The existing factual order is a transient negativity which can be transcended. One cannot even comprehend the existing order, let alone free its potentialities, unless it is critically opposed and ultimately transcended. The data are not "positives"; nor is the existing factual order inviolable. On the contrary, since that order imposes a subhuman condition of existence upon men, since they are therefore less than they can be, men must strive to change that order.

This approach is directly opposed to that of positivism, which treats facts *in their immediately given form* as truth. By their rejection of universal concepts and their reduction of truth to the immediately observable and verifiable, the positivists exclude "from the domain of knowledge everything that may not yet be a fact."[7] Marx, like Hegel—at least up to a given point in the latter's system—refused to limit truth to a particular "given"; he firmly believed "that the potentialities of men and things are not exhausted in the given forms and relations in which they may actually appear. . . ."[8]

Of course, all this should not be taken to mean that Marx had no use or regard for "the facts"; this would be patently false and absurd. The point is, rather, that he was always conscious of the transient character of any given facts which are but negative moments in a ceaseless historical process. The existing factual order of capitalism, for instance, had to be studied carefully if only to learn how to negate it. The possibility of revolution rested on certain apparently objective economic and political conditions, and these could be grasped through an analysis of the structure and tendencies of capitalism. Only with this factual knowledge could Marx develop (as was his intention) a general theory to guide the revolutionary action of the working class. Moreover, once he arrived at an empirical generalization or theoretical proposition which he regarded as true, he always pointed to the historically specific conditions to which they applied. The proposition, for example, that the "relations of production" tend to determine the character of men, including their consciousness, is regarded by Marx as a socio-historical fact; but this is precisely what he regards as man's alienated condition. At the same time, therefore, that he is describing that fact he is exposing the materialistic nature of the prevailing order in which relations of production are fundamental in forming and *deforming* human relations and in divesting man of his human character. Thus,

---

6 In this connection, Hannah Arendt has remarked that "the influence of Aristotle on the *style* of Marx's thought seems to me almost as characteristic and decisive as the influence of Hegel's philosophy." *The Human Condition,* (New York: Anchor Books, 1959) , p. 365. (Italics mine.)

7 Marcuse, *op cit.,* p. 113.

8 *Ibid.,* p. 113.

Marx's proposition is a *critical* one, implying that the prevailing relation between consciousness and social existence is a false one that must be overcome before the true relation can come to light. The truth of the materialistic thesis is thus to be fulfilled in its negation.

Marx emphasizes time and again that his materialistic starting point is forced upon him by the materialistic quality of the society he analyzes.[9]

Misunderstanding of this point has led to the worst distortions of Marx's theory, in which the very opposite of what he believed is attributed to him—namely, that his ideal was a materialistic society. Actually, his ideal was to invert the prevalent relationship between social being and social consciousness. Precisely what Marx meant by leaving the domain of "necessity" and entering the domain of "freedom" was that men would now begin *consciously* to determine their fate. This is the view Marx held not only in his early philosophical writings but in his maturity as well. In *Capital*, he wrote:

The life-process of society, which is based on the process of material production, does not strip off its mystical veil until it is treated as production by freely associated men, and is consciously regulated by them in accordance with a settled plan.[10]

In these terms, as was pointed out earlier, Marx viewed socialism and/or communism not as ends in themselves. The abolition of private property and the socialization of the means of production are the first steps in the abolition of alienated labor. That this will lead to "an association, in which the free development of each is the condition for the free development of all" is *not* at all inevitable. Everything will depend on what men do with the socialized resources. If men do not associate freely and utilize these resources to fulfill their human needs and to further their human development, then the socialization of the means of production has merely substituted one form of subjugation for another. Marx foresaw this danger and warned against reifying "society" and setting it up against the individual:

What is to be avoided above all is the reestablishing of "Society" as an abstraction *vis-a-vis* the individual. The individual is *the social being*. His life . . . is therefore an expression and confirmation of *social life*.[11]

The needs and freedom of the individual thus remain paramount in Marx's ideal; he therefore condemns any society that imposes a division of labor without considering the need for well-being and for maximum self-realization of each and every individual. This is his main criticism of class society: it is a situation in which an individual's entire fate tends to be determined by his class position and the function assigned him in the system of production. The

9 *Ibid.*, pp. 273–74.
10 Karl Marx, *Capital*, Vol. I (Moscow: Foreign Languages Publishing House, 1954), p. 80.
11 Karl Marx, *Economic and Philosophic Manuscripts*, p. 105.

difference between this condition and the one he envisioned in the future, Marx made clear in a famous passage:

> The division of labor offers us the first example of how, as long as man remains in natural society [i.e., governed by laws which are inexorable, like natural laws over which men have no control], that is as long as a cleavage exists between the particular and the common interest, as long therefore as activity is not voluntarily, but naturally, divided, man's own deed becomes an alien power opposed to him, which enslaves him instead of being controlled by him. For as soon as labor is distributed, each man has a particular, exclusive sphere of activity, which is forced upon him and from which he cannot escape. He is a hunter, a fisherman, a shepherd, or a critical critic, and must remain so if he does not want to lose his means of livelihood; while in communist society, where nobody has one exclusive sphere of activity, but each man can become accomplished in any branch he wishes, society regulates the general production and thus makes it possible for me to do one thing to-day and another to-morrow, to hunt in the morning, fish in the afternoon, rear cattle in the evening, criticize after dinner, just as I have a mind, without ever becoming hunter, fisherman, shepherd or critic.[12]

From Hegel, then, Marx took the emphasis on negative critical thinking which he integrated into his intellectual consciousness.[13] With Marx, however, dialectical thinking is not only critical and revolutionary but empirical and sociological as well. Conflict, for example, is explained not abstractly but in terms of concrete and specific social relationships. One class owns the means of production while the other does not; this is the basis of the various forms of conflict between them. Marx views the entire capitalist system as resting on conflicting principles and tendencies: "contradictions" exist between the social character of production and the institution of private property, or between the growth of the "productive forces" and the existing "relations of production"; between production for use and production for profit; between production and consumption, and still others—all arrived at inductively. For Marx, these conflicting principles are rooted in definite social relationships, and his dialectical reasoning is therefore quite the opposite of Hegel's closed ontological system. Marx's thought is in all respects a different order of truth from Hegel's, and not to be interpreted in terms of the latter's philosophical concepts. This can only be appreciated by further examining Marx's work.

---

12 Karl Marx and Frederick Engels, *op cit.*, p. 22.

13 However, unlike his friend and colleague, Frederick Engels, Marx made no attempt to codify dialectical reasoning into a rigid system equally applicable to nature and society. A critique of Engels' view of the dialectic and his vacillation between Hegelianism and Positivism may be found in George Lichtheim's *Marxism: An Historical and Critical Study* (New York: Frederick A. Praeger, 1962), and in Sidney Hook's *Reason, Social Myths and Democracy* (New York: The John Day Company, 1940). Also a brief critical discussion of the way Engels treats the dialectic sometimes as an ontology and sometimes as a heuristic device may be found in my own recently published study, *Marxism: A Re-Examination* (Princeton, New Jersey: Van Nostrand, 1967).

9

From
Social Philosophy
to Social Theory

Marx worked out his own theory of the relationship between social existence and social consciousness—the so-called materialist conception of history—in direct opposition to Hegel's idealistic conception of that relationship. Throughout his life Marx continued to honor his intellectual debt to that "mighty thinker" by coquetting with the Hegelian mode of expression. Nevertheless, he believed that dialectical thinking had suffered from mystification in Hegel's hands. "With him it is standing on its head. It must be turned right side up again, if you would discover the rational kernel within the mystical shell."[1] What was this rational kernel? "In its rational form," Marx wrote, "it [the dialectic] is a scandal and abomination to bourgeoisdom and its doctrinaire professors, because it includes in its comprehension and affirmative recognition of the existing state of things, at the same time also, the recognition of the negation of that state, of its inevitable breaking up; because it regards every historically developed social form as in fluid movement, and therefore takes into account its transient nature not less than its momentary existence; because it lets nothing impose upon it, and is in its essence critical and revolutionary."[2]

[1] Karl Marx, *Capital,* Vol. I (Moscow: Foreign Languages Publishing House, 1954), p. 20.
[2] *Ibid.,* p. 20.

In Hegel, moreover, the "existing state of things" appeared as an expression of the Idea or Spirit; he had held, apparently, to an inverted conception of the relationship between existence and consciousness. This prompted Marx to state once more in his maturity what he had already repeatedly insisted upon in his youth.

> My dialectical method is not only different from the Hegelian, but its direct opposite. To Hegel, the life-process of the human brain, i.e., the process of thinking, which, under the name of "the Idea," he even transforms into an independent subject, is the demiurgos of the real world, and the real world is only the external, phenomenal form of "the Idea." With me, on the contrary, the ideal is nothing else than the material world reflected by the human mind, and translated into forms of thought.[3]

This was the standpoint Marx had already arrived at in 1843—if not before—when he had developed the rudiments of his own theory in critical opposition not only to Hegel but to the Left- or Young-Hegelians as well. One of the latter, Bruno Bauer, had written two essays on the so-called "Jewish Question," in which his analysis of the causes of Jewish persecution, as well as the solution he proposed, remained within a theological framework. In effect, Bauer had argued that the Jews must overcome their religious parochialism, give up their Judaism, as a precondition of their political and social emancipation. In reply, Marx argued that religion is not the basis but the manifestation of secular conditions. "We do not claim that [men] must transcend their religious narrowness in order to get rid of their secular limitations. We claim that they will transcend their religious narrowness once they have overcome their secular limitations. We do not turn secular questions into theological questions; we turn theological questions into secular ones."[4]

Since Bauer was an implacable enemy of religion, as were the other Left-Hegelians, the solution he proposed was religious criticism. Bauer, Marx observed, had merely restated a theological question—Was a Jew or a Christian more likely to attain salvation?—in another, albeit more enlightened, form: Was a Jew or a Christian more capable of emancipation? Bauer was not proposing that the Jews give up Judaism for Christianity, but for Christianity in dissolution. They must join in negating Christianity; they must be critical and enlightened and in this way they will contribute to a "free humanity." Thus for Bauer the emancipation of the Jews was a matter of religious criticism. He reasoned that since it is the Christian *qua* Christian who finds Judaism offensive, he will cease to find it so when he ceases to profess Christianity. Therefore, by adopting a critical and enlightened attitude toward the Christian religion, by contributing to its dissolution, the Jews help to remove the cause of their presecution. The Jew is thus saddled with a

---

[3] *Ibid.,* p. 19.

[4] Karl Marx, *Early Writings,* translated and edited by T. B. Bottomore (London: C. A. Watts and Co., Ltd., 1963), p. 10.

two-fold responsibility: he must in addition to his own work take on the work of the Christian—the "criticism of the Gospels," of the "life of Jesus," etc.

In reply, Marx advances his own approach, simultaneously sociological and revolutionary. Sociological because he posits a *social* condition underlying the phenomenon of Judaism, and revolutionary because it is precisely this condition which must be abolished if the phenomenon is to disappear. Marx thus attempts to escape the theological formulation of the problem by transforming it into a secular, sociological one. What is the secular basis of "Judaism"? Self-interest, egoism, huckstering, money—in a word, *capitalism.* Marx was here exploiting the double meaning of *Judentum,* which in the language of the time meant "commerce" as well as Judaism.[5]

Marx took the opportunity afforded by Bauer's essays to put forward his own recently acquired point of view. The essence of the prevailing social system was huckstering; human worth was measured by the value of the commodities each held. In the sense, then, in which Marx used the term *Judentum,* all civil society was now dominated by its *practical* spirit. He paraphrases a passage from Thomas Hamilton's *Men and Manners in North America* to demonstrate the extent to which Mammon had become the idol of the devout New Englander: "In his view the world is no more than a Stock Exchange, and he is convinced that he has no other destiny here below than to become richer than his neighbor. Trade has seized upon all his thoughts, and he has no other recreation than to exchange objects. When he travels he carries, so to speak, his goods and his counter on his back and talks only of interest and profit. If he loses sight of his own business for an instant it is only in order to pry into the business of his competitors."[6] As Marx saw it then, the task of the age was to emancipate itself from huckstering and money. "An organization of society which would abolish the preconditions and thus the very possibility of huckstering, would make the Jew impossible."[7] The Jew, as others, must recognize this. "In the final analysis, the *emancipation* of the Jews is the emancipation of mankind from *Judaism*"—or from what he was later to call capitalism. By eliminating huckstering and its preconditions, the huckstering consciousness no longer becomes possible. Marx criticized Bauer for remaining in the realm of pure thought and for not recognizing the connection between forms of religious consciousness and the

---

[5] Sidney Hook, in his classic study, *From Hegel to Marx,* observed in this regard: "Although Marx was free of antisemitic prejudice, he unfortunately was not oversensitive to using the term, 'Jew,' often with unsavory adjectives, as an epithet of abuse." I hope it is superfluous to point out that in presenting Marx's argument as he states it, I am not defending his practice. Jews had apparently played a conspicuous role in European commerce since the Middle Ages and for this reason "Jew" became a synonym for merchant. In this connection it will be recalled that Werner Sombart attributed a fundamental role to the Jews in the formation of capitalism.

[6] Karl Marx, *Early Writings,* p. 35.

[7] *Ibid.,* p. 34.

real conditions of social life. Essentially, this was the same criticism Marx had of Hegel's view.

In his *Critique of Hegel's Philosophy of Right,* written about the same time as his reply to Bauer, Marx treats religion as a state of alienation and presents the premises of his own approach—a few of which can be quoted here:

> The basis of irreligious criticism is this: *man makes religion;* religion does not make man. Religion is indeed man's self-consciousness and self-awareness so long as he has not found himself or has lost himself again. But *man* is not an abstract being, squatting outside the world. Man is *the human world,* the state, society.

> It [religion] is *the fantastic realization* of the human being inasmuch as the *human being* possesses no true reality.

> Religious suffering is at the same time an *expression* of real suffering and a *protest* against real suffering. Religion is the sigh of the oppressed creature, the sentiment of a heartless world, and the soul of soulless conditions. It is the *opium* of the people.

> The abolition of religion as the *illusory* happiness of men, is a demand for their *real* happiness. The call to abandon their illusions about their condition is a *call to abandon a condition which requires illusions.*

> Criticism has plucked the imaginary flowers from the chain, not in order that man shall bear the chain without caprice or consolation but so that he shall cast off the chain and pluck the living flower. The criticism of religion disillusions man so that he will think, act and fashion his reality as a man who has lost his illusions and regained his reason. . . .

> It is the *task of history, therefore,* once the *other-world of truth* has vanished, to establish the *truth of this world.* The immediate *task of philosophy,* which is in the service of history, is to unmask human self-alienation in its *secular form* now that it has been unmasked in its *sacred form.* Thus the criticism of heaven is transformed into the criticism of earth, the *criticism of religion* into the *criticism of law,* and the *criticism of theology* into the criticism of politics.[8]

Marx goes on and adumbrates already in this early essay what was later to become his theory of social change and revolution and the role of the working class within it.[9]

This brief review of Marx's early writings should lend greater cogency to the assertion that Marx developed his own theory in critical opposition to the Old- and Young-Hegelians alike. With the exception of Feuerbach, whose great achievement, Marx believed, was to make "the social relationship of 'man to man' the basic principle of his theory," none of the Young-Hegelians had gone much beyond Hegel conceptually. But Feuerbach had committed a different type of error—that of the mechanical materialists: he had ignored

---

8 *Ibid.,* p. 43–44.
9 See *Ibid.,* especially pages 52, 58–59.

the active, creative side of practical human activity. Therefore, Marx's theory (which takes this active side into account) cannot be adequately understood as materialism in the traditional sense. His view, as he himself characterized it, was to be distinguished from both idealism *and* materialism "constituting at the same time the unifying truth of both."[10] It is to this view, as a theory of man, society, and history, that we now turn.

The General Theory

The premises from which Marx begins are real, flesh-and-blood human individuals. In the first instance, these real men are physical organisms with real physical needs. Like all other natural organisms, men, in order to survive, must enter into a metabolic relationship with nature. Men survive and develop only by interacting with nature, and this interaction, being the basis of their life process, is indispensable under any social circumstances. Essentially, then, as in the case of all other animals, man's major and most fundamental activity, laboring, is the production of life, the maintenance of the life process. "By producing their means of subsistence men are indirectly producing their actual material life."[11] Men, however, unlike all other animals do not *simply* take from nature what they need for the maintenance of life: they *produce* their means of subsistence. While it is true, therefore, that what and how men produce always remains in varying degrees dependent "on the nature of the actual means they find in existence and have to reproduce," it is equally true that men can and do modify these means, thereby reducing their *immediate* dependence upon natural conditions. In these terms, the labor activity of men is not a mere adaptation to nature but a conscious and purposeful transformation of natural conditions. Men appropriate the materials of nature and by their modification create a super-organic world of man-made artifacts. Man is not only an *animal laborans* but a *homo faber* who lives and acts in two worlds simultaneously—the artificial and the natural.

For Marx, the labor process is not only natural but *social:* Men produce not in isolation from one another but by interacting and cooperating with one another. Men act upon nature by interacting with other men. "The fact is," wrote Marx, "that definite individuals who are productively active in a definite way enter into . . . definite social and political relations." Individuals "produce materially and are active under definite material limits, presuppositions, and conditions independent of their will."[12] "Material limits" refers to both the natural and social conditions which are imposed

---

[10] Karl Marx, *Economic and Philosophic Manuscripts of 1844* (Moscow: Foreign Languages Publishing House, 1961) , p. 151.
[11] Karl Marx and Frederick Engels, *The German Ideology* (New York: International Publishers, 1960) , p. 7.
[12] *Ibid.,* p. 13.

upon men. Though these limits can ultimately be widened and the conditions changed, at any given moment men are born into, and act within, the framework of existing material conditions. In Marx's words, the

> . . . mode of production must not be considered simply as being the repro-duction of the physical existence of the individuals. Rather it is a definite form of activity of these individuals, a definite form of expressing their life, a definite *mode of life* on their part. As individuals express their life, so they are. What they are, therefore, coincides with their production, both with what they produce and with *how* they produce. The nature of in-dividuals thus depends on the material conditions determining their production.[13]

"Mode of production" is the general concept which Marx employed to encompass the complex process through which men simultaneously interact both with nature and with one another. There is a dialectical relationship between the two kinds of conditions: the interaction of men with nature determines the character of their social relationships, while the character of their social relations determines their mode of interaction with nature. These propositions are not dogmas for Marx. On the contrary, he insists that one must "bring out empirically, and without any mystification and speculation, the connection of the social and political structure with production."[14] Employing the concepts "productive forces" and "relations of production," Marx laid down the basic propositions of his general theory in his preface to *A Contribution to the Critique of Political Economy:*

> In the social production which men carry on they enter into definite rela-tions that are indispensable and independent of their will; these relations of production correspond to a definite stage of development of their ma-terial powers of production. The sum total of these relations of production constitutes the economic structure of society—the real foundation, on which rise legal and political superstructures and to which correspond definite forms of social consciousness. The mode of production in material life determines the general character of the social, political and spiritual processes of life. It is not the consciousness of men that determines their existence, but, on the contrary, their social existence determines their con-sciousness. At a certain stage of their development, the material forces of production in society come in conflict with the existing relations of pro-duction, or—what is but a legal expression for the same thing—with the property relations within which they had been at work before. From forms of development of the forces of production these relations turn into their fetters. Then comes the period of social revolution. With the change of the economic foundation the entire immense superstructure is more or less rapidly transformed.[15]

13 *Ibid.,* p. 7.

14 *Ibid.,* p. 13.

15 Karl Marx, *Contribution to the Critique of Political Economy* (Chicago: Charles H. Kerr and Company, 1904) , pp. 11–12.

By "material forces of production" or what here shall be called "productive forces," Marx is referring to the productive activity of real individuals in their relations of cooperation. A "productive force" is therefore first and foremost a *social force.* "By social we understand the cooperation of several individuals, no matter under what conditions, in what manner, and to what end. It follows from this that a certain mode of production, or industrial stage, is always combined with a certain mode of cooperation, or social stage, and this mode of *cooperation is itself a* 'productive force.' "[16]

Men produce—appropriate and transform the materials of nature—only by

> . . . cooperating in a certain way and mutually exchanging their activities. In order to produce they enter into definite connections and relations with one another and only within these social connections and relations does their action on nature, does production take place.
>
> These social relations into which the producers enter with one another, the conditions under which they exchange their activities and participate in the whole act of production, will naturally vary according to the character of the means of production.[17]

Marx illustrated the latter point—that relations vary with the means of production—saying, "Labor is organized, is divided differently according to the instruments it disposes over. The hand mill presupposes a different division of labor from the steam mill."[18]

There is therefore nothing mystical in the term "productive force" as used by Marx. It includes, first of all, the real labor power of working men. It is the social force of these living workers, by which they produce the means of satisfying the natural and social needs of their existence; it therefore includes the workers, the instruments of production employed by them, and the definite form of cooperation conditioned by the instruments and means of production. Anything that increases the productivity of human labor power increases the "productive forces" of a society. Thus while the concept denotes men's mastery of nature as expressed in the advance of technique, science, and instruments of production, it also includes the social organization of production, *i.e.,* the cooperation and division of labor among men. While technical problems can and do emerge as a result, for instance, of the inappropriateness of a certain organization of labor for certain instruments of production, this is *not* what Marx had in mind when he wrote that at a certain stage of their development the productive forces come in conflict with the existing "relations of production."

16 Karl Marx and Frederick Engels, *op cit.,* p. 18. (Italics mine.) .

17 Karl Marx "Wage Labor and Capital," in Marx and Engels, *Selected Works,* Vol. I, (Moscow: Foreign Languages Publishing House, 1950) , p. 83.

18 Karl Marx, *The Poverty of Philosophy* (Moscow: Foreign Languages Publishing House, N.D.) , p. 127.

"Relations of production," as he himself stated, refers to the fundamental *"property relations"* of the society in question. In the process of production men labor with other men but they also labor *for* other men. Under capitalism, those who owned and controlled the means of production had great power over those who did not; the latter, who had been separated from their means of production and who therefore owned only their labor power, served and obeyed. Thus the concept *property relations* becomes the starting point of Marx's theory of classes. But it is also an important concept in his theory of social change and revolution.

In the early phase of a system's development, the *property relations* facilitate the constant growth of the productive forces. In the later phases of its development, the productive forces are retarded and hampered in their growth by the existing *property relations*. These property relations have to be "burst asunder" in order to allow for the further growth of the productive forces. The workers, acting as a class, set free the forces potentially existing in social labor by their revolutionary action. In this sense the workers' revolution is a constructive act, because it frees social productivity of the constraints imposed by capitalist *property relations*. Marx's theory is therefore not merely technological. The tension between productive forces and property relations is not a mere lack of adjustment between technical innovations and their social application. According to Marx's theory, it is impossible to measure accurately the productive forces of a society apart from the formal social relationships in which they are at work; it is impossible to measure productive forces purely in terms of natural science and technology. At best, one can make only a reasonable estimate of what would be the potential of a given technology under different property relations. Merely technical changes are therefore inadequate for the liberation of the productive forces.

Thus, Marx saw the "mode of production" as composed of two parts: *property relations* and *productive forces*. The property relations either advance or block the growth of the productive forces. The potential of these forces cannot be measured by a technological calculation alone; rather, it can be released only by the elimination of outdated property relations. With the removal of these property relations and the establishment of newer and more flexible forms of organization, the further development of the productive forces and new forms of human activity are facilitated. As the "mode of production" changes, other spheres of social conduct (or subsystems), *e.g.*, legal, political, ideological, change in consequence. Thus stated, there is no ambiguity in Marx's theory. It unequivocally asserts that a society's changing economic structure determines changes in its social structure as a whole, and in the consciousness of the people within it.

For Marx, therefore, ideas and conceptions, far from having an independent existence, are intimately connected with the material activity and social intercourse of real men. Religion, morality, philosophy, and law—in a word, ideology—have no real history or development. When one speaks of the history of religion, of law, or the like, he is abstracting ideas from real life; he is engaged in the reification of concepts which have no existence apart from living men. Ideas neither exist nor change. Rather, it is living men who—along with the material conditions of their existence—change themselves, "their thinking and the products of their thinking."

To illuminate the connection between social existence and social consciousness Marx postulated a stage in which they had constituted a unity. Prior to any division of labor between the material and mental activities of men, their "doing" and their "thinking" were directly interwoven. Thus while all human activity had what one might choose to regard, for example, as political, religious, and legal (normative) aspects, these were not yet separate and distinct spheres. They were, in Marx's words, "the direct efflux of their material behavior."[19] Under these circumstances, there were no special individuals who were professional practitioners of politics, law, religion, etc. Mental activity, not yet divorced from man's general activity, had not even the semblance of an autonomous existence. The existing social relations between individuals expressed themselves simultaneously as political and legal relations. However, with a new division of labor, between material and mental activities, political and legal relations

. . . are bound to assume an independent existence *vis-à-vis* the individuals. In language, such relations can only be expressed as concepts. The fact that these universals and concepts are accepted as mysterious powers is a necessary consequence of the independent existence assumed by the real relations whose expression they are. Besides this acceptance in everyday consciousness, these universals are also given a special validity and further development by political scientists and jurists who, as a result of the division of labor, are assigned to the cult of these concepts, and who see in them rather than in the relations of production, the true basis of actual property relations.[20]

The new division of labor brought into being a variety of distinct ideological spheres, each with its own professional practitioners who were now interested in maintaining their respective spheres. Nevertheless, the spheres are still regarded by Marx as dependent in varying degrees—for their character, change, and development—upon the existing relations of production. For example, Marx asserts that the ruling ideas in every age are the ideas of the ruling class. This class, having the means of material production at its disposal, controls also the means of mental production and thereby attempts to impose its ideas upon those who own and control neither. The dominant ideas are nothing more than the mental expressions of the dominant relationships. The ruling class has no need to develop or disseminate these

19 Karl Marx and Frederick Engels, *op cit.,* p. 14.
20 *The German Ideology,* quoted in T. B. Bottomore and Maximilien Rubel, *Karl Marx: Selected Writings in Sociology and Social Philosophy* (London: Watts and Company, 1961) , p. 78.

ideas by itself. The division of labor has brought into being a special group of ideologists whose main concern and source of livelihood it is to develop and perfect the illusions of the class about itself and ideologically to defend its interests.

But one must not assume a one-to-one relationship between the class and its spokesmen. On the contrary, the development of a cleavage, of hostility, and even opposition, is altogether possible between the two. There are, however, certain objective limits to such a cleavage. In one of his earliest conceptualizations of this problem, Marx asserted that in the event of a collision between the class and its spokesmen, in which the interests of the class were endangered, the interests would ultimately win out. The cleavage would disappear and with it the illusion that the ruling ideas were not the ideas of the ruling class and had a power distinct from this class.[21]

The division of labor in general, it will be recalled, was a negative condition for Marx; for while it enhanced the productive power of men, it also imprisoned them in narrow spheres of activity from which they could not escape without losing their means of livelihood. The material basis of man's eventual emancipation—the developing productive forces—was in the meanwhile exacting from him a great human price. Marx explored this process in detail in his chief work: *Capital.*

[21] Karl Marx and Frederick Engels, *op cit.,* pp. 39–43.

10

Marx's Sociology
of
Alienated Labor

Das Kapital, or *Capital*, could just as appropriately have been entitled *Die Arbeit;* for by and large it is, especially the first volume, a sociological study of the world of alienated labor. At the same time, Marx explores in detail what he considers the fundamental aspects of the expanding capitalist system: its developing productive forces and its basic relations of production. In these terms, *Capital* is a careful examination of the changing existential conditions of men and, concomitantly, of their changing character and consciousness; it is a documentation of his thesis that in the process of material production men alter, along with the conditions of their existence, their entire psychological makeup.

The first phase in the development of the productive forces within the capitalist mode of production Marx called "simple cooperation." While cooperation is characteristic of all large-scale production, simple cooperation prevails during that period in which capital operates on a large scale, but division of labor and machinery play a subordinate part. "A greater number of laborers working together, at the same time, in one place, in order to produce the same sort of commodity under the mastership of one capitalist, constitutes, both historically and logically, the starting point of capitalist production."[1] Cooperation of this kind takes

---

[1] All citations in this chapter (hereafter found as page numbers after the quotation) are from Karl Marx, *Capital,* Vol. I (Moscow: Foreign Languages Publishing House, 1954). This particular statement appears on p. 322.

place mainly in manufacture in the strict sense, *i.e.*, hand production; thus production in these early stages is distinguished from handicraft production in the guilds only by the greater number of workers simultaneously employed by one and the same capitalist. The emphasis here is on the *socially* productive force that comes into being by bringing many men together to work side by side and to cooperate with one another. The capitalist pays each individual worker for his individual labor power and gets more than he bargained for. He now gains directly from their cooperation, from the new socially productive force. The capitalist could not have gained as much surplus value by employing 12 isolated men, each working 12 hours, as by employing 12 working together and cooperating for 12 hours. In addition, without anyone realizing it, the extension of the scale of production together with the contraction of the "arena," *i.e.*, assembling many workers under one roof, provide the requisite conditions for the further development of the "productive forces"—a consequence impossible when the workers and the means of production are isolated and scattered, as in the cottage system, for example.

For Marx, cooperation in this form characterized the earliest phase of capitalism and was an important new productive force. It was new, not in the sense that there were no examples of simple cooperation before in history, but in the sense that the utilization and further growth of this productive force was now dependent on specific "relations of production." The existence of large outlays of capital now became a precondition for the cooperation of many workers. The workers could not cooperate unless they were employed simultaneously by the same capitalist.

In the specific case of English capitalism in the period under consideration, these "relations of production" prevailed—capitalists with adequate means of production and money, on the one hand, and workers without either, on the other. In this phase, then, the "relations of production" had not yet become fetters, and the "productive forces" had not yet come into conflict with them. On the contrary, the existing relations provided the framework within which the productive forces could continue to develop. The concentration of the means of production in the hands of the capitalists became the precondition for the cooperation of many workers; the extent of their cooperation depended on the extent of concentration; the whole process rested on capitalist relations of production, or property relations.

If the early phase of manufacture was characterized by a relatively simple form of cooperation, then the later phase was based on a more complex division of labor. Manufacture arises out of handicrafts, in some cases uniting the formerly independent ones and in others uniting the members of the same craft. And it is this uniting of the crafts, forging them into one productive organization whose parts are *human beings,* which distinguishes manufacture as a new phase in the growth of productive forces. This phase retains the character of handicraft because each operation is still performed by hand and is therefore dependent on the skill and dexterity of the individual workman in handling his tools.

Since he is now engaged in one simple operation, however, the worker is alienated from some of the creative prerogatives he exercised before. His whole body becomes an "automatic, specialized implement of that operation." (p. 339.) What he loses in creativity he gains in efficiency. The worker now takes less time in performing the specific operation than the craftsman who performs the entire series of operations in succession. The division of labor among many workers, each with his specialized operation, is the basis of the productive system called manufacture, a new organization of labor under which the socially productive power of labor is increased. This new productive force under the capitalist system is gained in manufacture by concentrating the powers already existing in the *society at large*. Thus manufacture, according to Marx, " . . . produces the skill of the detail laborer, by reproducing, and systematically driving to an extreme within the workshop, the naturally developed differentiation of trades which it found ready to hand in society at large." (p. 339.)

The capitalist entrepreneur had already grasped at this early stage in capitalist development that anything which interrupts the "constant flow" of the labor process also cuts into his profits. The production of commodities with a minimum of labor time, not a consideration at all under the guild system, now became a consideration of central importance. Decreasing the labor time necessary for the production of commodities was impossible so long as the worker had to perform a series of fractional operations which required him at one time to change his place and at another to change his tools. These shifts interrupted the flow by creating gaps in the working day that had to be closed by tying the worker to one and the same operation for the entire day. For Marx the closing of these gaps, which manufacture achieved, resulted in a further increase in the productive power of labor, in the productive forces under capitalism.

The concentration of production, of the various skills and trades in one workshop, also made necessary changes in the tools employed. Unlike the craftsman who used a few tools for many operations, the worker now employed a specialized tool for each specialized operation. In Marx's words: "Manufacture is characterized by the differentiation of the instruments of labor—a differentiation whereby implements of a given sort acquire fixed shapes, adapted to each particular application, and by the specialization of those instruments, giving to each special implement its full play only in the hands of a specific detail laborer." (p. 341.)

This development was important to Marx for a number of reasons. In itself it constituted a further revolutionizing of the means of production. In addition it brought about radical changes in the world of work. Old social forms were decomposing and their elements becoming parts of a new social organization of work. The transformation of the worker into a detail laborer could not take place, Marx believed, without at the same time causing significant changes in the worker's character and personality. The increasingly complex division of labor was alienating the worker from his creative powers and thus diminishing him as a human being. The higher productivity of the new organization of labor is made possible precisely by dividing, classifying, and grouping the workers according to their very specific functions. What is taken away from the individual worker in artistic skill, creativity, and reflective powers is given to the organization. The deficiencies of the former become the virtues of the latter. The organization as a whole is enriched by alienating the worker from his individual powers.

Moreover, manufacture develops a hierarchy of labor. If the workers are now tied to limited functions, these are ranked in a hierarchy and are parcelled out among them according to their socially acquired capabilities. At the very bottom of the hierarchy are those who perform the simplest manipulations of which anyone is capable. Hence, in contrast with guild production, manufacture brings into being a class of unskilled laborers, a class unknown in handicraft production. Describing this change, Marx wrote: "If it [manufacturing] develops a one-sided specialty into a perfection, at the expense of the whole of a man's working capacity, it also begins to make a specialty of the absence of all development. Alongside the hierarchic gradation there steps the simple separation of the laborers into skilled and unskilled." (p. 350.)

Marx is intent upon showing the growth of the socially productive power of labor, its dependence upon capitalist property relations, and the price which the individual worker pays for this increased productivity. For Marx the main tendencies of the capitalist system assert themselves in this period. First, the expansion of capital simultaneous with its concentration into increasingly larger units is already clear in the manufacturing phase. Second, this together with the fragmentation of the old crafts and the conversion of the craftsmen into detail laborers has the consequence of alienating the worker from his creative human faculties. Knowledge, judgment, and will, which had previously been exercised to some degree at least by the individual craftsman, now become a function of the productive organization as a whole. The worker is "brought face to face with the intellectual potencies of the material process of production, as the property of another, and as a ruling power." (p. 361.) The process which began in *simple cooperation,* where the capitalist represented to the worker the power and will of associated labor, became more pronounced in *manufacture,* which reduced the worker to a detail laborer.

If in manufacture the revolution in the means of production began with the organization of labor power, in *modern industry* it began with the instruments of production. For Marx, machinery and its employment in modern industry is the most important phase in the development of the capitalist mode of production. Although in its inception it rests squarely on manufacture, machine production eventually departs radically from the previous system.

In contrast with manufacture, where the productive process was adapted to the skills of the worker, the machine system compelled the worker to adapt himself to it. The subjective principle disappears and the whole process is examined objectively. Production is analyzed into a sequence of phases, each of which is solved by means of machines. The total system is now considered superior the more the process becomes a continuous one, the less it is interrupted in its various phases, the more the shifts from one phase to another are made not by hand, but by machinery.

In his examination of the development of the capitalist mode of production, Marx was among the first to describe in detail the changing role of the worker and the effect of the machine upon him. He described, for example, how the older division of labor while being overthrown by machinery still hung on in the factory in an even "more hideous form." "The life-long specialty of handling one and the same tool, now becomes the life-long specialty of serving one and the same machine." In this way the worker's dependence upon the factory, and therefore on the capitalist, is rendered complete. In manufacture the worker used the tool; in the factory the machine uses him. Under these circumstances the intellectual powers of the worker become superfluous and vanish before the gigantic physical forces of the total factory organization and the hidden mind behind it all.

For Marx, this phase in the development of the capitalist mode of production was the *critical* one. During this phase modern industry accelerates the concentration of capital and leads to the exclusive prominence of the factory system. It destroys all the previous forms of production and replaces them by the modern capitalist form, and by the direct and open power of capital. But this process, according to Marx, also generates direct opposition to the sway of capital. The process which leads to the power of capital leads also to ". . . the contradictions and antagonisms of the capitalist form of production, and thereby provides, along with the elements for the formation of a new society, the forces for exploding the old one." (p. 503.)

It is clear, then, that for Marx the development of productive forces under capitalism, the social and technical basis of man's eventual emancipation, was in the meanwhile a manifestation of his growing alienation. Man is increasingly losing control over the productive process. Only by forfeiting more and more of his creative human faculties does the worker contribute to the growth of the productive organization. Far from having abandoned the concept of alienation, then, Marx sharpened and concretized its meaning: it referred to the growing dehumanization of man under capitalist-industrial conditions.

Marx's revolutionary reply to this condition is well known: While labor itself could never be altogether abolished—it being the process by which men produce and reproduce their very life—*alienated* labor, exploitation, and oppression could be eliminated from the human experience. Those who suffered most directly from these conditions, the laborers themselves, would sooner or later find them intolerable and wrest all capital and power from their oppressors. With this as a beginning, and with the eventual abolition of classes and class conflicts, men might some day reach a condition in which "the free development of each will lead to the free development of all."

If not in the eyes of his contemporaries, then definitely in the eyes of posterity, Marx's ideas became the most challenging of all those advanced in the course of the nineteenth century. In the present century, revolutions have been made in his name and various forms of "Marxism" continue to stir large masses of men throughout the world. In this book we cannot even begin to address ourselves to this phenomenon and to the relation of the various "Marxisms" to the original. Rather, attention will be confined to the intellectual reaction to Marx (and Marxism) which took place after he died, in the various academies of Europe.

This brings us to the second theme of this book: the critical reaction to Marxism. For just as "sociology" emerged in the nineteenth century as part of the conservative reaction to the philosophy of the Enlightenment, so in the twentieth century much of sociology took shape in a critical encounter with the theories of Karl Marx.

PART **IV**

THE
DEBATE
WITH
MARX'S
GHOST

11

Max Weber

(1864–1920)

Max Weber, who has been called the "bourgeois Marx," became a sociologist "in a long and intense debate with the ghost of Marx."[1] The title of one of his major works, *Wirtschaft und Gesellschaft*, his concern with the Protestant ethic, even his superb studies in *Weltreligionen*, all show his sustained interest in the problems and issues Marx had raised. Though Weber was influenced by the German historical school—itself engaged in a critical examination of Marx's (and Hegel's) conceptions—the main character of his total life's work was shaped by his debate with Marx; and among those who took up the Marxian challenge, Weber was perhaps the greatest. His main interest, a lifelong preoccupation, was the origin and nature of modern capitalism, which eventually led him not only to a fastidious examination of the economic system of the West but all its major social and cultural institutions. Ultimately, this became a matter of understanding the peculiar nature of Western Civilization and important contrasts with the civilizations of the East. In working on this and other problems, he generalized and revised Marx's method. He was not, it will be argued here, refuting Marx; for, as will be seen, he accepted as extraordinarily fruitful Marx's major methodo-

[1] See Albert Salomon's article, "German Sociology" in Georges Gurvitch and Wilbert E. Moore, *Twentieth-Century Sociology* (New York: The Philosophical Library, 1945), p. 596.

logical principles. Insofar as refutation of Marxism was involved, it was a matter of showing the inadequacy of certain of Marx's revolutionary conclusions and of challenging the alleged human and moral superiority of socialism as compared with capitalism. To say, therefore, as Parsons has, that after an early contact with the Marxian position Weber "soon recoiled from this, becoming convinced of the indispensability of an important role of 'ideas' in the explanation of great historical processes"[2] is quite incorrect and even has bizarre implications. For it implies that Marx, for whom class consciousness was fundamental in the transition from capitalism to socialism, did not know that ideas were important in history. But this allegation about Weber is also incorrect, for he retained throughout his life the greatest admiration for Marx as a thinker. If Weber "recoiled," it was from vulgar and dogmatic Marxism—as, indeed, Marx himself had done. The position taken here is that Weber's work must not be read as a repudiation of Marx's methodological principles but rather as a "rounding out" and supplementing of his method. The valadity of this assertion can best be assessed by a reexamination of Weber's work.

Methodological Foundations

Weber published his essays on methodology[3] in the *Archiv für Sozialwissenschaft and Sozialpolitik* after he, together with Edgar Jaffé and Werner Sombart, assumed the editorship of that journal. It was to be primarily a scientific journal but with useful knowledge for the layman as well as the specialist. Not only general knowledge of the "social conditions of all countries" but studies of practical social problems would be included. And while the journal would be open to critical discussions of practical social policy and legislation, it was to remain scientific at all costs. Are these various purposes compatible with the requirements of the scientific method?—Weber asks. The origin of social science has been practical, he replies; formerly it was an applied science or technique. As it assumed the character of a pure academic science, the distinction between existential knowledge, or "what is," and normative knowledge, *i.e.*, what should be, was blurred. Keeping this distinction as clear as possible was therefore to be a primary responsibility of all contributors.

The journal was to deal with "social-economic" problems, referring to the fact that conditions of scarcity impose upon men the requirement—if their material and ideal needs are to be fulfilled—of "planful provision and work,

---

[2] See the introduction to *The Theory of Social and Economic Organization*, translated by A. M. Henderson and Talcott Parsons (Glencoe, Ill.: The Free Press, 1947), p. 6.

[3] Here we are dealing only with the essays translated into English under the title, *The Methodology of the Social Sciences* (Glencoe Ill.: The Free Press, 1949). (All subsequent references will be noted only by page numbers, as previously.)

struggle with nature and the association of human beings." (p. 64.) Anything either directly or indirectly connected with this process constitutes a problem for the social sciences, given this specific orientation.

Weber clarifies the orientation of the journal by exploring the various ways in which the "economic" aspect of social life can be studied, and thus distinguishes the *strictly economic* from the *economically relevant*, and these in turn from the *economically conditioned*. These distinctions, which no doubt bring greater clarity into any discussion of economic problems and phenomena, were more often than not overlooked by many Marxists, who dogmatically adhered to the so-called materialist conception of history. By strictly, or predominantly, economic, Weber referred to those institutions in which the economic aspect was of primary significance and which were deliberately created for economic ends. Obvious examples would be a bank, a stock exchange, a factory. In addition, however, there are spheres of interaction, modes of conduct, institutions, and events which are in themselves *non*economic but which may be nonetheless *economically relevant*. Religion, for example, may not have any immediately obvious economic character; yet upon closer examination it may reveal certain consequences for economic conduct and development. This is what Weber attempted to demonstrate with his own researches into the economic relevance of various religious ethics. In part this is a polemical concept for he is arguing that the noneconomic orders of society not only enjoy a high degree of autonomy but also have a significant causal influence upon the strictly economic—something which some Marxists at least were inclined to deny. Finally, Weber speaks of *economically conditioned* phenomena. Here, to use his example, we might be dealing with an art form or the artistic taste of a given public, which is clearly a noneconomic phenomenon and whose consequences for economic conduct (economic relevance) are so slight as to be of little or no interest. Yet, given artistic tastes, why they emerged in a specific period and why certain groups have them can be understood by an analysis of the "social stratification of the artistically interested public," on the assumption of its having been conditioned and influenced by economic institutions and events.

These distinctions and the conception of society underlying them provide greater clarity in an analysis of the major institutions of society. Thus the state, for instance, can be viewed under a variety of aspects. Insofar as it engages in economic activities per se, it is at least in part an economic phenomenon; and insofar as the policies of the state have consequences for economic life, it is economically relevant; finally, to the extent that various governmental policies are influenced by economic interests, the state is an economically conditioned institution. Clearly, then, the term "economic," which had heretofore been used loosely and vaguely, is not at all self-evident or easy to define.

The "economic" for Weber, as for Marx, referred to the "material struggle for existence," (p. 65.) and this became the main orientation both of the journal and of Weber's own lifelong work: to study not only the strictly economic phenomena but the economically conditioned and economically relevant as well. Each was a point of view by means of which the completely interwoven skeins of human relations could be analyzed and the significance of each aspect assessed. In effect, this was Weber's methodological approach; one analyzes a total society as a social system by adopting these various perspectives and by following them through as systematically and objectively as possible. He was not, however, advocating a totally eclectic method.

Actually, when Weber and the other editors had decided "that the scientific investigation of the *general cultural significance of the social-economic structure of the human community* and its historical forms of organization" was to be the central aim of the journal, this was due to their recognition of its extreme fruitfulness despite its "one-sidedness." Weber grants the one-sidedness but goes on to insist that the adoption of this perspective was both intentional and well reasoned. For he believed

> that the analysis of social and cultural phenomena with special reference to their economic conditioning and ramifications was a scientific principle of creative fruitfulness and, with careful application and freedom from dogmatic restrictions, will remain such for a very long time to come. The so-called "materialistic conception of history" as a *Weltanschauung* or as a formula for the causal explanation of historical reality is to be rejected most emphatically. The advancement of the economic *interpretation* of history is one of the most important aims of our journal. (p. 68.)

The reaction against the dogmatic and vulgar type of Marxian explanations now brought with it the danger of underestimating the fecundity of Marx's method when employed as a heuristic principle, not as a key for unlocking all doors.

Profound and pervasive as economic conditions are, however, it is superfluous to remind the expert or sophisticate that explanations based on "economic conditions alone" can never be complete. Every perspective, Weber argues, whether from the standpoint of economic or religious institutions—the standpoint from which he himself carried out so much research—can never be more than a partial, limited, and necessarily one-sided explanation; and if one stops there, without exploring the phenomenon in question from additional perspectives, an understanding of the total complex cultural whole will never be gained. There is no way of overcoming or getting around this inherent one-sidedness of a single perspective; only by taking a variety of such approaches systematically can one gain an increasingly adequate knowledge of "reality" which in its infinite characteristics and complexity can never be grasped in its entirety. The justification for a one-sided approach is that though limited it has heuristic value. In addition, however, it may be justified as a technical expedient for it enables specialists and scholars to utilize a common conceptual apparatus and thus offers all the advantages of an academic division of labor. And as we shall see, while Weber is not altogether unambiguous on this score, he grants that the criterion of such a method is the degree to which "it is successful in producing insights into interconnections which have been shown to be valuable for the causal explanation of concrete historical events." (p. 71)

For Weber, "the '*one-sidedness*' and the unreality of the purely economic interpretation of history is in general only a special case of a principle which is generally valid for the scientific knowledge of cultural reality." (p. 71.) He insists that an absolutely "objective" scientific analysis of cultural or social phenomena is never to be had because all such analyses depend on "one-sided viewpoints according to which—expressly or tacitly, consciously or unconsciously—they are selected, analyzed, and organized. . . ." (p. 72.)

In this connection, a close examination of Weber's argument shows that he was not entirely successful in drawing the distinction between the *Naturwissenschaften* and *Geisteswissenschaften* that he was apparently so intent upon preserving. Everything—or almost everything—that in the realm of sociocultural phenomena presented according to him, unique methodological problems can, at least in principle, be accommodated in the general scientific methodology; but this is not to deny that the task may be considerably more complicated in the cultural realm. In both the natural and the social sciences, "total reality" can never be grasped; in both cases some sort of abstraction is necessary and this abstraction, along with the selection of problems, phenomena, and relationships to be studied, are always based to some degree on the values of the investigator, his sponsors, or others. And while Weber saw the *qualitative* aspect of socio-cultural phenomena as the primary concern in the social sciences as compared with the predominantly *quantitative* aspects of physical phenomena, he himself acknowledges that "this distinction in itself is not a distinction in principle, as it seems at first glance." (p. 74.) Obviously, the natural sciences employ qualitative as well as quantitative categories, and economics, among the social sciences, is a conspicuous example of the use of both categories. Nevertheless, Weber retained the view that there was a decisive difference between cultural and physical phenomena and hence a decisive difference between the methodological requirements of the cultural and physical sciences, respectively. He argues that *cultural significance* can never be "derived or rendered intelligible," on the basis of a system of analytical laws. Why not? Because "the significance of cultural events presupposes a *value orientation* towards the events. The concept of culture is a *value concept*." (p. 76.)

Most, if not all, of the arguments Weber mobilizes in support of this assertion can be seen as applying equally to the physical sciences. When he says, for instance, that (1) segments of reality become significant to us because of their value relevance; (2) only that portion of reality is significant to us which is related to our values; and (3) a "presuppositionless" investigation of empirical data is impossible; are these not equally true in the study of physical phenomena? Surely, to take but one example from the history of the physical sciences, the reason why the geocentric view of what today is called the solar system prevailed for so long as well as why it finally succumbed, would have to be sought in the value and interest relevance of the geo- and heliocentric views respectively. Why, then, did Weber hold to the need for a special method in the cultural sciences?

Of interest here is Weber's discussion of "laws." Hypothetical laws were, he believed, of great value as heuristic means; one could analyze cultural phenomena in terms of laws and general concepts but never really *understand* their significance and meaning by means of these general laws. It is not at all easy to make sense of Weber's many and varied assertions on this score, which often seem contradictory. To attempt it may nevertheless be worthwhile in order to salvage what may well be an important insight.

He recognizes that in the cultural as well as the natural sciences, general propositions are required, as is knowledge of regularities; therefore, it is entirely justified in the social sciences to attempt to formulate "laws." No science is possible without this, Weber admits. But he goes on to insist that, "In the cultural sciences, the knowledge of the universal or general is never valuable in itself," (p. 80.) and "an 'objective' analysis of cultural events, which proceeds according to the thesis that the ideal of science is the reduction of empirical reality to 'laws' is meaningless." This, he maintains, is not "because cultural or psychic events for instance are 'objectively' less governed by laws. It is meaningless for a number of other reasons." (p. 80.) The first reason Weber adduces probably would not hold up under careful scrutiny; he writes, ". . . knowledge of social laws is not knowledge of social reality but is rather one of the various aids used by our minds for attaining this end." (p. 80.) Today most philosophers of science would argue that "laws" of any kind, whether in the natural or social sciences, are in fact such aids which do not necessarily have any one-to-one relationship with "reality." Weber's second reason is also vulnerable but perhaps less so. When he argues that "knowledge of *cultural* events is inconceivable except on a basis of the *significance* which the concrete constellations of reality have for us in certain individual concrete situations," this may have greater cogency. For here Weber is asserting, it appears, something more than the proposition that values and interests have a much more profound influence on the investigatory process in the social than in the physical sciences. What seems to be important to him here is that one focus on the "characteristic uniqueness of the reality" in question. This is what is really interesting and significant, and not the general theoretical proposition which can never be more than a heuristic device.

To take an illustration of which Weber was very fond—namely, the Marxian proposition that the relations of material production tend to determine the character of other aspects of society—this, Weber would argue, as in fact Marx himself did, is not a universally valid law irrespective of time and place. It is a historically and culturally specific proposition, and it always

remains an empirical question whether and to what degree the proposition
may be valid for a specific cultural setting. Moreover, what is really interesting, is how it works itself out in a particular setting, which can never be
known in advance on the basis of the general theory. What is more, the
significance and meaning of a so-called "economic factor"—the term itself
being an unjustified reification of an aspect of social conduct—varies from
one place to another as does the significance of all other aspects of culture
isolated for study. This is quite different from the situation in physics, for
example, where the *law* of gravity does not require quotation marks since it is
in fact a universally valid law. In the final analysis, Weber writes,

> All knowledge of cultural reality, as may be seen, is always knowledge
> from *particular points of view*. When we require from the historian and
> social research worker as an elementary presupposition that they distin-
> guish the important from the trivial and that they should have the
> necessary "point of view" for this distinction, we mean that they must un-
> derstand how to relate the events of the real world consciously or uncon-
> sciously to universal "cultural values" and to select out those relationships
> which are significant for us. (pp. 81–82.)

The criteria for significance are subjective. This does not mean, however, that
"research in the cultural sciences can only have results which are 'subjective'
in the sense that they are *valid* for one person and not for others. Only the
degree to which they interest different persons varies." (p. 84.)

One ought not pretend that in his essays on methodology Weber makes his
position perfectly clear. To the extent, however, that an interesting point
emerges, it appears to be the following: precisely because they are universally
valid, laws are important and valuable in the natural sciences. However, for
"the knowledge of historical phenomena in their concreteness, the most
general laws, because they are most devoid of content are also the least
valuable. The more comprehensive the validity—or scope—of a term, the
more it leads us away from the richness of reality, since in order to include
the common elements of the largest possible number of phenomena, it must
necessarily be as abstract as possible and hence devoid of content." (p. 80.)
Weber is saying, then, that the more general and universal the propositions
are in the cultural sciences, the more trivial and innocuous they are; and,
more importantly, such generalizations obscure significant and essential differences. Certainly one can generalize about social phenomena as he himself
did. In his studies of the world religions, for example, he was quite willing to
generalize about Asiatic religions, which he attempted to show never developed a "rational, inner-worldly ethic," and further tried to show the historical
significance and implications of the absence of this condition. But the
generalization is interesting precisely because of the significance Weber
attached to a rational ethic in the West—an issue to which we shall later
return. Weber is arguing that no high-level generalizations about religious

practices, phenomena, and institutions could possibly take into account the diverse forms these phenomena assume in different settings. Dervishes and ecstatics—even quasi-prophetic movements—appeared in many cultures; but if one's study remained at this level one could never grasp the uniqueness of Israelite prophecy, or its significance for the development of Occidental culture. Only a patient and meticulous analysis of the special conditions of ancient Israel could reveal this uniqueness and its fundamental contrasts with the religious institutions of China and India. It is therefore clear that Weber is a historian as well as a sociologist, as interested in the distinguishing characteristics of cultures, as he is in what they have in common.

To be sure, here, too, one could reply to Weber that seeking after the characteristic richness of a certain cultural reality can also become a trap—preventing one from seeing the forest for the trees—and if pushed to an extreme, can become as fruitless and blinding as high-level abstractions. And, indeed, a careful reading of Weber's works on the *Weltreligionen* (to be discussed later) sometimes leaves one with the impression that he has so immersed himself in details that he has forgotten the purpose of his investigation.

To take yet another illustration of Weber's conception, his thesis on the significance of the Protestant ethic (the validity of which will be postponed for a later discussion) could not be deduced from any general law. Moreover, the significance Weber assigned to this ethic applied only to a certain historical context, namely, the origin and emergence of capitalism; for, once the modern economic system had consolidated itself, the significance of that ethic disappeared, and it became, in his words, a *caput mortuum*. The emergence of capitalism could not be deduced from any law; it was not historically inevitable; there is no historical necessity that can account for its emergence. Quite the contrary, modern capitalism is the product of the interaction and convergence of a variety of individual historical developments. It should be pointed out in this connection that Marx himself also intended his generalizations about the origin and development of capitalism to be understood as historically and culturally specific —*i.e.*, relating to a definite period in Western Europe and not to societies in general, irrespective of time and place. Marx vehemently dissociated himself from the attempt to turn his emphasis, which he believed to be accurate under certain historical circumstances, into a universal "law." In a letter to Mikhailovsky, he rejected the latter's attempt to transform his sketch of the origins of capitalism in western Europe into a historical-philosophical theory "of the general path every people is fated to tread, whatever the historical circumstances in which it finds itself. . . . But I beg his pardon. (He is both honoring and shaming me too much.)"[4] Similarly, in another letter, Marx wrote: "Hence the 'historical

---

4 Karl Marx and Frederick Engels, *Selected Correspondence* (Moscow: Foreign Languages Publishing House, N.D.).

inevitability' of the movement [the genesis of capitalism] is *expressly* limited to the *countries of western Europe*."[5] Surely, then, Marx would have been the first to agree with Weber that the reasons for the absence of indigenous capitalist development in China and India, or anywhere else for that matter, is an empirical-historical question which could only be answered by investigating the relationship of the *Wirtschaft* to the *Gesellschaft* in all its complex aspects. Indeed, this is precisely how Marx approached the problem, and before Weber.

Ideal Types

If Weber was a historian interested in the unique forms and combinations cultural elements assumed in specific cultural contexts, he was also equally interested in generalizations about various social phenomena. One of the conceptual tools he adopted for this purpose is the now famous *ideal-type* construct. Only by means of such a construct, by moving from it to empirical reality and then back to the construct, modifying it accordingly, could an increasingly adequate conception of the phenomenon in question be acquired. I say Weber *adopted* this tool because certainly it did not originate with him; here, too, he learned from many of his predecessors who employed this device, but particularly from Karl Marx, whom he expressly acknowledges.

Depending on the researcher's purposes, point of view, values, etc., "the most varied criteria can be applied to the selection of the traits which are to enter into the construction of an ideal-typical view of a particular culture."[6] If one is interested, for example, in certain aspects of modern economic life, *e.g.*, the exchange economy, free competition, or rational conduct, then one needs some kind of analytical construct with which to think about these phenomena. "Substantively," writes Weber,

this construct in itself is like a *utopia* which has been arrived at by the analytical accentuation of certain elements of reality. Its relationship to the empirical data consists solely in the fact that where market-conditioned relationships of the type referred to by the abstract construct are discovered or suspected to exist in reality to some extent, we can make the *characteristic* features of this relationship pragmatically *clear* and *understandable* by reference to an *ideal-type*.[7]

In the first instance, the ideal-type is not yet a hypothesis "but it offers guidance to the construction of hypotheses. It is not a *description* of reality but it aims to give unambiguous means of expression to such a description."[8] Thus what Weber had in mind at least as a point of departure was not a

5 *Ibid.*, p. 412.
6 Weber, *op. cit.*, p. 91.
7 *Ibid.*, p. 90.
8 *Ibid.*, p. 90.

hypothesis, not an "average," and not a faithful description of reality; nor was it a model of what "ought to be." Rather, it was an accentuation of what the researcher considered to be the essential characteristics and tendencies of the phenomenon in question. The possible pitfalls that accompany the use of this device are (1) that one might confuse the construct with "actual reality"; (2) that one will regard the construct as a procrustean bed into which to force the data; or (3) that one might hypostasize the ideas so that they assume the character of real forces. If these dangers are averted, the ideal-type can become an extremely useful instrument with which to confront reality.

However, an ideal-type need not be confined to accentuating aspects of reality in a "frozen state"; developmental sequences may also be posited and built into ideal-type constructs. If, for example, one speaks of stages of development and keeps firmly in mind that these are relatively arbitrary intellectual constructs, then the idea of stages and developmental sequences can have great heuristic value. Ideal types can also be formulated as hypotheses; and as we shall see in our discussion of the most famous case in which Weber mixed the two types of constructs, it led to considerable confusion and to methodological errors.

Generally, the most fruitful use of the so-called ideal-types, Weber believed, was exemplified in the work of Marx; and Weber's remarks in this connection are important enough to be quoted in full.

> We have intentionally avoided a demonstration with respect to that ideal-typical construct which is the most important one from our point of view; namely, the Marxian theory. This was done in order not to complicate the exposition any further through the introduction of an interpretation of Marx and in order not to anticipate the discussions in our journal which will make a regular practice of presenting critical analyses of the literature concerning and following the great thinker. We will only point out here that naturally all specifically Marxian "laws" and developmental constructs—insofar as they are theoretically sound—are ideal types. The eminent, indeed unique, *heuristic* significance of these ideal types when they are used for the *assessment* of reality is known to everyone who has ever employed Marxian concepts and hypotheses. Similarly, their perniciousness, as soon as they are thought of as empirically valid or as real (*i.e., truly meta-physical*) "effective forces," "tendencies," etc., is likewise known to those who have used them.[9]

Weber regarded Marx's method of abstraction, particularly his two-class model, as one that had yielded important insights into the nature of the modern economic system. Just as Marx had attached great importance to the locus of control over the material means of production, so Weber, in his analysis of political, military, and scientific institutions, centered his attention on the locus of control over the means of administration, violence, and research. In Weber's words,

9 *Ibid.,* p. 103.

To maintain a dominion by force, certain material goods are required, just as with an economic organization. All states may be classified according to whether they rest on the principle that the staff of men themselves *own* the administrative means, or whether the staff is "separated" from these means of administration. This distinction holds in the same sense in which today we say that the salaried employee and the proletarian in the capitalistic enterprise are "separated" from the material means of production.[10]

If Marx observed the increasing concentration of the means of production and the consequent separation of the worker from those means, so that a clear dichotomy emerged between those who owned and controlled the means of production and those who did not, Weber called attention to the increasing concentration of the means of administration, means of violence, means of research, etc. In this way he was arguing that the tendency which Marx dramatized as a special case in the sphere of production could be seen as part of a much more general process.

The bureaucratic structure goes hand in hand with the concentration of the material means of management in the hands of the master. This concentration occurs, for instance, in a well-known and typical fashion, in the development of big capitalist enterprises, which find their essential characteristics in this process. A corresponding process occurs in public organizations.[11]

And again, "War in our time is a war of machines, and this makes magazines technically necessary, just as the dominance of the machine in industry promotes the concentration of the means of production and management."[12] And as a final example, "In the field of scientific research and instruction, the bureaucratization of the always existing research institutes of the universities is a function of the increasing demand for material means of management. . . . Through the concentration of such means in the hands of the privileged head of the institute, the mass of researchers and docents are separated from their 'means of production,' in the same way as capitalist enterprise has separated the workers from theirs."[13]

This approach led Weber to some really significant observations about the institutions and trends of modern civilization. However, his methodological writings per se leave us with the impression that he was somewhat confused and ambivalent about how one might best use the scientific method in the study of human phenomena. As he himself stated, he believed that it is but a "hair-line which separates science from faith."[14] More interesting than his

10 Max Weber, *From Max Weber: Essays in Sociology*, translated by H. H. Gerth and C. Wright Mills (New York: Oxford University Press, 1958) .
11 *Ibid.*, p. 221.
12 *Ibid.*, p. 221.
13 *Ibid.*, pp. 223–24.
14 Weber, *Methodology*, p. 10.

purely methodological writings are his actual historical-sociological studies; and actually they are also more important for an evaluation of Weber's method, for it is in those studies that one can observe his methodological procedure in the study of substantive problems.

The Weber Thesis: Protestantism and Capitalism

If the studies on the Protestant ethic are viewed, as they should be, in the context of his total work in the *Weltreligionen*, then it becomes quite clear that while Weber was carrying on a dialogue with Marx, and introducing modifications to the Marxian method, he was by no stretch of the imagination attempting to refute Marx. (Actually, the thesis on the relationship between ascetic Protestantism and the spirit of capitalism was one Weber developed quite early; and though he never explicitly abandoned it, his emphasis in his later writings shifted to a variety of other fundamental conditions which can be subsumed under the "special peculiarity of Occidental rationalism," as he referred to it.) In all these studies—the earlier as well as the later ones on the religions of China, India, and Israel—he recognizes the fundamental importance of what he calls the "economic factor," and insists that one must "take account of the economic conditions."[15]

In *The Protestant Ethic*, however, he set himself a special task, *viz.*, to examine the economic relevance of a specific religious ethic, which he felt had not been given the consideration it deserved. Although he sometimes speaks of correlation and at other times of causal influence, he states very clearly that he is deliberately treating "only one side of the causal chain," *i.e.*, the impact of religious values on economic conduct. (In his later studies, he turned his attention to both causal directions, though certainly not systematically.) Again and again in *The Protestant Ethic*, he returns to remind the reader of his limited purpose—"to clarify the part which religious forces have played in forming the developing web of our specifically worldly modern culture, in the complex interaction of innumerable different historical factors."[16] Weber is simultaneously fighting on two fronts. First, he is seeking to disprove the idea that the Reformation was a historically necessary consequence of economic developments. But, on the other hand, he has "no intention

> whatever of maintaining such a foolish and doctrinaire thesis as that the spirit of capitalism (in the provisional sense of the term explained above) could only have arisen as the result of certain effects of the Reformation, or even that capitalism as an economic system is a creation of the Reformation. In itself, the fact that certain important forms of capitalistic business organization are known to be considerably older than the Reformation is a sufficient refutation of such a claim. On the contrary, we only wish to

15 Max Weber, *The Protestant Ethic and the Spirit of Capitalism* (New York: Charles Scribner's Sons, 1958) , p. 26.
16 *Ibid.*, p. 90.

ascertain whether and to what extent religious forces have taken part in the qualitative formation and the quantitative expansion of that spirit over the world.[17]

He wanted somehow to assess the contribution of the Protestant ethic in particular to the modern economic system and more generally to contribute to our knowledge of how "ideas become effective forces in history."[18]

Thus Weber is proposing to round out the Marxian method; he recognizes the fundamental importance of economic conditions and yet suggests that other influences be explored. He is certainly not saying that Protestantism *caused* capitalism or some other such foolishness. He believed that one could not quantify or assign precise weights to the various "factors," and this led him to what he considered to be the only possible methodological approach: to attack the same problem from a variety of viewpoints and perspectives. Generally, the methodological tone of these essays is that one cannot prove or disprove his hypothesis; when dealing with a problem as complex as this, all one can do is to make as good and as cogent a case as possible. In the very last paragraph he again reminds his reader that he has been tracing influence in one direction and admits that from his own point of view he has done only half a job since it is equally

. . . necessary to investigate how Protestant asceticism was in turn influenced in its development and its character by the totality of social conditions, especially economic. The modern man is in general, even with the best will, unable to give religious ideas a significance for culture and national character which they deserve. But it is, of course, not my aim to substitute for a one-sided materialistic an equally one-sided spiritualistic causal interpretation of culture and of history. Each is equally possible, but each, if it does not serve as the preparation, but as the conclusion of an investigation, accomplishes equally little in the interest of historical truth.[19]

Despite all these qualifications, if the thesis were to have any meaning at all, Weber knew that he had to establish some kind of correlation, however small it might be. Ascetic Protestantism, he believed, had contributed something to the overall development of the modern economic system. How much? One could never answer this question in quantitative terms. But Weber's critics have argued that he employed a very confusing if not dubious methodological procedure, the ideal-type; that the correlation he suggested is so small as to be insignificant; that his grasp of some of the basic facts was bad; and, finally, that there may not be any correlation at all. Before we consider these criticisms, it is necessary to review, at least briefly, what Weber was attempting in these essays and how he went about it.

As Weber defined capitalism, it was a modern phenomenon: a very complex

[17] *Ibid.,* p. 91.
[18] *Ibid.,* p. 90.
[19] *Ibid.,* p. 183.

system of institutions, highly rational in character, and the product of a number of developments peculiar to Western civilization. In these terms, capitalism was unique—both in the sense that it had not appeared before in the history of the West and in the sense that such a system never emerged spontaneously in the East. Capitalism was not as old as history and not to be confused with the various forms of capitalistic activity (speculative, commercial, adventurous, political, etc.) which were indeed known in previous periods of Western history and in the civilizations of the East as well. The emergence of the new socioeconomic system in the West could not be taken for granted as an automatic consequence of the growing rationalization of all aspects of life. It had to fight its way to supremacy "against a whole world of hostile forces," and its victory over the traditional forces of the Middle Ages was not "historically inevitable" or "historically necessary." As he stated in one of his final pronouncements on the subject: "In the last resort the factor which produced capitalism is the rational permanent enterprise, rational accounting, rational technology, and rational law, but again not these alone. Necessary complementary factors were the rational spirit, the rationalization of the conduct of life in general, and a rationalistic economic ethic."[20] In the early essays, he is exploring in a provisional way the source of the rational spirit and conduct in the ethic of Protestantism. Although he is not altogether clear on this score, he does seem to treat that ethic as a "necessary complementary factor." But what he really means, as becomes clearer from his later essays, is not that capitalism would not have arisen without it—indeed he himself acknowledged that it had in some places—but rather that the peculiarly energetic form it assumed in a certain historical period might be attributed to the "elective affinity" between the ethical injunctions of ascetic Protestantism and the spirit of capitalism—the emphasis here being on *spirit;* there was such great congruence, between the two, that they mutually reinforced each other to produce a methodical devotion to work and business activity and thus to a vigorous development of capitalism.

In *The Protestant Ethic,* Weber begins by drawing attention (on the basis of very limited and questionable kinds of studies and data) to what he considers important differences between Protestants and Catholics in terms of their inclinations toward technical, industrial, and commercial studies and occupations. Protestants were much more inclined to pursue these studies and to be engaged in capitalistic enterprise while Catholics seem to prefer the more traditional humanistic studies. Among workers, too, it appeared that Catholics remained in the more traditional occupations, *e.g.,* crafts, while Protestants acquired industrial skills and even filled administrative positions. These differences could not be accounted for in terms of advantages of inherited wealth but rather had to be explained by the character of the

20 Max Weber, *General Economic History* (New York: Collier Books, 1961), p. 260.

religious education and values which the two groups received in their respective homes and communities. What seemed all the more striking to Weber about the smaller representation of Catholics in "modern business life" was that as a minority, suffering certain political disabilities, they should have sought all the more forcefully to engage in economic activity (as had other minorities, notably the Jews). Contrary to expectation, however, Catholics had not, in the various countries where they were persecuted, manifested such patterns of economic rationalism. Protestants, in contrast, regardless of whether from upper or lower strata, whether a majority or minority

. . . have shown a special tendency to develop economic rationalism which cannot be observed to the same extent among Catholics either in one situation or in the other. Thus the principal explanation of this differ- ence must be sought in the permanent intrinsic character of their religious beliefs, and not only in their temporary external historico-political situa- tions.[21]

At first glance, Weber suggests, one might be tempted to explain these differences on the basis of the otherworldliness of Catholicism which would tend to encourage in its adherents an attitude of indifference toward matters of this world. Protestantism, in contrast, appears at first to have just the opposite orientation—secular, materialistic, hedonistic—generally, of this world. Actually, Weber argues, as in the case of so many other phenomena, matters are not as they immediately appear. "Eating well" may be important for contemporary Protestants, but things were quite different for their ancestors. The "English, Dutch, and American Protestants," he writes, "were characterized by the exact opposite of the joy of living. . . ." (p. 41.) Weber considered this a fact; but the illustrations he used provided his critics with powerful ammunition with which to challenge his facts as well as his method.

To illustrate the relationship between the methodical, ascetic norms of conduct enjoined by Protestantism (especially by certain denominations) and what he called the *spirit* of capitalism, Weber hit upon the figure of Benjamin Franklin, who presumably embodied both the ethic and the spirit. Here Weber was employing his ideal-type method; for as he saw it, Franklin's writings (at least those Weber examined) were "a document of that spirit which contains what we are looking for in almost classical purity. . . ." (p. 48.) From *Necessary Hints to Those That Would Be Rich* and *Advice to a Young Tradesman,* he selects some typical sayings which stress Franklin's apparent commitment to industry and frugality, hard work and punctuality. "Time is money," says Franklin and goes on to speak of money in almost idolatrous terms. Franklin was important to Weber because unlike Fugger and others— who also wanted to make more and more money, but for whom, Weber

---

[21] Weber, *The Protestant Ethic,* p. 40. (Subsequent, immediately following references will be cited only by page number in text.)

asserts, this "was an expression of commercial daring and a personal inclination morally neutral"—Franklin's utterances must be interpreted as the "idea of a duty of the individual toward the increase of his capital, which is assumed *as an end in itself*." (p. 51, italics added.) And while Weber was willing to admit that Franklin's moral attitude was colored with utilitarianism, so that "the appearance of honesty" seemed as good *and useful* as honesty itself, he insists that a closer look at Franklin's autobiography shows that he ascribed "his recognition of the utility of virtue to a divine revelation which was intended to lead him in the path of righteousness. . . ." (p. 53.) Weber takes Franklin at his word and believes that something more was involved here "than mere garnishing for purely egocentric motives." (p. 53.)

Franklin's motives for making money, Weber asserts, are completely devoid of "any *eudamonistic,* not to say hedonistic, admixture"; and if one wants really to understand his motives, they must be seen as rooted in his strict Calvinistic upbringing—*i.e.,* primarily if not exclusively religious. Why should men make money and why should "money be made out of men?" To this Franklin replies by quoting the Bible: "Seest thou a man diligent in his business? He shall stand before kings." The capitalistic spirit as personified in Franklin could not in this case be regarded, Weber avers, as an element of the "superstructure," since at least in Massachusetts, where Franklin was born, there was as yet no capitalist foundation. Therefore one had to seek elsewhere for the origin of this spirit and one could plausibly trace it to Protestant doctrine. Its main tenets became an essential ingredient in the psychology of those parvenus who engaged in business activities which the traditional ethic had looked askance upon and even condemned as avaricious. Flying in the face of the traditional ethic, they could find clear sanction and justification in the new Protestant teachings. Not all the Protestant groups, however, shared this particular emphasis that resulted in an ascetic way of life and, unexpectedly, in a great stimulation of capitalistic spirit and enterprise.

With Luther, Weber believed, a new concept had emerged, which heretofore had been absent from Christian theology and which could not be traced to roots either in German culture or in classical antiquity. This concept, expressed in the German word *Beruf* and even more clearly in the English word *calling,* referred to the morally dutiful fulfillment of a task assigned by God. This concept with its special connotation, first appearing in Protestant translations of the Bible and thereafter assuming especial importance among Protestants, imparted for the first time in the West a religious significance to man's daily, worldly activities. This was one important consequence of the Reformation and it was particularly Luther who increasingly emphasized "that fulfillment of worldly duties is under all circumstances the only way to live acceptably to God. It and it alone is the will of God, and hence every legitimate calling has exactly the same worth in the sight of God." (p. 81.)

Yet, Luther's general doctrine, far from being favorable to the ethos of capitalism, was positively hostile to it. His attitude toward usury, interest, and capitalistic activity generally, was quite traditional and in some respects even less accommodating than that of the later Scholastics. Moreover, after the peasant uprisings, when he had firmly aligned himself with the princes, he became more and more a defender of the status quo. The existing social order and the individual's place in it was divinely ordained, and hence, inviolable. Luther's economic traditionalism, as Weber says, "was originally the result of Pauline indifference [but] later became that of a more and more intense belief in divine Providence, which identified absolute obedience to God's will with absolute acceptance of things as they were." (p. 85.) Hence, while Luther had introduced the idea of the calling, it assumed a definitely traditionalistic meaning and did not provide a congenial atmosphere for capitalistic activity. Nothing in Luther's conception could have provided the parvenus with good consciences much less with a positive attitude toward their anti-traditional business conduct. It is not in Luther's teachings, therefore, but in Calvinism that one must seek those ethical elements so conducive, allegedly, to the furtherance of the capitalistic spirit. Weber does not, however, wish to imply that such was the declared aim of Calvin and the other reformers; rather, these were unforeseen, and even unwished-for, results of their labors.

How, according to Weber, did Calvin's teachings, on predestination in particular, translate themselves into diligent, methodical, worldly activity? The original doctrine of the founder, if it had remained unmodified, would have yielded no such results. Calvin himself was certain of his own salvation; he considered himself an agent of the Lord and therefore was not disturbed by the question: "Am I one of the elect?"

Accordingly, to the question of how the individual can be certain of his election, he has at bottom only the answer that we should be content with the knowledge that God has chosen and depend further only on that implicit trust in Christ which is the result of true faith. He rejects in principle the assumption that one can learn from the conduct of others whether they are chosen or damned. It is an unjustifiable attempt to force God's secrets. (p. 110.)

Clearly, such a doctrine was too heavy a psychological burden for ordinary men who needed to know their fate and who required a "sign." Thus, Calvin's followers increasingly gave way to the expressed need for "infallible criteria by which membership in the *electi* could be known." (p. 110.) When as a result of this pressure the original doctrine was not altogether abandoned it imposed

. . . an absolute duty to consider oneself chosen, and to combat all doubts as temptations of the devil, since lack of self-confidence is the result of insufficient faith, hence of imperfect grace. The exhortation of the apostle to make fast one's own call is here interpreted as a duty to attain certainty of one's own election and justification in the daily struggle of life. In the place of the humble sinners to whom Luther promises grace if they trust themselves to God in penitent faith are bred those self-confident saints whom we can rediscover in the hard Puritan merchants of the heroic age of capitalism and in isolated instances down to the present. On the other hand, in order to attain that self-confidence, intense worldly activity is recommended as the most suitable means. It and it alone disperses religious doubts and gives the certainty of grace. (pp. 111–12.)

In these terms, though good works are useless for the *attainment* of salvation, they are nonetheless indispensable as a possible sign of election; they serve to allay the anxiety of not knowing and reduce—if not totally eliminate—the fear of damnation. Hard work, the morally dutiful pursuit of a calling, the belief that God helps those who help themselves, keeping one's attention from the devil, and the absolute avoidance of anything which detracted from this generally ascetic way of life, all this was enjoined by the Protestant ethic. For Weber this ethic, embodied in varying degrees in Calvinism, Puritanism, Pietism, Methodism, and the Anabaptist sects, had the "greatest significance for the development of the spirit of capitalism." (p. 151.)

This brings us to the point at which Weber's method of presenting his thesis—the ideal-type—must be carefully examined if we are to understand the charges brought against him even by the most friendly of his critics. Just as earlier he had accentuated what he considered the characteristics of the new "spirit of capitalism" by employing Benjamin Franklin as its ideal representative, so now he treated ascetic Protestantism as a unified whole by placing one of its major representatives at the center of discussion. For Weber, it was Richard Baxter, an English Puritan minister and writer, who "stands out above many other writers on Puritan ethics, both because of his eminently practical and realistic attitude, and, at the same time, because of the universal recognition accorded to his works. . . ." (pp. 155–56.) So, if Franklin epitomized at one and the same time the new capitalistic ethos as well as the Protestant conception of the pursuit of a calling in a morally dutiful manner, so Baxter expressed through his religious writings, "a practical and realistic attitude." Baxter does not quite say "time is money," but he does say the spiritual equivalent, Weber argues. A waste of time is "in principle the deadliest of sins." Every "hour lost is lost to labor for the glory of God." Out of strictly religious motives, Baxter preaches "hard, continuous, bodily or mental labor"; but unlike St. Paul or Thomas Aquinas, who exempted some from the rule that "He who will not work shall not eat," Baxter exempts no one—not even the wealthy. Weber grants that there are certain secular, utilitarian elements in Baxter's thought, as when he expresses himself on the division of labor. The manufacturing system tends to serve "the common good, which is identical with the good of the greatest possible number"; yet even this has a characteristic Puritan element that becomes perfectly clear in his insistence on the methodical and systematic pursuit of a calling—everyday and for everyone. Baxter's doctrine detests both the "superior indulgence of the *seigneur* and the parvenu ostentation of the *nouveau riche,*" but "it has the highest ethical appreciation of the sober, middle-class, self-made man." (p. 163.) Puritanism, Weber writes, carried with it "the ethos of the rational organization of capital and labor," and "turned with all its force against one thing: the spontaneous enjoyment of life and all it had to offer." (p. 166.) Asceticism

. . . looked upon the pursuit of wealth as an end in itself as highly reprehensible; but the attainment of it as a fruit of labor in a calling was a sign of God's blessing. And even more important: the religious valuation of restless, continuous, systematic work in a worldly calling, as the highest means to asceticism, and at the same time the surest and most evident proof of rebirth and genuine faith, must have been the most powerful conceivable lever for the expansion of that attitude toward life which we have here called the spirit of capitalism. (p. 172.)

This becomes clear not only in Baxter's work but also in that of John Wesley, the founder of Methodism. And the latter, Weber notes, even anticipated his own thesis, for he actually wrote that

. . . the full economic effect of those great religious movements, whose significance for economic development lay above all in their ascetic educative influence, generally came only after the peak of the purely religious enthusiasm was past. Then the intensity of the search for the Kingdom of God commenced gradually to pass over into sober economic virtue; the religious roots died out slowly, giving way to utilitarian worldliness. (p. 176.)

Protestant asceticism thus provided a positive religious sanction for the exploitation of the worker's willingness to labor; it eased the employer's conscience and at the same time provided the worker with religious motives for treating his labor as a calling. Weber therefore concludes:

One of the fundamental elements of the spirit of modern capitalism, and not only of that but of all modern culture: rational conduct on the basis of the idea of the calling, was born—that is what this discussion has sought to demonstrate—from the spirit of Christian asceticism. (p. 180.)

Now if we keep in mind the many qualifications Weber drew around his thesis—that in these essays he is tracing causal influence only in one direction, that he recognizes the fundamental importance of the economic conditions, and that in a subsequent essay he hoped to trace the influence in a reverse direction—then he is asserting on the basis of half completed research that there was a mutually reinforcing convergence of the Protestant ethic and the capitalist ethos; and he is *examining* in this instance the degree to which the latter was derived from the former. Once the capitalist system had become established, the Protestant ethic was no longer a necessary ingredient for the maintenance of the system. Moreover, the ethic was not a necessary precondition for the emergence of the capitalist system per se, but rather for its markedly energetic character during the early phases of the system's development.[22] Only if *this* is Weber's thesis in these fragmentary studies, and not that the Protestant ethic had a primary causal influence in producing the spirit of modern capitalism, can Weber's method be defended. Whom did Weber select to illustrate the ethical injunctions of ascetic Protestantism? Never its founder!—which led some of his critics to wonder whether in Weber's view Calvin was a Calvinist. For if indeed it *were* Weber's position— and some of his critics have thus wrongly interpreted him—that Calvin's religious teachings were of crucial causal importance in generating the capitalistic spirit, then it would be methodologically impermissible to use anyone but Calvin and his contemporaries as representatives of the new religious doctrine and to show that this antedated capitalist enterprise. But Weber does not do this; instead, as we have seen, he used Richard Baxter (1615–1691), John Wesley (1703–1791), Benjamin Franklin (1706–1790), and others, all having lived a hundred or more years after Calvin. Obviously, Weber was not doing this in order to show what Calvinism was in the middle of the sixteenth century but rather to show what Calvinism became in the course of its development. Furthermore, he was showing what it became, not in isolation from other developments, but under the influence of economic and other developments. That is why the thinkers Weber cites embody elements of both Protestant asceticism and the capitalistic spirit. On the theoretical level, then, Weber is *suggesting* that these were relatively autonomous developments which intersected at a given historical point to contribute to the formation of the modern rational temperament: There was a great "elective affinity" between the norms of the new religious movement and the psychological requirements of the new economic system.

Yet, this is not the way most of Weber's critics have interpreted him. They have ignored Weber's limited purpose in these essays, his careful qualifications of his thesis, and, finally, his later writings on the world religions and on economic history in which it becomes crystal clear that ascetic Protestantism was but one among many historical developments that contributed to the special character of modern Western society. If Weber is *not* read in this way, *i.e.*, if the essays on the Protestant ethic are taken alone, then one can indeed get the impression that he was attributing a primary causal influence to the new religious ideas (although such an impression could only be the result of a very *careless* reading). And if this were his thesis, then indeed his critics would be quite right in arguing that in using Franklin, Baxter, and Wesley, seventeenth- and eighteenth-century figures, Weber had totally neglected the impact on religion of economic and political developments which from the time of Calvin had undoubtedly modified significantly the form and content of his original doctrine.

22 In his later essays, Weber was to shift his emphasis and argue that there were a number of conditions, all peculiar to Western civilization, which converged to produce not only the modern economic system but the peculiarly rational character of all the modern institutions in the West.

That Weber understood all this, however, cannot be doubted. Because he never examined, as he had promised, influences working in the opposite direction—*i.e.,* the effects of economic changes on the formation of ascetic Protestantism—he left himself open to all sorts of misreadings and nonsensical interpretations. He once remarked ironically in reply to one of his critics that, had he accomplished the entire project, he would probably have been accused of having capitulated to the Marxian position just as now he was charged with holding to an idealistic interpretation of the problem. Insofar, however, as Weber's critics have met him on his own ground and have correctly understood his limited purpose in these essays, they have raised a number of important objections.

Ephraim Fischoff, for instance, one of Weber's sympathetic critics, has argued that the ideal-type method led to a number of distortions and biases, as in the selection and overemphasis of the concepts "calling" and "predestination." Also, once Weber defined capitalism as he did, stressing its rational, novel, and ascetic character, "he did not have much difficulty in discovering elements of congruity with the schematic construction of the Protestant ethic slanted in the same direction."[23] In addition, Weber's method entailed the selection of a number of cultural components, isolating one and tracing its influence on others; this was to be done with each component until one could determine the relative causal weight of each in shaping the socio-historical reality in question. This is what he had planned when he completed the essays on the Protestant ethic. He never carried it out, probably because he sensed the enormous difficulty and complexity of such a task. Finally, his "interactionist" view, though a good antidote to a dogmatic monistic one, "offers no method for determining the interrelation of factors, the degree of influence pertaining to each, or their temporal variations, thereby leaving room for the play of personal evaluation in the choice and characterization of the particular historical atoms."[24] One's overall impression of the underlying rationale of Weber's method is that he had little or no hope of ever "demonstrating" a hypothesis when dealing with problems as complex as those with which he concerned himself.

Other important objections which have been raised against Weber's thesis pertain to matters of historical fact. In his *Anfänge des Kapitalismus,* Lujo Brentano argued that many of the developments Weber attributed to ascetic Protestantism had already appeared during the Renaissance; and other scholars, notably R. H. Tawney, have agreed that "Brentano's criticism that the political thought of the Renaissance was as powerful a solvent of conventional restraints as the teaching of Calvin is not without weight."[25] Other historians have also objected to Weber's assignment of anti-traditional

---

[23] See Ephraim Fischoff, "The Protestant Ethic and the Spirit of Capitalism: The History of a Controversy," *Social Research,* XI (1944), pp. 61–67.

[24] *Ibid.*

[25] See Tawney's Forward to *The Protestant Ethic,* p. 8.

values primarily if not exclusively to ascetic Protestantism. They have argued that these values were much more general than Weber's essays would have us believe and that they were common to Catholic as well as to Protestant writers. In general, then, since Weber in fact never fulfilled his promise of examining the reverse relationship of that suggested in these essays, they create a false impression, and are incomplete and methodologically deficient. For by choosing as his illustrations Baxter, Wesley, *et al.,* and not thinkers from the early phase of iron collectivism under Calvin, Weber had neglected (as he would have been the first to admit) the degree to which religious opinions had themselves been affected by economic and political developments.

Despite their various objections, many of Weber's critics have accepted his suggestion of some correlation, however small, between the Protestant ethic and the ethos of modern capitalism. Recently, however, a most extreme and damaging critique has been put forward, in which either such a correlation is totally denied or causal priority is given to economic developments.

Kurt Samuelsson has mobilized considerable evidence to show that, while there is some truth in the proposition that Protestant countries were more vigorous economically than Catholic countries, none of the regions reveals the symmetry Weber imputed to them. Furthermore, so many qualifications are necessary as to make Weber's "hypothesis," taken as a whole, untenable.

> By the time Luther and Calvin were born, the Low Countries and the northern and western districts of Germany had already been characterised for at least three to four hundred years by exceptionally brisk economic activity; textile manufacturing and commerce in the Netherlands and Flanders; ironfounding, saltdrying, and international trade in the Hanseatic territories. And in England, too, economic life had begun to exhibit great liveliness well before Henry VIII demanded the annulment of his first marriage.[26]

The Netherlands by the end of the thirteenth century were conspicuous for their leadership in trade and textile manufacturing, and the idea that Calvinism created or even contributed to the beginnings of the "spirit of capitalism" there has to be rejected. Amsterdam was a prosperous mercantile center long before Calvinism became the prevalent religion late in the seventeenth century. Even then it was the poorer classes who first adopted that religion. Likewise, in England, technical, industrial, and economic expansion, more generally, were evident from the beginning of the thirteenth century—which is why, perhaps, it never occurred to Marx to consider religious developments as crucial for the origins of the capitalist system. This expansion began "so long

[26] Kurt Samuelsson, *Religion and Economic Action* translated by E. Geoffrey French in 1961 (Stockholm: Scandinavian University Books, 1957), p. 103. (Immediately following references to this work cited only by page number appearing in text.)

before the Reformation and reached full maturity so long *after* it that it is fruitless to try to interpret the course of events in terms of a religio-economic correlation." (p. 108.) And in Scotland it was not until the eighteenth century that significant economic expansion took place and this was "after secularization and the Enlightenment had become more important influences than religious zeal." (p. 110.)

What about Switzerland, Calvin's home? Was Calvinism in any form the main impetus there? There is no evidence to support this, and other factors have to be invoked to explain the early and sustained capitalistic activity there. Switzerland was favorably situated as a center of trade between Italy and the northern and western parts of Europe, and gaining a livelihood from agriculture was especially difficult; also significant was the early weakening of traditional feudal ties by free cities based on trade and industry. Moreover, there is no evidence of accelerated economic growth during or immediately after the Reformation.

Even in Germany, Samuelsson argues, there was no clear relationship between Protestantism and economic progress.

Here too there are factors other than religious conditions that can more plausibly explain the situation in the various regions of the country: the deposits of iron and coal in the west, the trade routes along the Rhine, the extent and profitability of agriculture in the east and south. Moreover, the Protestant element in the major industrial and commercial districts is far from preponderant. In Essen about half the population is Catholic, in Dusseldorf a good two-thirds, in Cologne—the largest city of western Germany—at least three-quarters. Indeed, during the period of industrialization the Catholic predominance in all these places was even more evident. Furthermore, it may be noted that many of the most prominent industrialists, businessmen, and bankers were Catholics and/or descendants of families whose wealth and noble rank dated back for generations, whose mode of life and general outlook assort extremely ill with Weber's theories. (p. 112.)

As for New England, it is true that many of the *ideas* which Benjamin Franklin articulated were more in evidence there than in other regions. But Protestant sects were and are prominent in the South, which is still less developed economically than the North. Samuelsson adduces a number of other factors to explain the regional difference, all "material" and economic— *e.g.,* the greater extent of fertile and arable land in the South, and the generally unfavorable agricultural conditions in "New England [where] one had to go outside agriculture to attain wealth, or indeed even a slightly above average livelihood. The fur trade, fishing, maritime carrying, and the slave trade soon became the most important branches of economic life. And these were occupations in which, because they yielded larger profits than could be had from other trades, a surplus of capital was created that could be made available for new and more ambitious projects. If this theory is sound, then a particularly marked propensity to accumulate capital and take risks must have been prevalent in New England—because these qualities were necessary there for success and well-being." (p. 114.) Moreover, those who migrated to and settled in New England were, to begin with, well-to-do, skilled artisans and tradesmen.

Generally, in all those places where Weber saw economic vigor and regarded the new religious doctrines as an important contributing condition, one can sufficiently explain this vigor without recourse to that doctrine.

> England, Netherlands, Scotland, and the North Sea and Baltic districts of Germany, Switzerland—they all furnish examples: their locations on ocean shores of transcontinental routes that were in use hundred of years before the Reformation; the definitive shift of the center of gravity of European trade to the North Sea and Atlantic as a result of the great discoveries and the throttling of the Mediterranean routes by the Arab countries; the frequent inability of agriculture and stock raising alone to provide adequate sustenance. (pp. 115–16.)

And Samuelsson continues:

> Had Italy and Spain been converted to the Calvinist creed in the sixteenth century or later been flooded with Puritans and Pietists, trade would still not have remained centered on the Mediterranean but would have shifted to the coasts of Holland, England, and Germany. (p. 116.)

And it is in England especially that Samuelsson's analysis seems to support Marx's view as he sketched it in his chapter, the "Primitive Accumulation of Capital." "On the one hand," writes Samuelsson,

> . . . there was the comparatively early rise of a fairly broad "middle class," in the sense defined above, and on the other, the early disruption of older social forms through the growth of population, the transformation of agricultural operations by the enclosure movement, and the emergence of a large landless class from which the new industrial districts could quickly recruit their supplies of labor. (p. 118.)

An important final point relates to the considerable significance Weber attached to what he considered to be a fact: a definite preponderance of Protestant over Catholic children in the *Realgymnasien,* the *Realschulen,* and the *Oberrealschulen*—i.e., in those schools which stressed training and preparation for technical, industrial, and business occupations. Weber drew his conclusions on the basis of Martin Offenbacher's statistics which, it turns out, were very misleading indeed (see the data in *The Protestant Ethic,* p. 189). Among other criticisms, Samuelsson points out that a wholly distorted picture emerges from these data because "[n] either Offenbacher nor Weber tried to ascertain in what proportions the various denominations were represented among the inhabitants of those school districts where Protestants predominated in the schools." (p. 141.) If, then, one examines the data *by school district* rather than, say, for Baden as a whole, one sees that

. . . the proportions of school children classified by religious faith are almost exactly the same as the corresponding proportion of the total populations of the appropriate district. That the Protestants in Baden as a whole display a "school frequency" higher than their share in the aggregate population is thus due entirely to the fact that more Protestants than Catholics lived in districts where *Realgymnasien, Höhere Bürgerschulen,* and *Realschulen* were available. If one reckons not in terms of total population but of inhabitants of districts containing the respective categories of schools, there remain no differences worth mentioning. (pp. 141–42.)

And, Samuelsson concludes:

If the religious denominations of the children are compared with demographic conditions in each individual school district, Catholics and Protestants exhibit precisely the same "propensity for schooling." In brief, Weber's alleged difference is a myth. (p. 142.)

Thus he sees virtually no support for Weber's thesis.

Now, since Weber gave much attention to the alleged asceticism of Benjamin Franklin and the Puritans of New England generally, it will be instructive to examine the validity of this characterization. For Weber, asceticism aided capitalist development in that it repudiated the "joy of living" and thus prompted the English, Dutch, and American Puritans, and even the French Protestants, to save and invest their earnings rather than to spend them on articles of lavish consumption, or status-enhancing commodities.[27] American historians have shown, however, that this is not true. In South Carolina, for instance, "the characteristic French *joie de vivre* was by no means absent from the large settlement of *Huguenots,* right from the beginning of their establishment in the latter part of the seventeenth century."[28] The same was true of New York and Philadelphia where regardless of denomination the merchants adopted

. . . a modish and socially exclusive pattern of life and consumption which diverted potential capital into nonproductive activities, into the attempt to consolidate status on a level corresponding with their economic power. In Boston the pattern was no different. Sumptuary legislation, established in Virginia as well as Massachusetts, broke down functionally several decades after its introduction. (p. 186.)

Moreover, the dominant impression of New England at the time is so far from being ascetic virtue that it might better be described as unbridled hedonism. In their crucial trade with the West Indies the New England merchants traded their "produce, fish, wood, and goods for West Indian rum [which] was contingent on the decidedly unascetic customs of the farmers, mechanics,

---

27 Weber, *The Protestant Ethic,* p. 41.

28 See Gabriel Kolko, "Max Weber on America: Theory and Evidence," in *Studies in the Philosophy of History,* ed. by George H. Nadel (New York: Harper and Row, 1965), p. 186. (Immediately following references to this work cited only by page numbers in text.)

and fishermen throughout the colonies." (p. 186.) And Kolko cites James Truslow Adams to the effect that

> Throughout all the colonies drunkenness was a prevailing vice, as it was in England, and nearly every event, such as house raisings, harvestings, christenings, college commencements, funerals, and even the ordination of ministers, was frequently made the occasion of scandalous intemperance. (p. 187.)

Wherever manufacturing developed, it was a variety of "material" conditions which account for this; for instance, religious values played no apparent role in the growth of the iron industry, which developed where there was an abundance of resources and

> . . . as in the case of Pennsylvania, where the high cost of transportation for agricultural goods stimulated diversification. The textile industry later developed in New England for similar reasons: water power, ports, proper humidity for production, and a surplus labor supply. (p. 188.)

Kolko goes on to make the rather important point that the type of capitalism characteristic of the colonies was the precise opposite of Weber's image of a rational, sober, legal, and strictly calculable capitalism. If anything, the capitalistic activity of colonial New England approximated his conception of political, speculative, and other older forms of capitalism. Trade was based primarily on barter, not money; and *unpredictability* was characteristic of American commerce of the time. Often goods sent to a particular destination found a glutted market, no buyer, or no exchangeable cargo. Colonial wars decreased the predictability of business affairs, and, due to British mercantilist policy, much of the colonial trade was carried on "in a technically illegal fashion." (p. 190.) Moreover, if Weber stressed that land holdings and land speculation were not rational capitalistic activities, then he was wrong in believing that this was not a major source of profit making in New England. He was wrong too in seeing, in his words, a major contrast between ". . . adventurers, who wanted to set up plantations with the labor of indentured servants, and live as feudal lords, and the specifically middle-class outlook of the Puritans."[29] For if "free labor" was an essential ingredient of rational capitalism, as Weber believed, then the Puritan undertakings were no more rational than others.

> At least half of the total white population in the Thirteen Colonies [Kolko writes] arrived as indentured labor, and Massachusetts received its fair share. Indentured servants entering the colonies because of their criminal records were generally received in the South and Pennsylvania, but those voluntarily emigrating were distributed throughout the colonies. Massachusetts established laws governing indentured servants from the inception of the colony, strictly enforced their obligations to their masters,

29 Weber, *The Protestant Ethic*, pp. 173–74.

and fixed the length of their service at seven years, which was the general average in the early colonial period. When the supply lagged, bounties were offered. In 1710, the Massachusetts Legislature offered 40 shillings a head to any ship captain bringing in male servants between the ages of eight to twenty-five. Prisoners captured by the English in their wars were often sent to the colonies, and part of the labor force of Massachusetts' first iron mill consisted of captured Scottish soldiers.[30]

A final consideration of Weber's view of the Puritan, his motives, his daily life, and his business activities involves the adequacy of his understanding of Benjamin Franklin, a key figure in his essays. Here, the inescapable verdict is that Weber's understanding was incomplete and inaccurate, the result of a selective reading of Franklin's writings.

Franklin was much more of a physiocrat in his economic views than Weber seems to have suspected and "viewed manufacturers, merchants, professionals, and mechanics, as little more than useless in the economic process."[31] Agriculture became for him the only honest way for a nation to acquire wealth.

As for Franklin's alleged asceticism, this, too, turns out to be a myth. When, as a young man, he traveled to London, he

. . . did not save his money like a true Puritan but rather spent evenings at such notably ascetic activities as theaters, sports, drink, and women. He returned to America with an illegitimate son who eventually fathered another who in turn did the same. In Philadelphia Franklin set to work determined to make something of himself, living a well-scheduled life which included only eight hours a day for work. Franklin was a wise promoter, however, and his newspaper tried many things, from discussions of hypothetical adultery to Poor Richard's Almanac, to increase circulation.

Franklin was never a prude and never became one. He retired from business at what is still the ripe young age of forty-two in order to escape "the little cares and fatigues of business." His letter on how to choose a mistress is relevant to his asceticism, and while serving as American ambassador to France, Franklin in his old age left his wife at home and carried on several amorous affairs. In addition to women, Franklin indulged in good food and excellent wine.[32]

Even this cursory examination of the facts shows that Weber's knowledge of early America, the New England Puritans, and Ben Franklin was very scanty indeed. It might conceivably have been permissible for Weber to accentuate certain of Franklin's characteristics for the purposes of his ideal-type method; but this would have required that the other, non-ascetic aspects of Franklin's personality (apparently unknown to Weber), be negligible. Since, however, Franklin was quite remote from what Weber portrayed him to be—a devout Puritan who adapted his everyday conduct to the precepts of his

30 Kolko, *op. cit.*, p. 191.
31 *Ibid.*, p. 192.
32 *Ibid.*, p. 193.

stern Calvinist upbringing—indeed, quite the opposite, this together with the other criticisms discussed here cannot but undermine Weber's entire thesis. At the very least one would have to acknowledge that there is little if any justification for retaining his notion as part of our intellectual consciousness as if it were firmly established knowledge. Why, then, has this particular idea of Weber's held on so tenaciously? Part of the explanation, no doubt, lies in the widespread but erroneous view that Weber in this instance had refuted and bested Marx. This—as he would have been the first to admit—he had neither intended nor accomplished.

That he himself became unhappy with the impressions these early and fragmentary essays created and with the exaggerated importance they acquired as compared with his other writings, can be seen in the different emphasis which emerged as he progressed in his encyclopedic studies of the world religions.

The Religion of China

Here, as in his later study of India, Weber is concerned with the question of why rational capitalism, as he defined it, emerged as an indigenous development only in the West. Although it would be inaccurate to say that he eventually abandoned his thesis on the role of ascetic Protestantism, it does become clear that the further he progresses in these studies of the world religions, the more he is prepared to view capitalism as one aspect of a much more comprehensive and general historical process in the West—rationalization. And this led him to his most important conclusions, namely, the fundamental differences between the civilizations of the East and the West. If this new emphasis is only partially evident in his studies of China and India, it becomes crystal clear in his later work on ancient Judaism. To illustrate the shift in Weber's thinking, a brief review and discussion of his work on China and India is in order.

Students of economic development in the West had stressed two factors, which, among others, had contributed greatly to the rise of capitalism: the great influx of precious metals and a significant growth in population. Weber observes, however, that in the case of China similar developments were evident. The great increase in the stock of precious metals led to a greater development of the money economy, particularly in state finance. Yet this did not shatter traditionalism; if anything, it strengthened it. Likewise, the enormous growth in population "was neither stimulated by, nor did it stimulate, capitalist development. Rather, it was . . . associated with a stationary economy."[33]

In the West, Weber proffers, the cities of antiquity and the papal curia,

<hr>

[33] Max Weber, *The Religion of China*, translated and edited by Hans H. Gerth (Glencoe: The Free Press, 1951), p. 12. (Immediately following references to this work cited only by page numbers in text.)

cities, and emerging states of the Middle Ages "were vehicles of financial rationalization, of money economy, and of political capitalism." (p. 13.) In China, in contrast, there were no cities like Florence, and the state failed to establish a money economy due to the resistance of the salaried officials—"the most powerful interest group"—who were paid substantially in silver and whose income depended on trade. These officials, therefore, had common interests with the traders in opposing the interference of the Peking government and its centralization of currency matters.

The Chinese city was fundamentally different from the Occidental one; it did not become a center in which capitalist relationships and institutions could germinate, for it lacked political autonomy. Unlike the *polis* of antiquity and the commune of the Middle Ages, it had neither political privileges nor military power of its own, no "self-equipped military estate such as existed in Occidental antiquity." The Occidental city became sufficiently strong to repel an army of knights and was not dependent for its survival on any centralized bureaucracy. Political associations of merchant and craft guilds were nonexistent in the Chinese "city," and legal contracts, either economic or political, could not be made. In short, there did not emerge a relatively independent bourgeois class centered in relatively autonomous towns—the fruit of prolonged struggle and revolts. Revolts were indeed common in the Chinese city but these were to remove specific officials or to change specific practices, not to guarantee the freedom of the city. One of the reasons for this was that the "fetters of the sib were never shattered." The Chinese city dweller never became a citizen in the Western sense; for he "retained his relations to the native place of his sib, its ancestral land and temple. Hence, all ritually and personally important relations with the native village were maintained." (p. 14.) (This was the opposite of the West where Christianity, according to Weber, was to play an important role, at least ideally, in developing an ethic which transcended kinship obligations.)

These differences between the Occidental and Oriental cities can be traced to their different origins. The *polis* of antiquity was an overseas trading city, whereas in China trade was predominantly inland. And in order to preserve tradition, foreign trade and contact were limited to a single port, Canton. Furthermore, industrial development was not centered in the city where it could, as in the West, escape the control of traditional groups and interests. Thus the economic, political, and formal-legal foundations of an autonomous and rational organization of industry and commerce were absent.

Control of the rivers, in China as in Egypt and other ancient civilizations, led to some rationalization of the economy but was greatly limited due to religious and other conditions. The

laws of nature and of rites were fused into the unity of *Tao*. Not a supra-mundane lord creator, but a supra-divine, impersonal, forever identical, and external existence was felt to be the ultimate and supreme. This was to sanction the validity of eternal order and its timeless existence. The impersonal power of Heaven did not "speak" to man. It revealed itself in the regimen on earth, in the firm order of nature and tradition which were part of the cosmic order, and, as elsewhere, it revealed itself in what occurred to man. The welfare of the subjects documented heavenly contentment and the correct functioning of the order. All bad events were symptomatic of disturbance in the providential harmony of heaven and earth through magical forces. (p. 28.)

River regulation, the basis of imperial authority, was assured not by empirical-rational means alone but by the conduct of the emperor who had to abide by the imperatives of the classical scriptures. If, for example, the dikes broke, this was evidence that he did not have the qualities of charisma demanded by heaven and therefore had to do public penitence for his sins.

As in all large far-flung states with undeveloped systems of communication, administrative centralization remained negligible; nevertheless, this did not facilitate the growth of autonomous centers of power. The central government employed quite effective means in preventing officials from becoming independently powerful in their areas of assignment. The official was never assigned to his home province and had to shift every three years either to another province or to another office. Not knowing the provincial dialect, he was dependent on interpreters; and not being familiar with the local laws and traditions, he became wholly dependent on assistants from the province whom he paid from his own pocket.

> . . . this resulted in actual power being vested in the hands of the unofficial, native subordinates. And the higher the rank of the authorized official the less was he able to correct and control their management. Thus the local and central government officials were not sufficiently informed about local conditions to facilitate consistent and rational intervention. (p. 50.)

Yet, this did not lead to a Western type feudalism either, for appointment to office was based on educational qualifications rather than criteria of birth and rank.

The dependence of the central government on its officials, and these in turn on provincial assistants, enhanced traditionalism; even the "money economy" contributed to the strengthening of traditional structures. The officials became in effect "tax farmers," who extracted what they could from their provincial subjects, gave as little as they dared to their superiors, and kept the rest. They were prebendaries who had a paramount interest in maintaining the existing socioeconomic conditions and hence the profits from their prebends. Thus as the money economy expanded so did prebendalization, a great obstacle to attempts at internal change. To become prebendaries they were dependent on the central government; once they became officials and received their assignments, however, they acquired only a very limited power, for they remained dependent on the indigenous elements of the provinces in which they were strangers. This is in sharp contrast with the West where there were strong and independent forces. With these princely power could ally itself in order to shatter traditional fetters; or, under very special conditions, these forces could use their own military power to throw off the bonds of patrimonial power. This was the case in the five great revolutions which decided the destiny of the Occident: the Italian revolution of the twelfth and thirteenth centuries, the Netherland revolution of the sixteenth century, the English revolution of the seventeenth century, and the American and French revolutions of the eighteenth century. We may ask: Were there no comparable forces in China? (p. 62.)

The Chinese were highly acquisitive, and their capacity for work and industry was unsurpassed; there were even powerful and autonomous merchant guilds though not concentrated in the towns; there was a tremendous growth in population since the eighteenth century; and, finally, a constant increase in precious metals. Yet, no capitalism. How does Weber explain this?

Though "private property" emerged, it never became truly private as in the West: the sib in China was so powerful that true alienation of land from it was impossible. Land was not unconditionally or permanently sold; rather, the sib always retained the right to repurchase. There were moneylenders and other forms of politically determined capitalism but these did not lead to modern rational, capitalistic enterprise. "There was no rational depersonalization of business," Weber writes, "comparable to its unmistakable beginnings in the commercial law of Italian cities." (p. 85.) In China, the growth of wealth in the form of money led to different results. When officials retired, for instance, they invested their money in landholdings which enabled some of their sons to study so as to pass the state examinations and thus become eligible for "tax farming" careers of their own. In this way the whole familial community had a vested interest in the examination system and other traditional institutions. And this community was held together by powerful and rigid kinship bonds.

The power of the sib rested to a large degree on the ancestor cult; ancestral spirits acted as mediators between their descendants and God. The "city" then, never became a "home town" but remained "typically 'a place away from home' for the majority of its inhabitants." (p. 90.) Cities were mere urban settlements of farmers and "there remained only a technical administrative difference between city and village. A 'city' was the seat of the mandarin and was not self-governing; a 'village' was a self-governing settlement without a mandarin." (p. 91.) And autonomous military power developed, in contrast with the West, in the villages and not in the cities.

The sib and other traditional elements were in the long run stronger than the rational bureaucracy; illiterate old age, for example, carried a higher status and authority than the most learned mandarin; and Chinese justice, far from becoming formal, legal, and rational, remained patriarchal *cadi* justice.

There were still other developments which contributed to the formation of capitalism in the West and were patently missing in China. After the pacification of the empire, there was neither rational warfare nor even an "armed peace during which several competing autonomous states constantly prepared for war. Capitalist phenomena thus conditioned through war loans and commissions for war purposes did not appear." (p. 103.) An additional handicap to capitalist development was the empire's lack of overseas colonies.

Rational development in China also took a different form from that of the West. This is best seen from the specific kind of bureaucracy composed of *literati*. To be sure, they had to qualify for office by passing examinations, which in turn required a certain education. Their social honor was not the result of alleged magical powers—sorcery, healing the sick, and the like—but of knowledge of writing and classical literature. They were therefore quite far from being bureaucrats in the Western sense for their ideal, above all, was to be cultivated Confucian gentlemen.

> The Chinese examinations [writes Weber] did not test any special skills, as do our modern national and bureaucratic examination regulations for jurists, medical doctors, or technicians. Nor did the Chinese examinations test the possession of charisma, as do the typical "trials" of magicians and bachelor leagues. To be sure, we shall presently see the qualifications which this statement requires. Yet it holds at least for the technique of the examinations.
>
> The examinations of China tested whether or not the candidate's mind was thoroughly steeped in literature and whether or not he possessed the *ways of thought* suitable to a cultured man and resulting from cultivation in literature. (p. 121.)

Rational administration depended on subordinates who were skilled in the required technical and administrative tasks, for the *literati* themselves rejected the one-sided thoroughness and specialization characteristic of Western civilization from Plato to its restatement in the "calling" of ascetic Protestantism. Yet, while the *literati* viewed the examinations as tests of their cultivation and general humanistic knowledge, the popular view was different.

> In the eyes of the Chinese masses, a successfully examined candidate and official was by no means a mere applicant for office qualified by knowledge. He was a proved holder of magical qualities, which, as we shall see, were attached to the certified mandarin just as much as to an examined and ordained priest of an ecclesiastic institution of grace, or to a magician tried and proved by his guild. (p. 128.)

Orthodox Confucianism had renounced the beyond and in so doing had ignored the religious needs of the masses. Magic and animism, always strong among the peasants,

> had come under the patronage of a priesthood which was tolerated because it claimed to have originated with a philosophical personage, Laotzu, and his doctrine. Originally the meaning of this doctrine did not differ in the main from that of Confucianism. Later it became antagonistic to Confucianism and was finally considered thoroughly heterodox. (p. 177.)

There were repeated power struggles between the *literati* and the priests, in which the former were always victorious. Yet, ironically, the *literati* constantly availed themselves of the *Taoist's* priestly and magical services, affording *Taoist* heterodoxy a recognized place in religious practice. This

rested upon the fact that the victorious Confucians themselves never seriously aimed at uprooting magic in general and Taoist magic in particular. They only sought to monopolize office prebends. (p. 194.)

Not only were magic and animism tolerated, they were systematized and rationalized so that they became a tremendous power in Chinese life. All sciences which had empirical and naturalistic beginnings were completely rationalized as magical and supernatural practices and rituals. The Chinese world, despite its secular, rational-empirical elements, remained enchanted—a magic garden.

The *literati* were to a notable degree secular or "this worldly," but not consistently so. They not only tolerated magic as a means of taming the masses—they themselves believed in it. Under these circumstances it is understandable why they never waged war against magic, never strove to divest Chinese culture of magical beliefs and practices.

"Demagification" of religion, Weber believed, was carried out in the West most consistently and thoroughly by ascetic Protestantism; but the process had begun with the ancient Jewish prophets. This does not mean, he emphasizes, that the Puritans did not retain superstitious beliefs; that they did is obvious from their witch trials. Rather, it means that they came to regard "all magic as devilish." For Weber, then, one criterion of the rationalization of religion is the degree to which it has rid itself of magic. But there is still another criterion: "the degree to which it has systematically unified the relation between God and the world and therewith its own ethical relationship to the world." (p. 226.) In these terms, whereas Puritanism resulted in a "tremendous and grandiose tension toward the 'world,' " Confucianism regarded this as the best of all possible worlds. Above all, the Confucian was to adjust to the world; his conduct had implications for cosmic harmony so he exercised rational self-control and repressed all irrational passions that might disturb his poise. But this did not weaken the powers of magic; quite the contrary, it took the use of magic for granted. For though the educated Confucian adhered, or submitted, to magical practice with some skepticism, the masses were altogether steeped in it. And the *literati* (unlike the Old Testament prophets), far from having demanded that the masses abandon these practices, even connived in them—for material as well as spiritual reasons. "Tension toward the 'world' had never arisen because, as far as known, there had never been an ethical prophecy of a supramundane God who raised ethical demands." (p. 230.) A true prophecy which raised such demands and which viewed the world as matter to be shaped according to ethical norms was unknown in Chinese history.

As we see, then, Weber counterbalances the conditions apparently favorable to the development of capitalism by other unfavorable conditions. As he repeatedly stresses, his treatment of an enormously complicated problem with innumerable variables could hardly yield a simple answer. Yet, he wants to salvage his original thesis: "compared to the Occident, the varied conditions which externally favored the origin of capitalism in China did not suffice to create it." (p. 248.) What was missing? The ethical code of Puritanism or its functional equivalent. Or, stated otherwise, the religious norms which did in fact prevail in China precluded the spontaneous development of capitalism there. But again he is not arguing a strictly one-sided causal influence. "To be sure," concludes Weber,

> the basic characteristics of the "mentality," in this case the practical attitudes toward the world, were deeply codetermined by political and economic destinies. Yet, in view of their autonomous laws, one can hardly fail to ascribe to these attitudes effects strongly counteractive to capitalist development. (p. 249.)

The Religion of India

In India, too, Weber saw many social and cultural conditions which, it would seem, should have given rise to modern rational capitalism. Warfare, finance, and politics, for instance, had been rationalized, and the last of these even in quite "Machiavellian" terms. Many of the older type capitalist forms had at one time or another been in evidence: state creditors and contractors, tax farmers, etc. Urban development also seemed to parallel that of the West at many points. In addition, what Weber called rationality was prominent in many aspects of Indian cultural life: the rational number system, arithmetic, algebra, rational science, and in general a rational consistency in many spheres, together with a high degree of tolerance toward philosophical and religious doctrines. The prevailing judicial forms appeared compatible with capitalist development; there existed an autonomous stratum of merchants; handicrafts as well as occupational specialization were developed; and, finally, the high degree of acquisitiveness and high evaluation of wealth were a notable aspect of Indian social life. "Yet," Weber writes,

> . . . modern capitalism did not develop indigenously before or during the English rule. It was taken over as a finished artifact without autonomous beginnings. Here we shall inquire as to the manner in which Indian religion, as one factor among many, may have prevented capitalistic development (in the Occidental sense).[34]

Here, again, we see Weber's peculiar methodological approach of looking at the problem from one point of view. He regards Indian religion as "one factor

[34] Max Weber, *The Religion of India*, translated and edited by Hans H. Gerth and Don Martindale (Glencoe, Ill.: The Free Press, 1958), p. 4. (Immediately following references to this work cited only by page numbers in text.)

among many" which, he states cautiously, "may have prevented capitalistic development. . . ." Since there was no way of quantifying or weighting the elements, all one could do was to make as strong and as cogent a case as possible. If Indian religion had taken another form—*e.g.*, equivalent to that of ascetic Protestantism—then, perhaps, a modern, rational type of capitalism might have developed there too. Since economic, urban, scientific, and other developments were somewhat equivalent in India and the West, and modern capitalism emerged autonomously only in the latter civilization, the different religious ethos which took shape there must have made a significant causal contribution to the origin of the modern economic system. Ultimately, however, Weber sees more operative here than just the Protestant ethic; what he sees as really crucial is that despite the rational, scientific elements in the East, and the existence there of economic strata and forms seemingly conducive to the emergence of a modern rational economy, the East remained an enchanted garden. This meant that all aspects and institutions of Oriental civilization were permeated and even dominated by the magical mentality— which became a brake on economic developments in particular and on rationalization of the culture as a whole. On the other hand, Occidental civilization, already in its early stages of development, had undergone significant disenchantment, which has increased almost as a unilinear development right to the present. This disenchantment or rationalization began with the scriptural prophets; but Christianity, Greek formal logic, Roman law, the medieval papal curia, cities, and states, the Renaissance, the Reformation, the Enlightenment, the various bourgeois revolutions, etc., all contributed to the process which has made Western civilization as a whole fundamentally different from that of the East. This is the implicit and occasionally explicit emphasis in these works.

Actually, Weber's studies of the world religions embrace much more than religious phenomena and institutions. In effect, he takes the entire social structure of the society in question into his purview. In the case of India, clearly the caste system was of fundamental importance. The origin of the four main castes or categories—Brahmans, Kshatriyas, Vaishyas, and Shudras—is shrouded in mystery; more, however, is known about the proliferation of groupings, so that literally thousands of subcastes crystallized in the course of Indian history. Basing himself on the best Indological sources, Weber sketches the process by which new castes form and others undergo schisms.

With the increasing wealth of some strata, numerous tasks were defined by them as "lower" and unclean so that eventually the native, resident population refused to engage in them. This made room for alien workers, whatever their origin, who moved into these occupations and became a "guest" people tolerated for the economic function they fulfilled. They were not at first properly a part of the host village organization; they retained their own community organizations and had full jurisdiction over them. When, in addition, certain ritual barriers were raised against these guest peoples, Weber calls them a *pariah people*. (One example of this in the West was the Jews during the Middle Ages—except that in their case, as Weber shows, it was precisely the Jews who brought with them certain ritual practices which they voluntarily maintained against the host people.) Eventually, through a variety of forms of transition, a *pariah people,* having established itself in some of the formerly native Hindu occupations, develops an interest in maintaining its hold over these occupations and demands and receives certain Brahmanical services. The members of the pariah group, underprivileged anyway, come to prefer a legitimate status to that of an alien people since "caste organizations, like quasi-trade unions, facilitate the legitimate defense of both internal and external interests of the lower castes." (p. 17.) The hope and promise which Hinduism held out to these negatively privileged strata helps to explain "their relatively minor resistance in view of what one would expect of the abysmal distance Hinduism establishes between social strata." (p. 17.) Clearly, this is not the place to discuss the caste phenomenon in detail; what interests us here is the role Weber assigned to caste as a factor which may have imposed structural restraints on economic development.

The caste system, to be sure, had essentially negative consequences for economic development; but not, as one might at first expect, primarily because it imposed restrictions and prohibitions on social interaction. Rather, it was because the caste system became totally traditionalistic and anti-rational in its effects. And here Weber takes time to acknowledge an insight which reveals that in these studies as in others he took leads from Marx. "Karl Marx," writes Weber,

> . . . has characterized the peculiar position of the artisan in the Indian village—his dependence upon fixed payment in kind instead of upon production for the market—as the reason for the specific "stability" of the Asiatic peoples. In this, Marx was correct. (p. 111.)

Weber adds, however, that "not only the position of the village artisan but also the caste order as a whole must be viewed as the bearer of stability." (p. 112.) That order was quite flexible in the face of the requirements of the concentration of labor in large-scale enterprises; caste proscriptions on interaction with the ritually impure were not the main impediment to industrial development. All the great religions, he suggests, have placed such restrictions on modern economy. It was the traditional, anti-rational "spirit" of the whole social system which constituted the main obstruction; and this, along with the "artisan's traditionalism, great in itself, was necessarily heightened to the extreme by the caste order." (p. 112.)

The anti-rational spirit became manifest in the prevalence of magic and in the role of the Brahmans, whose very power was connected "with the increasing significance of magic in all spheres of life." This together with other religious developments had significantly modified the character of Indian economic conditions and strata. If, for example, there was an Indian "bourgeoisie," it was very weak for at least two reasons:

. . . first, was the absolute pacifism of the salvation religions, Jainism and Buddhism, which were propagated, roughly, at the same time as the development of the cities. (The possible causal interrelationship between urbanism and the salvation religions and its significance will be discussed below.) Second, there was the undeveloped but established caste system. Both these factors blocked the development of the military power of the citizenry; pacifism blocked it in principle and the castes in practice, by hindering the establishment of a *polis* or *commune* in the European sense. (pp. 88–89.)

The bourgeoisie as well as the guilds had no independent military organizations and therefore could be repressed whenever a prince found it expedient to do so. The Indian town enjoyed no true self-government or autonomy.

Also, apart from the implications which the sacred cow had for Indian animal husbandry, magico-religious practices retarded technical-industrial development. Often, "tools were worshipped as quasi-fetishes" and along with "other traditional traits, this stereotyping of tools was one of the strongest handicaps to all technical development." (p. 99.)

Indian religions, including Buddhism, had attained a highly technical virtuosity but this resulted in an extreme devaluation of the world; none of them enjoined the adherent to prove himself or his grace through action or work. Quite the contrary, the highest good was a contemplative flight from the world. Indian asceticism never translated itself into a methodical, rational way of life that tended in its effects to undermine traditionalism and to change the world.

Thus India, like China, remained an "enchanted garden" with all sorts of fetishism, animistic and magical beliefs and practices—spirits in rivers, ponds, and mountains, highly developed word formulae, finger-pointing magic, and the like. In contrast to the Hebrew prophets, who never made peace with the magicians, the Brahmans (a distinguished, cultivated, and genteel stratum like the Mandarins), in the interests of their power position, not only recognized the influence of magic but rationalized it and made numerous concessions to the unclassical magicians. (p. 295.) This despite the fact that ideally, according to the Classic Vedas, magic was to be suppressed —or at least merely tolerated among the masses. Weber believed that

The driving motive of the Brahmans in this reception and accommodation process was in part quite grossly material. They wished to protect the many prebends and incidental fees which were available if one accepted the service of these ineradicable folk deities. As well, there was the force of competition against the powerful salvation confessions of Jainism and Buddhism which had managed to get into the saddle only through adaptation to the folk tradition. (p. 297.)

The general character of Asiatic religion, Weber concluded (on the basis of his studies of China, India, Korea, Ceylon, etc.), was a particular form of gnosis; *i.e.,* positive knowledge in the spiritual realm, mystically acquired. Gnosis was the single path to the "highest holiness" and the "highest practice." This "knowledge" far from becoming a "rational and empirical means by which man sought with increasing success to dominate nature" became instead "the means of mystical and magical domination over the self and the world . . . by an intensive training of body and spirit, either through asceticism or, and as a rule, through strict, methodologically ruled meditation." (p. 331.) This gave rise to a redemption aristocracy, for such mystical knowledge was necessarily esoteric and charismatic, hence not accessible or communicable to everyone. The holy and godlike was attained by an "emptying" of experiences of this world. Psychic peace, not restlessness, was godlike; the latter, being specifically creature-like, was illusory, transitory, and soteriologically valueless.

Hence, in contrast to the soul-saving doctrines of Christianity, no emphasis was placed on "this life"; Asiatic religion led to an otherworldliness. "In Asia generally," writes Weber, "the power of a charismatic stratum grew." In sharp contrast to the Hebrew prophets, however, this stratum

> . . . succeeded in breaking the dominion of magic only occasionally and only with very temporary success.
> Not the "miracle" but the "magical spell" remained, therefore, the core substance of mass religiosity. This was true above all for peasants and laborers, but also for the middle classes. (p. 335.)

That this magical, anti-rational world had a profound impact on economic conduct and development could not be doubted. Magic was employed

> . . . for achieving all conceivable sorts of inner-earthly values—spells against enemies, erotic or economic competition, spells designed to win legal cases, spiritual spells of the believer for forced fulfillment against the debtor, spells for the securing of wealth, for the success of undertakings. (p. 336.)

The depth and tenacity of this magical mentality created conditions in which the "lust for gain" never gave rise to the modern economic system Weber called rational capitalism. What was notably absent from Asiatic religion therefore was that development which in the Occident ultimately broke the hold of magic over the minds of men and gave rise to a "rational, inner-worldly ethic." This historical process began

> . . . with the appearance of thinkers and prophets who developed a social structure on the basis of political problems which were foreign to Asiatic culture; these were the political problems of civic status groups of the city without which neither Judaism nor Christianity nor the development of Hellenic thought is conceivable. (p. 338.)

The ancient Jewish prophets then were fundamental; for it was to them and to the early Greek thinkers that the roots of the *Rationalisierungsprozess* in the West could be traced.

Ancient Judaism

For Weber, the development of Judaism was important for the profound impact it had on the beginnings of Western civilization. According to the Jewish religious conception, God created the world and intervened in history; the world in its present form was a result of God's reaction to the actions of men and particularly the Jews. The present condition of toil, trouble, misery, and suffering, the opposite of that promised for the future, was temporary and would "give way again to the truly God-ordained order. The whole attitude toward life of ancient Jewry was determined by this conception of a future God-guided political and social revolution."[35] For the attainment of the future order everything depended on the worldly actions of the Jews and their faithful devotion to the Commandments of God (*Yahwe*). In addition to ritual correctitude there was

> . . . a highly rational religious ethic of social conduct; it was free of magic and all forms of irrational quest for salvation; it was inwardly worlds apart from the paths of salvation offered by Asiatic religions. To a large extent this ethic still underlies contemporary Mideastern and European ethic. World-historical interest in Jewry rests upon this fact.[36]

The historical importance of Judaism, apart from being the source of Christianity and Islam, is to be found in its rational-ethical character and for this reason

> Only the following phenomena can equal those of Jewry in historical significance: the development of Hellenic intellectual culture; for western Europe, the development of Roman law and of the Roman Catholic church resting on the Roman concept of office; the medieval order of estates; and finally, in the field of religion, Protestantism.[37]

In this remarkably painstaking study, Weber defines the historical status of the Jews as that of a "pariah people"—a term which has been subject to considerable misunderstanding.[38] The term refers primarily to the social segregation of the Jews which resulted to a large degree from the ritualistic requirements of their religion. Weber understands the segregation of the Jews

[35] Max Weber, *Ancient Judaism,* translated and edited by Hans H. Gerth and Don Martindale (Glencoe, Ill.: The Free Press, 1952) , p. 4.

[36] *Ibid.,* p. 4.

[37] *Ibid.,* p. 5.

[38] For an illuminating discussion of Weber's use of this concept see the preface by Gerth and Martindale to *Ancient Judaism,* especially pp. XXIII–XXVII. (Immediately following references to this work cited only by page numbers in text.)

in this sense as self-imposed and long antedating their forced ghettoization for economic and other reasons in medieval Europe. If the young Marx sought to understand the phenomenon of Judaism by analyzing its social basis and "secular essence," Weber too was in this case deducing Jewry's attitude from its pariah existence; but he is intent upon showing that general social and historical conditions, though important, were not sufficient to explain how Jewry developed into a people "with highly specific peculiarities." For this never would have come about in the absence of the specific Jewish ritual and religious commandments. Here again, Weber is exploring the influence of religious ideas on social existence and development—but always against the background of social, economic, and political structures which he examines fastidiously.

Weber shows, for instance, how the older stratification system changed and how in its place there soon emerged a wealthy urban patriciate on the one hand and a number of economically heterogeneous strata on the other. These were the "poor." Ancient Israel, situated as it was in the midst of the great and powerful states and along major trade routes, became a center of trade with many cities. Evidence of class conflict between "indebted peasants and urban creditors existed from the beginning of recorded history." (p. 61.)

Conflict between the rich and the poor was exacerbated with the emergence of the monarchy, particularly under Solomon; and Weber calls attention to the ambivalence with which Jewish tradition had regarded the third king of Israel. It was against the background of this basic transformation of Israeli society that the prophets of social justice emerged. Now, increasingly, the kings, whose oppressive consequences Samuel had prophecied, were making of Israel a *corvée* state, a "house of bondage" like the Egyptian state the Jews despised as an abomination. These politically oriented prophets spoke out against this trend and voiced sharp criticism of the monarchs, their private sins as well as their public practices. The prophets, though not out of political motives per se, thus expressed the sentiments of the peasants and other oppressed groups who remembered that they had fought for freedom against the privileged strata, and that God had brought their forefathers out of the land of Egypt. Now the people saw themselves increasingly subjected to debt bondage, taxes, and *corvée* duties.

This should not be taken to mean, Weber emphasizes, that when the prophets rebuke the monarchs or speak out against the rich, they are direct ideological spokesmen of the oppressed. There is no doubt that the political content of their messages was drawn from the actual events of the day and from reflecting on the condition of the oppressed. But the real inspiration and meaning of their message, Weber insists, were purely religious. Yahwe and his Commandments were being forsaken and his Covenant violated. It was this primarily, if not exclusively, which motivated the prophets to say what they did and to foretell doom. They increasingly deprecated the patricians and their riches, and the kings and their chariots, and "hallowed the time when

Yahwe himself as war leader led the peasant army, when the ass-riding prince did not rely on horses and wagons and alliances, but solely on the God of the Covenant and his help." (p. 111.)

Here we may pause to note how Weber conceives the relationship between religious ideas and socioeconomic conditions. The prophets were a relatively autonomous stratum in Israeli society; they were religious practitioners with strictly religious interests. However, their political orientation, which became evident in a specific period, was clearly related to changes in social stratification and to the institutionalization of the monarchy. "It is no accident," he writes,

> . . . that the first appearance of the independent, politically oriented seers, who were succeeded by these prophets, coincided almost exactly with that great transformation which kingship under David and Solomon brought about in the political and social structure of Israel. (p. 110.)

Although the prophets were religious thinkers, and comprised a relatively autonomous stratum, their message, and the various forms it assumed, could not be explained in strictly immanent terms. There was a definite relationship between the prophetic movement and other aspects of the social structure, and the fact that prophecy acquired a political character in a given historical period can be understood only by viewing it in relation to the general social changes that had come about. The relative independence of the prophets was facilitated by the fact that in Israel the king was not a priestly dignitary at the apex of a hierocratic order and that the prophets received support and protection from wealthy and powerful Yahwistic families whom the monarchy could not suppress. However, if, in Weber's view, "rationalization" was a consequence of the prophets' unceasing war against magical and orgiastic practices, this was not out of any rational, secular, or political considerations on their part; rather, it had to be explained on the basis of their unswerving devotion to Yahwe.

This devotion was based on the unique relation of Israel to its God, expressed and guaranteed in a unique historical event—the conclusion of a covenant with Yahwe. The prophets and the anti-royalist Yahwistic nobles always hearkened back to that great and miraculous event in which God kept his promise, intervened in history, and liberated the Jews from Egyptian bondage. This was proof not only of God's power but of the absolute dependability of his promises. Israel, then, as the other party to the Covenant mediated by Moses, owed a lasting debt of gratitude to serve and worship Yahwe and to have no other gods before him. This rational relationship, unknown elsewhere, created an ethical obligation so binding that Jewish tradition regarded " 'defection' from Yahwe as an especially fatal abomination." (p. 119.) Moreover, the markedly rational nature of this relationship lay in the worldly character of God's promises to Israel; not some supernatural paradise or utopia was promised, but

> . . . that they would have numerous descendants, so that the people
> should become numerous as the sand of the seashore, and that they should
> triumph over all enemies, enjoy rain, rich harvests, and secure possessions.
> (p. 119.)

And to Moses was held out the hope of leading his people out of Egypt and
into the Promised Land—here on earth and, in fact, just across the border,
despite the circuitous route required to reach it. "The god," writes Weber,

> . . . offered salvation from Egyptian bondage, not from a senseless world
> out of joint. He promised not transcendent values but dominion over
> Canaan which one was out to conquer and a good life. (p. 126.)

Of course, the conception of Yahwe, as well as the degree of devotion to
him, varied through time and with the different social strata. The richness of
Weber's analysis of this phenomenon cannot be conveyed here. The main
point is that the eminently rational character of Judaism could be explained
by the convergence of a number of circumstances: (1) The Jews loathed
everything which emanated from Egypt, including the cult of the dead; (2)
bedouin practices were also rejected, for Amalek was a traditional enemy of
Israel; (3) as for Baal, once the Jews became a settled agricultural people in
Canaan, the attributes of Baal and other functional deities were soon
syncretized with those of Yahwe, so that he was no longer merely the "war
god of the confederacy" but could bring rain and assure a good harvest. In
addition, however, and perhaps most important, was Israel's peculiar relationship to God and his Covenant. When, in Weber's words,

> . . . Yahwe was angry and failed to help the nation or the individual, a
> violation of the *berith* with him had to be responsible for this. Hence, it
> was necessary for the authorities as well as for the individual from the out-
> set to ask which commandment had been violated? Irrational divination
> means could not answer this question, only knowledge of the very com-
> mandments and soul searching. Thus, the idea of *berith* flourishing in the
> truly Yahwistic circles pushed all scrutiny of the divine will toward an at
> least relatively rational mode of raising and answering the question.
> Hence, the priestly exhortation under the influence of the intellectual
> strata turned with great sharpness against soothsayers, augurs, day-choosers,
> interpreters of signs, conjurors of the dead, defining their ways of con-
> sulting the deities as characteristically pagan. (p. 167.)

In ancient Israel, the relation of priests to prophets was quite fluid so that
the Levites, for example, gained their prestige less by their special skills in
offering sacrifices than by their rational knowledge of Yahwe's Commandments. Oracular and magical means were systematically reduced to a minimum, and "became less and less important as against the rational case study
of sins, until the theological rationalism of Deuteronomy (18:9–15) in
substance discredited lot casting altogether or at least ceased to mention it."
(p. 179.) All forms of sexual and alcoholic orgiasticism were consistently

opposed until they became anathema to the various advocates and defenders of Yahwism—the Levitical Torah teachers, the prophets, and the wealthy and politically influential, pious Yahwistic families. In this way, although magic was never eliminated from popular practice, it was dislodged from its position of dominance in ancient Judaism—particularly in Judea—and this contrasts with all other ancient religions.

In Weber's view, classical prophecy acquired its most characteristic form when the great powers of the area, Egypt and Mesopotamia, resumed their expansionist policy. The classical scriptural prophets, *e.g.*, Amos, Isaiah, Jeremiah, Ezekiel, despite their purely religious motives were in effect political demagogues and even pamphleteers. It would be wrong, however, to view prophecy exclusively or even primarily as a response to internal developments and conflicts—as the expression of the interests and sentiments of the "people" who were now oppressed by the overlords and the monarchy. Prophecy in its classical form, Weber insists, never would have arisen in the absence of the great-power conflict which constituted a threat to the existence of Israel. When the monarchy was strong or protected by a great power, the prophets "remained silent—or rather [were] reduced to silence. With the decreasing prestige of the kings and the growing threat to the country, the significance of prophecy again increased and the scene of the prophet's activities moved closer and closer to Jerusalem." (p. 269.)

They spoke in the streets and addressed their publics directly; their inspiration was spontaneous and their major concern was "the destiny of the state and the people. This concern always assumed the form of emotional invectives against the overlords." (p. 269.) When they prophesied doom and a catastrophe actually befell the country, they showed no sign of personal jubilation; instead they mourned but also expressed hope for better times now that God's wrath had passed. Objectively, they were involved in conflicting political interests and party antagonisms; but they had no personal political interests or motives. They were mere mouthpieces through which Yahwe spoke. In Weber's words,

. . . according to their manner of functioning, the prophets were objectively political and, above all, world-political demagogues and publicists, however, subjectively they were no political partisans. Primarily they pursued no political interests. Prophecy has never declared anything about a "best state" (disregarding Ezekiel's hierocratic construction in the Exile) nor has it ever sought, like the philosophical *aisymnete* or the academy, to help translate into reality social-ethically oriented political ideals through advice to power holders. The state and its doings were, by themselves, of no interest to them. Moreover, unlike the Hellenes they did not posit the problem: how can man be a good citizen? Their question was absolutely religious, oriented toward the fulfillment of Yahwe's commandments. (p. 275.)

Thus Weber is demonstrating the enormous complexity of prophecy in Israel and implicitly arguing that no simple formula is sufficient for an understanding of the phenomenon. Their pronouncements on internal affairs must not be understood as direct ideological manifestations of class relationships and conflicts. The prophets did not stem from the oppressed and disadvantaged strata; most of them were wealthy and came from distinguished families. Even Amos, who was described as a poor stockbreeder, was an educated man; and like Isaiah (who was wealthy and distinguished) he cursed the rich and the great but "yet pronounced the rule of the uneducated, undisciplined demos as the worst of all curses." (p. 277.) They were therefore neither defenders of democratic ideals nor spokesmen for the "people"; and their main support came not from the oppressed but from individual, pious, and distinguished families in Jerusalem. That their motives were purely religious becomes clear, in addition, from their condemnation at one and the same time of both debt slavery and the fertility cults and shrines of Baal "which meant much to the rural population for economic as well as ideal reasons." (p. 279.)

The prophets and the Torah teachers were of major importance in the rationalization of Judaism. However, the documentation of the radical "disenchantment" of Judaism was only one of the tasks Weber set himself in this copious and meticulous study. Another important problem was how the Jews came to constitute a pariah community. This, Weber shows, must be viewed as the result of both prophecy and the special ritual requirements of Judaism the Jews took with them into exile and held to stubbornly and tenaciously.

With the destruction of the Temple and the exile of the Jews, sacrifice, permissible only in Jerusalem, became impossible. However, above all, especially in the Babylonian community, that the prophetic tradition should be preserved was essential; Jews were to remain ritually pure and guard themselves against any and all pagan practices and worship. This was particularly important since the *Diaspora* was regarded as a temporary situation and the hope of returning to the homeland remained alive. Slowly, there emerged a specific religious community organization with new institutions peculiar to the Exile.

If, for Weber, the Jews had produced a rational religious ethic which influenced Western culture at its roots, this did not lead to rational economic conduct as did Puritanism. The peculiar ethical dualism of the Jews, their in-group, out-group morality, prevented this; for allegedly it permitted, or was morally indifferent to, "certain forms of behavior toward the outsiders which were strictly forbidden with respect to brothers in belief." (p. 343.) Christian ethics, Weber believed, had important implications for economics in the West not only because it weakened the power of the sib and other kin ties (meanwhile having adopted the Jewish hostility toward magic) but also because it produced a uniform ethic. This reached a high point with the Protestant sects, whose "superior, religiously determined economic ethics gave them superiority over the competition of the godless according to the principle 'honesty is the best policy.' " (p. 344.) Thus here again Weber returns to his older theme but now views this as one aspect of a general historical process in the West, to which a large number of historical events had contributed.

That he was now prepared to view modern capitalism *and* Protestantism, along with other aspects of modern Western civilization as the complex product of a historical process that reached back to ancient Israel, may be gathered from his last pronouncements on the subject in his posthumously published *General Economic History* (esp. pps. 232–70) and more especially in the introduction he wrote just before he died to the book edition of *The Protestant Ethic*. The emphasis is on the fundamental importance of the general rational quality of Western culture, and modern industrial capitalism is viewed as one aspect of this process which had many complex antecedent conditions. This interpretation of Weber's conclusions is also borne out by the discussion of the problem by his wife, Marianne Weber.

This recognition [she writes] of the particular character of Western rationalism and the role it played in Western culture constituted for Weber one of his most important discoveries. As a result, his original question of the relation of religion to economics became the wider, more general question of the particular character of the entire Western culture. Why does rational science which produces verifiable truths exist only in the West? Why only here rational harmonic music, or architecture and plastic art which employ rational construction? Why only here a rational state, a trained bureaucracy of experts, parliaments, political parties—in a word, the state as a political institution with a rational constitution, and rational law? Why only here the fateful power of modern life—namely, modern capitalism? Why all this only in the West? . . .

He finds that the birth of the modern Western state just as that of the modern churches was the work of jurists, and that juridical rationalism was a special accomplishment of the Romans; that modern enterprise capitalism is to a large measure codetermined by the special character of Western science, which makes it possible to calculate its technical factors precisely, etc. . . .[39]

Thus Weber's conception is far wider and much more complex than the conception conveyed in the early essays on the Protestant ethic taken by themselves. And it is his analysis of the special character of Western civilization as a whole which must be regarded as his most important contribution by far.

Political Sociology and Political Values

Thus Weber came to view the Occident as that civilization in which the "disenchantment of the world" had been carried out more thoroughly than elsewhere. Virtually all aspects of Western culture had undergone this rationalization process, so that now in principle there were no mysterious,

39 Marianne Weber, *Max Weber: Ein Lebensbild* (Heidelberg: Verlag Lambert Schneider, 1950), p. 381. (My translation.)

unknowable, or inscrutable powers and man could master all things through rationalization. Science was the most eminent example of this, but the other spheres of human conduct also bore this quality of rational mentality and organization. In its ideal-typical form, this is what he called *zweckrationales Handeln,* or rational-purposeful conduct. As a general orientation it was based on the assumption that things *and humans* behave in certain predictable ways and that one could therefore use this knowledge for any given purpose. This was one type of knowledge yielded by modern Western science and in fact its main practical-technical significance.

Science, Weber believed, like Nietzsche, could provide men with *means* but not ends; it could never show us the way to "true values." A conflict of values, or gods, as he sometimes spoke of it, was inevitable. And particularly in the complex, modern societies of today, values could never be arranged, through science or otherwise, in one universally agreed-upon scale.

What, then, can science offer? *Clarity,* Weber replies; clarity with respect to our conduct, its motives, ends, means, and consequences. Science, and in this case social science, can provide insight into the value-oriented nature of man's actions and into the kinds of values he holds; it affords insight into the means of attaining certain values and some of the costs and consequences this entails for other values. Men are oriented to a plurality of values so that the realization of any one may be impeded by its excessive cost or by the need to sacrifice others. This is what is involved in Weber's concept, *Zweckrationalität.* This kind of knowledge and clarity about one's acts and their consequences makes possible and meaningful an *ethics of responsibility,* which Weber preferred to an *ethics of faith,* where success or failure are attributed either to God or other men.[40] When individuals can choose their values under conditions of greatest freedom, while respecting others to do the same, and choose, too, the means of actualizing them, and, finally, have a clear understanding of the consequences of a given choice, this is a most desirable situation which combines a high degree of reason, responsibility, and freedom. It may be instructive, then, as a final consideration of Weber and his work, to inquire, however briefly, into his own values and conduct.

In Weber's personal life, objectivity and freedom had a very restricted meaning; for he was above all a nationalist whose major ideal was the strengthening of the German *Machtstaat.* All other conflicting values were to be subordinated and sacrificed. Christian teachings on the dignity of man, for example, standing in clear opposition to his national ideal, could not be applied to matters of state and the attempt to do so was as dangerous as it was foolhardy. Whatever "clarity" he sought was for the purpose of furthering German national interests; and none of the existing social classes in

---

40 In addition, Weber speaks of three other types of orientations: Wertrationalität in which one pursues a value without regard for cost; and *affective and traditional,* respectively, which are self-explanatory. See Weber's *Theory of Social and Economic Organization,* pp. 118 ff.

Germany—neither the Junkers, the bourgeoisie, nor the workers—was "mature enough" to lead the country in this mission. Talented and responsible leaders were also lacking so that leadership positions were being filled by bureaucrats —so many cogs with no initiative. This being the situation as he saw it, he took upon himself the task of educating the Germans and alerting their leaders to the unanticipated consequences of their acts.

Like a prophet of doom—and there is no doubt that he considered himself a Jeremiah of sorts—he repeatedly warned during World War I against Germany's unrestricted submarine warfare and anticipated the results of the United States' entry into the war. Earlier, when he had studied the condition of the landworkers in Germany, he quite frankly acknowledged that his survey was carried out from "the point of view of *raison d'état;* this is to me not a question of the landworkers; I am not asking, do they live well or badly, or how can we help them."[41] What really concerned him was that the German landworkers were leaving the land and being replaced by Polish and Russian workers. This must be stopped, Weber urges, for only in this way can Germany's eastern frontier be secured.

This brings us to another of Weber's "political a priori convictions," his Russophobia. Throughout his life, he had "an unquestioning hatred and fear of the Russian colossus." (p. 34.) That Weber believed in the validity of certain judgments made outside the sphere of reason is clear. Discussing moral conscience in a letter to Emmy Baumgarten, he wrote:

Here we reach the frontiers of the human reason *(Begriffsvermögen)*, and we enter a totally new world, where quite a different part of our mind pronounces judgment about things, and everyone knows that its judgments, though not based on reason, are as certain and clear as any logical conclusion at which reason may arrive. (p. 35).

Apparently, nationalistic prejudice is one such certainty for elsewhere he wrote that economics becomes in effect a national science. "Economics, as an explanatory and analytical science, is *international,* but as soon as economics expresses values, it becomes bound up with the substance of our life as a nation. . . . The economic policy of a German state, as likewise the value standard of a German economic theorist, can therefore only be German." (p. 41.) And since the various German classes were incapable of leading Germany,

. . . there is no more serious duty for every one of us, for each in his narrow circle, than to collaborate in the political education of our nation which must remain the ultimate aim of our science. (p. 45.)

It may not be too wide of the mark to suggest that Weber's overwhelming nationalist sentiment profoundly colored and limited his view of other

[41] J. P. Mayer, *Max Weber and German Politics* (London: Faber and Faber Ltd., 1944), p. 33. (Immediately following references to this work cited only by page numbers in text.)

cultures, *e.g.,* England and the United States, and marred his scholarship as in the case of *The Protestant Ethic* where he shows no real firsthand knowledge of English and American society, historical personalities, or sources.

More striking, and perhaps more important, is Weber's nationalistic, even atavistic, attitude toward war. "This war," he wrote on October 15, 1914, "is with all its ugliness great and wonderful, it is worthwhile experiencing it. . . ." (p. 74.) As for his opinions on war aims, he advocated, among other things, German rights to fortresses north of Warsaw and permanent military occupation of Luxembourg, so that J. P. Mayer remarked that it is open to doubt whether Weber's war aims were different, in effect, from those of the *Alldeutsche.* (p. 75.) After the war he was asked by a pupil about his political plans and he replied that he had none "except to concentrate all my intellectual strength on one problem, how to get once more for Germany a great general staff." (p. 107.) Here as elsewhere Weber put his faith in "leaders."

Whether in business, politics, or military affairs, great leaders had to be created as an antidote to bureaucracy; only by keeping the charismatic principle alive could the world be saved from mediocrity. It was "horrible to think," wrote Weber, "that the world [Germany?] could one day be filled with nothing but those little cogs, little men clinging to little jobs and striving towards bigger ones. . . ." (p. 127.) However, not too long after he died the charismatic and bureaucratic principles were fused in his homeland into the most horrendous synthesis the world has ever known.

To what extent Weber's personal political values permeated and shaped his scientific work as a whole would require a full-scale study and cannot be taken up here. But that one of the greatest social thinkers of our time held such values is not an insignificant datum.

12

Vilfredo Pareto

(1848–1923)

The work of Vilfredo Pareto constitutes an exceedingly ambitious but largely unsuccessful attempt at rebutting and discrediting the principles of the Enlightenment in both its eighteenth- and nineteenth-century forms. His voluminous writings may be viewed as a sustained onslaught upon the liberal-democratic, socialistic, and Marxian theories, respectively. Like Weber, Pareto also developed his "sociology" in an intense debate with Marx's ghost; but fundamental differences may be discerned in the approaches of these two thinkers.

For Weber, as we have seen, rationality (in the formal if not in the substantive sense) remained central in his analysis of human conduct and appeared as an increasingly important principle underlying the major institutions of modern Western society. With Pareto, in contrast, "reason" was a negligible if not altogether irrelevant factor for an understanding of society and history. And while Weber accepted and employed a reconstructed version of the Marxian method, Pareto paid his respects occasionally to what he regarded as its very limited validity and proceeded to develop his two major ideas as a refutation of Marx.

Whereas Marx had viewed man as a rational and perfectible creature, Pareto viewed him as essentially nonrational and unchanging, and advanced his theory of "residues" with the aim of demonstrating that proposition. And while Marx viewed class conflict in history as resulting in progressively more "popular" social systems (at least in the sense of increasing man's potential for freedom, or control of his own destiny), Pareto regarded history as essentially cyclical. As a direct antithesis to Marx's theory of class struggle, Pareto advanced his theory of élites. The circulation of élites, the real stuff of history, had few, or perhaps no, positive consequences for the "people."

Throughout his work, Pareto affirmed his allegiance to "science" and insisted that his aims were strictly scientific; but a careful examination of his work reveals the polemical nature of his concepts, method, and theories. Although he fancied his method as inductive and empirical, and always emphasized the need for objectivity and verification, his own attempts at "proof" are more often than not mere illustrations. He has rejected metaphysics in all its forms, he repeatedly tells us; yet, in the end he has provided us with a metaphysic of his own, resting on a number of eternal and immutable a priori's. This will become clearer as we proceed with our careful but sometimes tedious analysis of Pareto's voluminous writings. First, however, a few biographical details are in order, for Pareto came to sociology by means of a rather circuitous route.

Pareto had a strong background in French language and culture and knew French as well as or perhaps even better than Italian.[1] He was born in France to French parents and spent thirty years in French-speaking Switzerland. It was in Italy, however, that he received his secondary education. He studied primarily physics and mathematics at the University and Polytechnical School of Turin; it was there, in 1869, that he wrote his thesis, "The Fundamental Principles of the Equilibrium of Solid Bodies." Thus, "equilibrium," a concept which he was later to apply to social phenomena, first engaged his interest in the physical context.

As even a cursory glance at his illustrative material shows, Pareto knew Greek and Latin and had a great passion for Greek and Roman literature and history. But since there is no evidence of his having studied these subjects during his formal schooling, he must have acquired this knowledge well after his adolescence, as his interest in society and history grew. His general sociology is as much a study of antiquity as of contemporary society.

Although the intellectual influences on Pareto, particularly in sociology, were varied, he chooses for some reason never to acknowledge his debt to them. Mainly this seems to be because he feels that he has bested all his predecessors, including Aristotle, Machiavelli, Marx, Darwin, and others, and that their work has now become obsolescent. Not until he reaches the fourth and last volume of his general treatise on sociology does he acknowledge that he owes something to his antecedents, whom he nevertheless does not cite by name because, as he says, this is of no interest in the scientific study of social

[1] For these and other biographical details, I rely on G. H. Bousquet, *Pareto: Le Savant et L'Homme* (Lausanne: Payot and Cie. S. A. Librairie De L'Universite, 1960). [Author Note: All translations from the French are mine.]

phenomena. This prompted his editor and translator, Arthur Livingston, to remark: "All the same, in a work of a million words with not a few asides and containing not a few strictures on great writers of past and present, a few hundred words more might not have come amiss to describe what Pareto in particular owed, for his general method to Auguste Comte, for his theory of derivations to Bentham (some of whose categories Pareto adopts verbatim), for his theory of class circulation to Gaetano Mosca, for his theory of residues to Frazer and others, and for a number of phrases and items of detail even to Hegel, William James, and many others."[2]

Obviously not a religious man, neither was he anti-religious in the sense of desiring to suppress religious institutions. Christian and all other dogmas, for that matter, Pareto regards as so much nonsense, and Christian "miracles" have the same objective value as pagan "miracles." Eventually he would argue that as stupid and absurd as certain notions and practices may be, they may nonetheless have useful consequences for a given society. The aura of sanctity surrounding universal suffrage, democracy, socialism, or Christianity, etc., is foolish and "nonlogical," yet it may, perhaps, have some utility.

Religion, as other "sentiments" for Pareto, is constant and fundamental, regardless of the form it may assume. In 1907, for example, he writes that at the moment the "religions" of socialism and humanitarianism are growing, while belief in a personal god is declining; but religion of some kind will always remain, for it is absolutely essential to society. The particular "theology" is not important, only its social effects. In an authoritarian situation the religion of freedom has "utility" and, conversely, where "anarchy" threatens, an authoritarian religion becomes indispensable to prevent the so-called "dissolution" of society. "Fatherland," "honor," "virtue," etc. are manifestations of "sentiments," which have no objective existence but are nevertheless the prime movers of human conduct and the crucial factors determining the character and evolution of societies. As we shall see, however, he is far from consistent in his use of the concept "sentiment" which he sometimes treats as a synonym for cultural value but more often than not as an "instinct,"—i.e., a biopsychic determinant of behavior which remains constant and, hence, does not vary with socio-historical conditions. This despite the fact that his own "sentiments" changed conspicuously in the course of his intellectual development.

As a young man in Florence, for example, he was an active pacifist and humanitarian, a liberal in economic theory. In 1891, he wrote, "War and armed peace are the most costly luxuries which the ruling class offers at the expense of the nation."[3] He was also opposed to colonialism; in his opinion Tonkin cost France dearly and Tunisia would not benefit Italy except perhaps

---

2 Vilfredo Pareto, *The Mind and Society* [*Trattord di Sociologia Generale*], four volumes edited by Arthur Livingstone,Vol. IV, (New York: Harcourt, Brace and World, Inc., 1935) , p. 1477n.

3 Bousquet, *op. cit.,* p. 41.

to provide some administrative positions for the sons of the bourgeoisie. Later, for some unknown reason, Pareto does a complete turnabout, to reveal an almost obsessive hatred and contempt for humanitarianism, a sentiment of the weak in the subject class and of the decadent in the governing élite. G. H. Bousquet argues that despite this change Pareto held to his former views on the evils of war. This, as we shall see, is an untenable view in the light of Pareto's unsparing praise of *force,* in class conflict as well as in conflicts between nation-states.

Before the basic transformation in Pareto's outlook came about, however, he was a "democrat" and even, on occasion, favored the working class in its struggle with the bourgeoisie. In 1893, for example, he deplored the violence committed by workers but blamed protectionism, corruption, and militarism. He was so convinced a liberal that he believed one day commercial treaties would appear as the peculiarities of a barbaric epoch in which free exchange was unknown. And in the same period he writes that the abuses and scandals of government then so evident provide a rough idea of "what awaits us when socialism will reign in all its glory."[4] But this early critique of socialism was quite different from what it was to become. As a young man he attacks the ruling bourgeoisie for not realizing its ideal of liberty; he supports temporary alliances with the socialists to resist oppression and comments that it is they who almost single-handedly fight the superstitions of "patriotism." And, finally, when they are persecuted by the government he extends them aid—personal, moral, and intellectual. But all this was to change. Around the turn of the century there was a great transformation both in his daily habits and in his thought. He became what the intellectual world has called "the hermit of Celigny," the adversary, as Bousquet has phrased it, of humanitarian democracy.

Pareto and Science

For Pareto, there were basically two independent and mutually exclusive domains of human conduct: that of science and logic on the one hand and of sentiment on the other. Science involves logic, observation, and objective experience, and "truth" rests on these processes. The other domain is "non-logico-experimental"—which is just the beginning of Pareto's cumbersome vocabulary. These are two independent domains, and science has nothing to say about "reasoning" that leaves its realm. Pareto has chosen "science" but denies that it can ever replace the other realm or even make serious inroads upon it. In fact, *sentiment* is the fundamental and predominant force in society, *the determining factor* of human conduct (outside the very restricted sphere in which Pareto arbitrarily confined logico-experimental norms).

Pareto's first task as he saw it was to distinguish carefully between

4 *Ibid.,* p. 61.

scientific and nonscientific propositions. Objective experience is the sole criterion of scientific theory, which is arrived at inductively by describing the relationships among facts; in short, scientific theories are "logico-experimental." Other "theories," which he calls "nonlogico-experimental" add something to experience and seek to dominate the "facts." (Thus Pareto's brand of positivism did not view as problematic how one decides what may be regarded as a "fact," the degree to which "data" are taken and not merely "given," and hence the extent to which theory does in effect organize, "dominate," and interpret the "facts.") Pareto subscribed to the methodological view, which treated "laws" as strictly heuristic devices, not necessarily as the workings of "reality." When uniformities, or relationships among facts, become evident, "law" is the name one gives to these patterns; "law" is not some *force* to which the facts are actually subject. The scientist selects certain observable phenomena and organizes and classifies them according to some relatively arbitrary scheme so that the phenomena appear to be subject to a certain "law." There are no "necessary" laws; rather, phenomena behave "as if" there were, and the scientist states the degree of probability with which the phenomena in question will follow a specified pattern. Scientific relativity, then, was for Pareto, as for Vaihinger, Mach, Poincaré, *et al.,* a basic assumption.

Pareto's sole aim, he assures us again and again, is scientific truth, which can be attained in the social realm by applying the methods of the physical sciences. In all his works, he stresses that he is not interested in improving or changing the world; he is not concerned with providing theoretical guidance for practical affairs. Rather, he has one single and exclusive aim in view: to study the uniformities phenomena present, their "laws." (Unlike Weber, Pareto insisted that the methodological approach in the natural and social sciences must be one and the same.) And like many economists before him, Pareto advocated the method of successive approximations. Since no concrete phenomenon can be known in all its details, some sort of abstraction always becomes necessary. What aspect one singles out for study depends on one's interests. One begins with some simplifying assumptions, taking into account additional complicating factors as one proceeds—a method equally applicable to natural and social phenomena. For instance, the various assumptions built into the hypothesis of *homo economicus,* as a first approximation, are not essentially different from the physicist's assumption of a vacuum in which bodies fall.

There is, however, an important characteristic of social phenomena Pareto is intent upon accentuating: the utility of an idea and its truth are not necessarily identical in the social sphere. As a matter of fact, they are often independent of each other. He reminds his reader periodically that when he argues for the absurdity of an idea, this does not necessarily mean that it is injurious to anyone; and when he argues that an idea has utility, the reader should not assume that it is experimentally true. Clearly, a great many ideas have currency among men which are patently false, or whose relative truth is not known. Who holds these doctrines and why? What are the consequences of holding these beliefs and for whom? These are the questions, Pareto tells us, that interest him and that he wants to answer by means of a scientific sociology. Yet, as will be seen, he rarely approaches these questions either scientifically or sociologically; instead he offers us a primitive psychology and a philosophy of history.

Les Systèmes Socialistes

In this two-volume critique of socialist and communist doctrines, from the earliest schemes of antiquity through the so-called "utopian socialists" and concluding, finally, with the theories of Marx, one clearly perceives the outline of the theoretical framework which Pareto later elaborated in his general sociology. An examination of the Systèmes leaves no doubt as to the polemical nature of Pareto's "sociological" concepts and propositions. After examining the various socialist theories Marx himself had regarded as "pre-scientific" and of course finding them all wanting, he is thus prepared for a scrutiny of so-called "scientific socialism." The last two chapters, in many respects the most interesting, deal with Marx's thought. Of course, in itself the fact that Pareto's theories are polemical is no reason to reject them, for a theory may be polemical and valid at the same time. Here, however, we are considering only their polemical aspect postponing for later the question of their validity.

Pareto came to the study of sociology through his critique of socialism, which in effect contains all the ideas one later meets in his Traité de Sociologie. His explicit critique of Marx may be found first of all in the Systèmes, but also in a number of articles and in his "Introduction to Capital." His Systèmes is so far from being systematic that it appears to be quite without plan. He promises us a rather interesting study: "On the one hand, we shall inquire into the real facts which have favored the establishment of certain social systems, or the appearance of certain projects for social systems; in other words, what are the things or facts which reveal themselves to us in these forms; on the other hand, we shall examine the 'reasonings' which have been employed to justify these systems or projects for systems and we shall see to what extent the premises are drawn from experience and from logical deductions."[5] Pareto never keeps his promise, either in a methodical or in any other way. Oddly enough, he acknowledges, in passing, the limited validity of Marx's sociological theory: "This research will show us often that there are economic facts which modify social institutions and doctrines and

---

[5] Vilfredo Pareto, Oeuvres Complètes, Tome V, Les Systèmes Socialistes (Geneve: Giovanni Busino, Librairie Droz, 1965), p. 25. (All immediately following references to this work will be cited merely by page numbers in the text.)

which are thus reflected in the consciousness of men, as in the view of the 'materialist conception of history.' " (Vol. V, pp. 26–27). But he never uses its guidelines to assess its fruitfulness as an analytical tool and in fact never returns to it except to "refute" it by assertion. Socialism in general and Marxism in particular are regarded by Pareto as religions that emerged and gained popularity because they appealed to certain "sentiments" (a term, as previously mentioned, that has a special meaning in Pareto's system, *viz.*, a nonlogical principle of conduct). Never in this work does he relate doctrines and beliefs to social conditions, for this in effect would have taken him back to Marx's conception; nor does he ask whether and to what degree rational interests rather than blind sentiments might better explain the popularity in a given period of socialism or Marxism. Pareto rarely pauses to analyze the existential conditions of men, but speculates instead about their sentiments and instincts.

Marx's theories, Pareto writes, are neither more nor less erroneous than others, *e.g.*, the so-called optimistic economists. They are all nonlogical! Nevertheless, there is a scholarly-scientific view of Marx's work, particularly his conception of class struggle. But whereas classes and class conflict were transient historical phenomena for Marx, Pareto insists that class conflict is destined to continue forever. Its forms may change but the substance remains the same. "Suppose collectivism to be established," he writes, "and that 'capital' no longer exists; then only a particular form of class struggle will have disappeared and new ones will emerge to replace it. New conflicts will appear between the different kinds of workers and the socialist state, between the intellectuals and the non-intellectuals, between the various politicians, between the politicians and those they administer, between innovators and conservatives, etc. Are there really such people who imagine seriously that with the advent of socialism the sources of social innovation will be dried up? That men will no longer envision new projects, that interests will not push some men to adopt these projects in the hope of acquiring a dominant place in society?" (Vol. II, p. 455.) Why, in Pareto's view, is class conflict destined to be an eternal human condition? Not so much because a complex, heterogeneous society is bound to have a variety of groups with different and conflicting interests; but rather because it is rooted in the nature of men and is a form of their struggle for life. "The struggle for life or well-being is a general phenomenon for living things, and everything we know about this leads us to recognize it as one of the most powerful forces for the conservation and amelioration of the race. It is therefore extremely improbable that men will be able to transcend this condition. . . . All our efforts can never result in a fundamental change of this condition, only slight modifications of its forms." (Vol. II, p. 455.) Pareto thus views class conflict as an inseparable aspect of men's struggle with nature, and hence as inevitable and unending. Social conflicts are rooted in natural conditions, not least in the very nature of man, who is pushed into action by essentially "natural" and therefore "nonlogical" forces. This is the substance of Pareto's theory of human conduct as he later elaborates it in his "sociology."

As he develops his critique of socialism and shows us how one must "scientifically" analyze the phenomenon, he presents us with all the notions we shall later meet in the obscure and awkward terms of his *Traité*. First, he discusses a number of concepts to illustrate that one cannot employ these terms logically. Take, for example, "liberty" and "constraint"; the first is associated with agreeable feelings and the second with disagreeable ones. All one has to do to get people to accept constraint is to give it the name of liberty. Why?—because these and similar concepts advanced by the socialists and optimistic liberals, draw their force from sentiment and not from logic. Is there then anything salvageable in the general socialist idea? Any worthwhile elements?

Inheritance, he grants, is a very "imperfect" means of distributing the wealth of a society. The way is therefore open to reformers of good will, but they must take care not merely to criticize the existing system but rather to bring forth preferable alternatives. But Pareto still sees a number of problems —reformers ought to use clear and precise terms, and more importantly, the new social arrangement must be compatible with the character of men. "Every human society," argues Pareto, "includes some elements unadapted to the conditions of life of the particular society, and if the actions of these elements are not confined to certain limits, the society will be destroyed." (Vol. II, p. 131.) This poses a difficult problem for socialists, because humanitarian sentiments (which he grants are "useful" up to a certain point) oppose the "necessity" of selecting and eliminating these elements. So Pareto sees two problems requiring solution: (1) Can the birth of unadaptable elements be reduced? (2) If not, can they be eliminated with a minimum of error in choice, with a minimum of suffering, and without violating too much humanitarian sentiments? Pareto thus offers us a "scientific" approach to the problem of selecting and eliminating the "poorly adapted," the "misfits."

Throughout his *Systèmes*, as in his later work, Pareto maintains that sentiment is the dominant and overwhelming force in social conduct, and that logic and rationality are of minimal significance. One must not stop at the "reasonings" of men—which are anything but reasonable—but go on to examine the underlying sentiments; sentiment for Pareto thus becomes what the so-called economic foundation was for Marx. But whereas for Marx, changes in the economic system ultimately induced changes in men's character and psychology, Pareto's sentimental foundation is an unchanging entity. Only the "reasonings" (or what he later calls "derivations") that justify and "explain" human conduct vary, not the sentiments. Just what are these sentiments or real forces masked by, among other things, socialist rhetoric?

Pity, says Pareto, is one such prevalent sentiment, which impels men to sympathize with their fellows who suffer wrongs or pain and to seek a remedy. This is a very "useful" sentiment, he assures us, for it is the cement of society and the real basis of all ameliorative social doctrines. In the lower classes there exists a sentiment which "has its source in the suffering which those in these strata endure and in the desire to try to put an end to it by getting hold of the means which men in the higher strata enjoy, or quite simply by coveting what the other has." (Vol. I, p. 64.) So, Pareto argues, this sentiment manifests itself in socialist doctrine and men accept it for this "reason" and not for the "logico-experimental validity" of the doctrine. Why this "sentiment" manifests itself in socialism rather than a resurgence of Christianity or the like does not seem to interest Pareto. And why does socialism appeal mainly to the proletariat? Do they have a monopoly on the sentiment of pity? Well, it has not escaped Pareto that socialist ideas have also appealed to individuals of the upper classes so he "explains" this as a result of the degeneration of the sentiment of pity, corresponding to a general degeneration of these classes. (Vol. I, 65.)

In short, Pareto sees a different "psychology" in the higher and lower classes, but this is always a result of nonlogical sentiments. Individuals of the lower classes in particular never obtain anything even remotely resembling a conscious, rational understanding of their existential conditions. In addition to this assertion we are also exposed to the rudiments of his scientific utilitarian calculus: A certain amount of goodwill on the part of the upper for the lower classes has utility, but an excess is injurious and a symptom of decadence. In all epochs, humanitarian sentiments have given rise to sentimental reveries. When there is but a faint echo of this attitude in poetry or literature, this is a sign that the élite is strong, vigorous, and self-assured; but as the élite "decays," the expression of humanitarian sentiment grows. This, then, is Pareto's first major idea, i.e., the theory of sentiment, the manifestations of which he will later call "residues" and "derivations." His second major idea also appears for the first time in his Systèmes.

Sentiments change little or not at all. What does change is the form of appeal to certain sentiments and/or the justifications of certain actions motivated by sentiments. But here, to anticipate our later discussion somewhat, Pareto sees a distinction between the élite and the non-élite. The élite acts primarily on the basis of enlightened self-interest, while the lower, subject classes are moved largely by sentiment. To further their interests, the élite find it expedient to appeal for support to the sentiments of the lower classes. Thus the non-élite, the mass, is impelled into action by blind forces, while the élite conducts itself according to a rational understanding of its situation. It may be somewhat tenable to argue that historically the lower classes have been moved predominantly by nonrational forces and the upper classes more by rational considerations. But instead of viewing the different "psychologies" as functions of the different conditions of life of the two classes, Pareto views these psychological differences as eternal traits. Sentiment is basic and all the rest is trapping.

"Scientific socialism," writes Pareto, "was born of the need to give a scientific appearance to humanitarian aspirations. In our epoch the scientific form has become *à la mode,* as in other times was the religious form." (Vol. I, p. 73.) Marx's analyses of the economic system, the relationships between the classes, the structural tendencies of the system, the sources of political power, etc. were just so many meaningless exercises for Pareto, since the "people" are in any case never moved or guided by a rational analysis of their condition.

Sentiments vary in kind and are unequally distributed in a society; modifications in the forms of society are a result of the shifts of these sentiments. One can observe that in history great oscillations are more or less rhythmic: Periods of faith alternate with periods of skepticism. Each individual occupies a determined position in the social pyramid and if one arranges individuals according to their degree of influence and political power, then in most societies those highest in influence and political power will also be the men with the greatest wealth. This is the élite. (Vol. I, p. 8.) But Pareto is not here saying what we might at first expect. Like Marx, he does indeed see a correspondence between economic and political power; but whereas the economic power, for Marx, tended to determine the political, Pareto viewed both as determined by the presence in individuals of certain élite characteristics—élite sentiments.

Élites and aristocracies do not last. They degenerate rather rapidly. Every élite therefore has the need to reinvigorate itself with reinforcements from the lower classes—its best elements. The decadence of the élite expresses itself in an outburst of sickly humanitarianism, while a new élite full of *strength* and *vigor* (Pareto's favorite terms) forms in the midst of the lower classes. "Every élite," writes Pareto, "that is not ready to fight to defend its position is in full decadence; there remains nothing for it to do but to vacate its place for another élite having the virile qualities which it lacks. It is by means of force that social institutions are established and it is by means of force that they are maintained." (Vol. I, p. 40.) The struggle and circulation of élites is the stuff of history; therefore, popular uprisings are of no real consequence for the people. They serve merely to facilitate the fall of the old élite and the rise of the new. The élites use the lower classes, by paying lip service to their sentiments, in order to retain or to take power. "Most historians," writes Pareto, "do not see this movement. They describe the phenomenon as though it were the struggle of an aristocracy or oligarchy, always the same, against the people, always the same." (Vol. I, pp. 35–36.) In reality, however, two aristocracies are struggling for power. The various revolutions of history, *e.g.,* the triumph of the bourgeoisie over the feudal aristocracy, achieved nothing for the people and neither will they do so in the future. There will be no definitive liberation of man, no classless society.

Pareto was not quite satisfied with his rebuttal and decided to strengthen it in his *Traité*. There he continues to insist that his single aim is scientific truth—despite the most obvious fact, however, that the entire structure of his general "sociology" is shaped by his debate with Marxism.

Pareto's Sociology

Pareto defined sociology as the study of human society in general, and his declared aim in this work[6] was a general theory of society. More precisely, he wanted a theory of human conduct and chose as his point of departure an examination of the norms of a very specific type of conduct, namely, scientific. Scientific conduct, as we have seen, was "logico-experimental" as was the typically rational conduct of *homo economicus*. Economic man acts on the basis of observation, experience, and logical reasoning. Do these logico-experimental norms so characteristic of scientific and economic conduct carry over into other areas? Do they guide man's other actions? There can be little doubt that Pareto had settled these questions in his own mind long before he undertook this copious study whose ostensible purpose was to answer them scientifically. His conclusions were not, contrary to what he would have us believe, the result of any inductive method.

Man's actions in general are nonlogical. This is the "hypothesis" Pareto wants to prove and account for in his sociology. How does he proceed? He does not ask in this study whether, to what degree, and under what social circumstances, man's general conduct is either logical or nonlogical. Rather, he defines logico-experimental conduct, confines it more or less exclusively to scientific and economic actions (though he might include certain military and political arts), and then by means of his residual definition classifies all other actions as nonlogical. He then proceeds to inundate us with illustrations of man's nonlogical or nonrational actions. Having convinced himself of the alleged fact that all of man's acts which were "nonscientific" and "noneconomic" were also nonlogical, he needed a scientific explanation. And apparently he believed he was providing one in his vague and crude concepts of "sentiments" and "residues." These he occasionally uses as synonyms for "values" but more often than not as unchanging, instinctual, bio-psychic forces.[7]

The latter is also implied throughout Pareto's work in his treatment of residues (soon to be defined) as "constants." It makes no difference to him whether it is a matter of worshipping fetishes or idols, saluting a flag, examining a creature's entrails to foretell the future, supporting universal

6 Pareto, *op. cit.*

7 I find it very difficult to understand how Talcott Parsons in his *Structure of Social Action* could interpret residues as values; this interpretation may suit his thesis that the works of Weber, Pareto, Durkheim, *et al.* converged conceptually and theoretically, but it can be upheld only by means of a very selective reading of Pareto's work.

suffrage, voting socialist, etc.—they are all varying manifestations of the relatively unchanging psychic state of man. All these actions, different as they may appear, are motivated essentially by the same force, the same constant. What does change and what has varied historically are the "explanations," "reasons," and theoretical justifications men have provided for their actions. But these, the "derivations" as Pareto calls them (apparently because they are in his view, derived from the sentiments), are to be regarded under all circumstances as the effects of the sentiment, *the ultimate cause* of both the nonlogical action and the nonlogical explanation. Only the action ("residue") and the rhetoric provided to justify it ("derivation") are observable, and both are the manifestations of a nonobservable, unchanging force, namely, the "sentiment." *How* this "constant" determines a variety of actions and how, according to any logic, constants can determine variables, Pareto never takes the pains to tell us. Furthermore, he does not attempt anywhere in this work to determine scientifically whether in fact man's conduct is predominantly nonrational but rather asserts it again and again, as he does his "purely scientific" intention. "We have no preconceptions, no a priori notions," he says somewhat naïvely and then proceeds, after he has distinguished the logical from the nonlogical, to give examples *only* of the latter. Logical or rational action is the appropriate linking of means to ends, appropriate not subjectively but objectively, *i.e.*, from the standpoint of an informed outside observer. Such rationality, Pareto would have us believe, is minimal if not altogether absent from most human conduct. He does occasionally grant somewhat inconsistently that logical actions are "very numerous" among "civilized" peoples, thereby implying that they are few and far between among the "non-civilized"; one is forced to wonder how man survived with little or no rationality and how the "primitives" survive if they have as little naturalistic knowledge as Pareto suggests.

As for "logical actions," even among the civilized, Pareto drops them unceremoniously, never to weigh the proportion of these in man's total conduct. By means of the rather dubious "method" of citing examples of nonlogical conduct, Pareto believed, no doubt, that he had *demonstrated* the nonrationality of human conduct. (There is no doubt that in this work Pareto thought he was proving a hypothesis rather than generating one.) More, that man is *by nature* nonrational and moved primarily if not exclusively by nonlogical forces. "Nonlogical actions," writes Pareto, "originate chiefly in definite psychic states, and sentiments, subconscious feelings, and the like. It is the province of psychology to investigate such psychic states. Here we start with them as data of fact without going beyond that."[8]

In Pareto's system, A = sentiments, B = nonlogical conduct, and C = pseudo-logical theory or rationale. People imagine that it is "C" which impelled them to act. In actuality, A determines both B and C, so that the

---

[8] Vilfredo Pareto, *op. cit.*, Vol. I, p. 88. (All subsequent references appear as previously noted in the text.)

causal relationship is AB, AC. He is, however, prepared to assign some influence to C: The "existence of the theory C reacts upon the psychic state A and in many cases tends to reinforce it. The theory consequently influences B, following the line CAB." (Vol. I, p. 89.) And, of course, actions can also have influence "upon the psychic state A and consequently upon the theory C, following the line BAC," etc. A few paragraphs later, although he describes the psychic state very much as an effect of various social conditions, he continues for some arbitrary reason to treat it as the main underlying cause of conduct. "For example, C is the theory of free trade; D, the concrete adoption of free trade by a country; A, a psychic state that is in great part the product of individual interests, economic, political, and social, and of the circumstances under which people live. Direct relations between C and D are generally very tenuous. To work upon C in order to modify D leads to insignificant results. But any modification in A may react upon C and upon D. D and C will be seen to change simultaneously, and a superficial observer may think that D has changed because C has changed, whereas closer examination will reveal that D and C are not directly correlated, but depend both upon a common cause, A." (Vol. I, p. 91.)

Here, clearly, social conditions, and economic, political, and other *interests* are assigned considerable importance. Do these interests and conditions conduce to rational conduct? Apparently not! In the very next paragraph, he ignores the sociological implications of the previous one and proceeds as Pareto the psychologist to make a number of assertions that are never substantiated by the scientific empirical method he so celebrated: "Theoretical discussions, C, are not, therefore, very serviceable directly for modifying D; indirectly they may be effective for modifying A. But to attain that objective, appeal must be made to sentiments rather than to logic and the results of experience. The situation may be stated, inexactly to be sure, because too absolutely, but nevertheless strikingly, by saying that in order to influence people thought has to be transformed into sentiment. (Vol. I, p. 91.) Inexact and "too absolute" as the proposition is, he nonetheless remains wedded to it: Sentiments, not rational interests, determine human conduct.

Throughout his exposition, *e.g.*, in his discussion of magic and religion, he regards magical beliefs and practices as just so much nonsense. His approach is neither historical nor sociological, for he never stops to relate social conditions to certain beliefs and practices in various times and cultures. Since he is determined to show just how nonrational man is, he has nothing to say about the naturalistic knowledge and rational actions which play, no doubt, an essential role even in the most "primitive" of societies. Magic, religion, etc., are regarded by Pareto as effects of "sentiments in which they originate (and which) are fairly common throughout the human race," not as correlates of the conditions under which men interact with each other and with the natural environment. The emphasis throughout is on institutionalized conduct as a manifestation of a psychic state, never vice versa. When he notes, for instance, the marked prominence of *law* in Roman culture, he "explains" it solely by reference to the prevailing psychic state. So important to him is this concept that he compares whole societies on that basis: "Among modern peoples, the English, at least down to the last years of the nineteenth century, have more than any other people resembled the Romans in their *psychic state*." (Vol. I, p. 168. Italics added.) And this is all he has to say on the subject.

This, therefore, is the heart of the Paretian system, already adumbrated in his *Systèmes Socialistes*: Men are essentially nonlogical because they are impelled into action by nonlogical forces of action, *sentiments*. But men also have a persistent "need" to "rationalize" their conduct; this they do by means of pseudo-logical formulae. This together with his theory of élites, which occupies a very minor position in his treatise, constitutes the major theme of his work. He dresses these two ideas up in a cumbersome and contrived vocabulary which adds nothing to our understanding and perhaps even detracts from it. Nevertheless, to assess Pareto's work a brief examination of his vocabulary, concepts, and the use he makes of them is necessary.

The Theory of Residues

In his one-volume discussion of "residues," Pareto focuses exclusively on what he has defined as nonlogical conduct and its alleged cause, which he labels "A." Element "A" he now tells us corresponds to "certain instincts of man, or more exactly men" and "is virtually constant in social phenomena."[9] Some instincts still remain outside his treatment. "Unaccounted for still," he adds, "would be simple appetites, tastes, inclinations, and in social relationships that very important class called 'interests.'" Pareto thus manufactures "instincts" as he requires them, and, moreover, always subsumes "interests" under his general rubric of nonlogical action. Why interests should be thus regarded and not as a relatively rational category, he does not say.

Pareto, who repeatedly calls for scientific precision, provides us with concepts which are anything but precise. Sometimes he really means "instinct" in the sense of a biological urge, such as sex. But at other times his use of the term either approximates the sociological concept of "value" or resolves itself into plain nonsense. In the United States, he writes, "the improvident instinct has fathered a theory that people ought to spend all they earn; and so analysis of that theory yields a quantum a which will be improvidence." (Vol. II, 853.)

What Pareto himself never explains, but which becomes clear if one understands whom and what he is arguing *against*, is why "interests" should be conceived as nonrational. That social classes have interests which are served by certain theories he readily acknowledges; but that the pursuit of

---

[9] Vilfredo Pareto, *op. cit.,* Vol. II, No. 850, p. 501. (Hereafter, references are to paragraphs or sections which Pareto numbers and not to pages.)

interests is rational conduct he denies. "Interests" for Pareto are a nonlogical category, always subordinate to instinct and synonymous with sentiment. Animals have instincts *only*, but no theories, he assures us. Men, on the other hand, have instincts (clearly a wastebasket term for Pareto), "interests," and theories.

Now he introduces his peculiar terminology, simply, he says, to avoid embarrassing his exposition with symbols and letters and to make it easier to follow. Element A from now on will be called *residues*, what is left over, that is, when conduct is divested of its variable elements; residue is therefore the constant element and always reducible to the principle underlying nonlogical action or "reasoning." "Residues," writes Pareto, "correspond to certain instincts in human beings. . . ." (Vol. II, 870.) Element B in the Paretian system is called *derivations* and refers to the nonlogico-experimental theories. In addition, he introduces an element C, which he calls *derivatives;* apparently he regarded this as a kind of secondary theoretical manifestation of A, but never again uses this term.

No sooner does he introduce these terms than he cautions us about their use: "The residues *a* must not be confused with the sentiments or instincts to which they correspond. The residues are the manifestations of sentiments and instincts just as the rising of the mercury in a thermometer is a manifestation of the rise in temperature. Only elliptically and for the sake of brevity do we say that residues, along with appetites, interests, etc., are the main factors in determining the social equilibrium. . . . The completed statement would be: 'The sentiments or instincts that correspond to residues, along with those corresponding to appetites, interests, etc., are the main factors in determining the social equilibrium.' " (Vol. II, 875.) We are thus returned to the original, simple formula: the underlying instinct or sentiment is the key force—in the strictest sense, the Paretian source or "principle" of nonlogical action. "Residue," then, refers to the overt conduct (verbal or nonverbal) which is a manifestation of the sentiment and/or instinct; and "derivation" is the strictly verbal "explanation," justification, or rationale one provides for his act.

At times, sentiment is a fundamental individual property and at others a group characteristic. Pareto never settled in his own mind whether it was to be regarded as part and parcel of an individual's bio-psychic drives or as a cultural belief acquired through tradition. Often he uses the term to refer to a nonlogical idea, or superstition, which has been perpetuated over so long a period of time as to become merely a residue: "The bad omen . . . that is associated with the presence of thirteen persons at a table may be a derivative from a sentiment of horror at Judas' betrayal followed by his suicide; but that derivative has become a residue by this time, and people feel ill at ease at a table of thirteen without the least thought of Judas." (Vol. II, 877.) That Pareto himself sensed his lack of clarity, consistency, and precision may be gathered from his periodic warnings to the effect that "all the pointers just given must be kept in mind at all times in the investigations following. Anyone forgetting them will get everything askew." (Vol. II, 878.)

Now, instincts or sentiments (residues) differ among themselves and Pareto distinguishes six types:

I. *Instinct for Combinations.* A term he uses synonymously with "ability to think," "inventiveness," "imagination," "ingenuity," "originality," etc. In terms of its consequences, this residue has led to human "progress," a term he does not define.

II. *Instinct of Group Persistence, or Persistence of Aggregates.*
   Persistence of relations between a person and other persons or places:
   Relationships of family and kindred groups
   Relations with places
   Relationships of social class
   Persistence of relations between the living and the dead
   Persistence of relations between a dead person and the things that
      belonged to him in life
   Persistence of abstractions
   Persistence of uniformities
   Sentiments transformed into objective realities
   Personifications
   Need of new abstractions.

As we see, relationships of social class are included here and thus summarily *defined* as nonrational; his "proof" consists of examples of nonrational conduct among workers.

III. *Need of Expressing Sentiments by External Acts.*
   Need of "doing something" expressing itself in combinations
      Religious ecstasies.

IV. *"Residues Connected with Sociality."* This refers to the "need" for uniformity and conformity. Neophobia, self-pity, repugnance to suffering, etc., are also included, as are "risking one's life," "sharing one's property with others," "sentiments of superiors," and "sentiments of inferiors," "need of group approbation," and "asceticism."

V. *"Integrity of the Individual and His Appurtenances."* Here Pareto includes "resistance to the social equilibrium" (always nonrational by definition), "sentiments of equality in inferiors," the restoration of individual integrity, etc.

VI. *The Sex Residue.* Though he has given us six types of residue, he employs primarily the first two and rarely has anything to say about the remaining four.

Class I Residues

"Taking Class I as a whole," Pareto writes, "one notes: (1) a propensity for combinations; (2) a search for the combinations that are deemed best; (3) a propensity to believe that they actually do what is expected of them."

(Vol. II, 889.) This class is "experimental" not in the sense of "logico-experimental" but in the sense of playfully trying all sorts of combinations, toying with things, making unexpected discoveries, and doing things having unexpected consequences. All this, says Pareto, has led to "progress." The combinations residue is the common basis of theology, metaphysics *and* experimental science. "Those three kinds of activity are probably manifestations of one same psychic state, on the extinction of which they would vanish simultaneously." (Vol. II, 974.) We never learn, however, how one and the same psychic state leads to what he regards as fundamentally different activities.

Though derived from the same psychic condition, there is an insuperable barrier between the logical and the nonlogical. If A is always seen in conjunction with B, logico-experimental science infers that it is highly probable that they will continue to appear together. No "necessity" is ascribed to this proposition, for then one is superimposing something nonexperimental to the proposition—an act of faith. The scientist adds something too; he "imagines" and "invents" and is guided by preconceptions, guesses, and assumptions. But in his case, Pareto avers, "Experience will be there to rectify any error that may develop from the sentiment he feels." (Vol. II, 977.) For the nonscientist, in contrast, sentiment plays a key role, and propositions are accepted on faith. This is the rule among the majority of men, and the more intimate the contact between the scientist and the population at large, the greater the likelihood that he will succumb to popular conceptions and be blinded to the conflict between experience and beliefs based on sentiment. "That is why the student of the social sciences finds it more difficult to adhere to the logico-experimental method than, for instance, the chemist or the physicist." (Vol. II, 979.)

Occasionally, we are surprised to learn that despite the "constant" sentiments, superstition has declined among the masses, which can be attributed to the advance of science and the "enormous development of industrial life." Recognizing, however, that he is thereby opening the door to the possibility of growing rationality—even among the "people"—he drops the point and never treats as an empirical question whether, to what degree, and in which areas of social life, Everyman is guided by rational norms. By and large, rationality remains for Pareto the exclusive province of the scientific, economic, political, and military élites, and nonrationality, the province of the "masses."

Class II Residues

This brings us to class II residues, the persistence of aggregates—habits, customs, traditions, and other beliefs and practices that persist through time. Basic to Pareto's theory of social equilibrium and circulation of élites, and to his conception of society and history, these "persistences" reside primarily in the masses—or more correctly in the individuals making up the mass. Livingston offers the following interpretation: "The tendency of the mind (the instinct, sentiment, impulse) that creates such units is the force now of first, now of second, importance in determining the social equilibrium. The intensity of the impulse or sentiment in individuals determines what we ordinarily call 'character.' In society at large it determines the type of civilization or culture." (Vol. II, 991 n.) The aggregate of persistent elements may refer to beliefs in the "devil," in "Santa Claus," in "democracy," etc. For Pareto they are all substantially the same—nonlogical elements, passively received, accepted, and tenaciously held. And this again is traced by Pareto to an "instinct." "After the group has been constituted," he writes, "an instinct very often comes into play that tends with varying energy to prevent the things so combined from being disjoined. . . . This instinct may be compared roughly to mechanical inertia: it tends to resist the movement imparted by other instincts."

It is among the "masses" at large that this residue is most active; the social equilibrium and the decline of one élite and the rise of another depend on the degree of success with which an élite can invent formulae that appeal to the dominant sentiments of the masses. The mass is passive in its reception and retention of virtually unchanging sentiments and the élite is active in exploiting these sentiments by means of its ingenious formulae. Just as the sentiments remain unchanged, so do the conditions of the masses regardless how often élites change positions. In the final analysis, it is not the existential conditions of the masses which determine their sentiments, but quite the reverse. The mass always remains blindly nonrational because it is controlled or moved by sub- or unconscious "forces," "impulses," "instincts," or "sentiments." The masses are damned and this is their permanent condition.

Nowhere in his exposition does Pareto systematically consider any causal forces outside his residues, the prime mover to which he returns again and again. There is no attempt anywhere to relate the contrasting character and conduct of the "élite" and the "mass" to their respective cultural conditions. The "stupidity" of the mass is an eternal trait because it is a result of those constant residues. There will always be an élite and always a mass—and all this follows from Pareto's "method" and ultimately from his own sentiments. Despite his admonishments about the need for "objectivity," he transforms what may be a tenable proposition under certain socio-historical conditions into a supra-historical philosophy, and provides us with a new theory of "historical inevitability." There is nothing metaphysical, he apparently believed, in the assertion that "forms" change but the "thing in itself" (sentiment) remains constant. It is only a change in form, he insists, if yesterday "witches" were burned and thieves hanged, and today "sex heretics and thieves alike get off with mere terms in prison." (Vol. II, 1010.)

In almost every case, the "sentiment" is employed as the chief explanatory principle; then, suddenly, as an aside, he injects a remark which is supposed presumably to refute simultaneously the idealistic and "materialistic" viewpoints. "Erroneous the idealistic theory that regards the residue as the cause of the facts. Likewise erroneous, but at times less so, is the materialistic theory that regards the facts as the cause of the residue. In reality, the facts reinforce the residue, and the residue the facts. Changes occur because new forces came into play to affect either the facts or the residue or both—new circumstances occasion changes in modes of life. (Vol. II, 1014.) Thus he almost, but not quite, makes a concession to the Marxian view: *"New circumstances,"* he says, *"occasion changes in modes of life."* What are these "new circumstances?" Are they new social facts? And if so, does this not tend to undermine the theory of residues, particularly if the new facts lead to changes in the mode of life? At best, his formulation above is an equivocal "theory," in which everything interacts with everything else and nothing is quite determinable. But this "interactionist" view, presumably superior to any one-sided one, is never developed. He continually reverts to the causal priority of sentiments and believes, apparently, that he is confirming the proposition by piling up hundreds of cases of ostensibly nonrational behavior— *substantially* the same everywhere and at all times because they are the product of the underlying, unchanging sentiments. The "forms" of this behavior vary from place to place and from one period to another, and this may be due to varying "social facts." Defining the latter as "form" enables Pareto to argue that social change is merely "formal," never substantive.

Classes III and IV.

Pareto now argues that acts not only manifest and strengthen sentiments but "may even arouse them." People have a "need" to do something, "to act;" but then "doing something" can engender the "need." He proliferates "needs" as required to "explain" the various phenomena which have caught his eye. So now as he presents his Class IV, *i.e.,* Residues Connected with Sociality, he says: "This class is made up of residues connected with life in society"—whatever that is supposed to mean—and adds: "A need for particular associations is observable among the majority of peoples. They are of many different kinds. Some are for purposes of mere amusement, others for purposes of individual advantage. Still others have religious, political, literary, or other purposes." (Vol. II, 1114.) There is a "need" for particular associations and whether one joins a church, political party, social club, etc. is all the same, since it is determined by the single common underlying need. Pareto goes on to enumerate still other subcategories of this residue, *e.g.,* the need for uniformity, conformity, and imitation. Especially interesting is his residue called Self-Pity Extended to Others. This, we are told, accounts for the phenomenon of humanitarianism, as does his Instinctive Repugnance to Suffering: "This is a sentiment of disgust at the sight of all suffering, regardless of whether it be beneficial or otherwise. . . . The sentiment is often observable in weak, submissive, spineless individuals. If they chance to succeed in overcoming it, they are likely to show themselves exceedingly cruel. That explains a remark one sometimes hears to the effect that women are more tender-hearted and at the same time more cruel than men." (Vol. II, 1142.) Here as elsewhere one cannot help wondering in what sense Pareto fancies this to be science.

We learn, in addition, that there are sentiments of social ranking—of superiors and inferiors, of group approbation and asceticism, which he views as a uniquely human phenomenon and explores at some length. Though he attributes varying "utilities" to ascetic practices, he treats them all, not surprisingly, as effects of the same residue and, of course, as nonrational conduct. But he fails here as elsewhere to give even passing attention to the possibility that certain acts of asceticism may be very rational indeed—as, for example, a hunger strike or the like designed to achieve certain political or economic ends, which in their meaning are fundamentally different from all the examples he has selected to accentuate their "non-logical" character. Asceticism, as he sees it, is really a perversion "of the instinct of sociality, and without this instinct human society could not exist." (Vol. II, No. 6.)

Class V. The Integrity of the Individual, His Appurtenances and Possessions.

This class is a complement of the previous one and refers to the sentiment (whether natural or learned he does not say) which prompts one "to defend one's own things and strive to increase their quantity." This he relates to what he calls the "social equilibrium."

In a slave system, as, for example, in ancient Greece, even if one is not himself a slave-owner, he may feel that the slave-owner is wronged by having the slave taken from him. This, we are told, flows from "sentiments of resistance to alterations in the [prevailing] social equilibrium." A partially ideal equilibrium would be one in which another citizen would make all Greeks free men and all barbarians slaves. An altogether ideal equilibrium, for the times, would be the demand for the total abolition of slavery. If the existing equilibrium is disturbed or altered, "forces" come into play which tend to reestablish it. These forces are, of course, the sentiments which manifest themselves in the various types of residues, themselves in turn masked by derivations. The masses know nothing of "equilibrium," "forces," etc. These, we are told, are "scientific" terms utilized only by the scientist. "Just" and "unjust," "right" and "wrong" are the words plain people use to express whether they approve of something or whether it offends their sentiments. Pareto tells us little or nothing more about his concept of social equilibrium, but the illustrations he employs fit into his total picture of man as a nonrational being. Man is "not inspired by any 'ideal of justice,' but by his instinct of self-preservation, an instinct that he shares with animals and which has nothing to do with any 'ideal' of 'justice.' "[41] (Vol. II, 1213.)

Self-preservation, a quasi-biological concept suits his purposes, for it serves to accentuate the animal-like character of human action in general. Again he seeks to eliminate from the question of "social equilibrium" anything remotely resembling interest in the rational sense. He studiously avoids looking at social acts in any way which might disclose some degree of rationality. His own example, however, lends itself to rational interpretation, for when individuals feel threatened, physically or otherwise, the course they adopt to protect and defend themselves may be altogether rational. Whether, and to what degree, reactions to "threats" are rational ought to be an empirical question for Pareto; but he never treats it as such. If, to pursue another of his own examples, slaveholders respond to a slave uprising by repressing it harshly, this may or may not be to their "interest"; but if Pareto's "objective outside observer" determines that the success of the uprising would have adversely affected the wealth and power of the slaveholders, then their reaction was, at least in part, rational. Similarly, there is no good reason why the uprising should be regarded as nonrational from the standpoint of the slaves. Of course, the problem is complicated by short- and long-run interests and the like; but if the concept of rationality is to have any meaning at all, then there is no sound reason why either the uprising or its suppression should be viewed as inherently nonrational, which, in effect, is Pareto's position.

Pareto consistently views "sentimental" and rational conduct as mutually exclusive. If his intentions had been as scientific as he claimed, he would have adopted a different methodological approach designed to measure the degree of rationality of the acts in question, and, equally important, he would have distinguished types of rational conduct. From this angle, Max Weber's typology of actions—traditional, affective, *Zweckrationalität,* and *Wertrationalität*—is far superior to Pareto's, for it distinguishes types of nonrational conduct and types of rationality. That Pareto did not regard the degree to which interests and acts are rational as an empirical question is evident from his many illustrations. Here one will suffice to show that his polemical aim led him to deny dogmatically the rational character of certain acts.

Discussing the sentiment of equality in social inferiors, he says that it "is often a defense of integrity on the part of an individual belonging to a lower class and a means of lifting him to a higher one." If the demand for equality is indeed a means for lifting an individual from a lower to a higher social position, why is this nonrational? Because Pareto prefers to see this taking place "without any awareness, on the part of the individual experiencing the sentiment, of the difference between his real and apparent purposes. He talks of the interest of his social class instead of his own personal interest simply because that is a fashionable mode of expression." (Vol. II, 1220.) For Pareto, it is inconceivable, apparently, that an individual from the lower class might arrive at the rational conclusion that he could further his personal interests by furthering those of his social class. Sensing that he might have gone too far, that he has, in effect, emptied social life of *all* rational content he returns now and again to say that "non-logical actions play a great part in social life." And if this is all he meant, who would disagree?

Even when he himself has provided an example of eminently rational conduct, he refuses to view it as such. The following, for instance, is for some reason nonrational for Pareto: The "tendency is to admit to the advantages all whose cooperation helps one toward obtaining them so that their introduction yields more in profit than in costs; and to exclude all who do not help, or help less effectively, so that their participation costs more than it yields." (Vol. II, 1221.) What, one wonders, could be more rational than that? And even if, as Pareto insists, the demand for equality on the part of the socially disadvantaged is really a demand for inequality, but this time in their favor, this only illustrates the possible deception of self and others but does not diminish the rationality of the demand.

Pareto's dichotomy of rational/nonrational allows for no gradations between polar opposites; acts are always either one or the other. Since the effectiveness of his polemic rests on "proving" that it is the nonrational which dominates social life, and must continue to do so, he ignores the subtle mixtures of rational and nonrational one encounters in any society. The fact that some human associations may rest predominantly on a "sentimental" and affective basis, and others on a cognitive-rational one, is not given any consideration. In Pareto's scheme, therefore, one finds none of the insights afforded by the various sociological dichotomies viewed as opposite ends of a *continuum; e.g.,* Tönnies's typology in which the trend from *Gemeinschaft* to *Gesellschaft* is a historical process and, in addition, a conceptional device for measuring the *degree* of rationality of a given social system. Neither does one find in Pareto the insights provided by Weber's approach to the problem of rationality; *i.e.,* that certain social institutions and cultural values retarded its development in the East and accelerated it in the West. Right or wrong, Weber's conclusions are the results of a sociological inquiry. For Pareto, in contrast, cognitive-rational man is *always* and *everywhere* subordinate to and dominated by sentimental-affective man. The very "method" he employed—defining logico-experimental conduct, arbitrarily assigning it to very narrow spheres, and then proceeding to examine the other spheres of conduct, a priori *defined* as nonlogical—led him unswervingly to the very conclusion he had as a hypothesis: Human conduct is so thoroughly nonrational as to preclude any possibility of consciously and rationally altering the social order. Man acts as a result of sentimental causes, which are so pervasive and powerful that they cannot be counteracted or overcome by his weak, insignificant, and occasional efforts at conscious, rational action. Thus Pareto's work, its title notwithstanding, can hardly be regarded as sociology, for he virtually ignores the question of *social* conditions that tend to facilitate or impede the possibility of rational action. And when he arrives at his sixth and final class of residues, it becomes even more evident than before that he is putting forth an instinctual psychology.

The Sex Residue

"Mere sexual appetite," writes Pareto, "though powerfully active in the human race, is no concern of ours here. . . ." The sex "instinct" interests him "only so far as it influences theories, modes of thinking—as a residue." (Vol. II, 1324.) This instinct is "often . . . 'logicalized' and 'dissembled' under the guise of asceticism; there are people who preach virtue as a way of lingering, in their thoughts, on sex matters." Here, Pareto clearly employs the concept of residue as a manifestation of an instinctual urge rooted in the bio-chemical bodily processes. If in the case of the other residues he appears never to have decided whether "instinct" is a biological force or a cultural factor, now it is unequivocally the former. The sex instinct "gives rise" to actions which are constant, which have persisted throughout history, and which are ubiquitous in the present. These actions, the residues, are attempts to control, regulate, repress, pervert, and invert the natural instinct. This has resulted in the "religion of sex" and "as in many other religions, inflexibility in forms gives rise to perversion and hypocrisy. . . ." (Vol. II, 852.) The various sex taboos, forms of prudery, abstinence, and asceticism are just so many ways of hiding sexual desire—just so many forms of a "nonlogical" (a term which becomes in this case even more awkward and curious than before) reaction to a powerful internal force.

Again it is Pareto the psychologist talking: The "sex residue is active not only in mental states looking to unions of the sexes or lingering in recollections of such things, but also in mental states that evince censure, repugnance, or hatred towards matters of sex. . . ." (Vol. II, 1331.) One seeks in vain an attempt to explain certain taboos, proscriptions, ascetic practices, etc. by relating them to other socio-cultural conditions; and the absence of such an attempt is all the more striking when one recalls that Pareto has been honored as one of the founders of functional analysis in sociology. Actually, one finds no analysis of any kind—only illustrations of "omnipresent" residues. Thus we learn that the residue is "active" in speech and writing; it "figures actively" in literature, and when moderns talk of "immoral" literature, for instance, this "oftentimes is a mere matter of hypocrisy, people shrinking at the word and not at the thing, and doing the thing but avoiding the word. . . ." (Vol. II, 1334.) Pareto is here engaged in an "unmasking" venture. Virtue, sexual morality, etc. are just so much rhetoric designed to hide one's lust.

The sex residue is a "constant" as are the others. This is evident, says Pareto, from the "constant" [?] types of reaction one witnesses throughout history to violations of taboos. Such violations of the dogmas of the "sex-religion" engender reactions not unlike the reactions to violations of other religious dogmas. The changes through time in sexual morality and the variations from one culture to another are viewed as mere changes in "form." Why do the "nonlogical" manifestations of the sex residue so annoy him?

Because in the United States, for example, that "paradise of sex hypocrisy" the "mails refuse to carry an English novel because it is deemed 'sensuous'; but they carry without the slightest scruple publications that preach slaughtering the moneyed class and robbing them of their property. But, really, can anyone keeping strictly to logic and experience consider such activities less harmful to individual and society than a little 'sensuality' in print?" He continues: "In some cities in the United States the authorities send policewomen about the streets to provoke 'mashers' and arrest them, but they never [?] hire detectives to provoke anarchists to crimes of violence and then arrest them." (Vol. II, 1345.) In general, Pareto's discussion in this area is quite superficial, unimpressive, and even primitive—especially when compared with the work of his contemporary, Sigmund Freud.

The sex residue, for Pareto, epitomizes the general character of residues: unchanging, invincible forces over which man has little or no control. Only the "derivations" change, but these do not significantly affect the nature of man's existence.

Sentiment in Thinking: The Theory of Derivations

People have a "need" to make their nonlogical conduct appear logical; they therefore provide pseudo-logical explanations for their acts and mistakenly believe the "explanation" is the cause of their conduct. In actuality, however, says Pareto, they are impelled into action by sentiments. Derivations "derive the force they have, not, or at least not exclusively, from logico-experimental considerations but from sentiments." (Vol. III, 1397.) The qualifying phrase, "or at least not exclusively," which Pareto sees fit to insert from time to time, would seem to indicate some reservation on his part. Yet, he does not deem it scientifically worthy of his attention to ask certain obvious sociological questions: (1) Which areas of social life seem to be dominated by sentiment and which by rational considerations? (2) Have there been any historical changes in this respect? (3) What appear to be the *social* correlates of greater rationality in certain contexts and periods and, conversely, of the greater role of sentiment in other contexts and periods? (4) What is the significance of a preponderance of rationality or nonrationality in given contexts?

Further, is it a fruitful way of viewing things to argue that all nonrational conduct is the same? That magic, nationalism, sex, idol worship, class solidarity, socialism, etc. are all different "forms" of the same psychic force? To pursue the problem of the relationship of the rational to the nonrational, it may be worthwhile to contrast Pareto's procedure with that of another sociologist.

Pareto notes that in certain primitive societies men are confronted with the phenomenon of a storm and seek ways of dealing with it—all nonlogical. Another "functionalist," Bronislaw Malinowski, studied the same phenomenon among the Trobrianders. He observed the use of canoe magic and sought to understand it, not by inventing a series of residues, but by relating magic to the social context in which it was employed—deep-sea fishing. As he proceeded to study this and other enterprises, he concluded that these people are both rational and nonrational; they employ both naturalistic and supernatural techniques and the degree to which one dominates, or supplements, the other depends on the circumstances in question.

These "primitives," Malinowski noted, understood very well indeed that, for instance, the outrigger canoe had to be constructed according to definite specifications if it was to be serviceable at sea; a minimum of "scientific" or technical knowledge was necessary. They knew what kind of equipment was most appropriate for deep-sea fishing; they had learned from experience that certain forms of social cooperation were most effective in that type of undertaking and they also had and used experiential knowledge about weather conditions at sea. They were not so foolish (in Pareto's terms, nonlogical) as to begin the expedition when the sky was overcast and a storm seemed likely. In all these terms, then, they were rational, and employed, in however rudimentary a way, naturalistic knowledge (logico-experimental norms, in Pareto's terms).

Yet, much to their chagrin, these stalwart fishermen had learned that their "scientific" knowledge was not enough to ensure their success and their safe return home. Why not? Because after they had carefully taken into account and controlled all the factors they could, unanticipated disasters befell them. Occasionally, they embarked on an expedition when the sea behaved as an inland lake on a summer day. Then, at sea, suddenly a bolt from the blue, an unexpected storm, and disaster. Here was an event they could neither foresee nor control. Hence, notes Malinowski, it was the task of the canoe magician to cope with this force to forestall unforeseen disasters. Now, to be sure, from the standpoint of a modern Western observer, magic here as elsewhere is "nonlogical," or supernatural nonsense; but Malinowski provides insight into the conditions in which magic supplements "science." When magic is employed, some of its *latent functions, e.g.,* allaying anxiety, are now better understood than before. To strengthen his thesis that magical practices are resorted to only under certain circumstances, he investigated lagoon fishing and found that where men have complete control and where naturalistic knowledge is sufficient, magic is *not* employed.

Surely, this "functional" approach is a much more fruitful one than Pareto's, in which no insights are given into the conditions of social life under which men tend to be more or less rational. Pareto's treatment of residues as constants obscures the extent to which all conduct, and not least what he calls nonlogical, varies with other conditions. If Marx's method made it possible to ask how social consciousness varied with the conditions of social existence, Pareto's method, in contrast, is designed to deny historical change and cultural differences. For he always comes back to the "sentimental" determination of thinking and doing and insists that despite "apparent" changes, the sentimental force remains dominant.

Derivations are persuasive because they are, together with the residues, manifestations of the sentiments. They are persuasive not only because they are derived from an individual's own sentiments, but because they appeal to the dominant sentiments: to the authority of maxims prevalent in the community; to the authority of outstanding individuals; to the authority of supernatural beings. But all these derivations are just so much "fatuous, inconclusive 'talk' " covering up the ultimate cause—sentiment—where Pareto always stops his analysis. When, he writes, a student of human conduct "sets out to study social phenomena, he halts at manifestations of social activity, that is to say at derivations, and does not carry his inquiry into the causes of the activity, that is to say, into residues." (Vol. III, 1402.) Did Pareto not see that he, too, has halted arbitrarily—with the sentiments? He was dogmatically committed to the proposition that in order to induce "people to act in a given way, one must necessarily resort to derivations, for they are the only language that reaches the human being in his sentiments. . . ." (Vol. III, 1043.)

Not surprisingly, the residue is a force that transcends different cultures, or, in other words, it is one and the same determinant of action in all cultures: "A Chinese, a Moslem, a Calvinist, a Catholic, a Kantian, a Hegelian, a Materialist, all refrain from stealing; but each gives a different explanation of his conduct. In other words, it is a case of a number of derivations connecting one residue that is operative in all of them with one conclusion which they all accept." (Vol. III, 1416.)

Two problems must be kept distinct, says Pareto: first, how residues and derivations function; and, second, their bearing on social utility. He wants to examine the problems in that order but as he proceeds, his definitions, one finds, are confused and even contradictory. Henceforth, we are told, it would be better to view "derivations" (presumably itself a "manifestation") under two aspects: "derivation proper and the manifestation to which it leads." By "derivation proper" he refers to "the need for logical developments which human beings feel." This "need" also has a "manifestation"—"reasonings of different kinds." So cryptic is Pareto's discussion here, that the editor, A. Livingston, is brought to remark: "The 'manifestation' would really be a 'derivative' and why Pareto discards this term, which is quite his own, for an obscurer 'manifestation' must remain a mystery." (Vol. III, 1688.[2])

The impression is inescapable that Pareto himself is not sure how he wants to use his terms. He writes that "since sentiments are manifested by residues we shall often, for the sake of brevity, use the word 'residues' as including the sentiments that they manifest." Therefore, when he says that residues are the elements which determine the social equilibrium, Pareto wants us to translate this to mean: "The sentiments manifested by residues are among the elements which stand toward the social equilibrium in a relationship of reciprocal determination." He is still not satisfied, however, for he notes that this remains too elliptical and might be taken to mean that he is ascribing objective existence to sentiments, something he assures us he does not want to do. "What we observe in reality," he writes, "is a group of human beings in a mental condition indicated by what we call sentiments." So, again we are requested to translate his proposition into the following terms: "The mental states that are indicated by the sentiments expressed in residues are among the elements that stand in a relation of reciprocal determination with the social equilibrium." Recognizing that he has gained nothing by this, he adds: "But if we would express ourselves in a language altogether exact, that is still not enough. What in the world are those 'mental states' or, if one will, those 'psychic conditions'? They are abstractions. And what underlies the abstractions? So we are obliged to say: 'The actions of human beings are among the elements that stand in a relationship of reciprocal determination with the social equilibrium. Among such actions are certain manifestations that we designate by the term 'residues' and which are closely correlated with other acts so that once we know the residues we may, under certain circumstances, know the actions. Therefore, we shall say that residues are among the elements that stand in a relationship of reciprocal determination with the social equilibrium.' " (Vol. III, 1690.) So we are back to residues and these really mean actions which are correlated with other actions. Acts now seem to be the key factor. Now that he has "clarified" matters for us, to avoid being pedantic, he will use the short form of the proposition: "residues are among the elements that determine the social equilibrium." But in a footnote to the same proposition, he reverts to the term "sentiment" which corresponds, he says, to the term "force" in the study of mechanics. Having sensed, perhaps, that speaking of acts and acts alone might undermine his entire thesis, he refuses to abandon the underlying nonlogical force and returns, in the next paragraph, to the older formulation: ". . . derivations also manifest sentiments. Directly they manifest the sentiments that correspond to the residues in which they originate. Indirectly they manifest sentiments through the residues that serve for purposes of derivation." (Vol. III, 1690.)

The old causal chain is thus restored. It begins with "sentiment," or "instinct," which motivates nonlogical actions (residues), which in turn are "logicalized" (always with pseudo-logic) as "derivations." Pareto continues to view what he regards as the nonlogical acts of humans as *instinctive* in the same sense as is true of chicks: "The hen defends her chicks" expresses a uniformity, and "present in the hen is a sentiment that prompts her to defend her chicks," and "that defense is a consequence of a given psychic state." Likewise, says Pareto, uniformities in human conduct may be explained "by saying that human beings—or some human beings—sacrifice their lives for their countries, that present in them is a sentiment which prompts them to sacrifice their lives for their countries, that such sacrifice is the consequence of a given psychic state." (Vol. III, 1690.) On the one hand, he traces acts to sentiments *et al.*, and, on the other, acknowledges that in speaking of sentiments, instincts, psychic states, etc., he is adding something nonempirical to his proposition. "All that experimental observation shows is a set of simultaneous facts—men dying for their countries and using certain modes of speech." But he has closed himself off from a sociological analysis of this datum, *viz.*, Under what social circumstances do men act this way?—and never abandons "sentiment" and "instinct" as his chief explanatory principle.

Ultimately, his theory of the structure of society is *psychological*: the so-called social equilibrium is determined by the distribution of psychological attributes or, more precisely, by the distribution of individuals holding these attributes. All other conditions are virtually ignored. What emerges, then, is a conception in which societies change little or not at all. Pareto argues this by means of his distinction between "substance" and "form," which when used by others is metaphysical but used by him is "scientific." "Observable in . . . historical societies are phenomena that vary little in substance, but widely in forms. As the various religions succeed one another in history, their forms may be as different as one pleases, but after all they are all expressions of religious sentiments that vary but slightly. The same may be said of the various forms of government. . . ." (Vol. III, 1695.)

"There is nothing new under the sun," said Ecclesiastes; there are no substantial changes in history nor will there ever be, says Pareto. And how does Pareto explain the absence of "substantial" change? By the substantial proportion of people who believed, and continue to believe, nonlogical nonsense. "We have no accurate statistics," he writes, "to show the exact number of such persons and therefore whether and to what extent their relative proportion to population has changed. Certain it is that the proportion has been and remains a very considerable one, that it has never been and is not now small." This proportion can never be reduced and the "people" will remain eternally incompetent and stupid. All religions are "varying forms of a single substance. . . . Socialism made room for itself by crowding back some of the prevailing faiths such as Catholicism and nationalism, and assimilating others. . . ." (Vol. III, 1702.) Pareto's "social equilibrium" thus rests on the unchanging sentiments. All religions stem from the same sentiment. In any single society, therefore, the decline of one form is accompanied by the rise of another. "Religion" in general will remain constant, since it is forever generated anew by the sentiments. Similarly, the "submissiveness" of the "people" has not changed; the sentiments of subordination which in the past led to the submission of the lower to the higher classes express themselves today in the submission of the lower classes to the leaders of the trade unions and political parties.

Pareto therefore sees "advantages" for "society" in "having a community divided into two parts, the one in which knowledge prevails, ruling and directing the other in which sentiments prevail so that, in the end, action is vigorous and wisely directed." (Vol. III, 1786.) And "the art of government lies in finding ways to take advantage of such sentiments, not in wasting one's energies in futile efforts to destroy them. . . ." (Vol. III, 1843.) As he proceeds to apply his "utilitarian calculus," his ideological position occasionally becomes more explicit. He unabashedly tells us, for instance, that "it is advantageous to society that individuals not of the ruling classes should spontaneously accept, observe, respect, revere, love, the precepts current in their society. . . ." (Vol. III, 1932.) Pareto has determined what is best for "society" and how it is best maintained—by an élite which exploits the sentiments of the ignorant masses. For a while this ignorance could be explained by the "difficulties that lay in the way of teaching the ignorant. But that excuse is no longer valid," says Pareto, for now "it is evident even to the blind that if the ignorant do not learn, it is because they will not." (Vol. III, 2016.) And this brings us more directly to Pareto's conception of "society."

Society, Élites, and Force

Social differentiation, for Pareto, refers primarily to the fact that individuals are "physically, morally, and intellectually different." More, some individuals are "superior" to others. Like Kolabinska, Pareto uses the term *élite* to refer to "superiority"—in intelligence, character, skill, capacity, power, etc. And although he allows for the possibility that some are given the label of élite without in fact possessing these qualities, on balance he sticks to the proposition that those who possess élite qualities become élites. One can measure the degree of excellence in every human endeavor, in prostitution and theft as well as in law and medicine and assign to the individuals in each an index ranging from 0 to 10. A grade of 10 may thus be assigned to the very best in each field, reserving 0 for the man who is a good-for-nothing or "out-and-out idiot." Napoleon, he says, "was certainly not an idiot, nor a man of little account, as millions of others are. He had exceptional qualities. . . ." (Vol. III, 2029.) Thus the élite of a society consists of those with the highest indices in their branches of activity. This Pareto divides into two: a *governing élite, i.e.,* those "who directly or indirectly play some considerable part in government, and a *nongoverning élite,* comprising the rest." (Vol. III, 2032.) Together these constitute the higher stratum, or class, of the society. The lower stratum or non-élite, in contrast, are those with whose political influence "we are not just here concerned"—which influence turns out to be practically nil from Pareto's standpoint. Pareto continues to talk about *élite* and *non-élite,* higher class and lower class, rulers and ruled, and thus employs an abstraction (a two-class model) which he censured in others (*e.g.,* Marx) as gross oversimplification. To the rulers and the ruled, Pareto relates his residues—but only the first two classes of residues, for he has nothing more to say about the remaining four.

There is, according to Pareto, a predominance of Class I residues in the higher stratum, and a predominance of Class II in the lower. More precisely, in the higher stratum "Class II residues gradually lose in strength, until now and again they are reinforced by tides upwelling from the lower stratum." Revolutions are in fact great religious tides, the upward thrusts of lower classes strong in Class II residues. Residues are also invoked to explain why "history is the graveyard of aristocracies"; for the élite decays in quantity and quality, *i.e.*, in the requisite residues that "enabled them to win their power and hold it. The governing class is restored not only in numbers, but—and that is the more important thing—in quality, by families rising from the lower classes and bringing with them the vigor and the proportions of residues necessary for keeping themselves in power. It is also restored by the loss of its more degenerate members." (Vol. III, 2054.) If the circulation ceases, the governing class collapses and "sweeps the whole of a nation along with it. Potent cause of disturbance in the equilibrium is the accumulation of superior elements in the lower classes and, conversely, of inferior elements in the higher classes." (Vol. III, 2055.) Thus the rudiments of Pareto's theory of revolution. But this "theory" includes another important element, *force*, which, for Pareto, may be the more important one. "Superior elements" are not only those "fit to rule" but those willing to use force. Inferior and decadent elements are unfit and fear its use. The "decaying" élite, shying away from the use of force, tries to buy off its adversaries; it becomes less the lion and more the fox and, therefore, increasingly vulnerable to the new lions.

"Societies in general subsist," writes Pareto in one of his typical "explanations," "because alive and vigorous in the majority of their constituent members are sentiments corresponding to residues of sociality (Class IV)." A gregarious instinct in men binds them together. "But," he adds, "there are also individuals in human societies in whom some at least of those sentiments are weak or indeed actually missing." Whether the society will subsist or dissolve depends on the relative proportion and strength of social sentiments within it. Corresponding to the distribution and intensity of these sentiments (*i.e.*, individuals holding them) one will find a society either more or less "uniform" or inclined to change: the greater the proportion and intensity of the residues of sociality, the greater the uniformity; and conversely, the weaker they are, the greater the tendency toward change. Societies are essentially "heterogeneous," says Pareto, in the distribution of residues; "the requirement of uniformity is very strong in some individuals, moderately strong in others, very feeble in still others, and almost entirely absent in a few." And "one may add as a datum of fact that the number of individuals in whom the requirement of uniformity is stronger than the average requisite of the intermediate state in which the society is situated is much greater than the number of individuals in whom the requirement is weaker than the average, and very, very much greater than the number in whom it is entirely missing." (Vol. IV, 2172.) Why is this a "datum of fact" for Pareto? Because "if the requirement of uniformity [apparently his term for unity and soli-darity] were to fail, society would not hold together, and each individual would go his own way, as lions and tigers, birds of prey, and other animals do." So societies hang together due to the predominance in them of individuals with strong social instincts; and the proof of this lies in the fact that societies do not dissolve.

This is not all. What Pareto calls derivations, theologies, etc. correspond to the "greater or lesser potency of the sentiments of uniformity." Thus one theology "will glorify the immobility of one or another uniformity, real or imaginary, the other . . . will glorify movement, progress, in one direction or another." (Vol. IV, 2173.) This is what actually happened in history. Men have sought merely to justify whatever sentiments they have held; moved by these blind forces they "explain" and justify their practice post hoc by talk. The same is true with respect to force, which "is used by those who wish to preserve certain uniformities and by those who wish to overstep them. And when each says he abhors the use of force, he means by the other.

Pareto goes on to suggest that the question whether "the use of violence to enforce existing uniformities is beneficial to society, or whether it is beneficial to use force to overstep them," can be solved by a kind of utilitarian (functional) calculus. The

. . . various uniformities have to be distinguished to see which of them are beneficial and which deleterious to society. Nor, indeed, is that enough; for it is further necessary to determine whether the utility of the uniformity is great enough to offset the harm that will be done by using violence to enforce it, or whether detriment from the uniformity is great enough to overbalance the damage that will be caused by the use of force in subverting it; in which detriment and damage we must not forget to reckon the very serious drawback involved in the anarchy that results from any frequent use of violence to abolish existing uniformities, just as among the benefits and utilities of maintaining frankly injurious uni-formities must be counted the strength and stability they lend to the social order. So, to solve the problem as to the use of force, it is not enough to solve the other problem as to the utility in general, of certain types of social organization; it is essential also and chiefly to compute all the ad-vantages and all the drawbacks, direct and indirect. (Vol. IV, 2175.)

But this calculus, to determine what is "beneficial to society," we now learn, is best left to the scientific élite and to the ruling class, for "social utility is oftentimes best served if the members of the subject class, whose *function* it is not to lead but to act, accept one of the two theologies according to the case—either the theology that enjoins preservation of existing uniformities, or the theology that counsels change." (Vol. IV, 2175, italics mine.) In spite of the cautious wording, this is a thinly veiled assumption of the incom-petence of the "people" to decide for themselves what is or is not good for them; "social utility" is best served if they follow passively and accept the judgments of the various élites.

When the rule of the governing élite is threatened, and out of humanitarian (or other) sentiments it declines to meet force with force, even a small group can impose its will upon it. And if the governing class shies away from the use of force for reasons of expediency, and resorts instead to fraud and deceit in order to outwit its adversaries, this eventually brings about a change in its composition—power passes "from the lions to the foxes." Foxiness, resting on the residues of the combinations instinct (Class I), becomes preponderant and intensified in that class while Class II residues decline. It is precisely the increase of Class I residues, supplying the "artistry and resourcefulness" now needed to outsmart one's opponents, that makes the governing class increasingly vulnerable to those willing and able to use force—the lions, that is, either from within that class or from the subject one.

The leaders of the subject class, ready, willing, and able to employ force, topple the governing class; this is accomplished all the more easily if it is moved by humanitarian sentiments and if it has found few or no ways of assimilating into its midst the élite of the subject class. A closed aristocracy is most vulnerable and insecure. On the other hand, the more adept is the governing class in absorbing those subject elements who are skilled at "chicanery, fraud, and corruption," the more secure is its rule; for it undercuts the possibility that these "talented" elements will "become the leaders of such plebeians as are disposed to use violence. Thus left without leadership, without talent, disorganized, the subject class is almost always powerless to set up any lasting regime." (Vol. VI, 2179.) Despite the qualification, "almost," the overwhelming thrust of the argument is, *contra* Marx, that there will always be a subject class. This is inevitable because it has no real leadership; its élite elements are consistently co-opted by the governing élite.

While the governing élite, being small, is greatly strengthened by the influx of Class I residues (*i.e.,* individuals holding them who are inclined to rule), the subject class is enfeebled not only by the loss of these elements, but also by the fact that though it "is still left with many individuals possessed of combinations-instincts, [these] are applied not to politics . . . but to arts and trades independent of politics. That circumstance lends stability to societies, for the governing class is required to absorb only a small number of new individuals in order to keep the subject class deprived of leadership. However, in the long run the differences in temperament between the governing class and the subject class become gradually accentuated, the combinations instincts tending to predominate in the ruling class, and instincts of group-persistence in the subject class. When that difference becomes sufficiently great, revolution occurs." (Vol. IV, 2179.) This is Pareto's theory of revolution, based on residues, sentiments, and temperament. The general formula, he tells us, can be applied to nation-states. Those who have not lost "the habit of applying force" will win over those who have lost the "habit"; and in the long run the latter situation "leads a country to ruin." (Vol. IV, 2179.) In general, the ideal of replacing the use of force by unarmed law is a grievous hallucination.

As for the oppressed, or those who think they are, derivations, such as humanitarianism, are used to arouse them or to bring the neutrals over to their side, or to get them to condemn or otherwise weaken the governing powers. Pareto has nothing but contempt for "those whose spinal columns have utterly rotted from the bane of humanitarianism." (Vol. IV, 2186.) The temptation is irresistible to present just a few examples of Pareto's "scientific-sociological" approach to "force." In a country where the ruling class, A, out of humanitarian or other considerations, "is becoming less and less capable of using force," it is "shirking the main duty of a ruling class. Such a country is on its way to utter ruin." But then the B's, the subject class, "apply force on a far-reaching scale, and not only overthrow the A's but kill large numbers of them—and, in so doing, to tell the truth, they are performing a useful public service, something like ridding the country of a baneful animal pest." Owing to this, "the social fabric is acquiring stability and strength. The country is saved from ruin and is reborn to a new life." Again, ". . . slaughter and rapine are external symptoms indicating the advent of strong and courageous people to places formerly held by weaklings and cowards." And commenting on the French Revolution of 1789, if the governing class "had had the faith that counsels use of force and the will to use force, it would never have been overthrown and, procuring its own advantage, would have procured the advantage of France." Failing in its function, however, it "was a good thing that power should pass into the hands of people who showed that they had the faith and the resolve requisite for the use of force." (Vol. IV, 2191.) He has much to say about force, about the spineless and the courageous, etc.; but one finds nothing more than this in his functional calculus for determining what is good for "society."

Other phenomena which Pareto takes up further illustrate his dependence on the notion of instinct. There are, he notes, *rentiers* and speculators, or "savers" and entrepreneurs. And how, ultimately, are we to understand "saving?" "All human conduct based on instinct may be more or less modified by reasoning, and it would be going too far to assert that that does not apply also to conduct based on the instinct for saving. But that does not prevent that instinct from being the primary element in saving, which remains none the less a nonlogical act." (Vol. IV, 2232.) *Rentiers* and speculators are not sociological but psychological categories, for each rests on basically different instincts. In the category "speculator," he tells us, "we are putting together all persons who directly or indirectly speculate and in one way or another manage to increase their incomes by ingeniously taking advantage of circumstances." (Vol. IV, 2233.) This includes not only capitalistic entrepreneurs but "lawyers, engineers, politicians, working people, [and] clerks. . . ." Of course, they all share an "ingeniousness" which can be traced to the Type I instinct just as the behavior of the *rentier* can be traced to Type II.

Pareto occasionally reminds us, contrary to his practice, that residues are not to be regarded as the only determining factor. However, Pareto can explain almost any problem in terms of the proportion of Class I and Class II residues. If, for instance, Alcibiades persuaded the Athenians "against the better judgment of the conservative Nicias, to undertake the Sicilian expedition," this was due to the preponderance among them of Class I residues. And Pareto adds: "Had sentiments of group-persistence been at all strong in the Athenians, they would have followed the view of Nicias, or would at the most have been satisfied with sending a small expedition that would have been no great tax on their resources." (Vol. IV, 2421.) This is typical of what Pareto considers to be "explanation." After recounting some of the historical events in very superficial terms, he concludes: "It is plain enough that what was lacking in Athens was such a balance between the combinations-instincts and the residues of group-persistence that while the combination-instincts encouraged to adventure, the group-persistences would supplement them with the perseverance and firmness of resolve required for success in the schemes imagined." (Vol. IV, 2424.) More, the fact that Alcibiades could be more effective leading the "slow-thinking" Spartans than the natives of his own city, "demonstrates how desirable it is that combination-instincts should predominate in the leaders and the instincts of group-persistence in subordinates." It is desirable, in other words, that the "masses," in any case predominantly nonrational, blindly follow and leave to the élite the work of making ingenious combinations. Both Sparta and Athens would have been easily defeated had they fought "with a people possessing ability to innovate combined with ability to make the proper use of novelties, a situation that arises in countries where our Class I residues predominate in the leaders and Class II residues in the subject classes." (Vol. IV, 2429.) Pareto's "proof": Thebes and Macedonia were equally endowed in a number of respects—both made improvements simultaneously in the arts of war, both had leaders with highly developed combination-instincts, who commanded peoples with "the group-persistences required for steadfastness of purpose." Why then did the Macedonians fare better? This is Pareto's profound reply: "Through a greater intensity in their Class II residues, the Macedonians stood by their leaders more consistently than the Thebans did." (Vol. IV, 2429.)

In effect, the combination-instinct, for Pareto, is the intelligence of the élite to take advantage of the superstitions of the masses but never to believe the absurdities themselves. He relates how Nicias, when commanding the Athenians, "was induced by his group persistences to place his trust in oracles and so led the army under him to complete ruin." And he concludes "that oracles are good things if they are used by rulers, who perhaps have no faith in them, as means of persuading their subordinates, but harmful if they are taken at face value by rulers and used as an end in themselves, not as means of persuasion. To make the proposition general, and so applicable to times that know no oracles, one need merely replace the term 'oracles' with the term 'group-persistences.' " (Vol. IV, 2440.) Pareto goes on to say that the élite will achieve its ends all the more efficiently, the more the masses are kept unaware of this doctrine, suggesting thereby that they are able to learn of their deliberate manipulation and, given such knowledge, could prevent it. He thus leaves himself open to the inference that the stupidity and acquiescence of the "people" need not be permanent. Explicitly, however, this is his formula for success: A people's prejudices (Class II residues) should be strong enough to assure its obedience to the leader, but not so strong as to prevent certain innovations. It is this "scientific-sociological" proposition which explains victory in war and prosperity and progress in peace.

Forms of government do have some influence on social events and development, Pareto acknowledges, but these forms are themselves "products of the character traits of the peoples involved, the traits, therefore, being far more important as causes of the social phenomena. . . ." (Vol. IV, 2445.) He quotes Von der Goltz's remarks about conditions in Prussia before the battle of Jena to the effect that in France the civil authority always defers to the military "whereas in Germany the prevailing spirit in the civil government, as well as in the public at large, is always to block the military authority." (Vol. IV, 2447.) Pareto notes parenthetically that in his time the situation has reversed itself. The "constant" character traits have *not only changed* but have switched places—with no further light thrown on the phenomenon.

Having the right traits and using force will ensure the maintenance of the governing class. And how might a governing class best defend itself and eliminate those who threaten it? "The infliction of death," replies Pareto, "is the surest means, but also the most harmful," since it could lead to a destruction of society's best individuals. Persecution is also not very practical since this tends to create martyrs, who are even more dangerous to the élite. In general, then, he leaves one effective formula for rulers: "One may say . . . that a governing class offers effective resistance only as it is disposed to go to the limit in resistance, without hesitation, using force and resorting to arms whenever necessary." (Vol. IV, 2480.) This, the reader might protest, is for Pareto, as it was for Machiavelli before him, more in the nature of a description than a prescription. Perhaps. Yet, the entire structure of his "sociology," his personal hopes that his "society will one day be saved from decadence by the heirs of the Syndicalists and Anarchists of our day," and finally, his attitude toward fascism, suggest something more than mere description.

Pareto and Fascism

It is not known how much direct influence Pareto had upon Mussolini, or even whether there was any direct contact between the two men when the latter was a political refugee in Lausanne. Before the march on Rome, Pareto had a very reserved and occasionally even hostile attitude toward the fascist movement. It is indisputable, however, that once the Italian dictator had established himself in power, Pareto gave his wholehearted approval to what he apparently regarded as the "moderate form" fascism assumed in its early phase. Later, he maintained his support and approval of the regime but, according to his biographer, G. H. Bousquet, underscored "the necessity of safeguarding a number of liberties."[10]

Fascism, for Pareto, seemed not only to confirm his theories but also to hold out hope for a "new era." That he identified with the new order is borne out by the fact that on March 23, 1923, he accepted an appointment as senator—a position he had declined to accept in the pre-fascist government. In a letter to an acquaintance at the time of acceptance, he wrote: "I am happy to see that you are favorably disposed to the new regime, which, in my opinion, is the only one capable of saving Italy from innumerable evils."[11] And, in the same vein, "France will save herself only if she finds her own Mussolini."[12]

In general, Pareto's attitude seems to have been that since the pre-fascist regime did not, or could not, save the country from "anarchy" by legal means, fascism had to do it by force. Having accomplished this, however, the regime should have strived to establish a "new legality." Fascism would be good for Italy if it avoided wars and if it refrained from imposing "exaggerated" restrictions on freedom. In short, fascism would be good if it were not fascism! His call for "liberties," however, was typically Paretian: What is most essential is that the new élite govern "effectively"—and this requires that it concede a "certain dose of liberty" to the people. Reflecting on fascism a year or so before he died, Pareto wrote, "We have arrived today at a point where there appears, among . . . the clouds of the future, the beginning of the transformation of democracy, of parliamentarism, of the cycle of demagogic plutocracy; and Italy which formerly was the mother of so many forms of civilization, could very well have a grand role to play in bringing into the world another."[13]

In his attitude toward fascism, then, we have a clearer view of Pareto's own firmly held sentiments, whose manifestations may also be found throughout his work which he fancied as "logico-experimental." In actuality, as we have seen, this work is neither scientific nor sociological, for his grandiose structure of peculiar terms and concepts adds little, and perhaps even nothing, to our understanding of the phenomena and patterns he singled out.

10 See G. H. Bousquet, *op. cit.,* p. 89.
11 *Ibid.,* p. 193.
12 *Ibid.,* pp. 193–94n.
13 *Ibid.,* p. 197.

13

Gaetano Mosca

(1858–1941)

Mosca, like Pareto, conceived of his life's work as an effective repudiation of the prevailing democratic and collectivistic theories, particularly Marxism. These theories, elements of which could be traced to ancient Greece, were given a more explicit formulation by the representatives of the Enlightenment in the eighteenth century; and in the nineteenth century were logically extended by Karl Marx and thus given a renewed impetus. Rousseau, in these terms, was the real parent of Marx, and Marx the true heir of the Enlightenment. Though Marx is regarded as the founder of modern socialism, writes Mosca, its "first intellectual and moral parent was undoubtedly Rousseau."[1] The various doctrines emanating from these sources are precisely the ones Mosca is "combating all along in these pages." (p. 152.) Like Pareto, he wants once and for all to destroy the Rousseauian-Marxian fantasy "that once collectivism is established, it will be the beginning of an era of universal equality and justice, during which the state will no longer be the organ of a class and the exploiter and the exploited will be no more." (p. 447.) Mosca's entire output, in

[1] Gaetano Mosca, *The Ruling Class*, translated from *Elementi di Scienza Politica* by Hannah D. Kahn. Edited and revised by Arthur Livingstone (New York: McGraw-Hill Book Company, 1965), p. 170. (Subsequent references to this work will appear by page numbers in the text.)

particular *The Ruling Class,* is intended as a refutation of this "utopia" against which he advances his own, more "realistic" theory: There will always be a ruling class!

To support this thesis, Mosca relies ultimately, as did Pareto, on the assumption of "constant psychological tendencies determining the behavior of the human masses." (p. 1.) Yet, what emerges from his total work is a theory which is, on balance, less dogmatic and less rigid than Pareto's as well as more *sociological*—though he prefers to describe his work as political science rather than sociology. His sociological view is evident not only in his rejection of geographic, climatic, social-Darwinian, and racial theories, but especially in his explicit use of concepts such as "social structure," "social types," and "social forces." It is, he writes, "social structure, upon which, after all, decision as to whether a people is to rule or to be ruled depends." (p. 61.) These concepts lead him to the view that it is not categories such as race, topography, climate, struggle for existence, etc. which account for the relative cultural backwardness of certain groups but definite social relationships: "We are obliged to agree . . . that European civilization has not only hindered but actually thwarted any effort toward progress that Negroes and Indians might have made of their own accord." (p. 23.) Given identical social and cultural conditions there is no reason to believe that Negroes could not distinguish themselves as well as whites. When Negro children recognize their condition, *i.e.,* "realize that they belong to a race that is adjudged inferior, and that they can look forward to no better lot than that of cooks and porters, they lose interest in studying and lapse into apathy." (p. 24.)

Mosca is also aware that "every individual is wont to adopt the ideas, the beliefs, the sentiments that are most current in the environment in which he has grown up." (p. 26.) His more consistently sociological approach may be further illustrated in his insistence that it is not any alleged organic differences among peoples that determine "the differences in social type that they have adopted, but rather the differences in social contacts and in historical circumstances to which every nation . . . is fated to be subject." (p. 28.) The doctrine which has mechanically transposed the Darwinian view from the natural to the social realm is also erroneous: It is not primarily a struggle for *existence* which prevails in society but a struggle for *preeminence;* this is "a constant phenomenon that arises in all human societies. . . ." (p. 29.)

Struggle for preeminence is Mosca's term for the social competition and conflict over wealth, power, and prestige; for "control of the means and instruments that enable a person to direct many human activities, many human wills, as he sees fit. The losers, who are of course the majority in that sort of struggle, are not devoured, destroyed, or even kept from reproducing their kind, as is basically characteristic of the struggle for life. They merely enjoy fewer material satisfactions and, especially, less freedom and independence." (p. 30.) In opposition to the various nonsociological doctrines, Mosca emphasized that it is the accumulation of experience and positive knowledge which accounts for the advance of civilization, and that the rise and decline of societies must be viewed as the effects of "changes in their types of social structure." (p. 35.) If Frenchmen, for example, are different today from what they were one hundred years ago, then this is due to the radical changes that have taken place in "the economic and political situation in France" and to the different intellectual atmosphere now prevailing there.

Mosca gives so much attention to social and cultural variables that his so-called "constant psychological laws" are relegated in his system to a relatively subordinate position. In Pareto's system, as we have seen, "sentiments" and the basic irrationality of man play so fundamental a role as virtually to exclude a consideration of socio-cultural conditions. Mosca, on the other hand, keeps these conditions constantly in view. The "great psychological laws," he writes, "reveal their operation . . . in administrative and judicial institutions, in religions, in all the moral and political customs of the various nations; and it is therefore upon these last categories of facts that we must concentrate our attention." (p. 46.) While his general argument rests somewhat less than Pareto's on psychological laws, Mosca too, ultimately falls back upon such "laws" for his explanation of why the struggle for pre-eminence, as well as the ruling class, must be eternal phenomena.

The Ruling Class

The observation that rulers and ruled have existed throughout history obviously did not originate with Mosca, as he readily acknowledged. But thinkers such as Plato and Machiavelli, to name just two, had made only casual allusions to this phenomenon. It was only in the work of Saint-Simon, Mosca believed, that one could see a definite and clearcut anticipation of his own doctrine: that once a society reaches a certain stage of development "political control in the broadest sense of the term (administrative, military, religious, economic, and moral leadership) is exercised always by a special class, or by an organized minority. . . ." (p. 239.) Saint-Simon had not only asserted "the inherent necessity of a ruling class. He explicitly proclaimed that that class has to possess the requisites and aptitudes most necessary to social leadership at a given time and in a given type of civilization." (pp. 329–30.)

In 1883, in his first work, *Teorica dei Governi e Governo Parlamentare*, Mosca elaborated on Saint-Simon's view and argued "that even in democracies the need for an organized minority persists, and that in spite of appearances to the contrary, and for all of the legal principles on which government rests, this minority still retains actual and effective control of the state." (p. 331.) And to emphasize that he was the *first* among his contemporaries to give this thesis explicit form, he adds: "In years following came the first edition of the present work, *Elementi di scienza politica,* and, among others, works by Ammon, Novikov, Rensi, Pareto and Michels."[2] (p. 331.)

Now this thesis—that under all systems, including politically democratic ones, a ruling class prevails—was obviously one with which Marx or the Marxists would not have disagreed. They knew very well that the "history of all hitherto existing society is the history of class struggles." This was, after all, the first observation Marx and Engels made in the *Communist Manifesto.* And three paragraphs later they also state quite clearly that modern bourgeois society "has not done away with class antagonisms. It has but established new classes, new conditions of oppression, new forms of struggle in place of the old ones." If Marx had stopped there, his thesis would have been identical with Mosca's. But, of course, Marx did not stop there and went on to argue that classes (including ruling classes) and class conflict rest on definite socioeconomic conditions and that the elimination of those conditions could lead to a society in which a ruling class would be superfluous and unthinkable. What was inevitable under some conditions was altogether avoidable under others. The point for Mosca, in contrast, was that history gives us no realistic basis for such a vision, since it is a fundamental and inexorable psychological law, and not primarily social conditions, which determines man's nature. What has been true "of all hitherto existing society" will continue to be true in all future societies. In this way Mosca reversed the implications of Marx's thesis and transformed it into a conservative one. The ruling class is a permanent attribute of society as is the struggle for preeminence. In all societies there have been and will continue to be two classes: one that rules and the other that is ruled. In Mosca's scheme, however, the ruled are assigned a somewhat less passive role than in Pareto's.

The ruled masses, Mosca acknowledges, are able to bring pressures to bear upon the rulers. The "pressures arising from the discontent of the masses who are governed, from the passions by which they are swayed, exert a certain amount of influence on the policies of the ruling, the political class." (p. 51.) Popular discontent may even result in the overthrow of a ruling class; but another such class would inevitably emerge from the "masses themselves to discharge the functions of a ruling class. Otherwise all organization, and the whole social structure, would be destroyed." (p. 51.) The ruling or political class assumes "preponderant importance in determining the political type, and also the level of civilization, of the different peoples." (p. 51.)

The power of the ruling class as well as the inevitability of its dominion rests on the fact that it is an *organized minority*—which is accompanied in Mosca's system by an *unorganized majority.* The unorganized state of the majority renders each of its individual members quite powerless before the

---

[2] For an account of the dispute over who had priority in this regard, see James H. Meisal's *The Myth of the Ruling Class* (Ann Arbor: The University of Michigan Press, 1962) , p. 170 *ff.*

organized might of the minority. Precisely because it is a minority, a relatively small group, it can achieve what the majority cannot: mutual understanding and concerted action. "It follows," writes Mosca, "that the larger the political community, the smaller will the proportion of the governing minority to the governed majority be, and the more difficult will it be for the majority to organize for reaction against the minority." (p. 53.)

Not only difficult, perhaps even impossible. There is an inexorable social law rooted in the nature of man which makes it inevitable that the representatives of the people—whether elected or appointed—will transform themselves from servants into masters. Appointed to represent and defend the common interests of the group as a whole, they soon develop special interests of their own; and in their zealous pursuit of these interests they become a well-organized, powerful, and dominant minority. The ruling minority is strengthened not only by its organization but by the superior qualities—material, intellectual, moral—which distinguish it from the mass. Members "of a ruling minority regularly have some attribute, real or apparent, which is highly esteemed and very influential in the society in which they live." (p. 53.)

The basic psychological law which impels men to struggle for preeminence always results in the victory of the minority, which by virtue of its organization and other superior qualities gains decisive control over certain "social forces." Control of any one social force—e.g., military, economic, political, administrative, religious, moral, etc.—may lead to control of others. The military power of warrior lords, for instance, enabled them to demand and receive "the community's whole produce minus what was absolutely necessary for subsistence on the part of the cultivators; and when the latter tried to escape such abuses they were constrained by force to stay bound to the soil, their situation taking on all the characteristics of serfdom pure and simple." (p. 55.) This has been true generally of societies in which land was the chief source of wealth: military power led to wealth just as later wealth in the form of money led to political and military power. When "fighting with the mailed fist is prohibited whereas fighting with pounds and pence is sanctioned, the better posts are inevitably won by those who are better supplied with pounds and pence." (p. 57.) In all societies, including, of course, representative democracies, the rich have readier access to agencies of social influence than the poor. In some societies during specific periods, control of "religious forces," as might be the case with priests, leads to wealth and political power; in other societies, specialized scientific knowledge becomes an important political force.

The various advantages of the ruling minority—organization, superior qualities, and control of social forces—conduce to the situation in which "all ruling classes tend to become hereditary in fact if not in law." There "is no eliminating that special advantage in favor of certain individuals which the French call the advantage of *positions déjà prises*." Among others, these are the "connections and kinships that set an individual promptly on the right road, enabling him to avoid the gropings and blunders that are inevitable when one enters an unfamiliar environment without any guidance or support." (p. 61.)

Arguing against social Darwinism and against the racial theories of Gumplowicz, Mosca adamantly insists on the social and cultural basis of the "superiority" of the various aristocracies and ruling classes in history. They "owe their special qualities not so much to the blood that flows in their veins as to their particular upbringing, which has brought out certain intellectual and moral tendencies in them in preference to others." And again, "the truth is that social position, family tradition, the habits of the class in which we live, contribute more than is commonly supposed to the greater or lesser development of the qualities mentioned." (p. 63.)

Thus Mosca rejects any attribution of organic superiority to the members of the ruling class; but he rejects equally the sociological implications of his statement that "social position, family tradition, and habits of class" determine the character of men. He is unwilling seriously to entertain the possibility that the psychology of men could be changed by changing social conditions and institutions. For Mosca, the existing institutions, notably the ruling class, though owing their existence in part to other socio-cultural conditions, are ultimately the result of a basic, unchanging psychological nature in man. Only by clinging to this assumption can he support his theory: Men under all conditions will struggle for preeminence, and this must result in the basic dichotomy of rulers and ruled.

Although the organized minority has superior might and can therefore repel by force challenges to its rule, it does so only as a last resort. Generally, it succeeds in stabilizing its rule by making it acceptable to the masses. This is done by means of a "political formula," a term roughly equivalent to Marx's ruling-class ideology, Weber's "legitimation" of power, Sorel's "myths," and Pareto's "derivations." Every governing class, writes Mosca, "tends to justify its actual exercise of power by resting it on some universal moral principle." (p. 62.)

The "political formula" is not invented and employed "to trick the masses into obedience." (p. 71.) It is a "great superstition" or illusion that, at the same time, is a great social force; without it, Mosca maintains, it is doubtful that societies could persist. "Political formula," then, is a broader concept than the term suggests; it includes the common values, beliefs, sentiments, and habits that result from a people's community of history and make that people receptive to the fictions employed by the governing class to legitimize its rule.

Nationalism is an obvious example in the modern era of such a formula: " . . . a man feels, believes, loves, hates, according to the environment in which he lives." (p. 73.) In previous eras, rule by "divine right" was the prevalent formula. Formulae change with the socio-historical circumstances but under all circumstances the consent of the governed is based on a formula of some kind:

The majority of a people consents to a given governmental system solely because the system is based upon religious or philosophical beliefs that are universally accepted by them. To use a language that we prefer, the amount of consent depends upon the extent to which, and the ardor with which, the class that is ruled believes in the political formula by which the ruling class justifies its rule. (p. 97.)

Every successful regime rests on the careful cultivation of the beliefs of the lower classes in the ruling political formula. Failure to develop such all-embracing, general beliefs means that the rulers have failed to unify the different social groups and classes of the society.

Ruling ideas cannot depart too far from the culture of the governed without resulting in conflict and antagonism which threaten the very survival of the society. The principles underlying the formula must be rooted in the "consciousness of the more populous and less well educated strata of society." (p. 107.) When such principles have sunk deeply enough into the consciousness of the poorly educated, the governing class, however corrupt and oppressive, gets remarkable results: the unswerving devotion of the poor, exploited, and oppressed masses. Nationalistic political formulae, properly cultivated, can effectively counter the internationalist doctrine of social democracy; and Mosca saw a vivid demonstration of this thesis during World War I. It is of interest to note in this connection that nationalism was a greater social force than even he had believed. Before the war he wrote: "These theories [proletarian internationalism] might have a certain practical efficacy in the event of a war between the Germans and the French, or between the Italians and the English, since all these nations belong to approximately the same social type. But if it were a question of repelling a serious Tatar or Chinese invasion, or merely a Turkish or Russian invasion, we believe that the great majority of proletarians even in countries where they are most strongly imbued with doctrines of worldwide collectivism would eagerly cooperate with the ruling class." (p. 115.)

Thus even Mosca was probably astonished to see that it took less than a Tatar invasion to mobilize and unite the workers behind their respective governments. And if Mosca the "pessimist" erred in underestimating the force of the ruling "political formula," is it any wonder that some of the "optimistic" socialists thus erred? In that instance narrow-minded nationalistic sentiments had overwhelmed the peoples of Europe and had brought upon them a terrible carnage. Must, however, the ruling "political formula," *e.g.*, nationalism leading to war, always win out? Mosca grants that such formulae gain acceptance among the masses primarily because they have so little education and so little understanding of their condition. But he does not envisage the possibility of raising the general level of their consciousness to the point where they could act rationally—*i.e.,* reject political formulae obviously not to their interest.

Another major social process to which Mosca calls attention is the emergence within the lower classes of a "directing minority," a kind of plebeian ruling class, which is often "antagonistic to the class that holds possession of the legal government." (p. 116.) The directing minority becomes a state within the state, wielding more influence over the masses than the legal government. The greater the isolation of the classes from one another, and the greater the discontent of the lower classes, the greater, too, is the likelihood that they will support the overthrow of the existing legal government. One ruling class then replaces the other but this avails the masses little or nothing. The really great danger in the growing cultural differences among classes, and in their mutual cultural isolation, "is a decline in energy in the upper classes, which grow poorer and poorer in bold and aggressive characters and richer and richer in 'soft,' remissive individuals." (p. 117.) The more closed are these classes to aspiring individuals from the lower classes, the greater their vulnerability and degeneracy. For it is only from the lower classes that the vigorous and strong elements may be recruited. In these classes, "the hard necessities of life, the unending and carking scramble for bread, the lack of literary culture, keep the primordial instincts of struggle and the unfailing ruggedness of human nature, alive." (p. 119.) Here we recognize an idea Pareto formulated in a much less simple and straightforward fashion. Both of these thinkers, therefore, had a working-class mystique, fundamentally different, no doubt, from that of Marx, but a mystique nevertheless.

For Mosca, the fate of a ruling class depends on its energy, wisdom, and political sophistication. It has considerable control of its destiny. A ruling class of some sort is a permanent institution, and efforts to abolish it will always remain quixotic. The point, therefore, is to devise the best political system possible in the light of this fact; one could learn much in this regard from the great political thinkers of the past.

Aristotle and Montesquieu

Mosca became in 1908 a Liberal-Conservative member of the Italian Chamber of Deputies. Thus unlike Pareto, who had isolated himself from political life and had produced a correspondingly rigid system, Mosca was actively engaged in Italian politics. This, perhaps, contributed in his case to the formation of a more flexible political theory, which was reflected in his official party affiliation. Though he was indeed an élitist in some sense, he advanced what may more precisely be termed as a liberal-aristocratic theory of politics.

He was a liberal in the sense that he had great respect and admiration for liberal principles, traditions, and institutions. The liberal principle, he believed, "has had a more brilliant record than the autocratic principle. . . ." (p. 409.) Political systems based on liberal principles have been more successful than others precisely because they have rested "upon the consent of the majority of citizens"; but he is quick to add, "though only a small fraction of the inhabitants may be citizens." (p. 409.) The models for his "good polity," therefore, were the ancient city-state of Greece, about which Aristotle had written, and the English system before the institution of universal suffrage—the system Montesquieu had so much admired.

Liberalism is the proper mediation between two fundamental principles forever at work in all political systems, vying with each other for hegemony: aristocracy and democracy. Liberalism is best in the sense that it allows both principles to work side by side with neither overpowering the other. Officials are appointed or elected from "below," *i.e.*, directly or indirectly by their subordinates; they are drawn, however, from a limited pool of wise, experienced, responsible, and devoted men who are best fit to rule—the aristocratic minority. They have authority but not unlimited power, since definite limits are imposed upon their powers in relation to "individual citizens and to associations of citizens." These limits—checks and balances—are the essence of liberalism; they are the fundamental elements of what Mosca calls "juridical defense," which in turn is the real criterion of the advance of civilization.

Such limits [writes Mosca] were not entirely unknown to classical Greece and ancient Rome. They are almost always recognized in modern constitutions. They relate to such things as freedom of worship, of the press, of education, of assembly, and of speech. They guarantee personal liberty, private property, and inviolability of domicile. (pp. 409–10.)

The liberal principle does not preclude the existence of an aristocratic minority or even closed cliques within it. In fact, a certain degree of closure is essential and good. On the other hand, too much closure results in *autocracy,* something to be eschewed since it leads to the isolation of the rulers and eventually to their downfall. The proper balance may be found in liberal systems which "steer the inclinations of at least the whole second stratum of the ruling class, which, if it does not in itself constitute the electorate, at least supplies the general staffs of leaders who form the opinions and determine the conduct of the electing body." (p. 410.) The "second stratum" to which Mosca here alludes, though varying with the society, corresponds to Aristotle's great middle class, the basis of political moderation. For Mosca, too, it "forms the backbone of all great political organization." (p. 413.) The existence of a large and stable second stratum makes it possible for a government to succeed without "paying homage to the beliefs and sentiments of the more ignorant classes. Only under such circumstances can one of the chief assumptions of the liberal system be made, we do not say complete, but not wholly illusory—namely, that those who represent shall be responsible to the represented." (p. 413.)

In these terms, Mosca regards it as essential to preserve and properly to balance the aristocratic and democratic tendencies present in varying degrees of strength in all political organizations. "If it is confined within moderate limits," he writes, "the democratic tendency is in a sense indispensable to what is called 'progress' in human societies." (p. 415.) Excessive suppression of this tendency results in social stagnation: If the aristocracies of Homeric times, for example, had remained closed and stationary, then civilization never would have advanced beyond that stage.

Class conflict, Mosca acknowledges to the Marxists, has been a major force in the development of civilization. "The struggle between those who are at the top and those who are born at the bottom but aspire to climb has been, is, and will ever be the ferment that forces individuals and classes to widen their horizons and seek the new roads that have brought the world to the degree of civilization that it attained in the nineteenth century." (p. 416.) Now, however, the democratic tendency has gotten out of hand; if it could be brought under control, then it would again become the conservative force which it ought properly to be.

> When the democratic tendency does not exert too great an influence, to the exclusion of other tendencies, it represents a conservative force. It enables ruling classes to be continually replenished through the admission of new elements who have inborn talents for leadership and a will to lead, and so prevents that exhaustion of aristocracies of birth which usually paves the way for great social cataclysms. (p. 416.)

The best system, then, is one in which the democratic tendency is appropriately bridled and curbed. But the principle of balance and moderation is constantly being threatened and undermined in practice by the Rousseauian-Marxian dogma of equality—a fantastic uptopia; for "every time the democratic movement has triumphed, in part or in full, we have invariably seen the aristocratic tendency come to life again through efforts of the very men who had fought it. . . ." (p. 417.)

If, therefore, Mosca was combating the ideas of the Enlightenment, it was specific aspects of that intellectual movement which he opposed. He admired Montesquieu but rejected Rousseau. The former had asserted the need for checks, balances, in short—moderation. A system based on these was more realistic and hence superior to the unbridled democratic theory of Rousseau. Although the latter had called for popular sovereignty and absolute equality, he had also recognized, Mosca alleges, the need for a ruling class. In Rousseau's *Social Contract* Mosca found the following statement: "Taking the term in its strictest sense there has never been a real democracy and there never will be. It is against the natural order that the great number should rule and the small number be ruled." (p. 391.) But as Meisel has shown, this passage was quoted out of context, and it was only by so doing that Mosca could have used it for his purposes. Rousseau goes on to say: "It is inconceivable that the People should be in permanent session for the administration of public affairs. . . ."[3] The real point Rousseau was making in this context was, in Meisel's words, "that *government* by all would be as much against 'the natural order' (since the result would be anarchy) as would be *sovereignty* (which is and remains inalienable) if possessed by less than all the people."[4] What Mosca feared most was "a demagogic dictatorship by a few experts in mob leadership" and he used the passage from Rousseau quoted above to show that he had also recognized the dangers of that kind of "democracy."

From Mosca's standpoint, then, Montesquieu and *even* Rousseau had admitted to the necessity of a ruling class. Greatly impressed by the English system of restraining the ruling class, Montesquieu had extolled that system and suggested it be adopted as a model. But, after all, long before him the basis of political balance and moderation, and their virtues, had been explored by Aristotle, that great thinker of antiquity whose ideas on the subject were still viable.

Aristotle's "classification of governments," writes Mosca, "into monarchies, aristocracies, and democracies (a classification that might now be judged superficial and incomplete) was certainly the very best that the human mind could contrive in his day."[5] It was an "extraordinary intellectual feat." The genius of Aristotle, in Mosca's view, was to anticipate what modern scholarship has increasingly established as fact, namely, "that democratic, monarchical, and aristocratic principles function side by side in every political organism." (p. 52.) The philosopher had recognized that good government is "mixed" government, *i.e.*, one in which the monarchy, the landed aristocracy, and the moneyed classes were properly balanced. In Mosca's terms, there "were so many political forces, the interplay of which, so long as any one of them did not prevail to the exclusion of others, was such as to provide a type of political organization in which due process of law was, in ordinary times, relatively secure." (p. 137.)

Aristotle had maintained, moreover, that the stability and efficacy of a political organization depend on the existence of intermediate strata sufficiently large, prosperous, and independent to mediate between the extremes at the top and the bottom. To assure this, and thus the proper functioning of the Greek city-state, moderate property ownership was essential. Aristotle had thus intuited a principle which held true not only in his own time but in Mosca's as well. For Mosca had observed that wherever and whenever the middle strata have declined economically, and thus politically, "the modern representative system has yielded its worst results." (p. 391.)

What Mosca liked particularly about Aristotle's system was that in it "not even the working classes, let alone slaves and metics, would be admitted to public office." (p. 427.) Furthermore, he had already perceived clearly in his

---

[3] Quoted in Meisel, *op cit.*, p. 254.

[4] *Ibid.*, p. 255.

[5] Mosca, *op. cit.*, p. 43. (Subsequent references will appear, as previously noted, in the text.)

time what certainly could not be doubted in the twentieth century, *viz.*, that it is human selfishness, that basic psychological trait, which makes private property inevitable. This is something which extreme democrats and collectivists deny, asserting instead the precise opposite: Man is not inherently selfish; it is the institution of private property which has engendered selfish conduct in him.

One must follow Aristotle and adapt his teachings to present conditions: Make whatever economic concessions to the lower and more populous classes that are absolutely necessary without, however, "impairing the inviolability of private property too seriously and without laying unbearable burdens upon large and moderate fortunes. Among these concessions one might mention shorter working hours, insurance against old age, illness, unemployment and accidents, and restrictions on labor by women and children." (p. 472.) Concessions may be made but they must not be carried "too far." They must be sufficient to assure political stability; and toward this end it has become evident that "improved economic conditions have on the whole made the laboring classes less prone to resort to desperate and violent acts." (p. 472.)

Mosca was thus reviving the "old doctrine of the golden mean" first found in Aristotle and later elaborated by others, notably, Montesquieu. Although the latter had replaced Aristotle's classification with his own—despotic, monarchical, and republican governments—he retained the theory of balance. Looking to England, he advocated a modified monarchy in which the executive, legislative, and judicial powers were separate, independent, and reciprocally checked and balanced. These principles could be found in their classic form in the English constitution whose advantages he described enthusiastically. Montesquieu had thus placed less emphasis than Aristotle on the role of social strata and forces and more on political, constitutional safeguards. Mosca therefore criticized Montesquieu and especially his followers who stressed the formal or legalistic aspect of the problem "rather than [its] substantial or social aspect. They have often forgotten that if one political institution is to be an effective curb upon the activity of another it must represent a political force—it must, that is, be the organized expression of a social influence and a social authority that has some standing in the community, as against the forces that are expressed in the political institution that is to be controlled." (p. 138.)

It is the "social forces" and the relationship among them that are of primary importance in maintaining a social equilibrium; but the formal and legal political devices, while only secondary, are nonetheless essential. Montesquieu's theory was perhaps incomplete but not "mistaken in any substantial respect." "To make his doctrine complete," writes Mosca, "one need add that a controlling and limiting political institution can be effective only when it represents a section of the political class that is different from the section represented by the institution to be limited and controlled." (p. 475.) Building in this way on the work of two great predecessors, Mosca develops the view that a ruling class is inevitable and the most one can hope for is a system of properly balanced social forces. Such balances have yielded the best political systems characterized by what he calls "juridical defense." The extension of juridical defense is the real meaning of progress.

Juridical Defense

The level of moral conscience of a people, as expressed in public opinion, religion, and law, is an indication of how far it has advanced from, say, barbarism to the various stages of civilization. In common with other nineteenth-century thinkers, Mosca accepted the evolutionary hypothesis— human history is an account of man's development from lower to higher cultural stages. A study of history shows that morality, justice, social order, and the like cannot be assured without instituting definite mechanisms to discipline the individuals and groups of society and to regulate the relations among them. The extent to which those mechanisms to assure respect for law have been developed determines the level of *juridical defense* and therefore the level of civilization a given society has achieved.

Men have instincts which are refractory to social order and discipline, and the control of those instincts cannot be entrusted to morality and religion alone. Adequate control requires a whole legislative system. The more a society succeeds in developing such effective systems, the better it is. In opposition to Rousseau (and Marx), then, who believed "that man is good by nature but that society makes him wicked and perverse," Mosca believed "that social organization provides for the reciprocal restraint of human individuals by one another and so makes them better, not by destroying their wicked instincts, but by accustoming them to controlling their wicked instincts." (p. 127.)

That religion alone is insufficient for the control of these instincts is proved by the fact that "if we place side by side two peoples of the same degree of barbarism, one of which has embraced Christianity and the other not, it will be found that in practice their behaviors are very much the same, or at least there is no appreciable difference between them." (p. 218.) Religious and moral sentiments are in themselves inadequate to afford the weak the protection they need. One sees, for example, that in "very religious countries, where the lower classes are completely at the mercy of the higher, it is no unusual thing to see masters beating their servants or other subordinates." (p. 129.) The conclusion is inescapable, therefore, that institutionalized juridical and legal means of defense are required if a society is to achieve some semblance of justice. The class structure of society and the consequent social inequalities and injustices will always be with us; such injustices can only be mitigated under an adequate political, legal, and juridical system. In Mosca's words:

The political organization proper, the organization that establishes the character of the relations between the governing class and the governed and between the various levels and various sections of the ruling class, is the factor that contributes more than any other to determining the degree of perfection that juridical defense, or government by law, can attain in a given people. (p. 130.)

Ultimately, such a system can prevail only where there are a number of "social forces" that mutually balance one another and where no single one of them is omnipotent or almost so. The absence or presence of such a balance explains, respectively, the difference between the system under the Czars, for instance, and the system in "England, where every arrest of an individual has to be legalized in earnest and very promptly." (p. 132.) For Mosca, as for Montesquieu, England was the model. There, presumably, juridical defense was more highly developed than elsewhere; classes and other social forces were reciprocally balanced; and government by law, civil liberties, and due process were firmly established principles. Moreover, the honesty and integrity of English governmental officials were beyond question. The more a political system departed from this model, the less just and moral it was.

Whatever the "political formula," whether it is divine right or popular sovereignty, "when no other organized social forces exist apart from those which represent the principle on which sovereignty over the nation is based, then there can be no resistance, no effective control, to restrain a natural tendency in those who stand at the head of the social order to abuse their powers." And in the absence of resistance, the ruling class undergoes a real moral degeneration, the degeneration that is common to all men whose acts are exempt from the restraint that the opinion and the conscience of their fellows ordinarily impose." (p. 134.) The absence of resistance leads to despotism or to what one might today call totalitarianism. There is no doubt, then, that Mosca was genuinely opposed to despotism. But in his scale of values, though this was "the worst of all political systems," it was "nevertheless preferable to anarchy, the absence of any government at all." (p. 137.)

Juridical defense depends on the ability of social forces to check and balance one another and on the separation of powers in the political system. Equally important is the separation of the ecclesiastical and temporal authorities and that the "political formula" should "have nothing sacred and immutable about it." If the rulers rule in the name of a formula which has a monopoly on truth and justice, then "it is almost impossible that its acts should be debated and moderated in practice." (p. 139.)

But there are still additional conditions on which juridical defense depends: (1) the distribution of wealth in a society, and (2) the organization of its military forces. From his discussion of the first point it becomes clear that Mosca felt that the issues raised by the socialists could not be ignored. The distribution of wealth had much to do not only with the social stability he desired, but with justice as well. Here important differences as between his approach and Pareto's emerge even clearer than before.

Whereas Pareto's élites seem to be floating above society, without roots in its class structure, Mosca gives explicit attention to the phenomenon of class. Political power is always rooted in definite "social forces," and the economic is among the most important of these. Although he does not arrange them in any permanent hierarchy of importance, since this would vary according to time and to place, he does regard the economic, political, legal, and military as the major social forces. In these terms, he generalized Marx's theory, much as did Weber, and argued that the control of the means of production, of political administration, of violence, etc. are all important in determining the structure of a society and its processes of change. Mosca also seems to have a greater concern with the issue of *justice* than Pareto, whose sociology often reads like a handbook for rulers. In the following passage, Mosca's treatment of the issue was not unlike that of the socialists in general and of the Marxists in particular.

Laws and institutions that guarantee justice and protect the rights of the weak cannot possibly be effective when wealth is so distributed that we get, on the one hand, a small number of persons possessing lands and mobile capital and, on the other, a multitude of proletarians who have no resource but the labor of their hands and owe it to the rich if they do not die of hunger from one day to the next. In that state of affairs to proclaim universal suffrage, or the rights of man, or the maxim that all are equal before the law, is merely ironical; and just as ironical is it to say that every man carries a marshal's baton in his knapsack, or that he is free some day to become a capitalist himself. (p. 143.)

Clearly, then, *real* juridical defense and just relationships require more than formal, legal mechanisms; and to the degree that liberal democracy ignores this fact, it connives in the perpetuation of sham liberalism and injustice. On the other hand, public ownership of the means of production, is also no solution, for it may result in something worse than the present system. Raising an objection to socialism not unlike Weber's, Mosca writes: "Insofar as the state absorbs and distributes a larger and larger portion of the public wealth, the leaders of the ruling class come to possess greater and greater facilities for influencing and commanding their subordinates, and more and more easily evade control by anybody." (p. 143.) For some reason which Mosca never provides, socialism and institutions of juridical defense cannot coexist in one social system. Neither socialism nor sham liberalism is the answer; the only real solution is to follow the leads of Aristotle and to work out a system based on the proper balance of liberal-democratic and aristocratic principles.

This means, first of all, that the distribution of wealth should be such as to eliminate the great extremes resulting in haves and have-nots. The good polity or what Mosca calls "a relatively perfect political organization" is one which "contains a large class of people whose economic position is virtually independent of those who hold supreme power." At least some of the members of this class must "have sufficient means to be able to devote a portion of their time to perfecting their culture and acquiring that interest in the public weal—that aristocratic spirit, we are almost tempted to say—which alone can induce people to serve their country with no other satisfactions than those that come from individual pride and self-respect. In all countries that ever have been, or now are, in the lead as regards juridical defense—or liberty, as it is sometimes called—such a class has been prominent." (p. 144.) Thus a large middle class and an aristocratic spirit are among the essential preconditions of the good society; and when these are lacking, "parliamentary government bears its worst fruits, as would any other political system." (p. 144.)

There are a number of social forces which militate against the establishment of a juridical equilibrium, chief among them being nationalism, the Church, large moneyed interests, and finally, social democracy. Any political system organized primarily on the basis of any single one of these forces, and its corresponding principles, makes it "difficult for all social forces to participate in public life, and more difficult still for any one force to counterbalance another. That is as true when power is in the hands of elected officials who are said to be chosen by the people as it is when power is entrusted exclusively to employees who are assumed to be appointed by a prince." (p. 147.) For Mosca, then, government in the name of the "people" may become as autocratic as any other.

Universal Suffrage

"Popular sovereignty" as a result of universal suffrage is a myth—a very dangerous myth, moreover, since through it the people are led to believe that they rule and that the elected officials are mere servants. In reality, however, the officials are just as much masters under this system as they are in all others. This, in essence, is Mosca's view of representative democracy; and, of course, it did not originate with him. The entire thesis was anticipated almost verbatim by Marx and Engels as Mosca knew very well. On the twentieth anniversary of the Paris Commune, Engels wrote:

> Society had created its own organs to look after its common interests, originally through simple division of labor. But these organs, at whose head was the state power, had in the course of time, in pursuance of their own special interests, transformed themselves from the servants of society into the masters of society. This can be seen, for example, not only in the hereditary monarchy, but equally so in the democratic republic. Nowhere do "politicians" form a more separate and powerful section of the nation than precisely in North America.[6]

But for Engels the process by which servants are transformed into masters was inevitable only under certain social conditions. The point of the Marxian analysis was to specify what those conditions were and by abolishing them to

---

[6] Karl Marx and Frederick Engels, Selected Works, Volume I (Moscow: Foreign Languages Publishing House, 1950), p. 438.

create new conditions of freedom. In Mosca's hands, however, Marx's *historically specific* thesis becomes a *universal law:* The transformation of servants into masters is inevitable in all systems, past, present, and future. Moreover, the so-called "servants" of the people under the representative system were never servants to begin with.

In actuality, the "representative" *"has himself elected";* and if this sounds "too inflexible and too harsh to fit some cases, we might qualify it by saying that *his friends have him elected."*[7] Elections do not change the fact that "those who have the will and, especially, the moral, intellectual, and material *means* to force their will upon others take the lead over the others and command them." (p. 154.) It is unavoidable in all social organizations that a minority will gain control of those *means* and thus over the lives and fate of the majority of men. Elections give the people no real freedom of choice "and the only ones who have any chance of succeeding are those whose candidates are championed by groups, by committees, by *organized minorities."* (p. 154.) And what are the criteria by which these minorities choose and support certain candidates? Mosca's reply, not unlike one Marx and Engels would have given, is that "as a rule they are based on considerations of property and taxation, on common material interests, on ties of family, class, religion, sect, or political party." (p. 155.)

But would Mosca go so far as to deny any and all influence on the part of the people? No! As was indicated in a previous comparison with Pareto's work, Mosca allows for some measure of influence on their part. The representative system, writes Mosca, "results in the participation of a certain number of social values in the guidance of the state, in the fact that many political forces which in an absolute state, a state ruled by a bureaucracy alone, would remain inert and without influence upon government become organized and so exert an influence on government." (p. 155.) After all, the candidates and other representatives of the ruling minorities cannot altogether ignore the various organized publics nor even the unorganized voters. They must win over their good will. The "sentiments and passions of the 'common herd' come to have their influence on the mental attitudes of the representatives themselves, and echoes of a widely disseminated opinion, or of any serious discontent, easily come to be heard in the highest spheres of government." (p. 155.)

Even the most despotic of regimes cannot ignore the sentiments of the masses or offend them with impunity. The representative system, however, allows for greater sensitivity to their discontent, since each incumbent knows that the grumblings and dissatisfaction of all the people could easily lead to his ouster and to the victory of another organized minority.

In Mosca's various discussions, the "people" is occasionally portrayed as a "common herd" whose behavior is governed by "sentiments" and "passions"

---

[7] Mosca, *op. cit.,* p. 154. (Subsequent references to this work will appear by page number in the text.)

—by irrational forces. There is some resemblance here between his conception and Pareto's, but Mosca remains, by and large, more consistently sociological. If the people generally have little or no rational understanding of their existential conditions and interests, it is because they are "poor and ignorant." They are uneducated, culturally impoverished, unorganized, and powerless. Normally, they have no means of control over the powerful. "In these circumstances," Mosca writes, "of the various organized minorities that are disputing the field, that one infallibly wins which spends most money or lies most persuasively." (p. 156.) The recurring emphasis on these social conditions leaves the door open to the *possibility* of changing them—a point to which we shall later return.

Disposition over social forces is what gives the various organized minorities their political significance. One of them will always win out, become the *political class,* and fulfill the political function. The point, then, is not to dream of a day when classes and ruling classes will be no more, but to devise, under the given circumstances, the best political system possible. Returning once more to Aristotle, Montesquieu, and the English political system, Mosca writes that such a system "enables all the elements that have a political significance in a given society to be best utilized and specialized, best subjected to reciprocal control and to the principle of individual responsibility for the things that are done in the respective domains." (p. 159.) In England, though it is true that officials are elected or appointed, it is nonetheless true that it is the "prominent people" who fulfill the main political functions, and without pay. These people have that aristocratic spirit expressed so well in the French saying, *noblesse oblige,* which is so essential for the good polity.

Parliamentarism

In Mosca's discussion of parliaments, one sees some similarities to Pareto's treatment of representative government, but these are mainly superficial, since despite Mosca's criticisms he regards parliamentary institutions as an essential aspect of liberal government—an opinion Pareto, judging from his later writings, did not share. It is true, Mosca acknowledges, that particularly the elective, lower houses of parliaments are often characterized by "prattlings," "long-winded speeches," and "futile bickerings." It is also true, as the socialists and anarchists allege, that it is not the majority's interests, opinions, and aspirations that are there represented, "but the interests of the wealthy ruling classes." (p. 255.) Finally, there is no denying the excessive interference on the part of individual members in the workings of the administration generally and in the distribution of wealth through taxation and other devices. These main defects of parliament as an institution had become so conspicuous by Mosca's time that they came to be designated by the pejorative term "parliamentarism." (Incidentally, Marx had already discerned them in the 1850's and had termed the state, "parliamentary cretinism.")

Yet, these defects are as nothing in their evil consequences compared with the situation that would result from the abolition of parliament and other representative institutions. Under prevailing conditions, Mosca insists, "the suppression of representative assemblies would inevitably be followed by a type of regime that is commonly called 'absolute.' " Suppression would result in a totalitarian system in which all social forces and values were subordinated to the ruling group and its bureaucracy. A disgust with "parliamentarism" and a fear of the revolutionary fervor of social democracy could lead, Mosca prophetically observes, to an "absolutely bureaucratic" order. "What we cannot admit is that such a step would be a wise one. We need give no long demonstration of that thesis in view of all that we have been saying as to the dangers and drawbacks involved in giving absolute predominance to a single political force that is not subject to any limitation or discussion whatever." (p. 256.)

Thus Mosca is unequivocally opposed to the weakening of the representative system. The repeatedly pronounced emphasis he places on the vital importance of liberal institutions is altogether absent from Pareto's later works. The collapse of these institutions, Mosca maintains, would lead to "moral ruin," to the violations of "juridical defense, of justice, of everything that we commonly call 'liberty'; and those violations would be far more pernicious than any that can be laid to the charge of even the most dishonest of parliamentary governments, let alone of representative governments." (p. 257.)

Mosca is thus directing this argument in two opposing directions. Against the more zealous opponents of democracy and socialism he is arguing that the destruction of representative and liberal government would result in something far worse. And to the socialists, Marxian and others, he is saying that they ought to abandon their utopian dogmas about the abolition of classes—including the ruling class. The best system (and best, too, because capable of realization) is not the classless society but the one advocated by Aristotle, Montesquieu, and himself—namely, a system permitting the various organized social forces to moderate and balance one another. The socialists would resign themselves to this if they were to realize that even under the most equalitarian of systems a ruling class would inevitably arise, since the people would still have to choose their representatives "from among candidates who would be put forward by groups, or committees, and these groups would be made up of persons who by taste and by interest would be actively devoted to political life." (p. 259.)

The primary evil of the parliamentary form of government is that more often than not it is the members of the lower, elected chamber who control the bureaucracy; and it is precisely these men who have only one eye on their professional responsibilities, the other being on the electorate. This makes for a situation in which their desire to govern well is "effectively thwarted by their no less natural desire to serve their own personal interests, and the sense of professional duty in ministers and representatives is always balanced by all sorts of ambitions and vanities, justified and unjustified." (p. 259.) What Mosca is here suggesting, once more, is that this "evil" results from the inadequate assertion of the aristocratic tendency, so necessary for sound and healthy government. If ministers were sufficiently independent of the electorate, they would be less subject to pressures of personal ambitions and party interests and hence more concerned with their professional responsibilities. What is required is that the "governors" be drawn from that stratum of citizens who are both wealthy enough to be incorruptible and educated enough to govern wisely.

Mosca was calling for the development of a public-spirited, nonbureaucratic civil service, "a special class of volunteer unsalaried officials," as it once prevailed in England. Eventually, the "democratic current" swept away this institution, revealing pointedly, again, the main dangers and evils of the democratic philosophy: It "recognizes no political act, no political prerogative, as legitimate unless it emanates directly or indirectly from popular suffrage." (p. 270.) The democratic principle has successfully suppressed the aristocratic, and with very undesirable results. Historically, it was a mistake to grant universal suffrage, but now it is too late to "go back on it without committing a second mistake which might have unforeseeable consequences of a very serious nature." (p. 492.) One must therefore make the best of the existing situation by strengthening the aristocratic principle. This, together with a large middle class, a system of balanced social forces, and institutions of juridical defense, makes for the best system possible. But the good system requires still another condition which, strange as it may sound, is a standing army.

Standing Armies

History teaches, writes Mosca, "that the class that bears the lance or holds the musket regularly forces its rule upon the class that handles the spade or pushes the shuttle." (p. 228.) This was also true of pre-modern Europe, where the class that controlled the means of violence acquired economic and political power as well. What Mosca found altogether intriguing, then, was the contemporary situation where the military was successfully subordinated to the civil authority. This became possible "only through an intense and widespread development of the sentiments on which juridical defense is based, and especially through an exceptionally favorable sequence of historical circumstances." (p. 229.) Ironic as it may appear, Mosca asserts, the control of the military and other groups with access to means of violence was facilitated by the institution called the *standing army*.

Mosca's reasoning rests on the assumption that in every society there are those who have a greater inclination than others toward adventure, belligerence, aggression, and violence. These make up the bands of armed men who in some societies, the "loosely organized," rule and terrorize every village and town. In other societies, the "better organized," they become a ruling class, "lords and masters of all wealth and political influence," as they did in medieval Europe. In bureaucratic states, finally, the standing army, being unrestrained and unchecked, has "no difficulty in dictating to the rest of society." (p. 228.) In none of these types of society is the military controlled by a civil authority. Only in those societies, therefore, in which (1) *the standing army is combined with* (2) *institutions of social balance and juridical defense* does one find the hegemony of the civil authority. One without the other would not have produced this result.

Before the standing army was institutionalized, it was the adventurers and criminals who were recruited as needed. But by the beginning of the eighteenth century the "necessity of keeping many men in arms and the difficulty of paying wages large enough to attract volunteers brought on conscription in most countries on the European continent. That system meant that common soldiers no longer came from the adventurous and criminal classes but were recruited from among peasants and workingmen. . . ." (p. 232.) It meant, too, that now the class structure of the society as a whole became the basis of the military structure—*i.e.*, that the authority of the upper classes as well as the submissiveness of the lower were transferred to the military sphere. Officers were recruited almost exclusively from the upper strata and common soldiers from the lower. The men at the top of the military hierarchy retained "close ties with the minority which by birth, culture, and wealth [stood] at the peak of the social pyramid." (p. 233.) This, together with the deeply rooted institutions of juridical defense explains, according to Mosca, why in England and the United States, for example, the army did not become "a tool for coups d' état." In those countries and others with similar conditions, "the standing army has so far stripped the class of persons who have natural tastes and capacities for violence of their monopoly of the military function." It follows, Mosca reasons, that enduring peace would bring with it the dissolution of the standing army and, hence, a regression to the state in which the bold and violent oppressed "the weak and peaceful." Therefore, he concludes, "war itself—in its present forms the root of so many evils, the parent of so many barbarities—becomes necessary every now and again if what is best in the functioning of our Western societies today is not to decline and retrogress to lower types of juridical defense." (p. 243.) Ultimately, Mosca was led to this pessimistic conclusion, which he himself called "grave and terrible," by his view of human nature as essentially *base, selfish, and brutish.*

Some Critical Remarks

Some of the criticisms earlier leveled at Pareto's theory are equally applicable to Mosca's, for both thinkers based their systems, ultimately, on a conception of "natural man" in all respects antithetical to that of Rousseau and Marx. Human nature, as Pareto and Mosca conceived it, is faithfully described by the final italicized words of the preceding paragraph: base, selfish, brutish. Though both thinkers made much of having stripped themselves "of every partisan passion, every interest, every fear," what Karl Popper has observed with respect to Pareto applies equally, or almost so, to Mosca: "His own prejudice is the anti-humanitarian religion. Had he seen that his choice was not between prejudice and freedom from prejudice, but only between the humanitarian prejudice and the anti-humanitarian prejudice, he might perhaps have felt a little less confident of his superiority."[8] If injustice, inequality, and the absence of freedom have been and continue to be the main characteristics of the human condition, then this "must somehow correspond," Mosca believed, "to the political nature of man."[9] This was the fundamental assumption of Mosca's social and political theory—a polemical and unwarranted assumption with which to combat Marx. But his understanding of Marx was inadequate.

In his excellent and thorough study, James H. Meisel has shown that Mosca knew firsthand only a few fragments of Marx's total work and relied for his judgment of that thinker on secondary sources. Mosca took "the word of a few experts, or, worse, of the journalists and social-democratic agitators whose Karl Marx was of the bargain-counter variety rather than the truthful image of the ponderous yet subtle scholar of *Das Kapital*." And, Meisel continues: "In all the 476 pages of *The Ruling Class* one finds not more than one direct quotation from Marx—a fact which would hardly merit notice if the subject matter did not play such a great role in Mosca's mind."[10] Perhaps that is the reason why Mosca never fully understood the subtleties of Marx's emphasis on the economic structure of society as the basis, for example, of political and military power. With his scanty knowledge of Marx's work he sought to relativize his theory by means of such categories as "social forces"; the result was a theory which not only failed to supersede that of Marx but never even attained its insights. This allegation may be supported by showing that Marx and Engels anticipated everything of value in Mosca's system but that he, in turn, failed to understand what was valid in theirs. In his introduction to Marx's *Class Struggles in France, 1848–1850*, Engels wrote:

> All revolutions up to the present day have resulted in the displacement of one definite class rule by another; but all ruling classes up to now have been only small minorities in relation to the ruled mass of the people. One ruling minority was thus overthrown; another minority seized the helm of state in its stead and refashioned the state institutions to suit its own interests. This was on every occasion the minority group qualified and called to rule by the given degree of economic development; and just for that reason, and only for that reason, it happened that the ruled majority either participated in the revolution for the benefit of the former or else calmly acquiesced in it. But if we disregard the concrete content in each case, the common form of all these revolutions was that they were

8 Karl Popper, *The Open Society and Its Enemies* (New York and Evanston: Harper Torchbooks, 1963), p. 318.

9 Mosca, *op. cit.*, p. 397.

10 Meisel, *op. cit.*, pp. 296–97.

minority revolutions. Even when the majority took part, it did so—whether wittingly or not—only in the service of a minority; but because of this, or even simply because of the passive, unresisting attitude of the majority, this minority acquired the appearance of being the representative of the whole people.[11]

Here one sees clearly all of Mosca's major concepts and even his central theme. He, on the other hand, did not see the connection between economic development and class formation. Marx and Engels understood very well the phenomena of "minority revolutions," "ruling classes," and "political formulae"—what they called "false consciousness" or "false representations." But for them, these were not eternal categories, the results of man's constant psychological nature. Since their view of human nature did not preclude it, they went on to formulate a proposition which was at the very least *sociologically* consistent and unassailable: "If, in all the longer revolutionary periods," Engels asked, "it was so easy to win the great masses of the people by the merely plausible false representations of the forward-thrusting minorities, why should they be less susceptible to ideas which were the truest reflection of their economic condition, which were nothing but the clear, rational expression of their needs. . . . ?"[12]

Moreover, once the majority did rise up, it was not at all inevitable that their representatives should degenerate into ruling élites, oligarchs, or ruling minorities. Describing the Paris Commune of 1871, Engels wrote:

Against this transformation of the state and the organs of the state from servants of society into masters of society—an inevitable transformation in all previous states—the Commune made use of two infallible means. In the first place, it filled all posts—administrative, judicial, and educational—by election on the basis of universal suffrage of all concerned, subject to the right of recall at any time by the same electors. And, in the second place, all officials, high or low, were paid only the wages received by other workers. . . . In this way an effective barrier to place-hunting and careerism was set up, even apart from the binding mandates to delegates to representative bodies which were added besides.[13]

This was to lead, ultimately, to social conditions in which the whole state apparatus would be thrown on the scrap heap of history. And while it is quite obvious that this vision has not been realized, it is equally obvious that the failure cannot be attributed, on the basis of the scientific knowledge available, to the basic psychological nature of man—particularly since an "experiment" such as the Commune has never been given a chance to succeed. Nevertheless, a disciple of Mosca, Robert Michels, also based his theory of the inevitability of oligarchy on causes "inherent in human psychology," in "the nature of the human individual."[14]

11 Marx and Engels, *op cit.*, pp. 113–14.
12 *Ibid.*, p. 114.
13 *Ibid.*, p. 439.
14 Robert Michels, *Political Parties* (New York: Dover Publications, Inc., 1959), pp. vii and viii.

14

Robert Michels

(1876–1936)

In common with Weber, Pareto, and Mosca, Robert Michels devoted a large part of his intellectual labors to the challenge of Marxism. And it was primarily the ideas of these antecedent thinkers which Michels employed and elaborated in the development of his own critique. Yet, despite certain criticisms of Marx's social thought, he remained something of a reconstructed Marxist himself; rejecting what he regarded as the utopian aspects of the Marxian vision, he retained elements of the Marxian method of analysis.

In 1927, sixteen years after *Political Parties* first appeared, Michels delivered at the University of Rome a series of lectures on political sociology. In these lectures, published under the title *Corso di Sociologia Politica*, he concerned himself with what he considered to be a major theoretical issue: the relative validity of Marx's conception of society and history. Noting a fact Marx himself was the first to acknowledge, *viz.*, that aspects of his economic interpretation of history had been anticipated by many thinkers before him, Michels writes: "The Arab philosopher, Ibn Kaldun, who lived in the fourteenth century, may have been the earliest scientific exponent of the economic conception of history."[1]

---

[1] Roberto Michels, *First Lectures in Political Sociology*, translated by Alfred de Grazia (New York: Harper and Row, Publishers, 1965), p. 10.

As for classes and class conflicts, these phenomena were also observed before Marx placed them at the center of his investigation. Michels cites Benjamin Disraeli, who had portrayed in his novel entitled *Sybil* the great cultural chasm that lay between the upper and lower classes. So great was this chasm, in fact, that English society could be viewed as *two nations*. In his novel Disraeli "repeated the idea that had caused him in his parliamentary discourse of 1840 to declare that the recognition of the proletariat's rights to its political emancipation and the betterment of its economic conditions was the only way to close the abyss that already separated the 'two nations.' "[2] Other thinkers— English, French, and German—had also anticipated elements of Marx's general conception; but this is not to deny, Michels emphasizes, the originality of the Marxian synthesis. It "is an indisputable merit of Marx and Engels to have been the first not only to erect as a system the particular part that the productive forces play in the historic process, but also to have assigned to them, with the creation of a new philosophy, their place in science."[3]

To underscore this point, Michels shows that even Pareto, a major opponent of Marxism, appreciated the scientific aspects of Marx's system. "Historical materialism," wrote Pareto in his *Trattato di Sociologia Generale,* "has been a notable scientific advance because it has helped to clarify the contingent character of certain phenomena, such as moral phenomena and religious phenomena, to which was given, and is given yet by many, an absolute character. Besides it certainly has an element of truth in insisting on the interdependence of economic phenomena and other social phenomena; the error stands in having changed this *interdependence* to a relationship of cause and effect."[4] Pareto also acknowledged the value of Marx's sociological principles which "discredited the unreal notion of those who want to explain facts with the ideas that men hold."[5]

This general attitude toward Marxism, shared in varying degrees by Pareto, Weber, and Benedetto Croce, was Michels' as well. There are invaluable principles and insights to be found in Marx's "materialist conception" which can be incorporated into a scientific sociology minus the "subversive flavor" of Marxism. Michels thus agreed with Croce who observed that "historical materialism, deprived of the elements of finality or inevitable utopia which Marxist socialism wanted to confer upon it, cannot give any support to socialism or to any other practical way of life. The economic conception of history is a doctrine that explains the reasons, the genesis, but does not help to illuminate socialism, which is a wishful vision of the future. It is silent on the outcome of the struggle it has traced through history."[6] In the remainder of his lectures, Michels seeks "to mark the boundaries within

2 *Ibid.,* p. 16.
3 *Ibid.,* p. 18.
4 Quoted by Michels in *Ibid.,* p. 19.
5 *Ibid.,* p. 21.
6 *Ibid.,* p. 21.

which historical materialism conforms to historical truth, and above all to examine its place in political science."[7]

Following Weber, Pareto, and Mosca, Michels reconstructs Marx's method and calls for a more pluralistic approach: "The complete view of things results from the action of several forces of dissimilar nature."[8] He fully acknowledges the fundamental importance of economic developments for social change; in this Marx was right. But what Marx had allegedly overlooked was that there were other forces or tendencies at work sufficiently strong to preclude the realization of democracy and socialism as he had envisioned it. For Michels, these tendencies were "dependent: (1) upon the nature of the human individual; (2) upon the nature of the political struggle; and (3) upon the nature of organization."[9] What Marx had not seen, according to Michels, was that as a result of these tendencies, "democracy leads to oligarchy, and necessarily contains an oligarchical nucleus." This is the central thesis which Michels develops in his classic study, *Political Parties*.

The most effective documentation of this thesis could be made, Michels reasoned, by describing the structure and tendencies of the various social-democratic parties in Europe. The aristocratic and oligarchical character of the various *conservative* parties was indisputable. But this, after all, was to be expected, and proved nothing since they had no commitment to democracy and based themselves quite frankly and unabashedly on conservative principles. If, on the other hand, oligarchical phenomena could be found "in the very bosom of the revolutionary parties" which professed to represent or to be working toward the negation of these phenomena, then this would constitute "conclusive proof of the existence of immanent oligarchical tendencies in every kind of human organization which strives for the attainment of definite ends." (p. 11.)

Ultimately, the "immanence" of these tendencies rests, for Michels, on certain innate human tendencies which urge man to transmit his material possessions to his legitimate heir or other kin. The same applies to "political power [which] comes also to be considered as an object of private hereditary ownership." (p. 12.) These tendencies prevail due to "the peculiar and inherent instincts of mankind," but they are also "vigorously nourished by the economic order based upon private property in the means of production. . . ." (p. 12.) Herein lies the theoretical dilemma he never managed to resolve: Is the quest for power and material goods to be regarded as a function of the socio-economic order in which men live, or is it a result of an immutable human psychology? By his own admission, an ideal democracy is impossible under "the existing economic and social conditions." But if he followed that logic

7 *Ibid.*, p. 21.
8 *Ibid.*, p. 54.
9 Robert Michels, *Political Parties* (New York: Dover Publications, Inc., 1959), p. viii. (All subsequent references to this work will appear by page number in the text.)

to the end, there could be no "iron law," since oligarchic and other social tendencies are contingent upon the existing social system. Michels therefore places great emphasis on so-called innate psychological laws.

Like Pareto and Mosca before him, Michels rested his general argument as to the inevitability of oligarchy on a conception of human nature precisely the opposite of that held by Marx. It is man's *inherent* nature to crave power and once having attained it to seek to perpetuate it. On the basis of this psychological assumption, Michels generates his theory that democracy requires organization which in turn leads *necessarily* to oligarchy. This, his "iron law of oligarchy" is, he says, "like every other sociological law, beyond good and evil"—and this so-called "sociological law" rests on what he took to be a constant, *his* conception of human nature. He never seriously considers what Marx had constantly emphasized: That what may appear as a law under certain social conditions—*e.g.*, capitalist institutions and values—must not be considered a law under all circumstances; that it is a fundamental error to treat a "social law" either as universally valid or as objective in the sense of being beyond good and evil and independent of men's will under all conditions.

In Marx's view social conditions typically elicit a subjective response from men; how they define those conditions, whether good or evil, can make a difference for the perpetuation or abolition of those conditions. There are, to be sure, certain periods when social conditions appear to impose insuperable limits on the actions of men; but there are other periods when opportunities for change emerge. Given the consciousness of these opportunities on the part of a sufficient number of men who are willing to act in concert, and such opportunities may be seized. Michels himself acknowledged that the "democratic currents of history," though they "break ever on the same shoal" are "ever renewed." And it would seem undeniable that at least part of the reason for this renewal is that the oligarchies are felt by the people to be oppressive and are thus overthrown. What Michels insists upon, however, is that the democratic currents will inevitably break again and again upon the same shoal. This is his "universally applicable iron law" which, however, can be entertained only if one accepts his underlying concept of man.

Nevertheless, there can be no doubt that the facts *qua* facts which Michels described were true. His study is a sound sociological description of what *is*—which is not to say that the pessimistic conclusions often drawn from his analysis are valid. Moreover, a brief review of that analysis will show that he himself had his more optimistic moments and that in the end he allowed for the interpretation that his "iron law" must not be regarded as anything more than a metaphor—a metaphor which he employed to dramatize certain conspicuous tendencies of men in organizations under specific socio-historical circumstances.

The people are incapable of governing themselves! Michels' support of this assertion is based first on the theory of crowds and crowd psychology: "It is easier to dominate a large crowd than a small audience." A crowd is easily given to suggestion and irrational outbursts; both serious discussion and thoughtful deliberation are impossible in its midst. Second, and more important, however, is the technical and practical problem of involving the huge multitudes in democratic decision making. If democratic is taken to mean that the multitude adopts resolutions and makes decisions *directly,* then democracy is indeed impossible. Rousseau understood this and so did most of the other later democratic theorists. Michels quotes Louis Blanc who in his polemic against Proudhon asked "whether it is possible for thirty-four millions of human beings (the population of France at the time) to carry on their affairs without . . . the intermediation of representatives." (p. 25.) What is true of nation-states is also true of modern organizations. The staggering demographic proportions of the socialist parties Michels studied made both direct discussion and direct action impossible. The party in Berlin alone, for example, had a membership "of more than ninety thousand."

The enormity of the populations in modern party organizations renders it technically impossible for all members to govern or administer directly their common affairs. Unavoidably, then, once a collectivity is formed for any specific purpose and attains to a certain demographic size, a division of labor becomes necessary. As the organization grows larger, this growth is accompanied by an increasing complexity. New functions emerge and are distributed, and along with this differentiation of functions comes the delegation of authority. Men are chosen to "represent the mass and carry out its will."

In the early stages of this development—speaking more particularly about organizations based upon democratic and socialistic ideals—the various functions stand in a *coordinate* relationship to one another: no hierarchy is implied in the various functions and positions. They are all equal in the sense that differential amounts of wealth or power are not associated with the various positions. The social honor accorded the "chief" does not enable him to transform that honor into special perquisites and privileges. In Michels' words: "Originally the chief is merely the servant of the mass." (p. 27.)

At first the democratic and equalitarian character of the organization is assured by the strong commitment on the part of its members to the principles of democracy and equality. Functions are rotated, delegates and representatives are totally subject to the will of the collectivity, and in general a high degree of camaraderie prevails. This was true of the early English labor movement, for example. But this state of affairs is possible only when the organization in question is relatively small in scale. The growing scale of the organization makes this form of democracy increasingly inapplicable. In addition to size, however, there is still another important variable involved which is at least in part a function of the organization's growth. Within the division of labor, certain tasks and duties become more complicated and require ability, training, and "a considerable amount of objective knowledge." (p. 28.) Differentiation of functions now implies specialization and specialization, in turn, expertise. Party schools are established to train functionaries and officials, and what results is "a class of professional politicians, of approved and registered experts in political life." Michels notes that "Ferdinand Tönnies advocates that the party should institute regular examinations for the nomination of socialist parliamentary candidates, and for the appointment of party secretaries." (p. 29.)

Expertise becomes a "foot in the door." The experts increasingly resemble not servants but masters and the organization becomes increasingly hierarchical and bureaucratic. Acquiring to an ever greater degree the attributes of leaders, the experts withdraw from the masses and concentrate in their hands a variety of prerogatives. In Michels' words:

> It is undeniable that all these educational institutions for the officials of the party and of the labor organizations tend, above all, toward the artificial creation of an *élite* of the working class, of a caste of cadets composed of persons who aspire to the command of the proletarian rank and file. Without wishing it, there is thus effected a continuous enlargement of the gulf which divides the leaders from the masses. (p. 31.)

Thus, the familiar process by which men originally appointed to serve the interests of the collectivity soon develop interests of their own often opposed to that collectivity. What began as a democratic and equalitarian situation culminated in leaders and led, in rulers and ruled. It is organization *qua* organization which is the efficient cause of this transformation. Democracy implies organization and organization, in turn, "implies the tendency to oligarchy. . . . As a result of organization, every party or professional union becomes divided into a minority of directors and a majority of directed." (p. 32.) This general proposition Michels expresses in a variety of ways: "With the advance of organization, democracy tends to decline. Democratic evolution has a parabolic course. . . . It may be enunciated as a general rule that the increase in the power of the leaders is directly proportional with the extension of the organization." (p. 33.)

According to Michels, then, every organization, however democratic in its inception, given a growth in its membership and complexity, increasingly exhibits oligarchic and bureaucratic tendencies. What began as a technical and practical necessity is transformed into a virtue: Democracy and equality *within* the party are now no longer regarded as essential and a new ideology emerges to justify the changes wrought by the "inexorable" processes of organization.

> Not even the most radical wing of the various socialist parties [writes Michels] raises any objection to this retrogressive evolution, the contention being that democracy is only a form of organization and that where it ceases to be possible to harmonize democracy with organization, it is better to abandon the former than the latter. Organization, since it is only

the means of attaining the ends of socialism, is considered to comprise within itself the revolutionary content of the party, and this essential content must never be sacrificed for the sake of form. (p. 35.)

In this way and by insisting, in addition, "that true democracy cannot be installed until the fight is over" the members are persuaded that it is the highest revolutionary virtue to be disciplined and to follow faithfully a few individuals at the top. The organization as an instrument of class struggle now adopts rather easily the vocabulary of military science: "There is hardly one expression of military tactics and strategy, hardly even a phrase of barrack slang, which does not recur again and again in the leading articles of the socialist press." (p. 43.)

"Experience" and "expertise" are among the main words the leaders use to legitimize their positions of power. The impression is created among the rank and file that their leaders are indeed indispensable. Indispensability, whether apparent or real, becomes an efficient tool in the leader's hands. Whenever his decisions or judgments are challenged, he threatens to resign—which appears as a fine democratic gesture, but which in reality is intended to remind his followers of his indispensability and hence to force their submission to his will.

Generally, it is Michels' view that the masses have a need for leadership and are actually quite content to have others attend to their affairs. And, of course, this serves to strengthen the aristocratic and bureaucratic character of the party or union.

The masses are apathetic. None of the reasons for this, however, which Michels adduces need lead to the conclusion that this must be their permanent attribute—what he later calls the "perennial incompetence of the masses." That they are indifferent is evident, Michels writes, from the "slackness of attendance at ordinary meetings." And since the various political and ideological issues "are not merely beyond the understanding of the rank and file, but leave them altogether cold," they are incompetent. Some of the reasons for slackness of attendance, Michels himself notes, are really quite simple and prosaic: "When his work is finished, the proletarian can think only of rest and of getting to bed in good time." (p. 52.) There is, then, "an immense need for direction and guidance [which] is accompanied by a genuine cult for the leaders, who are regarded as heroes." (p. 53.) Add to this the great differences in culture and education between the leaders and the rank and file (the former more often than not being of bourgeois origin, as we shall see), and one understands the submissiveness of the ordinary members.

While these tendencies are "manifest in the political parties of all countries," Michels notes that Germany is a special case. And his observations in this connection must be considered important, because his own earliest experiences and impressions were in the German movement—where the submission of the masses and adulation of the leaders were greater than elsewhere. He writes:

The German people in especial exhibits to an extreme degree the need for someone to point out the way and to issue orders. This peculiarity, common to all classes not excepting the proletariat, furnishes a psychological soil upon which a powerful directive hegemony can flourish luxuriantly. There exist among the Germans all the preconditions necessary for such a development: a psychical predisposition to subordination, a profound instinct for discipline, in a word, the whole still persistent inheritance of the influence of the Prussian drill sergeant, with all its advantages and all its disadvantages; in addition, a trust in authority which verges on the complete absence of a critical faculty. (p. 53.)

And Michels notes further that Marx was quite aware of the "risks to the democratic spirit" of this national character and that "he thought it necessary to warn the German workers against entertaining too rigid a conception of organization." Marx insisted that in Germany, "where the workers are bureaucratically controlled from birth upward, and for this reason have a blind faith in constituted authority, it is above all necessary to teach them to walk by themselves." (p. 55.)

As for the German leaders, on the other hand, "Engels," writes Michels, "regarded it as deplorable that [they] could not accustom themselves to the idea that the mere fact of being installed in office did not give them the right to be treated with more respect than any other comrade." (p. 222.) The leaders of the German socialist party thought and acted in a manner reminiscent of the Sun King; each was inclined to think of himself, in Michel's phrase, *"Le Parti c'est moi."*

Michels cites the remarkable stability of both the German and the Italian socialist parties. The latter, he says, "for the same reasons as in Germany, has exhibited a similar stability." (p. 93.) It is interesting that these were the parties with which he had firsthand experience and the two main cases on which he based his generalizations.

The masses, then, are politically indifferent and incompetent (in need of guidance), and these factors together with the gratitude and veneration they show toward those "who speak and write in their behalf" strengthen the position of the leaders. Their need for a religion is evident from the idolatrous manner in which they venerate the party's secular books, symbols, and leaders; and this "is not peculiar to backward countries or remote periods; it is an atavistic survival of primitive psychology." (p. 66.) Moreover, they are easily hoodwinked and deceived, more inclined to follow mediocre men with a flair for showmanship than men of talent and cultivation. This explains why Eduard Bernstein and Paul Lafargue, for instance, remained relatively unknown to the rank and file of their respective parties: Both were men of outstanding intelligence and scientific sophistication but they were also lacking in oratorical talent.

There are still other "peculiarities of the masses" that contribute to both their incompetence and indifference and to the superiority of the leaders. These peculiarities are reflected in the age-composition of the general membership of the socialist parties and unions. "The great majority of the membership ranges in age from 25 to 39 years." The young have other things to do with their leisure; "they are heedless, their thoughts run in erotic channels, they are always hoping that some miracle will deliver them from the need of passing their whole lives as simple wage earners, and for these reasons they are slow to join a trade union." (p. 78.) The older men, on the other hand, who have become "weary and disillusioned, commonly resign their membership. . . . In other words, the leaders have to do with a mass of members to whom they are superior in respect of age and experience of life, whilst they have nothing to fear from the relentless criticism which is so peculiarly characteristic of men who have just attained to virility." (p. 78.)

Many factors contribute to the widening distance between masses and leaders. In many countries, party leaders are of a predominantly middle-class origin and therefore possess from the beginning a cultural or intellectual superiority. But even in those countries where there are few intellectuals in the leadership, as was the case in Germany in Michels' time, a similar *distance* develops between leaders of working-class origin and the general membership. This Michels explains in the following ways:

> Whilst their occupation with the needs of daily life render it impossible for the masses to attain to a profound knowledge of the social machinery, and above all of the working of the political machine, the leader of working-class origin is enabled, thanks to his new situation, to make himself intimately familiar with all the technical details of public life, and thus to increase his superiority over the rank and file. (pp. 81–82.)

And again:

> The questions which they [leaders of working-class origin] have to decide, and whose effective decision demands on their part a serious work of preparation, involve an increase in their own technical competence, and a consequent increase in the distance between themselves and their comrades of the rank and file. Thus the leaders, if they are not "cultured" already, soon become so. But culture exercises a suggestive influence over the masses. (p. 83.)

Finally:

> This special competence, this expert knowledge, which the leader acquires in matters inaccessible, or almost inaccessible, to the mass, gives him a security of tenure which conflicts with the essential principles of democracy. (p. 84.)

Again and again we are told that "the incompetence of the masses is almost universal throughout the domains of political life, and this constitutes the most solid foundation of the power of the leaders." (p. 86.) The expertise of the leaders also leads to oligarchy, since the incompetent masses submit to them and give them "an authority which is in the long run destructive of democracy." (p. 86.) However, a careful reading of Michels' work shows that his analysis is "one-sided," as he himself admits in the end.

If he was asserting something more than the thesis that there will always be a need for some kind of leadership—in the sense that a symphony orchestra probably will always require a conductor—then he did not distinguish carefully the difference between leaders and oligarchs. His positivistic posture prevented him from seeing that it is at least in part a moral and subjective issue to decide whether or not leaders are to be regarded as oligarchs. The very "law" which he asserts is beyond good and evil depends in the last analysis on such judgments. As an objective scientific proposition one could perhaps "demonstrate" the *technical* impossibility on the part of the masses of governing themselves *directly*. In that case one would be demonstrating the need for leadership, not for oligarchy.

To pursue the example of the symphony orchestra, many have tried, but have failed, *to conduct themselves*. It is generally agreed among students of this question that a conductor is a technical necessity for the functioning of a symphony orchestra. If this is the case, one can say that so-and-so is a good or bad conductor, depending on the aesthetic results he achieves, but it makes no sense to say that he is an autocrat because he has remained in "office" for a long time and has "ruled" with an iron hand.

Insofar as there may be objective criteria of oligarchy, Michels does not define them precisely; *i.e.*, he does not indicate at what point the elected representatives cease to be mere leaders and become oligarchs. At times Michels uses the term "oligarchy" simply to describe remarkable stability or longevity of leadership—*e.g.*, for more than thirty years. At other times, however, he uses the term to refer to the "aristocracy" of talent and expertise that inevitably emerges and separates itself from the mass. Specialization creates authority: "Just as the patient obeys the doctor," writes Michels, "because the doctor knows better than the patient, having made a special study of the human body in health and disease, so must the political patient submit to the guidance of his party leaders, who possess a political competence impossible of attainment by the rank and file." (p. 89.)

But this analogy does not seem really appropriate for Michels' purposes. Was the purpose of his study merely to demonstrate that specialization leads to authority, in the sense conveyed by the above-quoted passage? Surely he was after something more than this. Otherwise why call it oligarchy? What he really wanted to demonstrate was the inevitability of the *abuse* of power and authority—to the extent of undermining democracy: that those who are placed in positions of authority to serve the interests of the collectivity, soon develop interests of their own which are antagonistic to those of the collectivity. And it would seem that whether or not this in fact occurs is the best criterion by which to determine whether those in authority have become oligarchs. Yet, this is not the way Michels proceeds: too often he employs the concepts of leadership and oligarchy as if they were necessarily synonymous and interchangeable.

As compared with the leaders of other political parties, Michels acknowledges, the abuse of power was drastically reduced among the leaders of the social-democratic parties; party work was more often based on idealism and the leaders were enthusiastic volunteers. A few individuals carried on the party's work, for which they were "unpaid or almost wholly unpaid." In Germany, on the other hand, although many party functionaries were unpaid volunteers, certain positions, *e.g.*, party journals and newspapers, had "a paid editorial staff and paid contributors." But paying the leaders does not necessarily lessen either their idealism or their relative immunity to "temptations." Michels pays a high tribute to the socialist leaders: "It would . . . be quite wrong," he insists, "to suppose that socialist propagandists and socialist officials are paid on a scale which enables them with the hard-earned pence of the workers to lead that luxurious existence which, with an ignorance bordering on impudence, is often ascribed to them by the 'respectable' press and the loungers of the clubs." A leader's labors "demand an abundance of self-denial and sacrifice and are nervously exhausting; whilst the remuneration he receives is a modest one when compared with the gravity and the difficulty of his task." Finally, Michels notes, "Men of the ability and education of Karl Kautsky, Max Quarck, Adam Müller, and a hundred others, would have been able, had they chosen to devote themselves to some other service than that of the workers, to obtain a material reward much greater than that which they secure in their present positions." (p. 115.)

Nevertheless, idealism alone, at a number of levels at least, does not suffice to sustain the party; and paying for services does bring with it some negative results. It impairs somewhat the initiative of members and their socialist values and at the same time contributes both to the growing bureaucratization of the party and to the centralization of power. Ironically, however, paying and not paying, or paying poorly, all tend to lead, Michels observes, to the same results—*i.e.*, they conduce to oligarchy. For example, "In France, where it is still the rule to pay the trade union leaders very small salaries, there is lacking a new generation of leaders ready to take the place of the old, and for this reason at the trade union congresses the same members continually appear as delegates." (p. 127.) This results in a concentration of power that inevitably perverts the original aims of the party. The men at the top abuse their power, for example, to control the party press so as to diffuse their fame and popularize their names; and the parliamentary leaders often become "a closed corporation, cut off from the rest of the party."

The controls the masses have over this process are merely theoretical. In the constant struggle between the leaders and the masses the former are destined always to win out. "It cannot be denied," Michels writes, "that the masses revolt from time to time, but their revolts are always suppressed." (p. 162.)

The so-called masses never revolt spontaneously, *i.e.*, without leadership. The process of revolt presupposes that the masses are being led by certain leading elements of their own who, once having achieved power in the name of the people, transform themselves into a relatively closed caste apart from and opposed to the people. Moreover, in "normal," non-revolutionary situations, the most "talented elements," the potential revolutionary leaders, are always subject to a variety of seductive influences; they are smitten by the ambition to enter the privileged positions of the labor movement. This is a particular manifestation of the general process of *co-optation* described by Pareto whom Michels quotes: *"Si les B[nouvelle élite] prennent peu à peu la place des A [ancienne élite] par une lente infiltration, et si le mouvement de circulation sociale n'est pas interrompu, les C [la masse] sont privés des chefs qui pourraient les pousser à la révolte."* (pp. 161–62n.)

Thus it would appear unavoidable that "the rank and file becomes continually more impotent to provide new and intelligent forces capable of leading the opposition which may be latent among the masses." (p. 161.) The *real* struggle is not between masses and leaders but between the existing leaders and the new, challenging, ascending ones. Even when appearances are to the contrary and the existing leaders seem to be guided by the good will and pleasure of the mass, this is not actually the case: "The submission of the old leaders is ostensibly an act of homage to the crowd, but in intention it is a means of prophylaxis against the peril by which they are threatened—the formation of a new élite." (p. 165.) The struggle between the old and the new élites very rarely culminates "in the complete defeat of the former." Slightly modifying Pareto's doctrine, Michels states that "The result of the process is not so much a *circulation des élites* as a *réunion des elites,* an amalgam, that is to say, of the two elements." (p. 177.)

For Michels, the benefits which accrue to the majority of the party members as a result of this process are "practically nil." His description, in a brilliant passage, of the impact of bureaucracy on socialist values probably is as valid today as it was in his time:

As the party bureaucracy increases, two elements which constitute the essential pillars of every socialist conception undergo an inevitable weakening: an understanding of the wider and more ideal cultural aims of socialism, and an understanding of the international multiplicity of its manifestations. Mechanism becomes an end in itself. (p. 187.)

Furthermore, *decentralization* in itself cannot prevent this development from taking place. It does not lead to greater individual liberty nor does it enhance the power of the rank and file. More often than not it is a mechanism by which the weaker leaders seek to escape the dominion of the stronger; but this, of course, does not prevent the weaker from establishing a centralized authority within their own domains. The party is "saved" from one gigantic oligarchy only to fall into the hands "of a number of smaller oligarchies, each of which is no less powerful within its own sphere. The dominance of oligarchy in party life remains unchallenged." (p. 201.) And the causes of this, for Michels, are not only sociological—*e.g.,* need for organization, mass apathy, and so on—but psychological, that is, due to the leaders' "natural greed for power" and "the general characteristics of human nature." (p. 205.)

Earlier it was asserted that Michels, despite his criticism of Marxism, retained certain elements of the Marxian method of analysis. This is true; but he employed the reconstructed method to expose the apparent errors—primarily of omission—of the "master."

Classes, class conflict, and class consciousness are all essential categories in Michels' thinking. He agrees, for instance, that it is not oppressive conditions in themselves but the *recognition* of those conditions which has been "the prime factor of class struggles." (p. 236.) And historically it has been the bourgeoisie that has played a central role in generating proletarian class consciousness. The bourgeoisie, having to defend its existence on a number of fronts at once—against the aristocracy and against those sections of its own class whose interests are opposed to industrial development—and unable to carry on the struggle alone, is compelled to mobilize the proletariat and thus places in its hands a weapon (political consciousness and experience) which it can employ against the bourgeoisie itself. In addition, there have always been those bourgeois intellectuals who for a variety of reasons have detached themselves from their original class and have joined the ranks of the workers to give them direction. As a matter of fact, Michels regards it as a

> psychologico-historical law that any class which has been enervated and led to despair in itself through prolonged lack of education and through deprivation of political rights, cannot attain to the possibility of energetic action until it has received instruction concerning its ethical rights and politico-economical powers, not alone from members of its own class, but also from those who belong to what in vulgar parlance are termed a "higher" class. (p. 237.)

What better example of this is needed than the founders of modern socialism themselves? They "were with few exceptions men of science primarily, and in the second place only were they politicians in the strict sense of the term." (p. 238.) Moreover, Michels continues, it "was only when science placed itself at the service of the working class that the *proletarian* movement became transformed into a *socialist* movement, and that instinctive, unconscious, and aimless rebellion was replaced by conscious aspiration, comparatively clear, and strictly directed towards a well-defined end." (p. 238.) Finally, Michels concurs that "The proletariat is . . . perfectly logical in constituting itself into a class party, and in considering that the struggle against the bourgeoisie in all its gradations, viewed as a single class, is the only possible means of realizing a social order in which knowledge, health, and property shall not be, as they are today, the monopolies of a minority." (p. 247.)

But Marx had not anticipated the extent to which the entry of the bourgeois intellectuals into the socialist movement, and their occupation of leadership positions, would bring about basic changes in that movement that "may be summed up in the comprehensive customary term of the *embourgeo-*

isement of working-class parties." Also, while Marx had been quite aware of strata within the working class, on balance he tended to underestimate the conflicts that could arise among them; instead he viewed it as a much more unitary category than it turned out to be in practice. Ironically, moreover, the socialist movement itself, Michels argues, has created new petty-bourgeois strata. A variety of leadership and other functions are given over to workers —or more precisely to *former* workers—who now inevitably undergo a profound psychological transformation that creates as great a social distance between them and the rank and file as between bourgeois and proletarian. In this way, "Certain groups of individuals, numerically insignificant but qualitatively of great importance, are withdrawn from the proletarian class and raised to bourgeois dignity." (p. 271.) The socialist party and other organizations, in providing opportunities for social ascent to former manual laborers, generate the very same tendencies one sees in originally bourgeois leadership.[10]

None of the traditional democratic mechanisms, either within socialist parties and other working-class organizations or in larger national political systems, has been effective in countering the oligarchic abuse of power. The *referendum*, for instance, has not only proved to be for the most part impracticable due to the incompetence of the masses and the lack of time to submit every question to popular vote; it has also yielded *less*, not more, democracy; *e.g.*, the well-known phenomenon of plebiscitarian "democracy," in reality, a dictatorship. Michels notes that George Sand had regarded "the plebiscite, if not counterpoised by the intelligence of the masses, as an attack upon the liberty of the people." And he himself cites Bonapartism whose power was "based on the referendum." (p. 337.) Of course, that this was very well understood by Marx is clear from his classic account of the phenomenon in his *Eighteenth Brumaire of Louis Bonaparte*.

As for the syndicalists and anarchists, they are merely deluding themselves when they "reason as if they were immunized against the action of sociological laws of universal validity." (p. 347.) They have not avoided the situation in which "the masses do not represent themselves but are represented by others." (p. 348.) And often their "direct action," *e.g.*, "the strike, instead of being a field of activity for the uniform and compact masses, tends rather to facilitate the process of differentiation and to favor the formation of an *elite* of leaders." (pp. 349–50.)

None of the various proposed "prophylaxes," then, have proved effective in preventing what élite theorists have deemed an inexorable process. These prophylaxes include Marxism, too—Michels' primary target, of course; at first it seems the "only scientific doctrine which can boast of ability to make an effective reply to all theories, old or new, affirming the immanent necessity for the perennial existence of the 'political class.' " (pp. 381–82.) But Marxism also fails because the members of the new society in their very efforts to

---

[10] In some cases, Michels argues, former proletarians as leaders may be worse. See p. 302 *ff*.

abolish class distinctions will create new ones. This is inevitable because the delegation of authority will be necessary to administer and to allocate material resources. The administrators would thus acquire enormous "influence at least equal to that possessed by the private owner of capital." (p. 383.) And, Michels continues, there is no basis for assuming that these administrators "will not utilize their immense influence in order to secure for their children the succession to the offices which they themselves hold." (p. 383.) Once a group of men, elected or not, gain control of the existing instruments of power, they will do everything they can to retain it.

Thus the weakest link in the Marxian view of the new society is the whole gamut of problems relating to administration, *i.e.*, the concentration of power in the hands of administrators and the means these individuals might utilize to retain their privileges. It seems inescapable, concludes Michels, that conflicts of interests emerge between leaders and led, not unlike the class conflicts of the old society. This process appears to be subsumed under an absolute social law.

> By a universally applicable social law, every organ of the collectivity, brought into existence through the need for the division of labor, creates for itself, as soon as it becomes consolidated, interests peculiar to itself. The existence of these special interests involves a necessary conflict with the interests of the collectivity. Nay, more, social strata fulfilling peculiar functions tend to become isolated, to produce organs fitted for the defense of their own peculiar interests. In the long run they tend to undergo transformation into distinct classes. (p. 389.)

This Michels intends not as a refutation of Marx's theory of class struggle but of his utopia, the classless society. (pp. 390–91.) "The socialists might conquer," he writes, "but not socialism, which would perish in the moment of its adherents' triumph." (p. 391.)

Michels had written these lines before a single socialist regime had taken power anywhere. However, the victory of the bureaucratic organization over the socialist soul had already become evident in the violation of a fundamental socialist principle: international solidarity. The working-class masses were fated to suffer most from the violation of this principle. Yet, as Michels notes of the German workers during World War I, "throughout the proletarian mass there has not been reported a single instance of moral rebellion against the struggle which enlists socialists to fight on behalf of German imperialism and to contend with the comrades of other lands." Ultimately, this must be viewed as a consequence of *organization* itself "which gives birth to the dominion of the elected over the electors, of the mandatories over the mandators, of the delegates over the delegators. *Who says organization, says* oligarchy." And this is predicated, for Michels, on the inherent nature of the masses which, however much they may advance educationally, culturally, or morally, will remain *perennially* incompetent. The mass "per se is amorphous, and therefore needs division of labor, specialization, and guidance"—the very processes which lead inevitably to its manipulation and subordination.

However, nothing could be further from Michels' intention than to provide a rationale for resignation to these processes. He emphatically states that in this work he "desired to throw light upon certain sociological tendencies which oppose the reign of democracy, and to a still greater extent oppose the reign of socialism." He quite deliberately adopted a one-sided view and laid "considerable stress upon the pessimistic aspect of democracy which is forced upon us by historical study." (p. 405.) He employed the term "iron law" to dramatize the difficult and formidable obstacles that lay before the realization of democracy; but not in order to deny altogether the possibility of its realization. From his analysis, "it would be erroneous to conclude," Michels maintains, "that we should renounce all endeavors to ascertain the limits which may be imposed upon the power exercised over the individual by oligarchies (state, dominant class, party, etc.). It would be an error to abandon the desperate enterprise of endeavoring to discover the social order which will render possible the complete realization of the idea of popular sovereignty. (pp. 404–5.) Moreover,

the writer does not wish to deny that every revolutionary working-class movement, and every movement sincerely inspired by the democratic spirit, may have a certain value as contributing to the enfeeblement of oligarchic tendencies. (p. 405.)

In the end, furthermore, he emphasized that free inquiry, and criticism and control of the leaders, so essential for the strengthening of democracy, can be developed increasingly among the masses themselves: "A wider education involves an increasing capacity for exercising control." And as Michels develops this point it becomes clear that while there are in his view at any given time certain limits on the degree of perfection democracy can attain (here as elsewhere the actual falls short of the ideal), still, the ideal can more and more be approximated. "It is," he insists, " . . . the great task of social education to raise the intellectual level of the masses, so that they may be enabled, within the limits of what is possible, to counteract the oligarchical tendencies of the working-class movement." (p. 407.)

In the concluding paragraphs of his work, Michels goes on record, unequivocally, in favor of democracy: "The defects inherent in democracy are obvious. It is none the less true that as a form of social life we must choose democracy as the least of evils." (p. 407.) And finally he writes: "It may be said, therefore, that the more humanity comes to recognize the advantages which democracy, however imperfect, presents over aristocracy, even at its best, the less likely is it that a recognition of the defects of democracy will provoke a return to aristocracy." (p. 407.)

It is in this spirit, therefore, that Michels' classic study should be read, namely, as "a serene and frank examination of the oligarchical dangers of democracy [which] will enable us to minimize these dangers, even though they can never be entirely avoided. (p. 408.)

15

Émile Durkheim

(1858–1917)

To understand the sociology of Émile Durkheim one must, in his case as in the case of so many of his contemporaries, examine his relation to socialist thought and to the socialist movement of his time. Apparently Durkheim had begun to concern himself with the problems of socialism as early as 1883, about the same time that he had drawn up the first plan of his *Division of Labor.* As he progressed in his work on the *Division of Labor, Suicide, The Family,* and *Religion,* all eventually to become full-scale studies, his interests shifted from socialism to sociology and then mainly to social problems. As Marcel Mauss observed, however, Durkheim never lost sight of his point of departure.[1] When, in 1895, he again took up the study of socialism and delivered a series of lectures on the subject at the University of Bordeaux, he sought to treat it both objectively and sociologically: How does one explain the various forms of socialist ideology? What were the social conditions and pressures which prompted Saint-Simon, Fourier, Owen, and Marx to advance their respective theories? Thus Durkheim's studies of socialism were to be an "analysis of the causes of an idea."[2]

[1] See Mauss' Introduction to the First Edition of Durkheim's *Socialism and Saint Simon,* edited with an Introduction by Alvin W. Gouldner (London: Routledge and Kegan Paul Ltd., 1959).

[2] *Ibid.,* p. 2. (All immediately following references to this work will be cited only by page number in the text.)

Durkheim had an intimate knowledge of socialist literature, including the works of Karl Marx, "whom a Finnish friend, Neiglick, had advised him to study during his stay in Leipzig." (p. 3.) Nevertheless, he remained throughout his life opposed to socialism though his closest friends and students were committed to it in its Marxian, Guesdist, and other forms. The features of socialism which, according to Mauss, he disliked were "its violent nature, its class character—more or less purely workingmen's—and therefore its political and even politician-like tone." (p. 3.) Thus in opposition to a conception of society and social change based on classes and class conflict, Durkheim put forward a theory based on "organic solidarity," which ignored for the most part the implications of class cleavages. Change was good only if it benefited society as a whole.

Though he never completed his studies of socialism, which were to include a critical examination of Marx's theories, what he did complete, taken together with his other works, may be viewed as an effort to construct a model of society essentially antithetical to that of Marx. And, as we shall see, despite his criticisms of Comte, Durkheim's organic consensual model owes much to that thinker. As in the case of Comte, Durkheim was proposing a positive, constructive philosophy to counteract the negative-critical philosophy of the socialists. Social stratification, class cleavages, problems of power and political conflict play no significant part in Durkheim's "positive polity."

However, the statement that Durkheim was profoundly influenced by Comte must be qualified. Not only for the reasons noted earlier in this study, that all Comte's major ideas came from Saint-Simon (which Durkheim was among the first to demonstrate), but also because he remained generally ambivalent toward the Comtean legacy and betrayed this fact intermittently in his various works. Durkheim was, in the apt phrase of Alvin Gouldner, an "uneasy Comtean." (p. viii.)

Durkheim's concern with "solidarity" was related to his fear of the social and political conflicts of his time. The strength and prominence of the socialist movement, as well as the sociological analyses and solutions it proposed, pressed him to seek some kind of intellectual mediation between two prominent theoretical systems: the Comtean and the Marxian. This he attempted to do by exploring the work of their common intellectual ancestor, Saint-Simon; and it is in his study, *Socialism and Saint-Simon,* that much of Durkheim's later thinking is anticipated. In the end, he failed to effect the ideological compromise he so ardently desired. Chronologically as well as ideologically, Saint-Simon had straddled two epochs: the Revolution, on the one hand, and the Conservative Reaction, on the other. If Marx accentuated and developed the elements in Saint-Simon's thought which derived from the former epoch, Durkheim did the same with the elements from the latter epoch. In short, Durkheim developed the conservative tendency in Saint-Simon, ignoring the radical one taken over by Marx. Taken as a whole, Durkheim's system bears an overwhelmingly conservative bias. Only occasionally does he react to an issue in a way similar to Marx. This despite his alleged "convergence with Marx,"[3] which as we shall see, is a momentary and superficial one. It is true that ultimately Durkheim "capitulates" to Marx (but denies it) by adopting at least one of his major theoretical propositions—that "social existence determines social consciousness." This is most clear in his *Elementary Forms of Religious Life;* even here, however, he uses the theory for his own purposes and diverges from Marx in certain important respects (to be explored later). To see how Durkheim put together and developed his conservative model of society, one must begin by examining his relation to Saint-Simon.

Durkheim and Saint-Simon

Although class conflict, for Saint-Simon, played an important role in the transition from the feudal to the bourgeois order, it lost virtually all significance once the new scientific-industrial order was established. While he clearly recognized the existence of classes and strata in the new society, he believed that the new conditions could lead to a hierarchical *but nonetheless organic* order of social peace and stability. Integration was to be achieved primarily by instituting the appropriate moral ideas. This becomes the leading idea of Durkheim's system as well. The new division of labor, *i.e.,* science and industry, need not lead, as Comte had feared it would, to "disorganization" and "anarchy." Everything depended, for Saint-Simon as for Durkheim, on whether the *appropriate* moral order could be developed to suit the new social and technical conditions.

By reviewing the basic principles of Saint-Simon's philosophy, the degree to which Durkheim was indebted to him will become clearer; for it is quite evident that it was Saint-Simon and *not* Comte whom Durkheim regarded as his intellectual master. The "idea, the word, and even the outline of positivist philosophy," wrote Durkheim, "are all found in Saint-Simon. . . . Therefore, it is to him that one must, in full justice, award the honor currently given Comte." (p. 104.) In these essays, Durkheim vehemently defends and proves this proposition. It was important for him to establish this fact, since the Saint-Simonian principles (which Durkheim summarizes rather well) all reappear in his own works; in fact, these same principles form the basis of his own sociology.

Moral ideas for Saint-Simon as for Durkheim are the real cement of a society. For both thinkers a society is above all a community of ideas: "The similarity of positive moral ideas is the single bond which can unite men into society." (p. 91.) If Saint-Simon saw as his major task to determine what kind of moral system post-Revolutionary European society required, Durkheim viewed his own work in a similar light: to provide a secular, moral system that would bind together into a solidary social order the classes, strata, and

---

[3] See Gouldner's discussion of this in *Ibid.,* p. xxiii.

occupational groups of contemporary France. Like Saint-Simon, he viewed the role of theory as essentially positive and constructive, and shared with the founder of positive philosophy a certain disdain for the negative-critical outlook of the *Philosophes* and the Revolutionaries. Durkheim wholeheartedly agreed that contemporary philosophy must be constructive and organizational, not critical and revolutionary. His emphasis on the constructive and organizational, however, was to serve as an antidote to the critical and revolutionary ideas of the socialists in general and the Marxists in particular.

It was Saint-Simon's conception of society as enunciated in his *Physiologie Sociale* and elsewhere that led Durkheim to his own positivistic and functional view and that inspired the organismic analogies and metaphors we find throughout his work. Durkheim's fundamental premise, which he never tires of repeating, that "society" is not a simple aggregate of individuals but a reality sui generis, had already been explicitly defined by Saint-Simon:

Society is not at all a simple conglomeration of living beings whose actions have no other cause but the arbitrariness of individual wills, nor other result than ephemeral or unimportant accidents. On the contrary, society is above all a veritable organized machine, all of whose parts contribute in a different way to the movement of the whole. The gathering of men constitutes a veritable being whose existence is more or less certain or precarious according to whether its organs acquit themselves more or less regularly of the functions entrusted to them. (p. 99.)

Likewise, Durkheim's evolutionary conception of society is anticipated in Saint-Simon's "law of progress." The Saint-Simonian emphasis—that men are the instruments rather than the authors of this law—remains a dominant theme in Durkheim's treatment of the individual and in his reification (and sometimes even deification) of society and social processes. For both thinkers, social laws dominated men with absolute necessity and all they could do was to submit. The best men could hope for was to discover the course or direction of these laws—the task of positive science—so as to adjust to them with the least pain.

Saint-Simon had described, in essentially a dialectical way, the origins of the scientific-industrial order within the womb of the feudal-theological system. The two contradictory systems could not co-exist indefinitely, and the tensions and conflicts ultimately resulted in the French Revolution. The conflict and anarchy of the post-Revolutionary epoch could be eliminated by finding and imposing a religious-moral order *appropriate* to the new scientific-industrial conditions. Eventually, this led to his call for a "new Christianity."

That Durkheim took over this view in its essentials is quite clear, notably in his *Division of Labor* in which *mechanical* solidarity was giving way to a "higher" solidarity he called *organic*. While both thinkers viewed the older social order as based on conflicting principles, classes, and class interests, they both read conflict out of their respective higher, organic societies. There was nothing normal about conflict in the new society; the existence of classes and strata did not preclude the moral unity and solidarity of the society as a whole. Durkheim believed that the mission Saint-Simon had set himself—to elaborate a new and appropriate body of universally acceptable moral and rational beliefs—still remained unaccomplished in his time. He agreed that the old order could not be restored; therefore the new one had to be "integrated." This was essential to avoid the recurring economic and political crises, the chronic mood of exasperation and discontent, and, finally, the "disintegration" of society. The "revolution" Saint-Simon had envisioned was still incomplete in his own time, Durkheim believed, because the new integrative institutions appropriate to the modern division of labor had yet to be established. A new law and morality must be developed to express the diverse shades and variations of industrial society and thus serve to integrate all its parts and functions.

This appeared feasible to Durkheim because he accepted the Saint-Simonian view of industry as a unifying and pacific force. Describing Saint-Simon's view, Durkheim writes: "From military—which it was formerly—the human spirit became pacific. Industry was offering nations a means—as fruitful as war—of becoming rich and powerful." (pp. 130–31.) Once the old feudal, military, and theological functions had lost their significance, there was no apparent reason for social conflict in the new "organic" society. The main source of conflict in the older system had been the conflicting interests and principles of the feudal and industrial classes—ergo, to achieve this "organic" quality, the new society had to be based on only *one* of these principles. Modern societies, writes Durkheim, following Saint-Simon's formula, "will be definitely in equilibrium only when organized on a purely industrial basis." (p. 131.) Like his master, Durkheim saw a homogeneity of interests not only among the many and varied occupational groups ("functions") but between the industrial capitalists and workers as well. He adopts Saint-Simon's formula that "the producers of useful things—being the only useful people in society—are the only ones who should cooperate to regulate" the course of the new industrial society. (p. 134.) This formed the basis for the role Durkheim assigned to "occupational guilds." Only those who live on unearned income, Saint-Simon argued, should be placed beyond the pale of regular society. "As for those who themselves make their wealth productive, who enrich it with their toil—they are industrials. Consequently, industrial society comprises all those who actively participate in the economic life, whether they are owners or not." Durkheim's own view is merely a paraphrase of Saint-Simon's. There was no *necessary* conflict of interests between those who owned the means of production and those who did not; there was no reason, therefore, why the existence of classes could not provide a basis for an organic solidarity.

To be sure, Durkheim will note some injustices in the industrial system based on structural inequalities, but these occupy a very minor part of his system, to which he gives only occasional attention. His theory of the integrative consequences of the growing division of labor is likewise derived from Saint-Simon. That Durkheim elaborated in his *Division of Labor* ideas that had already appeared in all their essentials in Saint-Simon's scheme, may be seen from the following excerpts from *Système Industriel*. In that work and others, Saint-Simon held that the growing division of labor would lead to greater interdependence and mutual responsibility among individuals, and to a greater dependence upon society as a whole.

> In the measure that civilization makes progress, the division of labor —considered from the spiritual as from the secular side, grows in the same proportion. Thus men depend less on others as individuals, but more on the mass. . . . [The] organization of a well-ordered system requires that the parts be strongly tied to the whole and subordinated. (p. 138.)

Even Durkheim's frequently reiterated idea of the integrative role of occupational guilds and corporations was first expressed by Saint-Simon. In order that the division of labor should result in a solidary industrial society, it was necessary "that in the large majority of the nation, individuals be joined in industrial associations, more or less numerous and connected . . . to permit their formation into a generalized system by being directed toward a great common industrial goal." (p. 139.) Like Saint-Simon, Durkheim sees the industrial system as possessing an inherent unity. His summary of Saint-Simon's conception describes his own equally well. Somehow, the growing division of labor was, in his view, leading to a solidarity of interests among all classes ("parts") of society. Classes are termed "functions" and are regarded as coordinative, cooperative, and unifying—never as conflictive. "Each people today," he writes, "forms a homogeneous whole, not because it acquired the habit of identifying itself with such and such a function or class, but because it is a system of functions inseparable from one another and mutually complementing each other." (p. 148.)

If the industrial system was only a system of functions, all that was necessary to assure their harmonious operation was proper regulation. Here, too, the rudiments of his theory appear first in Saint-Simon. Durkheim is very receptive to the positivistic formula proposed by his master; as we shall see, he quite sincerely believed in the scientific determination of moral values. He approvingly summarizes the Saint-Simonian formula. In the new society, " . . . it is not the strongest who control but those most capable in science or industry. They are not summoned to office because they have the power to exercise their will but because they know more than others, and consequently their functions do not consist in saying what they want, but what they know. They do not dictate orders, they only declare what conforms to the nature of things." (p. 150.) And again, "Those who direct are not above those who are directed; they are not their superiors. They fulfill a different function—that is all." (p. 151.)

This state of affairs presupposed for Saint-Simon the elimination of certain basic inequalities—*e.g.*, rights of birth and "even all types of privilege." (p. 151.) While it is true that Durkheim shared this view and even went so far as to view the institution of inheritance as a barrier to equality and a source of injustice and conflict, this remains a minor aspect of his system. For making this theme the center of his thesis would have meant capitulating to the Marxian and other socialists. If Marx considered the abolition of classes and class cleavages a precondition for the development of a truly human community, the impression is unavoidable that Durkheim envisioned such a community even while class cleavages continued to persist.

Moreover, Durkheim remained throughout his life blind to the authoritarian implications of both Saint-Simon's and his own systems. For while both talked of equality, both left the class structure intact and simultaneously professed to believe that in the "new" industrial society there would be no government in the accepted sense of the word. "Anarchistic," "nonauthoritarian," were the words Durkheim used to describe Saint-Simon's vision of the new society; and his use of these terms appears especially ironic, even grotesque, to modern readers in the light of intervening historical developments. The new society "has no leaders," he writes; "Each has the position which is *natural* for him to occupy, and executes no measures except those *ordered by the nature of things.*" (p. 153.) Force and compulsion will not be necessary. Science is the only authority the reorganized society recognizes and in fact it is science that makes the automatic accord of all social functions possible. For science teaches, among other things, what moral ideas are best suited to the new industrial conditions.

It is true that Saint-Simon saw the need to change certain property relations in order that the new society should emerge as he wished. "There is no change whatsoever in the social order," he wrote, "without a change in property." (p. 157.) But his point was to avoid the separation of talent and property. Durkheim also wanted the social order to rest on ability. Classes and strata would remain; but now, presumably, the owners, for example, would be the most capable—*naturally* capable, that is. Later, Durkheim suggests the abolition of inheritance so that property will not be separated from natural capacity.

Throughout Durkheim's work, one encounters the injunction, "Fight egoism!" For egoism left unbridled "would of necessity finally result in the dissolution of society." But these words are Saint-Simon's and first appear in his *Système Industriel.* What Durkheim regarded as the best antidote for egoism, namely, an altruistic moral commitment to "Society" was derived from Saint-Simon's *New Christianity.* "Love one another" was Saint-Simon's motto. "The fundamental principle established by the divine author of Christianity commands all men to regard themselves as brothers and to cooperate as completely as possible for their well-being. This principle is the most general of all social principles. (p. 165.) The real task was to organize "temporal power in conformity with this divine axiom." A new charity and a new philanthropy were required, Saint-Simon emphasized, "to improve as much as possible the fate of the class which has no other means of existence but the labor of its hands." (p. 166.) This is important not for its own sake but for the sake of social peace. The point for Saint-Simon as for Durkheim was that imposing the social order by force upon the proletarians was difficult and costly if not altogether impossible. Therefore, it is more desirable, in Durkheim's words, to "make them love it." (p. 166.) Durkheim correctly observed about this aspect of Saint-Simon's doctrine (and his own as well) that it was inspired by "compassion for the unfortunate, along with a fear of their dangers to the social order." (p. 168.)

Durkheim follows Saint-Simon in still another point, namely, the integrative role of moral sentiments. When he argues that the division of labor conduces to a higher solidarity, he does so only in the sense that men are increasingly dependent on one another; but he recognizes at the same time that this alleged interdependence is not sufficient to bring about real solidarity —which can only be effected through a moral education and commitment to "society as a whole." Again, Saint-Simon.

In his discussion of Saint-Simon, Durkheim's ideological commitment clearly emerges. He despised and feared restlessness, social conflict, and "anarchy"; the insatiable appetites of modern man were a sign of his morbidity. Along with Bonald, Maistre, and Saint-Simon, Durkheim believed that the decline of religious forces had left a moral vacuum. A morality of contentment was required because social peace could never be achieved so long as men were not contented with their lot. "What is needed if social order is to reign," writes Durkheim, "is that the mass of men be content with their lot. But what is needed for them to be content, is not that they have more or less but that they be convinced they have no right to more. And for this, it is absolutely essential that there be an authority whose superiority they acknowledge and which tells them what is right." (p. 200.) What is necessary above all is a strong moral force capable of moderating and regulating the various "functions" and of curbing "egoism" and special interests. And while Durkheim proposed a specific solution, *i.e.*, that professional and occupational groupings should eventually be formed to exercise this moral force and at the same time to mediate between the individual and the State, until that day arrived he was prepared to demand total allegiance to "Society"—which under the circumstances could only mean total allegiance to the State. Eventually, he would even take up his pen to defend the French point of view in the great "war to end all wars," while some of his closest friends, Jaurès among them, tried to expose the folly and horrors of such a doctrine.

Durkheim wanted to pose the social question in a manner entirely different from the way Marx did. This resulted in a conservative and authoritarian ideology that dominated his entire sociological system. His way of posing the question, he believed,

no longer stirs questions of classes; it no longer opposes rich to poor, employers to workers—as if the only possible solution consisted of diminishing the portion of one in order to augment that of the other. But it declares, in the interest of both, the necessity of a curb from above which checks appetites and so sets a limit on the state of disarrangement, excitement, frenzied agitation, which do not spring from social activity and which even make it suffer. Put differently, the social question, posed this way, is not a question of money or force; it is a question of moral agents. What dominates it is not the state of our economy but, much more, the state of our morality. (p. 204.)

That this view dominated his sociology may be documented by an examination of his major works.

The Division of Labor in Society

In his first major work Durkheim set himself the task of demonstrating that the growing division of labor, a historically necessary process, brings with it an ever higher form of solidarity. This idea, borrowed from Saint-Simon, was not only a positive thesis but a polemical one as well. Contemporary socialists, and particularly the Marxists, had also regarded the growth of science and industry as an inevitable process; but for them, in order that men in general should reap the benefits of modern technical developments, a fundamental restructuring of social relationships was necessary. In the Marxian view the "division of labor" was not merely a distribution of coordinate functions; quite the contrary, it was a system of structural inequalities. The so-called "functions" were fulfilled by men in definite strata: a hierarchy of positions with varying degrees of wealth, power, and social honor attached to them. Furthermore, the concept of hierarchy was inadequate to describe the existential conditions of men in the modern capitalist system; economic and social reality, most realistically conceived, was composed of socioeconomic classes with antagonistic interests. For Marx the term "division of labor" was an equivocation, if it obscured the basic social inequalities of the prevailing order.

Comte, too, had understood rather well that the new industrial developments, and the dispersion of interests accompanying them, were liable to undermine the solidarity of the existing society and to preclude social unity and peace in the future. He had opted for the opposite solution, however: a moral consensus of society as a whole, enforced by the State.

What Durkheim attempted to do, then, was to provide a cogent rebuttal to both the Marxian position, on the one hand, and the Comtean position, on the other. To Comte he was willing to concede that moral consensus was *one* precondition of social order; but against him he argued, in this work, that the division of labor *need* not lead to dispersion and conflict of interests. There were other, *non-moral* conditions that were at least equally important for the establishment of solidarity. The development of science and industry, permitting an increasing interdependence among individuals and groups within society as a whole, could serve as the objective basis of a new and higher solidarity.

This view constituted, at the same time, a polemic against the Marxian and other socialist positions: No fundamental restructuring of socioeconomic relationships was necessary; not revolution, but the determination and institution of the moral norms most suited to the new economic conditions is called for. To be sure, Durkheim does acknowledge the need for certain reforms without which there can be neither true justice nor true solidarity; but, again, this is more in the nature of an afterthought than a central tenet. Thus Durkheim's *Division of Labor* is a restatement of the Saint-Simonian position. What could be more logical, Durkheim apparently reasoned, than to bridge the chasm between Marx and Comte by developing the central ideas of their common intellectual ancestor.

Inspired by Saint-Simon, Durkheim attempted to show that the division of labor must be viewed in a new light. The "economic services that it can render are picayune compared to the moral effect that it produces, and its true function is to create in two or more persons a feeling of solidarity. In whatever manner the result is obtained, its aim is to cause coherence among friends and to stamp them with its seal."[4] Once upon a time, society was solidary because it was homogeneous; everyone was alike. However, with the growing differentiation of functions, the increasing heterogeneity and complexity of society, this original solidarity was undermined and eventually lost. But this does not mean that solidarity has been forever destroyed; a new and higher type of social solidarity is being generated by the division of labor. This is the thesis Durkheim developed in his first major work, proceeding from a consideration of what he called "mechanical solidarity," or solidarity through likeness.

Employing as his model some hypothetical primitive societies, Durkheim posits an original, solidary condition based upon common collective sentiments, his *conscience collective,* which in French carries the connotation of both a common consciousness and a common conscience. The collective sentiments are engraved, rather strongly, on all the individual consciences. The best empirical indication of the existence of a "totality of social similitudes" is the social reaction to crime. In fact, an act is "criminal," for Durkheim, precisely because it is carried out in opposition to the collective sentiments. We "must not say," he writes, "that an action shocks the common conscience because it is criminal, but rather that it is criminal because it shocks the common conscience." (p. 81.) Crime is "an offense against an authority in some way transcendent." (p. 85.) Anything which offends or violates the common conscience threatens the solidarity—the very existence— of society. An offense left unpunished weakens to that same degree the social unity. Punishment, therefore, allegedly serves the important function of restoring and reconstituting social unity. In the primitive context, it is expiatory

4 Émile Durkheim, *The Division of Labor in Society* (New York: The Free Press, 1965), p. 56. (All immediately following references to this text will be merely cited by page number.)

and retaliatory; it is a passionate reaction by society against those who dared violate its basic rules. Restitution is not enough; the social body "must have a more violent satisfaction. The force against which the crime comes is too intense to react with very much moderation. Moreover, it cannot do so without enfeebling itself; for it is thanks to the intensity of the reaction that it keeps alive and maintains itself with the same degree of energy." Thus Durkheim describes a social state based on a uniform conscience present in all members of society.

If repressive and expiatory law is characteristic of mechanical solidarity, it is *restitutive* law which is most typical of organic solidarity. Here the point is not punishment, but restoring damaged interests; law becomes "a means of reviewing the past in order to reinstate it, as far as possible, to its normal form." And now, since society is a complex of many and diverse groups and interests, law acts through specialized organs. Nevertheless, it is *society* which empowers these organs and acts through them. Even contractual relations, which are ostensibly private and individual, are binding precisely because society gives power to such relations; society sanctions "the obligations contracted for. . . . Every contract thus supposes that behind the parties implicated in it there is society very ready to intervene in order to gain respect for the engagements which have been made." (p. 114.)

Not all the relationships in the complex society, Durkheim acknowledges, conduce to solidarity. Some are negative. For instance, the rights of some persons are different from those of others. " . . . I cannot enjoy my right without harming someone else; such is the case with certain servitudes." (p. 118.) Law is then necessary to repair wrong and to prevent it. But these rules and relationships do not demand real cooperation; "they simply restore or maintain, in the new conditions which are produced, this negative solidarity whose circumstances have troubled its functioning." (p. 118.) Rules governing these relationships do not lead to "positive social links"; they lead to the separation of spheres but not to cooperation. The other rules of restitutive law, the residue, Durkheim writes, "express a positive union, a cooperation which derives, in essentials, from the division of labor." (p. 122.)

Durkheim begins now to develop his thesis on the positive consequences of the division of labor: it leads to exchange of services, reciprocity of obligations, interdependence, etc. Contracts and other formal-legal relationships governing these exchanges lead to what he defined as organic solidarity. It is true that later he will qualify this thesis but meanwhile we are told that ". . . Spencer has not without justice qualified as a physiological contract the exchange of materials which is made at every instant between the different organs of the living body." (p. 125.) In this way Durkheim conceives of the complex social system as a multiplicity of distinct functions which need to be coordinated. "Coordinated" is precisely accurate here because he views these "functions" in a *coordinate* and harmonious relation with one another, like the separate organs of a living being. His concept "division of labor" is therefore a device which enables him to accentuate the "cooperative" aspect of the social system while ignoring the others. He systematically divests the "division of labor" of all relationships of domination, and conflict—particularly *class* conflict. Durkheim will continue to insist, in this work as in others, that the division of labor *normally* engenders cooperation and solidarity. *Normally* is a very important term in his system; for, as we shall see, it is only the pathological, or abnormal, forms of the division of labor which bring with them "anarchy" and conflict.

But there is more: the growing division of labor—specialization of functions—not only leads to solidarity but also enhances man's individuality. Since mechanical solidarity results when likenesses are at their maximum, this is the same as saying that the common conscience completely envelops the conscience of each individual—"individuality is nil." Conversely, organic solidarity resulting from the division of labor rests on individual differences. By some curious reasoning Durkheim concluded that, since each now has a sphere of action peculiar to him, this develops his individuality and personality. "In effect," he writes, "on the one hand, each one depends as much more strictly on society as labor is more divided; and, on the other, the activity of each is as much more personal as it is more specialized." (p. 131.) If one had thought that specialization had the opposite effects, *i.e.*, that it fragmented the personality and stifled the free play of one's faculties, he would have been wrong. True, the individual who fulfills a special function does so by suffering certain constraints and a circumscription of his activity. Nevertheless, this state of affairs "leaves much more place open," Durkheim tells us, "for the free play of our initiative." (p. 131.)

It must have been the professions Durkheim had in mind and certainly not the industrial workers when he asserted that "the individuality of all grows at the same time as that of its [society's] parts." (p. 131.) And even then the thesis would not hold without a number of important qualifications. For Durkheim, the new social solidarity is accompanied by, and is even a result of, the "fact" that now each of society's "elements has more freedom of movement. This solidarity resembles that which we observe among the higher animals. Each organ, in effect, has its special physiognomy, its autonomy. And, moreover, the unity of the organisms is as great as the individuation of the parts is more marked. Because of this analogy, we propose to call the solidarity which is due to the division of labor, organic." (p. 131.)

This analogy suited Durkheim's polemical purpose and conservative bias. The decline of the *conscience collective,* the erstwhile moral consensus, could not be doubted; that its restoration was impossible both Saint-Simon and Comte had recognized. The cult in behalf of individual dignity in its utilitarian and other forms was unappealing to Durkheim because "it is not to society that it attaches us; it is to ourselves. Hence, it does not constitute a true social link." (p. 172.) Comte's solution was also inadequate for he had assigned the solidifying function to moral consensus alone.[5] Finally, there was the position of the Marxian and other radical socialists who called for a fundamental transformation of society, a position Durkheim rejected out of hand. In opposition to them, he wished to demonstrate that the modern economic developments need not lead to social conflict, disorder, discontent, and "dissolution." A "higher," organic solidarity could be achieved without revolution; for it "is the division of labor which, more and more, fills the role that was formerly filled by the Common Conscience. It is the principal bond of social aggregates of higher types." (p. 173.) Yet, Durkheim felt a certain uneasiness with this proposition, for, after all, it was quite evident that the division of labor was not *in fact* engendering the solidarity he predicted and longed for. How did he deal with these embarrassing facts?

If the division of labor did not result in solidarity, this was an *abnormal* condition, a consequence of the pathological forms it had momentarily assumed. "Though *normally*," writes Durkheim, "the division of labor produces social solidarity, it sometimes happens that it has different, and even contrary results. Now, it is important to find out what makes it deviate from its natural course, for if we do not prove that these cases are exceptional, the division of labor might be accused of logically implying them." (p. 353.) So, if Marx had accentuated the essentially conflictive character of the modern division of labor (capitalism)—had viewed it as a condition which alienated men from one another and from themselves; a condition in which exploitation, conflict, and domination were normal and unavoidable so long as the existing "relations of production" prevailed; a condition in which the solidarity of society as a whole was unthinkable—Durkheim proposed quite the opposite view. It is only in its pathological forms that the division of labor produces negative consequences.

In Durkheim's treatment of the so-called pathological forms, one sees clearly the attempt on his part to deal with the issues raised by Marx and to provide an alternative solution. For example, there were the recurrent industrial and commercial crises Marx had regarded as inherent in the capitalist relations of production. For Durkheim, these crises were to be explained by the lack of adjustment among the various "functions" of the social organism. He acknowledges that "insofar as labor is divided more, these phenomena [crises] seem to become more frequent, at least in certain cases. From 1845 to 1869, failures increased 70%." (p. 354.) Nevertheless, these cannot be attributed "to the growth in economic life."

"The conflict between capital and labor," he continues, "is another example, more striking, of the same phenomenon. Insofar as industrial functions become more specialized, the conflict becomes more lively, instead of solidar-

5 This, as we shall see, is not quite accurate since for Comte it is the State which enforces the "consensus."

ity increasing." (p. 354.) So Durkheim saw these facts and even agreed that the conflict of these classes assumes its most intense form with "the birth of large-scale industry." (p. 355.) He employs almost Marxian language when he says that this is the phase in which the "worker is more completely separated from the employer." (p. 355.) With the growth of the "division of labor," revolts have become more frequent and class warfare more violent. For Durkheim, however, all this is not a consequence of the division of labor in its *normal* form, but of its abnormal forms, one of which he called the *anomic* division of labor. This concept is polemical and is directed against both Comte and Marx.

Comte had noted what he chose to term the dispersive and disintegrative consequences of the growing division of labor; while it permits "a felicitous development of the spirit of detail otherwise impossible, it spontaneously tends, on the other hand, to snuff out the spirit of togetherness or, at least, to undermine it profoundly."[6] Private interest is accentuated while public interest is vague, not clearly perceived, and submerged. But the growth of industrial forces was inevitable; there was no going back to the *status quo ante* as Bonald and Maistre had wished. Since the very opposite of solidarity was the *natural* consequence of scientific and industrial developments, solidarity had to be imposed from above. And the State, Comte believed, was the organ best suited to fulfill this function.

The social destiny of government [wrote Comte] appears to me to consist particularly in sufficiently containing, and preventing, as far as possible, this fatal disposition towards a fundamental dispersion of ideas, sentiments, and interests, the inevitable result of the very principle of human development, and which, if it could follow its natural course without interruption, would inevitably end by arresting social progress in all important respects. . . . It is clear, in effect, that the only real means of preventing such a dispersion consists in this indispensable reaction in a new and special function, susceptible of fittingly intervening in the habitual accomplishment of all the diverse functions of social economy, so as to recall to them unceasingly the feeling of unity and the sentiment of common solidarity (pp. 358–59.)

What Comte is arguing here is that the alleged collective conscience of the pre-industrial period has declined and that this is the real cause of the dispersive effects of the new industrial forces. A new moral consensus must therefore be imposed from above. This is where Durkheim differs with Comte. The enfeeblement of the collective conscience was normal and inevitable for Durkheim and could not be regarded as the cause of this abnormal form of the division of labor. "If, in certain cases," he writes, "organic solidarity is not all it should be, it is certainly not because mechanical solidarity has lost ground, but because all the conditions for the existence of organic solidarity have not been realized." (p. 365.) How does one realize these conditions? By

---

6 Quoted by Durkheim in *The Division of Labor in Society*, p. 357.

learning how to regulate, moderate, and equilibrate the diverse functions. What is required if organic solidarity is to be realized is "an adequately developed regulation determining the mutual relations of functions." (p. 365.) This is essentially a Saint-Simonian argument which Durkheim employs against both Comte and Marx. Against Comte he is arguing that conflict and disorder are not a result of the decline of the older moral order but of the absence of an appropriate new one. And against Marx he is arguing that the growing division of labor can lead to a higher solidarity *without* a fundamental transformation of the existing structure of socioeconomic relations. The higher form of human community will be achieved if the various functions and the relations among them can be properly regulated and adjusted. Durkheim is not so naïve as to suggest that this would eliminate all social conflict. "Of course," he writes, "as precise as the regulation may be, it will always leave a place for many disturbances. But it is neither necessary nor even possible for social life to be without conflicts. The role of solidarity is not to suppress competition, but to moderate it." (p. 365.)

Marx, too, saw a need for the regulation of production, the administration of things, or, in a word, planning. But this was possible and could have salutary effects only *after* the most basic structural inequalities had been abolished. Durkheim, on the other hand, though prepared to make a concession to Marx in this regard, wanted regulation and planning *before* these basic social changes had been made. For Durkheim it was primarily a matter of devising the proper moral rules by which the interests in conflict could be "equilibrated." This required knowledge (positive science), patience, and a moderation of appetites. (Later we shall see that duty, discipline, and devotion to "Society" become the cardinal virtues of moral education.) At the same time, however, he acknowledges that class antagonisms are not due merely to "lack of adjustment,"—*i.e.*, that morality has not caught up with the rapid developments of industrial life—but "in good part, to the still very great inequality of the external conditions of the struggle. On this factor time has no influence." (p. 370*n*.)

If earlier we were told that the growing division of labor enhances individuality, this must now be qualified; pathological forms both debase and ruin the individual. To prevent and overcome his debasement, the worker, for example, must enter into solidary relations with "others"—apparently also with his employer—and "understand that his actions have an aim beyond themselves."

Durkheim understood very well that rules—even appropriate ones—cannot be the whole solution and that "sometimes the rules themselves are the cause of evil. This is what occurs in class wars. The institution of classes and of castes constitutes an organization of the division of labor, and it is a strictly regulated organization, although it often is a source of dissension. The lower classes not being, or no longer being, satisfied with the role which has devolved upon them from custom or by law aspire to functions which are closed to them and seek to dispossess those who are exercising these functions. Thus civil wars arise which are due to the manner in which labor is distributed." (p. 374.) Thus Durkheim introduces a second major pathological form—the *forced division of labor*. This was his concession to the Marxian view.

As Durkheim saw it, pain and suffering were a result of the fact that the division of labor was forcibly imposed upon individuals without regard for their "hereditary dispositions." For this problem, he says clearly, there is only one solution: " . . . there is no other way out than to change the established order and to set up a new one." (p. 375.) If the class structure produces anxiety and pain instead of solidarity, "this is because the distribution of social functions on which it rests does not respond, or rather no longer responds, to the distribution of natural talents." (p. 375.) Presumably, then, it once did correspond to the distribution of "natural talents." When this was the case, he does not tell us. This turns out to be a very poor concession and in fact no concession at all.

For Marx, the "division of labor" was a situation in which the individual was unfree; a situation in which the individual was deformed mentally and physically precisely because he was chained to a particular function. He therefore envisioned a time when, as a result of both an increased productive capacity and a change in social relationships, men could be liberated entirely from the necessity to fulfill a particular function and could instead, as Marx says in *German Ideology*, be free to fish, hunt, write poetry, and discuss philosophy. He never presumed to be able to determine the "natural" abilities of men; and even if one could, his ideal was not to place them accordingly into special functions. Durkheim, in contrast, envisioned a system in which some men have a "natural" bent for the "functions" which, as he himself acknowledged, are humanly debasing. His good society therefore becomes one in which some are still more equal than others, but now, presumably, the inequalities are based on "natural" abilities.

The opposite of a forced division of labor is one which "is established in virtue of purely internal spontaneity, without anything coming to disturb the initiative of individuals. In this condition, harmony between individual natures and social functions cannot fail to be realized, at least in the average case." (p. 376.) Some men, freely and of their own accord, will choose to fulfill the debasing functions and be happy in their lot because it suits their natural capacities. The good society is one in which "social inequalities exactly express natural inequalities." Durkheim recognized that this presupposed "absolute equality in the external conditions of the conflict" and that the "hereditary transmission of wealth is enough to make the external conditions under which the conflict takes place very unequal, for it gives advantages to some which are not necessarily in keeping with their personal worth." (p. 378.) At the same time, he was prepared to believe that "if the institution of castes corresponds to the natural apportionment of capacities, it is, however, only in a very proximate and rough-and-ready manner." (p. 378.) The higher solidarity might result in a new system of castes but now, at least, this would correspond to the natural inequalities among men.

As becomes gradually evident, despite Durkheim's occasional call for reforms (*e.g.*, the abolition of the institution of inheritance), the main thrust of his philosophy is to demand an unswerving devotion and subordination of individuals to "Society"—and this he demanded long before the external conditions had even begun to resemble equality. Durkheim recognized that some men profited from the social circumstances in which others must either yield or die. "If one class of society is obliged, in order to live, to take any price for its services, while another can abstain from such action thanks to resources at its disposal which, however, are not necessarily due to any social superiority, the second has an unjust advantage over the first at law. In other words, there cannot be rich and poor at birth without their being unjust contracts." (p. 384.) In short, he insists that the "task of the most advanced societies is . . . a work of justice." p.387. In the meanwhile, however, for the sake of social peace and unity, "our first duty," he concludes, "is to make a moral code for ourselves." The problem of *anomy,* not the forced division of labor, is the first and more important order of business. This is the overwhelming emphasis in all Durkheim's later works in spite of his occasional return to the problem of equality and justice.

There were therefore two possible directions Durkheim's work could have taken. He could have pursued the problems and implications posed by the social conditions he himself observed and called attention to both in the *Division of Labor* and again in the preface to its second edition—*viz.*, "as long as there are rich and poor at birth, there cannot be just contract, nor a just distribution of social goods." (p. 29.) Or, he could have pursued, as in fact he did, the Comtean and more generally conservative concern with social unity, peace, and solidarity. Had he chosen the first path, this inevitably would have led him to an approach not unlike that of the Marxian and other socialist traditions: a careful and systematic consideration of the consequences of social stratification and class conflict, *and* the possibilities of social change. For a variety of reasons, Durkheim gave only scant and momentary attention to these sociological questions and opted instead for a conservative standpoint. Justice was important but social unity even more so.

Yet, Durkheim recognized early that his thesis of the solidarity-producing effects of the "division of labor" was "incomplete," if not altogether untenable. What he had defined as its pathological forms were normal and prevalent in his day and what he had defined as normal was virtually nonexistent. His original thesis had alleged that the separate and diverse functions, "when they are sufficiently in contact with one another, tend to stabilize and regulate themselves." Not only was this vague but, as he admits in his preface to the second edition, "this explanation is incomplete. For if it is true," he continues, "that social functions spontaneously seek to adapt themselves to one another, provided they are regularly in relationship, nevertheless this mode of adaptation becomes a rule of conduct only if the group consecrates it with its authority. A rule, indeed, is not only a habitual means of acting; it is, above all, *an obligatory means of acting. . . ."* (p. 4.)

Here we clearly see the theme that was to remain central in all of Durkheim's work: social order at all costs. Society with a capital "S" is, and must be, the sole arbiter of conflicting interests, and it is for "Its" sake that conflicting interests must be settled and each assigned "its *suitable* limits." Society "has the chief interest in order and peace; if anomy is an evil, it is above all because society suffers from it, being unable to live without cohesion and regularity. A moral or juridical regulation essentially expresses, then, social needs that society alone can feel. . . ." (p. 5.) This is no mere metaphor for Durkheim; his reification of "Society" is an expression of his ideological concerns. "Society" becomes for him, as for the conservatives generally, a polemical concept and value with which to counter critical-revolutionary theses. There is no getting around the fact that as he matured, his call for justice became more and more infrequent and faint; individual dignity and freedom as well as working-class interests were increasingly relegated to an insignificant position as compared with the interests of "Society."

At the same time, a "new" theme emerged and became a leading idea in Durkheim's proposal for reform. If the prevailing absence of orderly and regulated relations among functions is to end—if, in other words, anarchy and anomy are to decline and ultimately to disappear—what is required is the resurrection of an old social institution and its reintroduction, in a modified and appropriate form, into modern social life. Comte was wrong in assigning the regulative function exclusively to the State; modern economic life is much too complex for its regulation to be given over to that institution. Instead, that tried and tested institution the *occupational corporation or guild,* which was already known in antiquity and which flourished during the Middle Ages, can be readapted to modern conditions and can again serve the regulatory function it had served so well in the past. The men of the French Revolution acted rashly when they destroyed this institution instead of only modifying it. The occupational group should become the basis of an occupational ethic, for "[a]n occupational activity can be efficaciously regulated only by a group intimate enough with it to know its functioning, feel all its needs, and able to follow all their variations."

The occupational guilds must again become a public institution. These are to be based on the existing class structure and their function would be to lay down general moral and legal principles according to which relations among the various occupations and classes would be regulated. As Durkheim saw it, the representatives of both the employers and employees would be elected to the corporation assembly "in proportions corresponding to the respective importance attributed by opinion to these factors in production." (p. 25n.) And he adds: "But if it is necessary that both meet in the directing councils of the corporations, it is no less important that at the base of the corporative organization they form distinct and independent groups, for their interests are too often rival and antagonistic. To be able to go about their ways freely, they must go about their ways separately. The two groups thus constituted would then be able to appoint their representatives to the common assemblies." (p. 25n.) This will be not only in the best interest of society but of the individual as well; for the individual finds "anarchy" painful and regulation, joyful. (p. 15.) The occupational groups, their relations with one another and with society as a whole, are the issues Durkheim considers in his book *Professional Ethics and Civic Morals*. It is there that he develops his philosophy of society and the individual but still with some ambivalence, as we shall see, since he returns in the end to the question of equality and justice, a question he never again raises afterwards, or at least not in any prominent way.

Professional Ethics and Civic Morals

Just as Saint-Simon had called for a new secular religion, Durkheim now began to call for a new secular morality. A theme that would become stronger as he grew older—the need for altruism, and the individual as well as social hazards of egoism—already finds expression here. "We are not naturally inclined," he writes, "to put ourselves out or to use self-restraint; if we are not encouraged at every step to exercise the restraint upon which all morals depend, how should we get the habit of it? If we follow no rule except that of a clear self-interest, in the occupations that take up nearly the whole of our time, how should we acquire a taste for any disinterestedness, or selflessness, or sacrifice?"[7] The employer as well as the worker "is aware of no influence set above him to check his egotism; he is subject to no moral discipline whatever and so he scouts any discipline at all of this kind." Moral standards have to be raised "so that the conflicts which disturb [economic life] have an end. . . . There should be rules telling each of the workers his rights and his duties, not vaguely in general terms but in precise detail, having in view the most ordinary day-to-day occurrences." Employers and workers must, in their respective groups, impose restraint upon their special and selfish interests; they must see the interests of the whole, and then conflict will diminish and become moderate while the solidarity of society is correspondingly enhanced.

Eventually, in this book, Durkheim will suggest that private inheritance of wealth be abolished and that it be given over to the authority of the occupational organizations—his functional equivalent of Marx's public ownership of the means of production. But while for Marx this was to lead to the abolition of classes, in Durkheim's scheme the classes remain intact just as

[7] Émile Durkheim, *Professional Ethics and Civic Morals* (London: Routledge and Kegan Paul Ltd., 1957), p. 12. (All immediately following references to this work will be cited by page numbers in the text.

they did in Saint-Simon's. Durkheim believed it possible to develop a truly *social* morality in a class system; he wanted to revive and reorganize the guilds "so that economic activity should be permeated by ideas and needs other than individual ideas and needs"; it is for this reason "that it should be socialized." (p. 29.) He wanted somehow to bring "men's minds into mutual understanding," even while the great structural inequalities remained. "It is only through the corporative system that the moral standard of economic life can be raised." (p. 29.)

The main problem and task, therefore, was moral, not structural; while Durkheim draws attention to institutionalized inequality, he believes that even after structural changes the "state of anarchy would still persist; for let me repeat, the state of anarchy comes about not from [the means of production] being in these hands and not in those, but because the activity, deriving from it is not regulated." (p. 31.) Rational planning and mutual understanding would be necessary after basic inequalities have been abolished; why not begin now to raise the moral standards of everyone? He did not see or perhaps would not see that in the existing conditions, preaching the same moral message to everyone meant preaching a morality of submission to the disadvantaged.

It is interesting that in this book his attitude toward the classes and their respective roles in the occupational organizations is not precisely what it became later. In his preface to the second edition of the *Division of Labor,* written many years after *Professional Ethics,* he saw the need for a degree of employee autonomy within the larger organization. In *Professional Ethics,* however, he is not yet sure. Employers and workers are treated simply as "categories of industrial personnel" represented in the same corporation à la Saint-Simon; at this stage, Durkheim merely *wonders* whether it might not be necessary for the employers and workers to have separate and independent electoral bodies, at least "when their respective interests were obviously in conflict." (p. 39.)

In his discussion of *civic morals,* Durkheim's conception of society emerges in classical conservative terms. Political society, or the State, is "formed by the coming together of a rather large number of secondary social groups, subject to the same one authority which is not itself subject to any other superior authority duly constituted." (p. 45.) And further: "When the State takes thought and makes a decision, we must not say that it is society that thinks and decides through the State, but that the State thinks and decides for it." (p. 49.) The principal function of the State is to think. And in almost Hegelian terms, Durkheim writes that its "representations are distinguished from the other collective representations by their higher degree of consciousness and reflection." (p. 50.) And, somehow, paradoxically, except for abnormal cases(!), "the stronger the State, the more the individual is respected." (p. 57.)

At this stage of Durkheim's thinking, the individual is not *totally* submerged as he later appears to be. He recognizes that the power of the State left unchecked can tyrannize over the individual. On the other hand, the power of the secondary groups must be curbed, for otherwise they, too, can gain "a mastery over their members and mold them at will."(p. 62.) The State, then, must prevent the absorption of the individuals by the secondary groups and serve "to remind these partial societies that they are not alone and that there is a right that stands above their rights. The State must therefore enter into their lives, it must supervise and keep a check on the way they operate and to do this it must spread its roots in all directions." (p. 65.) At the same time, the secondary groups, in turn, are to serve as a counterbalance to the State, restraining its excessive expansion. In this way, the various secondary groups "form one of the conditions essential to the emancipation of the individual." (p. 63.)

Yet, when Durkheim speaks of the emancipation of the individual, it is not the Kantian conception he has in mind. He is unwilling to make the freedom of the individual a moral imperative—at least not the real, concrete, flesh-and-blood individual. For Durkheim, the individual is an abstraction, submerged in a group, which is in turn subordinated to the Society (= the State). This is the ideology that eventuates in the "methodological tyranny" of his *Rules of the Sociological Method*. "It is not," writes Durkheim, "this or that individual the State seeks to develop, it is the individual *in genere,* who is not to be confused with any single one of us." The fundamental duty of the state "is to persevere in calling the individual to a moral way of life." (p. 69.) Ultimately Durkheim reverts to a Hegelian conclusion: "At the present day, the State is the highest form of organized society that exists. Some forms of belief in a world State, or world patriotism do themselves get pretty close to an egotistic individualism. Their effect is to disparage the existing moral law, rather than to create others of higher merit." In effect, this was the outlook that led Durkheim—despite his efforts to define patriotism in terms of setting one's own house in order according to the principles of justice—ultimately to defend the French point of view in World War I, while his close friend, Jaurès, the socialist, had been assassinated for exposing the folly and horrors of such a war.

Similarly, freedom and autonomy, for Durkheim, was not the process of eliminating and abolishing the various social forms that constrained and repressed the individual but rather bowing to the existing factual order. "To be autonomous," he writes, "means, for the human being, to understand the necessities he has to bow to and accept them with full knowledge of the facts. Nothing that we can do can make the laws of things other than they are, but we free ourselves of them in thinking them, that is, in making them ours by thought. That is what gives democracy a moral superiority." (p. 91.) What is more, in his conception of democracy, the individual constitutes a danger to the State; so if earlier we were told that the function of the secondary groups was to protect the individual from the State, now we learn that "they are also necessary if the State is to be sufficiently free of the individual." (p. 96.) It is this, as we shall see, which constitutes by far the dominant concern for Durkheim in his later works.

In *Professional Ethics,* however, in his concluding discussion of property, property rights, and contracts, Durkheim does return to the problem of justice and how it is impeded by certain institutions. Inheritance and exchange by contracts are the two main ways of acquiring property; and he tries to show by means of historical analysis that the former is "bound up with archaic concepts and practices that have no part in our present-day ethics." (p. 174.) Of "the two main processes by which property is acquired, inheritance is the one that is going to lose its importance more and more." (p. 175.) What remains then is the contract, and whether the conditions under which it is made can be just.

The contract is a juridical-moral bond between two subjects that specifies their mutual rights and obligations. Generally, says Durkheim, "a right exists on both sides." (p. 176.) He is quick to add, however, that "these mutual rights are not inevitable. The slave is bound in law to his master and yet has no right over him." (p. 176.) Thus Durkheim returns to an issue which, at this stage of his intellectual development, appeared to be fundamental: some "contracts" are made between social unequals where one dominates and the other serves and where the latter has no choice but to serve or to die. Can such a contract, though sanctioned by "a moral authority that stands higher," be just? To this question Durkheim replies with an unequivocal no.

In tracing its development as an institution, Durkheim shows that a *bona fide* consensual contract "could not be one of good faith except on condition of its being one by mutual consent." (p. 203.) But consent "binds truly and absolutely the one who consents only on the condition that it has been *freely* given. Anything that lessens the liberty of the contracting party, lessens the binding force of the contract." As Durkheim proceeds to develop this argument, one sees just how close he had moved in that instance and at that moment to the Marxian point of view. "This rule should not be confused with the one that requires the contract to be made with deliberate intent. For I may very well have had the will to contract as I have done, and yet have contracted only under coercion. In this case, I will the obligations I subscribe to, but I will them by reason of pressure being put upon me. The consent in such instances is said to be invalidated and thus the contract is null and void." (p. 204.) Thus a contract cannot be viewed as just, simply because a man has subjectively willed it. What is crucial is how much freedom and power he has to resist entering into certain contractual relationships. Whether a contract is binding or not depends, therefore, not merely on subjective will but on the *objective* conditions under which it is made. If

contracts imposed by constraint, direct or indirect, are not binding, this does not arise from the state of the will when it gave consent. It arises from the consequences that an obligation thus formed inevitably brings upon the contracting party. It may be, in fact, that he took the step that has bound him only under external pressure, that his consent has been extracted from him. If this is so, it means that the consent was against his own interests and the justifiable needs he might have under the general principles of equity. The use of coercion could have had no other aim or consequence but that of forcing him to yield up something which he did not wish to, to do something he did not wish to do, or indeed of forcing him to the one action or the other on conditions he did not will. Penalty and distress have thus been undeservedly laid on him.

Such a contract, Durkheim observes, is increasingly regarded as invalid and this is not merely because "the determining cause of the obligation is exterior to the individual who binds himself. It is because he has suffered some unjustified injury, because, in a word, such a contract is unjust." Increasingly, a contract is regarded as moral and just if it is not a "means of exploiting one of the contracting parties." The *objective consequences* for the parties concerned, and not their formal, subjective consent, must constitute the real criterion of a just contract.

Here, in the final pages of *Professional Ethics and Civic Morals,* Durkheim draws certain conclusions from the stratification and class structure of society which may be regarded as evidence of a momentary concession to, or convergence with, Marx and the socialists. The institution of inheritance is again singled out by Durkheim as a "supreme obstacle" to just relations in society.

> Now inheritance as an institution [writes Durkheim] results in men being born either rich or poor; that is to say, there are two main classes in society, linked by all sorts of intermediate classes: the one which in order to live has to make its services acceptable to the other at whatever the cost; the other class which can do without these services, because it can call on certain resources, which may, however, not be equal to the services rendered by those who have them to offer. Therefore as long as such sharp class differences exist in society, fairly effective palliatives may lessen the injustice of contracts; but in principle, the system operates in conditions which do not allow of justice. (p. 213.)

Where he differed with Marx was in the view of how social change would come about. For unlike Marx, Durkheim conceived of social change not as a function of class conflict but as a result of the slow evolution of the collective moral conscience. One important change, however, was immediately possible, which would at one stroke eradicate a fundamental source of inequality and thus make for a qualitatively new stage of justice: "One primary reform is possible at once and almost without any transition. This is the discontinuance of inheritance *ab intestat* or by next of kin. . . ." (p. 216.) Who, then, will inherit this wealth? As noted earlier, Durkheim regarded the occupational corporations as best suited to fulfill this function. Like the socialists, he thus sees the need to socialize property and wealth; but it is the professional groups that, in his opinion, "would satisfy all the conditions for becoming in a sense, in the economic sphere, the heirs of the family." (p. 218.)

But Durkheim is prepared to go even further; even after the abolition of inheritance, inequalities will remain—differences of talents and intelligence. Can it not be said that these inequalities of merit are also fortuitous?

To us it does not seem equitable that a man should be better treated as a social being because he was born of parentage that is rich or of high rank. But is it any more equitable that he should be better treated because he was born of a father of higher intelligence or in a more favorable moral *milieu?* It is here that the domain of charity begins. Charity is the feeling of human sympathy that we see becoming clear even of these last remaining traces of inequality. It ignores and denies any special merit in gifts or mental capacity acquired by heredity. This, then, is the very acme of justice. (p. 220.)

And this, then, is the note on which Durkheim concludes *Professional Ethics and Civil Morals*—a note, however, to which he never returns.

Education and Sociology

In Durkheim's theory of education, particularly as defined in these essays —the influence adults exercise upon the young—one sees an increasing tendency not only to reify but, indeed, to deify "Society." Society becomes the veritable creator of the individual, which viewpoint lays the groundwork for his theory of religion—the divine is the symbolic expression of the forces of society. Society is increasingly regarded as an all-embracing entity, *"sui generis,"* an expression he uses again and again. The implications of structured inequality no longer occupy his attention; nor does he propose that certain changes are necessary for justice to prevail. Now his *idée fixe* becomes how best to *adapt* the individual to "Society," how best to prepare him to adjust to its irresistible forces and to fulfill his specific "function" in a morally dutiful manner.

The truth in Durkheim's major sociological proposition, that an individual becomes human in the process of interaction with others, he chose to formulate in other terms—Society implants in each individual an aspect of itself so that in effect it creates him. Insofar as individuals may be discerned in Durkheim's scheme, they are, to employ the terminology of G. H. Mead, predominantly, if not exclusively, "me's." Mead's "I" is nonexistent in Durkheim's system. Moreover, as we shall see, it is not only necessary but good that the individual subordinate himself to society. Though he is inconsistent on this score, there is generally no tension in Durkheim's system between the individual and society; insofar as such tension exists, it is always resolved in favor of society.

The significance of socioeconomic classes and strata is only dimly perceived, if at all, in Durkheim's educational scheme; as in the *Division of Labor,* they are viewed simply as coordinate functions rather than as groups with conflicting interests. Forced servitude, *i.e.,* the fact that some are constrained either to serve or to starve, apparently has no implications for education, whose exclusive function it is to prepare the individual for society *as it is*. *"Education,"* according to Durkheim's formula, *"is the influence exercised by adult generations on those . . . not yet ready for social life. Its object is to arouse and to develop in the child a certain number of physical, intellectual, and moral states which are demanded of him by both the political society as a whole and the special milieu for which he is specifically destined."*[8] The individual is "specifically destined" to fill a certain occupational role and to live in a special milieu, and the function of education is to facilitate his adjustment to his destiny.

Durkheim avers, however, that by nature man is not inclined to submit to political authority; self-discipline and self-sacrifice are not modes of conduct to which he is congenitally disposed. But does this mean that when society fashions "individuals according to its needs," that they are "submitting to an insupportable tyranny?" No, replies Durkheim. For "in reality they are themselves interested in this submission; for the new being that collective influence, through education, thus builds up in each of us, represents what is best in us." (p. 76.)

If, for the *Philosophes* as for Marx, the best in man was yet to be realized, and it was precisely the existing social order which frustrated its realization, it was quite otherwise for Durkheim. He transforms all individual values into egoism pure and simple and, on the other hand, turns into unadulterated virtues everything the individual forfeits to society. In his words: "It is society . . . that draws us out of ourselves, that obliges us to reckon with other interests than our own, it is society that has taught us to control our passions, our instincts, to prescribe law for them, to restrain ourselves, to deprive ourselves, to sacrifice ourselves, to subordinate our personal ends to higher ends." (p.76.) In this way, restraint, deprivation, self-sacrifice, subordination, all become the cardinal values education must inculcate to serve the ends of "Society"; and the more we have placed our inclinations under social control, the more fully human we are.

"Society" thus becomes an unadulterated *positive;* social processes are *humanizing,* by definition, while dehumanization and alienation are excluded, also by definition, from social life. "Society" is hypostasized by Durkheim for clearly ideological reasons. More than anything, he craved for social solidarity and order; therefore, an antagonism of any kind between the individual and society had to be denied. The "antagonism that has too often been admitted," he writes, "between society and individual corresponds to nothing in the facts." (p. 78.) If, earlier, he himself had clearly shown that the existing society definitely implied constraint, coercion, and, generally, social conditions that precluded the individual's free development, now we learn that it is far

---

[8] Émile Durkheim, *Education and Sociology* (Glencoe, Illinois: The Free Press, 1956), p. 71. Italics in original. (Subsequent references appear as page numbers in the text.)

from the truth that the individual and society stand in opposition and are able to develop only at each other's expense. "The individual, in willing society, wills himself. The influence that it exerts on him, notably through education, does not at all have as its object and its effect to repress him, to diminish him, to denature him, but, on the contrary, to make him grow and to make of him a truly human being." For Durkheim, "Society" is the highest end; and in order that it be solidary, individuals must be content in their special milieux. The State, therefore, must "remind the teacher constantly of the ideas, [and] the sentiments that must be impressed upon the child to adjust him to the milieu in which he must live." Otherwise, education "would necessarily be put to the service of private beliefs, and the whole nation would be divided and would break down into an incoherent multitude of little fragments in conflict with one another." (p. 79.)

Clearly, there is nothing in the proposition, "Man is a social being," that is inherently either conservative or revolutionary. In Durkheim's hands, however, it becomes essentially conservative, for his emphasis throughout is on man's adaptation to circumstances but never on the adaptation of circumstances to man's ends. Man must bow before the inexorable social facts. Even his assertion of the absence of instincts in men is a truth that becomes ideological in his hands; if the "innate predispositions in man are very general and very vague," (p. 82.) how could one argue that society or certain forms of society are repressive and antagonistic to man's nature? Both Marx and Durkheim recognized that men are what they are largely as a result of the modes of interaction with other men. But each thinker drew from this proposition diametrically opposed conclusions. Since man is infinitely perfectible, Marx believed, those social forms which repress and constrain him must be shattered and changed to allow for the greater development of his creative faculties in freedom; the elimination of certain social relationships and institutions facilitates individual development and widens the boundaries of freedom. For Durkheim, in contrast, since the human dispositions at birth were so vague and general and since, as a consequence, the human child was so malleable, the task of education was to render these dispositions more specific so that he could eventually "play a useful role in society." Here, "useful role" must be translated as the particular function one is destined to fulfill in the "division of labor" and in whatever "milieu" (Durkheim's euphemism for stratum or class) he happens to be born in. Education is a matter of getting the child to accept social authority and to learn his duty. Duty "is, indeed, for the child and even for the adult, the stimulus par excellence of effort." (p. 88.) "For to be free," Durkheim continues, "is not to do what one pleases; it is to be master of oneself, it is to know how to act with reason and to do one's duty." (pp. 89–90.) This increasingly is the main burden of Durkheim's educational theory. If earlier he vacillated between two positions—*i.e.*, (1.) fine tuning of the social system, by bringing moral rules into harmony with the developing division of labor, and (2.) effecting certain basic social changes—now it is the former position which becomes dominant. The function of moral education is to inculcate a deep sense of altruism, self-discipline, duty, and satiety, and at the same time to curb egoism and to moderate insatiable appetites.

Moral Education

The development of a secular morality suited to the conditions of the time now became for Durkheim *the* essential task for French society. He states quite clearly that his aim in this work "is not to formulate moral education for man in general; but for men of our time in this country."[9] Durkheim, whose ultimate social theory of knowledge is in many respects similar to Marx's, understood very well that there is a determinate relationship between the moral values of men and the conditions of their social existence. That there could not be one morality good for all times and places, for all societies, was evident. Yet, Durkheim was prepared to prescribe a single morality for all the sub-societies, *i.e.,* classes and strata, of the France of his day.

The issues he had raised in *Professional Ethics* relating to the unjust nature of contracts so long as basic inequalities and constraint remained essential aspects of society, are now virtually ignored. Since the majority of French children are being socialized in the elementary school system, it must become the guardian "par excellence of our national character." (p. 4.) In modern French society, or for that matter in western Europe as a whole, God is dead! —or at least dying, and cannot be resurrected. Earlier God was the supreme guarantor of the moral order; in giving God his due, men were in fact assuring that their relations would rest on a firm moral basis. Anticipating his thesis in *Elementary Forms of Religious Life,* Durkheim was suggesting that "God" was really a symbolic expression of the force of society as a whole. In a Saint-Simonian, or even Marxian, fashion, Durkheim viewed the decline of religion as a consequence of both the dissolution of traditional society and the growth of modern industry and science. If religion has become a moribund institution and no longer fulfills a moral function, present-day society is then faced with a great danger: the possible denial of morality altogether. If no secular substitute is found for religion, "we run the risk of also eliminating essential moral ideas and sentiments" (p. 19.) and threatening "public morality at its very roots." (p. 3.)

To be sure, Durkheim continues to raise the question of injustice, but exclusively in abstract terms without reference to its structural basis. Now, the "characteristic of injustice is that it is not founded in the nature of things; it is not based upon reason." (p. 20.) For Durkheim, however, reason does not refer (as it did for the *Philosophes* and for Marx) to the critical faculties

---

9 Émile Durkheim, *Moral Education* (Glencoe, Illinois: The Free Press, 1961), p. 3. (Subsequent references to this work appear as page numbers in the text.)

of an individual by which he assesses an institution and, finding it oppressive, acts with others in order to change it. Durkheim wants to use reason and science to discover the moral forces of a society and, once discovered, "to investigate how they should develop and be oriented under present social conditions." We are thus back to the problem of the anomic division of labor. Anomy is the most serious problem facing man; and this refers not to the absence of all moral norms but to the absence of the appropriate norms. The main task, therefore, is to develop in the child "those general dispositions that, once created, adapt themselves readily to the particular circumstances of human life." (p. 21.) And in order to discover the new morality Durkheim wants to employ the scientific method.

Morality is not to be viewed as a body of general precepts, but rather as a totality of specific and definite behavioral prescriptions. Rules are "like so many molds with limiting boundaries, into which we must pour our behavior." (p. 26.) By studying the past as well as the present, one discovers the true function of morality, which is "in the first place, to determine conduct, to fix it, to eliminate the element of individual arbitrariness." (p. 27.) Specific moral rules promote "regularity of conduct"; and those who spurn such regularity, as do "transients and people who cannot hold themselves to specific jobs, are always suspect. It is because their moral temperament is fundamentally defective—because it is most uncertain and undependable." (p. 27.) There can be no doubt that in Durkheim's system of values, disdain for regularized and controlled conduct was not only pathological but morally *bad;* it promoted endless instability both in the individuals concerned and in society at large. Furthermore, it threatened the established order of authority.

A rule implies more than regularized conduct, for it is invested with authority, a "moral power that we acknowlege as superior to us." (p. 29.) And morality is precisely that "category of rules where the idea of authority plays an absolutely preponderant role." (p. 29.) A concept which embraces both aspects of morality, *i.e.*, regularity and authority, is discipline, "the fundamental element of morality." Here Durkheim begins to develop a philosophical theme that dominates not only this work but all his later works as well: moral discipline is a *good in itself*. It is good not only for society as a whole but, as we shall see, for the mental health of the individual. Despite his cautious wording, the bias is unmistakable: "Those . . . whose preference for change and diversity prompts a revulsion at all uniformity are certainly in danger of being morally incomplete. Regularity is the moral analogue of periodicity in the organism." (p. 34.) In his eagerness to develop a morality for the society as a whole, Durkheim now invests rules per se with a sacred quality, so that the question is never asked whether the existing rules may be, in fact, unjust and repressive and, hence, *immoral.* A denial of their authority, an "inability to feel and to recognize such authority wherever it exists—or to demur when it is recognized—is precisely a negation of genuine morality."

The utilitarians, and Marx as well, justified constraint only to the degree that it was clearly unavoidable for the functioning of society. To these arguments Durkheim replies that discipline is socially necessary and useful; for society is a living being and to assure its proper functioning, rules are imperative. "[A]ll living organization presupposes determinate rules, and to neglect them is to invite serious disturbance." "Disturbance" of the "social organism" is what Durkheim feared most; so much so, in fact, that he now suggests that it is inconceivable that a social institution could violate an individual's nature: "If an institution does violence to human nature, however socially useful it may be, it will never be born, much less persist, since it cannot take root in the conscience. True, social institutions are directed toward society's interests and not those of individuals as such. But, on the other hand, if such institutions threaten or disorganize the individual life at its source, they also disorganize the foundation of their own existence."

Can discipline be regarded as a repressive, restrictive, and constraining force which impedes an individual's development? No, says Durkheim, for "an inability to restrict one's self within determinate limits is a sign of disease—with respect to all forms of human conduct and, even more generally, for all kinds of biological behavior." (p. 38.) Durkheim is here advancing a "sociology" *and* a psychological philosophy. In his sociology he insists that a society, just as a living organism, is a "complex equilibrium whose various elements limit one another; this balance cannot be disrupted without producing unhappiness or illness." (p. 39.) For Durkheim, it is always the disruption, but never the maintenance, of the "equilibrium" (status quo) which causes suffering and pain. As psychologist-philosopher Durkheim focuses on what he regards as the main source of modern man's malaise—his unlimited appetites. In *Moral Education* he summarizes the main points he makes again in *Suicide* where one finds a treatise completely devoted to the need for moderation and restraint. He writes: "A need, a desire freed of all restraints, and all rules, no longer geared to some determinate objective and, through the same connection, limited and contained, can be nothing but a source of constant anguish for the person experiencing it. . . . This is why historical periods like ours, which have known the malady of infinite aspiration, are necessarily touched with pessimism. Pessimism always accompanies unlimited aspirations. Goethe's Faust may be regarded as representing par excellence this view of the infinite. And it is not without reason that the poet has portrayed him as laboring in continual anguish." (p. 40.)

Durkheim is preaching the same moral message to all members of society regardless of the position in which they find themselves. Men must set themselves finite goals and learn to be sated. The social changes Durkheim had earlier regarded as necessary for a more just equilibrium were yet to be realized; nevertheless, those subject to unjust relationships should curb their appetites and aspirations. *Constraint* is transformed by Durkheim into a purely *positive* phenomenon for it keeps "our vital forces within appropriate limits." (p. 41.) Moral regulations form "about each person an imaginary wall, at the foot of which a multitude of human passions simply die without being able to go further. For the same reason—that they are contained—it becomes possible to satisfy them." (p. 42.) Constraint, containment, limitation, these are positive values. Discipline, the essence of moral education, is essential for individual health and social order. "Through it [discipline] and by means of it alone are we able to teach the child to rein in his desires, to set limits to his appetites of all kinds, to limit and, through limitation, to define the goals of his activity." (p. 43.)

Whatever the element of truth in this general philosophico-psychological theory, it had necessarily to resolve itself into a morality of submission and resignation for the working class and, more generally, for the disadvantaged strata. However, Durkheim did not seem to grasp this implication. It is an illusion, he insists, that the imposition of limits on our desires and faculties results in a reduction of power or in subordination; true power is a subjective entity. Imagine, he writes, the most absolute despot in history "liberated from all external restraint" and whose desires are irresistible. "Shall we say, then, that he is all-powerful? Certainly not, since he himself cannot resist his desires. They are masters of him as of everything else. He submits to them; he does not dominate them. . . . A despot is like a child; he has a child's weaknesses because he is not master of himself. Self-mastery is the first condition of all true power, of all liberty worthy of the name." (p. 45.) It is as if Durkheim, having abandoned all hope of mastering or changing external social conditions, and fearing the "disruptive" consequences of unbridled appetites, had little choice but to counsel "self-mastery." Self-control as a moral injunction should be implanted in the child to dispense with the need for constant external controls. And the internalization of controls is useful, desirable, and good for both the individual and society. With this line of reasoning Durkheim is able to conclude that discipline and limitation are the condition of one's happiness and moral health. "The rule, because it teaches us to restrain and master ourselves, is a means of emancipation and of freedom." (p. 49.)

Although Durkheim was not altogether blind to some of the implications of this position, in anticipating objections and dealing with them he reverts to his doctrine of "natural abilities." The limits he wants to impose are "based on the nature of things, that is to say, in the nature of each of us. This has nothing to do with insidiously inculcating a spirit of resignation in the child; or curbing his legitimate ambitions; or preventing him from seeing the conditions existing around him." Nonetheless, the child simply must be given to understand that to be happy is to set himself goals that correspond to his "nature"; he must not strain "neurotically and unhappily toward infinitely distant and consequently inaccessible goals." One must select a goal compatible with one's abilities, and not seek to surpass "artificially" one's "natural limits." Discipline is useful and necessary "because it seems to us demanded by nature itself." (p. 50.)

Durkheim thus believed it somehow possible to discover one's "natural" capacities and limits even while vast cultural inequalities persisted among the various social classes and strata. He did not see, somehow, that so long as these inequalities continued to exist, it was very insidious indeed to encourage children to recognize their so-called "natural" limitations. For there can be no doubt that the educational system in Durkheim's time—and this is equally true today—did not even begin to realize the potential of most children, even granting for a moment that such potentials have "natural" limits. In effect, Durkheim inverted quite deliberately the theory of the Enlightenment.

For the *Philosophes,* social institutions were to be criticized and changed, thereby widening the boundaries of individual freedom and facilitating the constant and continuing perfection of man. For Marx, too, it was precisely the extant social system which imposed limitations on man, not his own "nature." Man was infinitely perfectible and his dynamic potential was realizable only by removing those social conditions which served to block it.

To be sure, Durkheim recognizes that, "if discipline is a means through which man realizes his nature, it must change as that nature changes through time." (p. 51.) He is not suggesting that the child cannot, or must not, surpass his father; in fact he regards such suggestions as arrogant. What he is suggesting, however, is that though they are "not absolutely the same at different historical periods," there are forces that set limits in each period and at each stage in the evolution of a society. A *proper* morality is one suited to a given stage—one in which individuals recognize the limits of that stage and "adjust" to them. Durkheim did perceive certain dangers in a morality which was "beyond criticism or reflection, the agents par excellence of all change." (p. 52.) But he insists that the exercise of criticism, which leads to a weakening of the existing order of discipline and authority, is not required in *normal* circumstances. If "in critical and abnormal circumstances," he writes, "the feeling for the rule and for discipline must be weakened, it does not follow that such impairment is normal. Furthermore, we must take care not to confuse two very different feelings: the need to substitute a new regulation for an old one; and the impatience with all rules, the abhorrence of all discipline. Under orderly conditions, the former is natural, healthy, and fruitful; the latter is always abnormal since it prompts us to alienate ourselves from the basic conditions of life." (p. 53.)

But by his own admission in *Professional Ethics,* great social inequalities led to unjust relations, and these very conditions were still in effect when Durkheim wrote his *Moral Education.* For most of his contemporaries, these inequalities were in fact the basic and normal conditions of their lives. Should it not then also be regarded as normal when men who are subjected to injustice criticize and even rebel against the prevailing order of moral rules and discipline? Therefore, when Durkheim writes: "Our task is not to shape the child in terms of a nonexistent morality but in the light of moral concepts as they exist or as they tend to be"—what is he in effect counseling? (p. 55.)

Is this not an educational theory designed to discourage and dissuade the child from striving for just conditions because they constitute a "nonexistent morality"? What have we here if not a morality that sanctions the status quo—a morality that holds the existing rules for absolutely good?

It would be unfair to accuse Durkheim of abhorring all social change; but this change had to be orderly, gradual, and organic. Injustices which precluded the free development of the majority of individuals were prevalent; this was bad. But if he found these injustices morally offensive, he found social disorder, "anarchy," and conflict even more offensive—and frightening. " . . . [W]e are living precisely in one of those critical, revolutionary periods when authority is usually weakened through the loss of traditional discipline—a time that may easily give rise to a spirit of anarchy." (p. 54.) Therefore, the most immediate task was to develop as rapidly as possible a new discipline suited to the new social conditions. But if the "new" conditions were by his own admission still unjust, could the morality be otherwise? In spite of his efforts to reconcile social justice with social order, there can be no doubt that it was the latter value he cherished above all.

Moral goals remain throughout Durkheim's work supra-individual; they are goals "the object of which is *society*. To act morally is to act in terms of collective interest." "Society" is something above "those sentient beings who are other individual human beings. . . ." (p. 59.) And more often than not though he paid his respects to the ideal of "humanity," in practice it was the nation-state Durkheim regarded as the highest form of society. In short, "society," for Durkheim as for Comte, remained a polemical-ideological concept —an antithesis to those ideologies based on the dignity of the individual and the interests of a particular social class. Marx had linked individual to class interests and had conceived of the abolition of the fundamental inequalities of a class-based social system as the precondition for the emancipation of the individual: Only after these basic changes had been made could "the free development of each lead to the free development of all." The individual and his free development was his highest moral ideal and he therefore guarded himself against any reification of "society." Durkheim, in contrast, defined morality so that "the individual interest of each person taken separately is altogether devoid of moral character." (p. 65.)

Sometimes in Durkheim's scheme, "society" becomes everything and the individual nothing; at other times, they are both equally abstract and the alleged antagonism between them is illusory. Anticipating his theory of suicide, he insists that the greater one's identity with a group, the more he will cling to life. Egoism is not only immoral, and anomy individually and socially disorganizing, but they conduce to self-destruction as well. Altruism, on the other hand, is not only moral—it preserves life. Man, writes Durkheim, "also destroys himself less frequently when he has things to concern him other than himself. Crises that activate people's feeling of identity with the group produce the same results." (p. 68.) And what example does he provide of a situation in which man "destroys himself less frequently"? *Wars,* writes Durkheim, "in quickening the sense of patriotism, subordinate preoccupation with the self. The image of the threatened fatherland occupies a place in one's consciousness that it does not have in peacetime; consequently, the bond between individual and society is strengthened, and, at the same time, the linkage to life is also reinforced. The numbers of suicides decline." (pp. 68–9.) This is indicative of Durkheim's concerns and values: Suicide looms larger as a social and individual evil, and as a cause of human destruction, than war and the misery caused by the "normal" structure of society.

It was Durkheim's clear position that our allegiance is owed above all to the nation. "The evidence suggests," he writes, "that familial goals are and should be subordinated to national objectives, if for no other reason than that the nation is a social group at a higher level." (p. 74.) Like Hegel, Burke, Comte, *et al.,* he writes: "The state is actually the most highly organized form of human organization in existence, and if one may believe that in the future states even greater than those of today may be formed, there is nothing to justify the supposition that there will never emerge a state embracing the whole of humanity." (p. 76.) Meanwhile, Durkheim wanted each state to dedicate itself to "human ends"; the state ought to commit itself not to expansion "to the detriment of its neighbors . . . but to the goal of realizing among its own people the general interests of humanity. . . ." (p. 77.) How otherwise could one dedicate himself to "humanity"? he asks. His positivistic bias dictated that morality be determined by an existing factual order, an existing group. And since humanity was merely an intellectual construct, not a real group, how could one give it one's allegiance? The "Society" or, in effect, the nation-state was the highest "real group" and "the school is the only moral agent through which the child is able systematically to learn to know and love his country." (p. 79.)

It is this attitude which reached its logical and practical conclusion in Durkheim's patriotic articles during the great carnage that began in 1914. The translation into practice of his doctrine that the individual must be sacrificed to the State mortally wounded him; for he lost his son in the war and, broken-hearted, died himself soon afterward. Durkheim's tragic error was to call for love and devotion to "Society" before that minimal justice he himself had regarded as necessary had been attained.

Durkheim conceded to Marx that "taken apart from particular cases, the nature of the distress in a given society is a function of the conditions of economic life and of the way in which it operates—that is to say, a function of its particular organization." (p. 84.) And he recognized, in addition, that to cure the ills he saw, to act effectively, it was necessary to group "individual efforts in such a way as to counter social forces with social forces." (p. 84.) But this is little more than an aside in this work, nor does he explore the implications of this observation for moral education. Instead, anticipating his thesis in *Elementary Forms,* he moves closer to the position that the divine is the symbolic expression of society; and is it any wonder, since "Society" had become a divine and sacred entity in Durkheim's mind. From here it was not very far to his methodological realism: society must be something more than a word or abstract term. It must be a living reality distinct from the individuals comprising it. Otherwise, how would we come to cherish society and devote ourselves to it? We must never say that society is a mental construct. Why? Because one "doesn't [sic] cherish a mental construct." (p. 257.)

In general, Durkheim's theory of education, apart from being conservative, is often banal, unimaginative, and puritanical besides. Leisure is dangerous, he tells us, and art frivolous: "In serious life, man is sustained against temptation by the obligation of work." Art is a game whereas morality is "life in earnest." The distance separating art from morality is that separating "play from work. Not therefore by learning to play that special game, art, will we learn to do our duty." Society had to become in men's minds a living reality to be taken seriously, and this ideological position underlay the methodological view in Durkheim's *Rules of the Sociological Method.*

The Rules of the Sociological Method

If secular education were to have the moral authority once exercised by the Church, something as powerful as "God" once was, had to be put in His place. It was therefore appropriate and convenient, as George Catlin noted, that society acquire godlike attributes. Society and the State became Durkheim's god and the ideological basis of his methodological "realism." Catlin observes: "By his ill-considered and scientifically pretentious psycho-mysticism Durkheim has contributed to give the color of justification to the new religion of the altar of *divus Augustus* and to the neopagan philosophy of Caesar-worship."[10]

Durkheim was aware of his bias. He preferred his methodological approach because he deemed it less *dangerous* than any other. In the preface to the First Edition of his *Rules* Durkheim candidly acknowledged that his reasoning was "not at all revolutionary. We are even, in a sense, essentially conservative, since we deal with social facts as such, recognize their flexibility, but conceive them as deterministic rather than arbitrary. *How much more dangerous is the doctrine* which sees in social phenomena only the results of unrestrained manipulation, which can in an instant, by a simple dialectical artifice, be completely upset!" (P. xxxix. Italics mine.) If, then, Durkheim, in

---

[10] See the Introduction to the translation of Émile Durkheim's *The Rules of the Sociological Method* Paperback Edition (New York: The Free Press, 1964), p. xxvi. (Subsequent references to this work appears as page numbers in the text.)

this work, was making explicit the rules for a scientific study of society, it was not without an eye to the political-ideological implications of his rules as opposed to others.

Durkheim's most fundamental principle was "the objective reality of social facts." (p. lvii.) The same objections may be raised here as were earlier raised against Comte: that by terming the existing factual order "objective" and "real," those tendencies at work which tend to negate the existing order are obscured and, even when perceived, are defined as unreal. Secondly, this principle tends to exaggerate the degree to which social facts are independent of an individual's will. Of course, Marx would have agreed that from the standpoint of a single individual many "social facts" *appear* to be independent of his will; but since in concert with other individuals the so-called objective social reality can be changed, it must be regarded as only *apparently* objective. Marx acknowledged that men cannot make history just as they please; but that they make history remains nevertheless an essential principle of his theory. In Marx's work, moreover, social facts are obviously not unadulterated "positives"; there are certain tendencies at work in the existing factual order which tend to *negate* and change that order. Not so for Durkheim. The social fact is a "positive" and the focus is always on "the power of external coercion which it exercises or is capable of exercising over individuals" but never on the power of individuals to change the social facts. In place of "society" as a concept referring to the interactions and interrelationships of individuals, we are given a reified conception of society as a real, living entity—a *thing*.

Durkheim's first rule is *"Consider social facts as things."* (p. 14.) This view is advanced as an antidote to that which "gives itself up to boundless ambitions and comes to believe in the possibility of constructing, or rather reconstructing, the world"; and when he adds, "by virtue of its own resources exclusively and at the whim of its desires," he thereby hopes to discredit his opponent's view by making it appear naïve. Durkheim understood, of course, that "social things are actualized only through men; they are a product of human activity." But men are always the passive objects of this activity, never acting subjects. The active, creative side of human conduct disappears in Durkheim's scheme. His emphasis throughout is that "far from being a product of the will, [social facts] determine it from without; they are like molds in which our actions are inevitably shaped. This necessity is often inescapable. But even when we triumph over it, the opposition encountered signifies clearly to us the presence of something not depending upon ourselves. Thus, in considering social phenomena as things, we merely adjust our conceptions in conformity to their nature."

Objections may also be raised against Durkheim's definition of morality. At any given time, "society" is the best judge of what is moral. "To decide whether a precept belongs to the moral order, we must determine whether or not it presents the external mark of morality; this mark is a widespread repressive sanction, that is, a condemnation by public opinion that punishes all violations of the precept." (p. 41.) It is always the repressive reaction of "society" which determines what is moral but never rebellion and resistance on the part of those who consider themselves wronged. If the men whom Durkheim himself had earlier perceived as victims of unjust relationships rebel, and their rebellion is met with a repressive reaction, the rebellion would now have to be regarded as immoral and the repression, moral.

Durkheim's positivistic brand of science led him to the view that science could determine ends as well as means. "If science," he writes, "cannot indicate the best goal to us, how can it inform us about the best means to reach it? . . . If science cannot guide us in the determination of ultimate ends, it is equally powerless in the case of those secondary and subordinate ends called 'means.' " (p. 48.) Perhaps he really believed that science taught him to desire the "normal functioning of society"; that the "normal" state is the most desirable end to be sought after, while the "morbid" and "pathological" are to be eschewed—or at least kept to a minimum. What is his "scientific" definition of these terms "We shall call 'normal' these social conditions that are the most generally distributed and the others 'morbid' or 'pathological.' " (p. 55.) Morbidity, continues Durkheim, is no less natural than health; "it is equally grounded in the nature of things. But it is not grounded in their normal nature; it is not inherent in their ordinary constitution or bound up with the conditions of existence upon which they generally depend." (p. 58.)

A very curious allegation indeed. We are here back to the thesis of his *Division of Labor:* that, *normally* it conduces to a higher solidarity and when it does not, it is because the division of labor has assumed pathological forms, *i.e.,* its *anomic* and *forced* forms. By his own admission in *Professional Ethics,* the forced division of labor was very widespread, and it was precisely this institutionalized condition that rendered so many human relationships inherently unjust. Was this not grounded in the normal nature of the social system? For whatever reason, Durkheim could not admit to such a proposition, namely, that the existing social system was *normally* and *inherently* diseased, therefore requiring basic structural changes. "One cannot, without contradiction, even conceive of a species which would be incurably diseased in itself and by virtue of its fundamental constitution." (p. 58.)

Thus Durkheim's organismic thinking led him to conclude that what is most widespread is also best: "It would be incomprehensible," he asserts, "if the most widespread forms of organization would not at the same time be, *at least in their aggregate,* the most advantageous." Advantageous for whom? For the "social organism" as a whole, of course. Could it be advantageous for one social class or stratum and not for another? Do certain institutions prevail because, among other things, some have the power to perpetuate them? Questions such as these never come to the fore. The issues of power and stratification are altogether ignored. If Durkheim is not saying that this is the best of all possible worlds, he is saying that *at the present stage* of evolution the prevailing conditions are necessary for the survival and adaptation of the social organism and therefore useful and good. He is not, however, altogether happy with this conception of things. There are transition periods, he writes, when "[a] phenomenon can . . . persist throughout the entire range of a species although no longer adapted to the requirements of the situation. It is then normal only in appearance. Its universality is now an illusion, since its persistence, due only to the blind force of habit, can no longer be accepted as an index of a close connection with the general conditions of its collective existence. This difficulty is especially peculiar to sociology." (p. 61.) The science of sociology has to determine whether a given condition is "normal," and if it is, the criticism and indignation it arouses is pointless and quixotic.

That even here in the *Rules* Durkheim was arguing against the Marxian and other socialist positions is clear. " . . . [I]n order to determine," he writes, "whether the present economic state of Europe . . . is normal or not, we shall investigate the causes which brought it about. If these conditions still exist in our present-day society, this situation is normal in spite of the dissent it arouses." (p. 62.) The system under these conditions still has "utility." In Durkheim's conception of evolutionism, one can determine by means of science whether a particular stage of a society's evolution is in fact "adaptive," whether it has "utility," whether it is "advantageous." When practices not adapted to any vital end persist, these are treated by Durkheim as "survivals"; they continue "to exist by the inertia of habit alone." On the other hand, "if the usefulness of a fact is not the cause of its existence, it is generally necessary that it be useful in order that it may maintain itself." (p. 97.) Thus Durkheim insists upon talking about whether social facts are "useful," "harmful," "parasitic," etc., without asking for whom. In effect, he solves deductively the problem of "society's" survival: "If . . . the majority of social phenomena had this parasitic character, the budget of the organism would have a deficit and social life would be impossible." (p. 97.) The fact that society does survive shows that somehow "the phenomena comprising it combine in such a way to put society in harmony with itself and with the environment external to it." (p. 97.)

In this way, the language and concepts of evolutionism served Durkheim's preoccupation with "society" and its "survival." And this preoccupation was expressed in his studied refusal (after *Professional Ethics*) to address himself to the stratified structure of society and the implications of this condition. By and large, the conditions that aroused the indignation of the socialists were normal and necessary; therefore, their criticisms and rebellious activity led to senseless anarchy. If society represses and constrains, this "is not derived from a conventional arrangement which human will has added bodily to natural reality; it issues from the innermost reality; it is the necessary product of given causes."

Also [continues Durkheim] recourse to artifice is unnecessary to get the individual to submit to them of his entire free will; it is sufficient to make him become aware of his state of natural dependence and inferiority, whether he forms a tangible and symbolic representation of it through religion or whether he arrives at an adequate and definite notion of it through science. Since the superiority of society to him is not simply physical but intellectual and moral, it has nothing to fear from a critical examination. By making man understand by how much the social being is richer, more complex, and more permanent than the individual being, reflection can only reveal to him the intelligible reasons for the subordination demanded of him and for the sentiments of attachment and respect which habit has fixed in his heart. (p. 123.)

The conclusion, then, is inescapable; man must submit!

There is no doubt, therefore, that even Durkheim's "scientific" *Rules* were designed to "create a sociology which sees in the *spirit of discipline* the essential condition of all human life while at the same time founding it on reason and truth." (p. 124. Italics mine.) There could be no reason and truth, no real social science, he insisted, so long as it did not emancipate itself from all parties in the political sense; but he remained blind, it appears, to his own involvement in partisan issues—blind to the fact that his sociology was *engagé* —and that therefore if he had applied to himself the standards he applied to others, he also had "no right to speak loudly enough to silence passions and prejudices." (p. 146.)

Suicide

Durkheim's use of socio-cultural variables to explain an ostensibly idiosyncratic phenomenon such as suicide must be regarded as ingenious and brilliant. However, we shall not be concerned with the empirical aspects of his classic study but rather with its philosophical implications for modern man and its ideological foundations.

Durkheim chose to study suicide because he hoped that from such a study would emerge "some suggestions concerning the causes of the general contemporary *maladjustments* being undergone by European societies and concerning remedies which may relieve it."[11] If in his earliest works the problems of *both* the anomic and the forced division of labor occupied his attention, now he reached the point where he focused almost exclusively on the first. The problems of modern man were a matter of "maladjustment." It was of utmost importance, therefore, to develop for modern man an appropriate morality—a morality that would give him a sense of satiety, that would help him overcome his restlessness and discontent, and enable him to adjust happily to modern

11 Émile Durkheim, Suicide, translated by John A. Spaulding and George Simpson (London: Routledge and Kegan Paul Ltd., 1963), p. 37. (Subsequent references to this work appear as page numbers in the text.)

conditions. Durkheim chose to study "suicide" because the other aspects of the general malaise he perceived were bound up with the conditions of the working class, class conflict, and social change. Had he studied these conditions, he would no doubt have come closer to the Marxists and other socialists than he cared to be. He now clearly and unequivocally opted for the conservative tendency in Saint-Simon or, in other words, for the Comtean position.

In studying suicide rather than any other manifestation of the general malaise, Durkheim was in effect centering attention on the problems of the upper and middle classes and of the liberal professions, for suicide was "undeniably exceptionally frequent in the highest class of society." (p. 165.) He was anxious to show (and pleased that he had done so) "that those who suffer most are not those who kill themselves most. Rather it is too great comfort which turns a man against himself. Life is most readily renounced at the time and among the classes where it is least harsh." (p. 298.)

Modern man kills himself primarily as a result of two conditions: the loss of cohesion in modern society and the absence of the appropriate moral norms by which to orientate himself. Modern man is egoistic and anomic. Both conditions can be remedied by developing a new and appropriate moral code and by resurrecting and reorganizing the occupational guild so that it may serve an integrative and regulatory function under modern conditions. The primary and most essential task is to bring about a high degree of social integration—moral, domestic, political, and economic—because the data tend to support the proposition: *"Suicide varies inversely with the degree of integration of . . . society."* (p. 208.)

Of course, there was *altruistic* suicide, which occurred when social integration was too strong. This, however, was endemic to "lower" societies; the implication being that the "higher" contemporary societies had nothing to fear—at least not suicide—from social integration. Because cohesion, consensus, and solidarity represented his most cherished value, Durkheim ignored the implications of his sociological and moral doctrine for the individuals of the lower classes. He was asking them, in effect, to submit to those same social conditions he, himself, had formerly regarded as unjust; moreover, he now systematically ignored the enormous price (other than suicide) disproportionately paid by them for whatever "social integration" they acquiesced in—*e.g.,* patriotism and chauvinism resulting in war. Durkheim feared "the excessive individuation characteristic of civilization" but apparently feared not at all the "social integration" and "altruism" that perpetuated injustice and compelled men to kill one another en masse as their patriotic duty. Thus he notes with alarm the rise in the rate of self-destruction *after* a war, but has nothing to say about the general destruction of war itself.

> On the morrow of the war of 1870 a new accession of good fortune took place. Germany was unified and placed entirely under Prussian hegemony. An enormous war indemnity added to the public wealth; commerce and

industry made great strides. The development of suicide was never so rapid. From 1875 to 1886 it increased 90 per cent, from 3,278 cases to 6,212. (p. 244.)

But, one might object, Durkheim is here merely describing a factual situation. Precisely! And this description reveals that in his scale of values suicide was a problem of greater concern than war.

One of the facts Durkheim was happy to establish was that man pays a supreme price for his prosperity. "So far is the increase in poverty from causing the increase in suicide that even fortunate crises, the effect of which is abruptly to enhance a country's prosperity, affect suicide like economic disasters." (p. 243.) And again, "In the various French departments the more people there are who have independent means, the more numerous are suicides." (p. 245.) It is as if Durkheim were demonstrating to the poor that their "poverty . . . may be considered as protection" (p. 245), while to the rich he was demonstrating that prosperity is accompanied by certain hazards. If in "crises" of prosperity, as well as in industrial and financial crises, suicides increase, then this has nothing to do with either prosperity or poverty but with the fact that "they are crises, that is, disturbances of the collective order. Every disturbance of equilibrium, even though it achieves greater comfort and a heightening of general vitality, is an impulse to voluntary death." (p. 246.) In explaining this phenomenon, Durkheim elaborates his philosophy for modern man.

The needs of all other animal creatures are strictly organic in nature; they are driven instinctively to replenish the energy exhausted in their metabolic interaction with nature; and once having done so, they are satisfied and crave nothing more. Natural limits are set on their craving and striving. In contrast, "[n]othing appears in man's organic nor in his psychological constitution which sets" limits on his desires. Man has needs which transcend the strictly vital requirements of his organism; and these needs are "unlimited so far as they depend on the individual alone." In the absence of an "external regulatory force, our capacity for feeling is in itself an insatiable and bottomless abyss." (p. 247.) This can only be a "source of torment" to man. "Unlimited desires are insatiable by definition and insatiability," writes Durkheim, "is rightly considered a sign of morbidity." (p. 247.) The infinity of man's desires and goals is what really causes him pain and suffering; the only solution, therefore, is to limit his passions. Some regulative force must be imposed upon him which will "play the same role for moral needs which the organism plays for physical needs. This means that the force can only be moral." (p. 248.) Since these imposed limits will be effective only so long as men recognize them as just, they must receive this sense of what is just "from an authority which they respect, to which they yield spontaneously." (p. 249.) And, of course, as we have come to expect, it is "Society" which is the ultimate authority in this regard: ". . . society alone can play this moderating role; for it is the only moral power superior to the individual, the authority of which he accepts. It alone has the power necessary to stipulate law and to set the point beyond which the passions must not go. Finally, it alone can estimate the reward to be prospectively offered to every class of human functionary, in the name of the common interest." (p. 249.) "Society" can and should determine the rewards to be assigned to each "function"—to the men in each occupation. "A genuine regimen exists, therefore, . . . which fixes with relative precision the maximum degree of ease of living to which each social class may legitimately aspire." (p. 249.)

Durkheim perceived that the living standards of all classes, including the workers, continued to improve; nevertheless, there was no contentment. Restlessness, social conflict, and "anarchy" prevailed despite this betterment of material conditions for all. But there still remained the "relative deprivation" of those in the lower and disadvantaged strata. Therefore, society must exert moral pressure so that "each in his sphere vaguely realizes the extreme limit set to his ambitions and aspires to nothing beyond. At least if he respects regulations and is docile to collective authority, that is, has a wholesome moral constitution, he feels that it is not well to ask more." (p. 250.) The only real solution to man's malaise is to curb and bridle his aspirations; only then will he be contented with his lot and strive "moderately to improve it; and this average contentment causes the feeling of calm, active happiness, the pleasure in existing and living which characterizes health for societies as well as for individuals." (p. 250.)

Durkheim understood, however, that "society's" moral authority would be accepted by men only if they regard the existing "distribution of functions" as just. "The workman is not in harmony with his social position if he is not convinced that he has his deserts." (p. 250.) And now there is a definite shift of emphasis in Durkheim's argument as compared with *Professional Ethics.* There he argued that at least one structural change required immediate institution: the abolition of the private inheritance of wealth. This was necessary because without it the relations among men were inherently unjust. Now, in *Suicide,* he retreats from this position or, at the very least, is highly ambivalent. It is true, he writes, that "the nearer this ideal equality were approached, the less social restraint will be necessary. *But it is only a matter of degree.* One sort of heredity will always exist, that of natural talent." (p. 251. Italics mine.) And to demand of those "naturally superior" that they function without greater rewards, would require a discipline even stronger than the existing one. For Durkheim, there would always be some who were more "useful" to society than others, and hence more deserving. If earlier he argued that "natural inequalities" (which he was so certain could be precisely measured) need not be accompanied by material inequalities, now he changed his view. Since *all* social systems regulate and repress, since man can never escape altogether from social restraint, the abolition of institutionalized economic inequalities, he now tells us, would only result in a diminution in the *degree* of restraint. This being the case, there is no point in agitating oneself

Émile Durkheim 275
Émile Durkheim 275
275
275
275 275

about existing inequalities and injustices; their abolition will make only a minor difference for man's existence. The main task for Durkheim, therefore, is not to change social conditions so that constraint and repression are constantly reduced, but to bring about a collective order that is obeyed and respected. Man must be given a moral education that will teach him, above all, to be content with his lot and to improve it moderately. Durkheim wanted *improvement,* not change. "All classes contend among themselves," he painfully observed, "because no established classification any longer exists." (p. 253.) The task, then, was to arrive at a new "classification" that all would accept.

Durkheim was impressed with the greater immunity to suicide of the poor; but his discussion of this fact becomes a celebration of poverty and of the damned and wantless condition of the poor. " . . . [T]he less one has the less he is tempted to extend the range of his needs indefinitely. Lack of power, compelling moderation, accustoms men to it. . . . [Poverty] is actually the best school for teaching self-restraint. Forcing us to constant self-discipline, it prepares us to accept collective discipline with equanimity, while wealth, exalting the individual, may always arouse the spirit of rebellion which is the very source of immorality." (p. 254) Regulation, moderation, discipline, duty —these are the highest virtues. Durkheim wanted a "highly socialized" man, "for if one were highly socialized one would not rebel at every social restraint." (p. 288.) And to bring about such "socialization" moral education alone was clearly not enough; society had to be reorganized and reformed—à la Durkheim.

It was only the egoistic and anomic types of suicide Durkheim regarded as morbid. The former, for example, "results from the fact that society is not sufficiently integrated at all points to keep all its members under its control. . . . Thus the only remedy for the ill," writes Durkheim, "is to restore enough consistency to social groups for them to obtain a firmer grip on the individual, and for him to feel himself bound to them." (p. 373.) Durkheim therefore calls once again for the restoration of occupational groups. The individual would be firmly integrated in his group, and the groups subordinated to the State, thus yielding an "organic" solidarity. The conflictive character of the previous system would be eliminated. Not only would amicable and cooperative relations prevail within and among the various categories of worker— occupations, professions, etc.—but between employers and employees. How are conflicts of interests prevented in the "new" society despite the continuing existence of structural inequalities?

Standing above its own members, it [the corporation] would have all necessary authority to demand indispensable sacrifices and concessions and impose order upon them. By forcing the strongest to use their strength with moderation, by preventing the weakest from endlessly multiplying their protests, by recalling both to the sense of their reciprocal duties and the general interest, and by regulating production in certain cases so that it does not degenerate into a morbid fever, it would moderate one set of passions by another, and permit their appeasement by assigning them limits. Thus a new sort of moral discipline would be established, without which all the scientific discoveries and economic progress in the world could produce only malcontents. (p. 383.)

This is Durkheim's vision of the corporate, and hence good, society in which each must fulfill his "function" and curb his egoism.

We see, then, that Durkheim's so-called "convergence with Marx" was temporary and very superficial indeed.[12] Yet, there is a sense in which Durkheim "capitulated" in his final major work and adopted one of Marx's fundamental theoretical propositions.

Elementary Forms of Religious Life

The sociological theory of religion, and more generally, of knowledge, which Durkheim developed in his *Elementary Forms,* was clearly inspired by Marx's celebrated idea that the social existence of men determines their social consciousness. Yet, in the concluding chapter of this work, in his single allusion to Marx's theory, Durkheim denies his debt out-and-out: "[I]t is necessary to avoid seeing in this theory of religion a simple restatement of historical materialism: that would be misunderstanding our thought to an extreme degree."[13] This debt is, however, indisputable; for while he was quite right in saying that his was not "a simple restatement" of Marx's thesis, he was wrong in thinking that Marx treated consciousness as "a mere epiphenomenon." The real divergence occurs when Durkheim generalizes Marx's proposition beyond socioeconomic relationships to include other social relations. And Durkheim also differs in the purposes to which he puts the thesis; for in his hands "social consciousness" becomes a predominantly conservative force and not as in Marx's system a fundamental element in the revolutionary transformation of social relationships.

In *Elementary Forms* Durkheim concerned himself with the origins and causes of religion—for him a permanent and essential aspect of human life. "What we want to do is to find a means of discerning the ever-present causes upon which the most essential forms of religious thought and practice depend." (p. 8.) If one could study the most rudimentary forms of social existence known, and the thought forms which accompanied them, Durkheim reasoned, then perhaps one could understand the connection between collective existence and collective representations and understand, too, why religion was an essential and permanent phenomenon. It is for this reason that the

---

12 See A. Gouldner's Introduction to Durkheim's *Socialism and Saint Simon, op. cit.,* p. xxiii.

13 Émile Durkheim, *The Elementary Forms of Religious Life* (London: George Allen and Unwin, Ltd., 1964), p. 423. (Subsequent references to this work appear as page numbers in the text.)

various primitive groups of Australia and North America formed the basis of his study.

A number of the results from this method were clearly quite fruitful. For instance, Durkheim argues quite cogently that the most fundamental categories of thought, *e.g.*, time, space, class, number, cause, substance, personality, force, etc., are ultimately derived from the conditions of men's social existence; the cognitive structure of men's minds is determined by the structure of their society. With this approach, one could contribute to the resolution of the epistemological issue raised in the debate between the "empiricists" and the "apriorists." Time, space, and all the rest were social categories for Durkheim; they were not immanent in men's minds in the Kantian sense but given by the social environment. Time, for example, was the collective representation of the rhythm of social life: the "indispensable guidelines, in relation to which all things are temporally located, are taken from social life. The division into days, weeks, months, years, etc., correspond to the periodical recurrence of rites, feasts, and public ceremonies. A calendar expresses the rhythm of the collective activities, while at the same time its function is to assure their regularity." Similarly with space: "There are societies in Australia and North America where space is conceived in the form of an immense circle, because the camp has a circular form; and this spatial circle is divided up exactly like the tribal circle, and is in its image. There are as many regions distinguished as there are clans in the tribe, and it is the place occupied by the clans inside the encampment which has determined the orientation of these regions." (pp. 11–12.) Hence, the categories of thought are not *a priori* but derived from the structure of social existence; once implanted in men's minds, the categories do indeed appear *as if* they were immanent. Durkheim therefore concluded that the "empiricists" were wrong in assuming that knowledge was the result of an individual's *immediate* sensory perceptions; they were wrong in believing that knowledge was unmediated by thought categories. Knowledge is indeed mediated as the "rationalists" claimed; however, the categories are not immanent but social in nature. All *collective representations* depend on their common underlying social structures, which effect not only a minimal moral conformity but a minimal *logical* conformity as well.

For Durkheim, the "sacred and the profane have always and everywhere been conceived by the human mind as two distinct classes, as two worlds between which there is nothing in common." (pp. 38–39.) There is a logical chasm between the two domains, and it is precisely the totality of *sacred* beliefs and practices which constitutes a religion. Moreover, "religious beliefs are always common to a determined group, which makes profession of adhering to them and of practicing the rites connected with them." (p. 43.) Religion is a group phenomenon, for it is a group which gives a religion its specific character and unity. On the other hand, the religion unifies the group; it quite literally binds men together.

In this way Durkheim gives a conservative emphasis to his general thesis that religious ideas are derived from society and serve to bind the members of a society together. This essential and positive function of religion—solidifying a society—explains why it is a ubiquitous and permanent institution. Durkheim's purposes are here served by developing this thesis on the basis of the "primitive horde" whose simplicity and homogeneity he no doubt exaggerated. This enabled him to obscure the fact that in more complex societies religious beliefs and practices vary from one stratum to another and that these strata even have conflicting conceptions of the "same" religious doctrine. Thus when Durkheim defines a church as a "moral community formed by all the believers in a single faith," he is oversimplifying. Most striking, however, is his refusal to see the negative, alienating consequences of religion; he shows only an occasional awareness of this: The "power of souls is increased by all that men attribute to them, and in the end men find themselves the prisoners of this imaginary world of which they are, however, the authors and the models." (p. 52.) Such observations are quite rare and when he makes them he never pursues their implications.

Marx, in contrast, viewed religion as "false consciousness." If men worshipped spirits and idols, if they projected upon hypothetical beings their own powers and, unaware of this, worshipped these beings and submitted to them, this was a manifestation of their alienation. So when Durkheim writes "that a human institution cannot rest upon an error and a lie," Marx would have disagreed. It was clearly an error to view the idol or the spirit as possessing real powers. Men invested the creations of their own hands and imagination with powers superior to their own under specific circumstances. The point, then, was to discover and change those circumstances; by eliminating the source of their erroneous views, men thereby gained a truer consciousness of reality and a greater control over their fate. For Marx, the so-called materialist conception was *negative* in that the determination of men's consciousness by "material" conditions implied a negation of man's freedom; this negative condition would be overcome only when men freely associated with one another and consciously shaped social conditions. There is always the suggestion in Marx's conception that men could discover the conditions which determined their consciousness as well as the other aspects of their lives, and could liberate themselves by abolishing and changing those conditions. Durkheim believed that religion expresses social reality, while Marx insisted that it expressed that reality *falsely*. To see the differences between the two thinkers even more clearly, a closer look at Durkheim's thesis is required.

Durkheim developed his own sociological conception by pointing out the inadequacies of both the "naturistic" and "animistic" schools, which undertook "to construct the idea of the divine out of the sensations aroused in us by certain natural phenomena, either physical or biological." (p. 87.) The basis of the divine had to be sought not here, but in the nature of social organization—in Australia, for example, in the division of society into clans. Totemism was the elementary form of religion that corresponded to that elementary organization. Each clan had its own totem, in effect, its name and emblem. But the totem was more than this: "It is the very type of sacred thing." And interestingly, the *"images of the totemic beings are more sacred than the beings themselves."* (p. 133.) This fact made it evident that the totem had a special symbolic significance. Because it symbolized the moral unity of the clan as a whole, it was sacred and eventually transformed itself into a divinity. If, writes Durkheim, the totem "is at once the symbol of the god and of the society, is that not because the god and society are only one?"

God thus becomes for Durkheim the symbolic manifestation of the powers of society. Each man senses that there is a power greater than himself and superior to him; but he does not know the real nature and source of this power; he does not understand that the conditions of social life in the clan have led him to regard the totemic emblem as a divinity or its visible symbol. And Durkheim sees this as a situation in which religion "ceases to be an inexplicable hallucination and takes a foothold in reality. In fact, we can say that the believer is not deceived when he believes in the existence of a moral power upon which he depends and from which he received all that is best in himself: this power exists, it is society." (p. 225.)

But, one must reply to Durkheim, if men continue mistakenly to attribute their own collective powers to a totem or any other symbol, is this not in fact a false conception of things? Are they not in fact deceiving themselves? Durkheim does not view matters this way. He writes: "Religious force is only the sentiment inspired by the group in its members, but projected outside of the consciousnesses that experience them, and objectified." (p. 229.) This objectification is not a sign for Durkheim that men hold a false conception of reality. He cannot admit to this and at the same time hold that religion is the wholly positive institution he insists it is.

If Society equals God, then it follows logically that what society imparts to each individual is "what is best and most profound in ourselves, and the preeminent part of our being. . . ." (p. 249.) Indeed, what society imparted to each individual was, for Durkheim, the secular, functional equivalent of the soul. There "really is a particle of divinity in us," writes Durkheim, "because there is within us a particle of these great ideas which are the soul of the group." And further: "So the individual soul is only a portion of the collective soul of the group. . . ." How did men come to believe in the immortality of the soul? This too may be attributed to the "immortality" of the group. "For though the group may not be immortal in the absolute sense of the word, still it is true that it endures longer than the individuals and that it is born and incarnated afresh in each new generation." (p. 269.) And just as the divinity of the totem was rooted in the clan, the idea of one supreme "universal" god emerged on the basis of the "internationalism" of the clans, phratries, and tribes.

In the end, Durkheim's theory of religion became for him a way of extolling "society" and the ascetic demands it made on the individual. He firmly believed that "it is by the way in which he braves suffering that the greatness of man is best manifested. He never rises above himself with more brilliancy than when he subdues his own nature to the point of making it follow a way contrary to the one it would spontaneously take." (p. 315.) Whatever tenable hypotheses Durkheim derived from his approach apply only to small, homogeneous communities, or to such groups within a larger society, but not to a complex society as a whole. Therefore, the positive functions he assigned to "religion" must be hedged in with many qualifications. He, however, never even hinted at the possible *dysfunctions* of religion; it is the real society, he stresses time and again, which is expressed in religion. For all of society's ugly and repulsive aspects are also expressed in religious beliefs— *e.g.*, in the various forms of anti-God. "Satan," he writes, "is an essential piece of the Christian system; even if he is an impure being, he is not a profane one." And he concludes, "Thus religion, far from ignoring the real society and making abstraction of it, is in its image; it reflects all its aspects, even the most vulgar and the most repulsive."

Somehow, Durkheim the positivist did not want to recognize that belief in the Devil is not the same as understanding the real causes of social evils. Ultimately the real social evil for Durkheim was anomy—"the old gods are growing old or already dead, and others are not yet born." (p. 427.) Men needed new gods, but suited to the new conditions. To discover what the nature of the new gods should be, one must strip the mystical veil from reality, a task for which science is better fitted than religion. Durkheim's science led him to conclude that *society* is the appropriate new god; for it "is the highest form of the psychic life" . . . "the consciousness of the con-sciousnesses." Society "sees from above" and "sees farther." When one reads Durkheim's final description of society as the "Supreme God," one also understands why duty, devotion, discipline, and abnegation were his highest moral imperatives.

16

Karl Mannheim

(1893–1947)

Like Max Weber before him, Karl Mannheim has also been called a "bourgeois Marx," and for similar reasons. For while the intellectual influences upon each of them were varied, the most striking characteristic in both cases is their lifelong effort at a skillful and nondogmatic application of Marxian methodological principles to the study of man, society, and history. Weber had recognized the enormous heuristic value of these principles and had fruitfully generalized Marx's method to yield a clearer understanding of Western civilization. Similarly, and in a sense following Weber's example, Mannheim accepted the suggestion that the value of Marx's method lay in the "hint that there is a correlation between the economic structure of a society and its legal and political organization, *and that even the world of our thought is affected by these relationships.*"[1] Most conspicuously in his sociology of knowledge Mannheim treated political, legal, philosophical, religious, and other ideas in their intimate relationship with economic and social changes. That the ideas people hold vary with changing economic circumstances and that they are "somehow

[1] Karl Mannheim, *Systematic Sociology* (New York: Grove Press, Inc., 1957), p. 137, italics mine. For a brief discussion of Marxian and other theoretical influences on Mannheim, see Robert K. Merton's essay "Karl Mannheim and the Sociology of Knowledge," in *Social Theory and Social Structure* (Glencoe: The Free Press, 1957), p. 494.

connected with the social context in which they live," remained throughout his work a central and guiding principle.

But if Marxism was the chief, it was not, of course, the only influence which shaped Mannheim's work. The list of intellectual predecessors and contemporaries who left their mark on Mannheim's sociology would have to include such thinkers as Montesquieu, Saint-Simon, Hegel, Marx, Max and Alfred Weber, Durkheim, Husserl, Nietzsche, Scheler, Lukács, William James, John Dewey, C. H. Cooley, Freud, G. H. Mead—yet this list would be far from exhaustive. Ultimately, however, the most conspicuous influence remained Marxian; for though he gained important insights from these and other thinkers, they served, Mannheim believed, primarily to enhance the analytical power a modified, nondogmatic Marxian method could yield.

Mannheim's life's work may be divided into two distinct but interrelated phases and projects. The first, for which he is more famous, is his contribution to the sociology of knowledge. This began with his doctoral dissertation entitled "The Structural Analysis of Epistemology" and culminated in his classic work *Ideology and Utopia* and in his later essays published in one volume under the title, *Essays on the Sociology of Culture*. The second phase, the fruit of his reflections on the crisis of his time and of life in England during World War II, included such works as *Man and Society in an Age of Reconstruction, Diagnosis of Our Time*, and *Freedom, Power, and Democratic Planning*. It was in this latter phase that one sees most clearly the ethical commitment underlying all of Mannheim's work—namely, that sociological studies must be regarded "as a response to the challenging present." Bramsted and Gerth have observed that for Mannheim, "sociology was a specifically modern way of thought which contributes to the rational self-orientation of man in industrial society. By raising us to a new level of self-awareness, the intellectual tools that the sociologist forges open up for us an insight into the dangerous processes of the modern world with its drift toward social upheavals and world wars."[2] There was, then, a first, or German, phase in which Mannheim directed his main efforts toward a sociological analysis of knowledge and a second, or English, phase in which he attempted to use his sociology to sketch the guidelines for a rational and democratic reconstruction of society. To understand how Mannheim developed his sociology it is best to begin by examining its origins in German sociology.

Mannheim and German Sociology

There were three main intellectual currents in Germany whose elements in various combinations imparted to German sociology its specific form: (1) German classical philosophy, particularly the Hegelian school; (2) non-

2 See "A Note on the Work of Karl Mannheim," by Ernest K. Bramsted and Hans Gerth in *Freedom, Power and Democratic Planning* (London: Routledge and Kegan Paul, Ltd., 1950), pp. vii–xv.

academic sociological thought, notably Marxism; and (3) the *Geisteswissenschaften,* whose outstanding representatives among Mannheim's older contemporaries were Wilhelm Dilthey and Georg Simmel. These were also the three currents most evident in Mannheim's early work. From Hegel (and Marx) he derived the conception of history as a structured and dynamic process. Seeing facts and events not as isolated phenomena and occurrences but in relation to the dominant social forces and trends "and to the whole social situation existing at any given moment derives from Hegel."[3] Since Marx, however, had already incorporated these and other insights into his own conception of historical change, Mannheim was indebted primarily to him for his basic approach: The changing class structure of a society resulted from changes in productive techniques and the division of labor. The ideologies of a given society in a given period bore some determinate relationship to the existing classes and to the objective conflict of interests among them.

Originally, Marxism was an "opposition theory" and was therefore outside the German academy. Eventually, however, the issues raised by Marxism not only penetrated the universities but generated so much interest and debate that the work of such outstanding thinkers as Max Weber, Troeltsch, Simmel, Sombart, Scheler, and Mannheim himself may be viewed as the fruitful results of a critical encounter with Marxism. In Mannheim's words, what began as "a mere dispute over principles was turned into an advancement of knowledge." (p. 215.) Marxism, then, together with aspects of Hegel's philosophy, were two main currents which profoundly influenced Mannheim's thinking.

The third influence, most notable in Mannheim's early essays on "styles of thought" and *Weltanschauungen,* was that of German humanistic studies. In common with Weber, again, he accepted Dilthey's assumption that there was a fundamental difference between the physical and cultural sciences, and that the latter required a specific method. If the physical sciences were concerned exclusively with calculable external phenomena, then the cultural sciences were (and must be) concerned with the motives and values of men and the meanings of their acts. In the physical sciences, explanation (*Erklärung*)— the correlation of external facts—was quite sufficient; not so in the human sciences where "explanation" alone is most superficial. What one should strive for in studying human conduct is not mere explanation but *understanding* (*Verstehen*); and for this, "sympathetic intuition" is required. Of course, explanation and interpretive understanding were not mutually exclusive; but the main point for Dilthey, Simmel, Weber, and Mannheim was that, whereas explanation is sufficient in the study of physical phenomena, an *adequate understanding* of human acts always requires an involvement with the

3 Karl Mannheim, *Essays on Sociology and Social Psychology* (London: Routledge and Kegan Paul, Ltd., 1953), p. 214. (Immediately following references to this work noted only by page numbers in the text.)

purposes, motives, and values of the actors concerned; *understanding,* in short, requires a concern with the mind.

In these terms, Mannheim was interested in *meaning,* because in his view the most important interrelationships and interactions of men were meaningful and communicative acts. Interpretive understanding had to be applied not only to works of art, literature, and music, but to everyday speech and acts as well. In this Mannheim followed Max Weber, whose work he knew very well. Thus it may be worthwhile at this point to recall Weber's approach as a way of illustrating Mannheim's.

For Weber, human conduct is "meaningful"—regardless of whether or not the persons involved realize this or understand the meaning of their conduct. Given the assumption that human actions are purposeful, communicative, and goal-oriented—even if this applies to some actions more than others—it becomes essential for the social scientist to understand the meanings, purposes, goals, and means of attaining them. Weber recognized, as did Mannheim, that it is an enormously complicated matter to distinguish between meaningful and nonmeaningful aspects of conduct. Nevertheless, one must not abandon the ideal of understanding by adopting instead the easier but more superficial behavioristic method.

Understanding is essential for Weber precisely because one deals in the social sciences neither with mere physical elements nor with mindless creatures. Knowing *why* men act the way they do is necessary if something more than a mere datum is desired, if something more than a mere correlation is the goal of an analysis. Why, for example, did the ancient prophets of Israel urge unswerving devotion to Yahwe? How did they conceive of themselves and their role? Did they regard themselves as spokesmen for those Hebrews who were now oppressed under the monarchy, *i.e.,* subject to *Corvée* and to high taxes? Were they, in short, ideological spokesmen for the oppressed masses or were they mouthpieces of Yahwe, as it were, enabling him to speak through them? Weber, it will be recalled, was more inclined to the latter interpretation of their motives and tried to support it with documentary evidence.

Or to take another well-known problem that engaged Weber's interest: why did the early capitalistic entrepreneurs pursue their tasks so energetically and diligently? Their motives, Weber believed, were predominantly religious and could be traced to the ethical injunctions of ascetic Protestantism. The motives of these parvenus could not be explained simply as a function of the requirements of the "primitive accumulation of capital." The motive for hard work and saving—the reinvestment of the profits in the expansion of the means of production—was not simply a mental reflection of economic requirements. Without denying the influence of capitalistic economic developments upon Protestantism, Weber insisted, nonetheless, that the religious movement had to be regarded as a somewhat autonomous one; and it was the teachings of this religious movement that were a major source of the entrepreneur's motives and values.

Mannheim admired Weber's elaboration and refinement of Marx's method and in fact emulated in his own work both of those mighty thinkers. He saw clearly that Weber had adopted Marx's general view that changes in the minds of men could not be understood adequately without relating them to the changes in their concrete existential conditions. "The greater art of the sociologist," writes Mannheim, "consists in his attempt always to relate changes in mental attitudes to changes in social situations. The human mind does not operate *in vacuo;* the most delicate change in the human spirit corresponds to similarly delicate changes in the situation in which an individual or a group finds itself, and, conversely, the minutest change in situations indicates that men, too, have undergone some change." (p. 219.) This remained the leading idea of Mannheim's sociology of knowledge. In his earliest essays, however, it is not yet the Marxian approach that is most evident but the ideas of Hegel, of the German historical school, and of Dilthey, Windelband, Rickert, and others. An examination of the early essays will be followed by a consideration of those in which he employed a more consistently Marxian approach.

The Sociology of Knowledge

In his doctoral dissertation Mannheim worked with some of the fundamental assumptions of Hegel and of the *Geisteswissenschaften:* a cultural element is always to be regarded as a part of a greater logico-meaningful whole. Understanding, therefore, consists in systematically placing an element in its larger logico-meaningful context. The larger *Gestalt* ("whole," "structure," "context," or "form") is what imparts meaning to its component elements. Every intellectual and cultural field has a structure of its own, asserts Mannheim, and adds in Hegelian terms: "The simpler forms can be understood, in our opinion, only in terms of this 'highest,' 'all-embracing' form." (p. 16.) "System," "context," "complementariness," "correlatedness," etc. are already implied in every concept; there is no such thing as an isolated concept, which can be demonstrated by the fact that one has a "sense" of where a given concept properly belongs "and that it will show at once if it is 'transferred' into an alien sphere, where it can only be applied 'metaphorically.' " (p. 23.) Even the process of "thinking" is a matter of placing a concept in its proper total framework; "a thing is taken to be explained, comprehended, insofar as we have discovered its place in the currently accepted orders, series, levels." (p. 22.)

The postulate of "system" holds for the exact physical sciences as well as for philosophy, art, and literature. In the physical sciences, however, an older system is superseded by a newer one because the latter is now considered true and the former, false. The Ptolemaic and Copernican systems, for example, cannot be regarded as equally true. Art forms, on the other hand, can exist side by side without contradicting one another even while expressing different truths. Clearly, different criteria of truth and validity are involved in the arts as compared with the sciences. Once a work of art has achieved aesthetic validity it acquires something of a "timeless glory"; and although the criteria for philosophical truth are closer to those of science than to those of art, certain of its "abandoned" solutions or insights may nevertheless have a timeless quality. Each cultural endeavor has its own criteria for validity; yet all such endeavors are parts of a meaningful whole which lends them a mutual affinity and a common "spirit."

What Mannheim is concerned with at this early stage of his thinking is preserving criteria for truth and validity in all cultural endeavors even while viewing them in a specific structural-historical context. He was already anticipating the accusations of "relativism" which critics would later level at his sociological theory of knowledge. His dissertation may be viewed as his earliest attempt at reconciling what appeared to many as irreconcilable: that on the one hand there is a certain affinity among the cultural creations of a given epoch, that they share a certain "historico-philosophical contemporaneity"; and, on the other hand, that truth and validity are not merely relative to a given historical epoch. In Mannheim's words, "To say that a certain creation of the mind can be explained with reference to its period is far from involving a relativistic stand as to its validity." (p. 39.) In the remainder of his dissertation Mannheim attempts to show how one might mediate between the doctrine of stable criteria of validity and truth, on the one hand, and the doctrine that things must be viewed in their socio-historical context, on the other.

The history of philosophy revealed, Mannheim believed, a "priority contest" among three basic epistemologies: (a) psychology, (b) logic, and (c) ontology. Which of these epistemologies will prevail at any given time depends on the philosophical "slant" of that epoch. Psychology insists that *experience* provides the data of knowledge and hence is the source of knowledge. To this logic replies that experience is mediated through logical categories; that "psychology itself is a science and must as such 'work out' these ultimate pre-scientific data with logical means in order to make them intelligible." (p. 50.) Logic, it is claimed from this standpoint, must therefore be regarded as the ultimate presupposition of knowledge. Ontology, finally, argues that everything man encounters, including himself, is an "instance of 'being' in the most general sense." Experience and logic are also manifestations of "being" and therefore all experiential and logical connections must be interpreted as ontological ones. Each of these epistemologies corresponds to a certain discipline, and each discipline has its own criteria of truth: For psychology, a proposition is true if it accords with the evidence; for logic a proposition must be accepted as true if it conforms to "logical necessity," or formal logical norms; for ontology, finally, a proposition is true if it corresponds to being or reality.

It is clear, therefore, that the respective criteria "are closely related to the particular science that supplied the analytic means for the quest after ultimate presuppositions." (p. 67.) The important conclusion Mannheim draws after a careful analysis of the competing epistemologies is that although the standards of truth have varied with the epistemological disciplines (*i.e.*, psychology, logic, ontology), ". . . truth-value remained a constant in every one of the criteria—the only variable being the standard." (p. 69.) Though the choice of discipline and criteria for truth may vary from one historical epoch to another and though the solutions and answers may be placed in their socio-historical context, this in no way precludes one's asking whether or not the solutions are true or valid. So in his first learned *étude*, Mannheim establishes his intention of preserving a durable standard for truth that, in his view, was altogether compatible with what he called, at this stage of his thinking, a structural and historical approach to knowledge. Perhaps the best illustration of his early conception of a structural approach may be found in his study of *Weltanschauung*.

On the Interpretation of Weltanschauung

What seemed self-evident to Mannheim was that the manifold cultural creations of men constituted a unity. This truth had been increasingly obscured by the splitting up of the whole culture into apparently separate and isolated domains. Mannheim believed that the fragmentation of the concept of culture into religion, art, literature, philosophy, etc. was a product of the various theoretical standpoints from which culture was analyzed. He should have added that the division of labor, in which there emerged professional practitioners of religion, art, literature, etc., had something to do with the subsequent theoretical treatment of these activities as separate and autonomous domains. As a result of the division of labor and of theoretical abstraction, the concrete cultural-experiential wholes had been neglected. The "whole," of course, can refer to an individual work of art, to the pattern which emerges from the total *oeuvre* of the artist, or, finally, to "the still more comprehensive 'whole' of the culture and *Weltanschauung* of an epoch."[4]

Interpretation, then, requires that one refer to the cultural unity underlying and tying together the various creations of a given society (or societies) in a given epoch. To understand, for example, art styles and art motives one "must make reference to even more fundamental factors such as *Zeitgeist*, 'global outlook,' and the like. Bringing these various strata of cultural life in relation to each other," Mannheim continues, "penetrating to the most fundamental totality in terms of which the inter-connectedness of the various branches of cultural studies can be understood—this is precisely the essence of

4 Karl Mannheim, *Essays on the Sociology of Knowledge* (London: Routledge and Kegan Paul, Ltd., 1952), p. 36. (Immediately following references to this work noted only by page numbers in the text.)

the procedure of interpretation which has no counterpart in the natural sciences—the latter only 'explain' things." (p. 36.)

Weltanschauung is thus conceived as an atheoretical entity; it is an idealistic concept, or construct, referring to the highest, all-embracing "spirit" that permeates all cultural creations ranging from the arts through customs and including even "the tempo of living, expressive gestures and demeanor. . . ." (p. 38.) Mannheim recognized that this method could degenerate into subjectivism. After all, when one posits a *Zeitgeist,* one has already had in mind some of the specific manifestations from which he has derived the general term. How this approach, which he termed atheoretical, could be translated into a more rigorous methodology, he regarded as a central problem for the so-called cultural sciences. Although his work in this area is rather interesting, he never really succeeds in developing such a method and it is perhaps for this reason that he eventually subordinates (but never abandons entirely) this approach to the more rigorous Marxian method of analysis. It may be of interest, nonetheless, to see how Mannheim employs in this essay the concept of *Weltanschauung* (the widest context of meaning) and levels of meaning for an understanding of the events of everyday life.

Mannheim suggests that every cultural product and/or social event will reveal, if one probes deeply enough, three levels of meaning: (a) the objective, (b) the expressive, and (c) the documentary. To take his own illustration, he is walking down a street with a friend. A beggar beckons to them, they stop momentarily, and the friend gives the beggar alms. This simple state of affairs—a "meaningful" situation—can be in the first instance interpreted from the "outside," as it were. "Beggar," "assistance," "giver," and "charity" are sufficient to reveal the meaning of the social interaction taking place; the "objective social configuration" *without* a knowledge either of the beggar's or the friend's consciousness gives us what Mannheim calls the *objective* meaning of the situation, the most superficial level of understanding.[5] To proceed beyond this superficial level, it would be necessary to grasp the individual intent of the almsgiver. In his giving of the alms, the objective meaning and result of which was "assistance," the friend may have intended to convey that he was engaging in a personal act of "mercy, kindness, and compassion." To determine this one must know the almsgiver intimately; only then can one grasp his act authentically, *i.e.,* as he intended it. This is the *expressive meaning* of his act. But, knowing the almsgiver intimately means that we know him in a variety of contexts; and in this light his so-called "act of charity" may reveal itself as an act of hypocrisy. The act of giving was not at all in keeping with his general character so that the *documentary* or *evidential* meaning of his act is really inauthentic and hypocritical. Of course, these are merely analytical levels, not clearly distin-

---

[5] In art, this level of meaning would be revealed by the purely visual content, in music, by melody, rhythm, harmony, etc.

guishable from one another in real situations. In this early phase of his thinking Mannheim believed that these devices provided one with greater insight into works of art and into everyday social interaction.

Could this approach be regarded as scientific? Yes, Mannheim replies, but in the special sense of the *Geisteswissenschaften*. Surely anyone who has had, for example, considerable listening experience can perceive significant differences in the music of Mozart, Tchaikowsky, and Debussy. And when it is said that these composers represent the Classical, Romantic, and Impressionistic movements, respectively, this is not a wholly subjective and arbitrary judgment. Experienced listeners tend to agree that the mood conveyed in the works of each of these composers and movements is representative of a certain cultural period. Furthermore, art connoisseurs, students of philosophy, *and* experts in musical styles may agree that their respective cultural areas share in a given period a common theme or spirit—or, as Mannheim would say, they express a common *Weltanschauung*. Can this be *demonstrated* in any positive, empirical sense? Mannheim was not so foolish as to suggest it could. But if positivistic standards cannot be applied, does this mean that studies of cultural creations might as well be abandoned? One can apply relatively rigorous scientific standards, Mannheim argued, to problems of *objective* and *expressive* meaning; given sufficient background, one can describe with precision the "visible" aspects of a work of art and the relevant aspects of an artist's biography which may have affected his style, choice of subject, materials, themes, etc. However, the third level, the *documentary*, presents special problems and difficulties. And here Mannheim raises an issue to which he will often return in his later works: the influence of his spatio-temporal location upon the interpreter.

Unlike the two other types of interpretation [writes Mannheim], documentary interpretation has the peculiarity that it must be performed anew in each period, and that any single interpretation is profoundly influenced by the location within the historical stream from which the interpreter attempts to reconstruct the spirit of a past epoch. It is well known that the Hellenic or Shakespearian spirit presented itself under different aspects to different generations. This, however, does not mean that knowledge of this kind is relative and hence worthless. What it does mean is that the type of knowledge conveyed by natural science differs fundamentally from historical knowledge—we should try to grasp the meaning and structure of historical understanding in its specificity, rather than reject it merely because it is not in conformity with the positivist truth-criteria sanctioned by natural science. (p. 61.)

To impose upon the interpretive sciences the standards of the physical sciences is to forfeit the possibility of knowledge in many areas of life. Each area of study imposes certain requirements and limits and in a sense dictates the appropriate methodological approach. Standards of precision and verification cannot be mechanically transferred from the physical to the cultural sciences without exacting a price; and this price, more often than not, is that a mechanical transfer of method yields the most superficial understanding in the cultural realm.

The interpretive or logico-meaningful method is quite different from and not to be confused with the historical or genetic method. Neither does one make the other superfluous. The point rather is that the interpretive method (relating the parts to one another and fitting them into a meaningful totality) presumably yields a deeper understanding of meanings. Mannheim notes in this connection an ambivalence in the work of Max Weber. "In his theoretical writings, he insists upon causal explanation [while] in his historical works, he very often proceeds according to the 'documentary' method." (p. 81 n.) Mannheim, too, uses both of these methods often shifting from one to another without notice—a source of no little confusion to his readers and critics. In effect, his studies of *Weltanschauung* had a twofold purpose: (1) he wanted to demonstrate the need in the study of certain aspects of culture to emancipate oneself from the methodology of the natural sciences and (2) to show that "In the realm of the mental, we cannot understand the whole from the parts, we can only understand the parts from the whole." (p. 82.) If this exemplifies his early conception of a "structural" approach, we have to turn to his essay entitled "Historicism" for his conception of historical analysis.

Historicism

In this essay the influences of Hegel, the German historical school, and the *Geisteswissenschaften* still predominate. "Historicism" is an aspect of a *Weltanschauung* that emerged in a certain period in response to definite historical conditions. After all, it was no accident, as Mannheim was fond of saying, that such concepts as "movement," "process," and "flux," conceived *organically* and applied to socio-cultural phenomena and institutions, first appeared in a definite historical period. The emergence of metaphors, concepts, and theories based on the "organism" as opposed to the "mechanism" had some determinate relationship, Mannheim believed, to the social conditions prevailing in Europe after the French Revolution.[6] "Historicism," then, refers to the writing of history under the influence of this *Weltanschauung,* or in Mannheim's words: "We have historicism only when history itself is written from the historistic *Weltanschauung.*" (p. 85.)

Under this *Weltanschauung* historians view all aspects of human life— institutions, customs, art, etc.—either developmentally or organically. Thus the structure of history, its ordering principle, may be studied from two directions: (a) the vertical or historical and (b) the horizontal or cross-sectional. One can take any social institution or cultural phenomenon and trace "it back into the past, trying to show how each later form develops continuously, organically from the earlier. If one gradually extends this

[6] Mannheim's exploration of these conditions will be discussed later when considering his essay, "Conservative Thought."

method to all the spheres in cultural life, then one will obtain, so to speak, a bundle of isolated evolutionary lines." (p. 86.) With this the historian has completed only half his task; for while one now sees development in each of the lines or spheres, they are isolated and disconnected, without any recognizable relationship among them. The remainder of the task, therefore, is "to show how, at one temporal stage, the *motifs*, which have just been observed in isolation, are also *organically bound up with one another.*" (p. 87.) "Organically bound up" in the "logico-meaningful" and not necessarily in the causal sense.

Mannheim realized very well that this method was in some sense "metaphysical," but he insisted that it is a necessary and valuable method in the study of culture. (p. 135.) The Hegelian notion of Spirit or Idea as the real subject of history was at the very least a fruitful heuristic device in the study of cultural *motifs*. In rather straight Hegelian terms, Mannheim writes: "The separate *motifs* are, rather, mutually conditioning at the successive stages of evolution and are components and functions of an ultimate basic process which is the real 'subject' undergoing the change." (p. 87.) Throughout this essay Mannheim employs a Hegelian mode of expression and speaks, for instance, of the historical process as permeated by "reason" and "form-giving categories"; and he retains the notion of a higher, all-embracing totality that imparts meaning and unity to the apparently separate events. Hegelian influence is also evident in the historicist view of truth: Present-day systems and conclusions of philosophy are based on a reality not yet known to earlier systems. The earlier systems, therefore, are not false but incomplete. Thus one must eschew an out-and-out rejection of previous systems by attempting to incorporate them in the newer systems. "This means," writes Mannheim, "at the stage we have reached that the ostensibly universal significance of the earlier systems should be reduced to a partial, parochial one, and that its elements—insofar as they retain any validity at all—should be reinterpreted from a new systematic center." (p. 90.)

More important, however, is Mannheim's related historicist conception of the greater truth and validity embodied in the thought of a later as opposed to an earlier historical stage. The philosophy of the Enlightenment, for example, held to "*a doctrine of the supra-temporality of Reason.*" (p. 90.) Those who held to this doctrine in the nineteenth century tended, therefore, to reject the later historical, organic, developmental conception of "reason." For Mannheim, this rejection was fundamentally wrong; for the nineteenth-century exponents of the Enlightenment view failed to see the greater validity of the *historical* conception, namely, "that the most general definitions and categories of Reason vary and undergo a process of alteration of meaning—along with every other concept—in the course of intellectual history." (p. 91.) By rejecting the historical conception, the philosophers of static reason closed themselves off from the insights derived from a dynamic organic model based on living and growing organisms. There can be no doubt, Mannheim believed, of the superior validity of the dynamic-historical conception of socio-cultural reality. This newer conception must be viewed as the theoretical counterpart of the general transformation taking place in the social structure. The changed socio-historical situation is "the basis for the emergence of a new theoretical superstructure." (p. 96.) Historicism, or the historical approach, rejects the rigid alternatives of true and false and seeks instead the "truth in history itself." (p. 100.) Getting at this truth, however, is not a simple matter.

Mannheim explores some of the problems involved by developing further the distinction between the *Naturwissenschaften* and the *Geisteswissenschaften*. In the exact physical sciences the historical and social position (*Standort*) of the knowing subject and his corresponding value orientations do not penetrate the scientific content. This is too strong a statement, and "penetrate less" would probably be a more tenable position. The point, however, is that Mannheim did see a qualitative difference in the impact of one's *Standort* in the physical as compared with the cultural-historical sciences. In the latter it is incontrovertible that, depending on whether one is a Positivist, a Hegelian, or a Marxist, the principles of selection, the direction of the study, and the categories of meaning will differ. One cannot posit an abstract, impartial knowing subject in the study of history. This is true because "historical knowledge is only possible from an ascertainable intellectual location . . . [and] it presupposes a subject harboring definite aspirations regarding the future and actively striving to achieve them. Only out of the interest which the subject at present acting has in the pattern of the future, does the observation of the past become possible." (p. 102.) That is why the "historical picture of the past changes with every epoch." (p. 103.)

Does this imply the relativity of all historical knowledge? Mannheim denies this and insists that *"historicism veers away from relativism."* (p. 104.) The "solution" he suggests at this stage and elaborates in his later writings is that social and historical knowledge is not relative but *perspectivistic* and *relational*. This was the view, so poorly understood, held by Max Weber in his historical studies. The so-called "materialistic conception" and his own thesis on ascetic Protestantism, far from being mutually contradictory, were in fact complementary. It was not, and never could be, a question of which view was right and which wrong. Both views were simply different perspectives of a given reality and presumably our knowledge of that reality became more adequate and was enriched as a result of the additional perspective provided by Weber. Mannheim expresses the same idea by citing Husserl's theory that even our conception of physical objects depends on the "location of the observing, interpreting subject." The "different historical pictures," Mannheim continues, "do not contradict each other in their interpretations, but encircle the same materially identical given historical content from different standpoints and at different depths of penetration." (p. 105.) The dialectical inter-

action of the theories of successive periods results in the progress of knowledge.

Thus Mannheim strives, now as later, to impart the status and dignity of
science to his perspectivistic, "dialectic-dynamic type of knowledge." (p.
115.) The efforts he made to distinguish the two "kinds" of science and to
harmonize perspectivistic knowledge with non-relativistic criteria of truth
are noteworthy. He firmly believed that perspectivism did not imply relativism.
Rather it led "to a widening of our concept of truth which alone can save us
from being barred from the exploration of these fields in which both the
nature of the object to be known and that of the knowing subject makes [sic]
only perspectivistic knowledge possible." (p. 120.) This brings to a close our
consideration of what may be termed the early phase of Mannheim's sociology
of knowledge. The dominant influences here were Hegel, the historical school,
Husserl, and the methodology of the *Geisteswissenschaften*. In his second
phase these influences, though not abandoned, are subordinated to a more
consistently Marxian approach.

Conservative Thought

If in the essays thus far considered Mannheim concerned himself with
thought forms or *Weltanschauungen* and their connection with other aspects
of social life, this was mainly in a general and philosophical manner. Though
he pointed here and there to underlying socio-historical conditions that
presumably determine a given world outlook, he did not as yet explore that
relationship in any systematic manner. In his essay "Conservative Thought,"
on the other hand, one sees a transition to a sociology of knowledge which was
to be more characteristic of his later phase: Now he concerns himself not only
with styles of thought, their relationship to one another, and their place in the
larger cultural context, but more explicitly and systematically with the social
basis of a given movement of thought. His main efforts are now directed toward demonstrating that "the key to the understanding of changes in ideas is
to be found in the changing social background, mainly in the fate of the social
groups or classes which are the 'carriers' of these styles of thought."[7] This
approach, clearly Marxian, may be taken as paradigmatic, for it exemplifies
the method he employed throughout his later essays in the sociology of
knowledge. To be sure, he retains and utilizes elements derived from the other
"schools" described earlier, but the dominant influence now becomes Marxian.

To support his thesis that there is a determinate relationship between forms
of thought and the existence and fate of social groups, Mannheim selects for
study the conservative movement, its class basis and its historical context.

---

[7] Karl Mannheim, *Essays on Sociology and Social Psychology, op cit.,* p. 74.
(Further, immediately following references to this work to be found in the text.)

Although he examines the bases of conservatism in general, he focuses eventually on one group and one country during a specific period: German conservatism after the French Revolution. In this study his "styles" and movements of thought are predominantly political, approximating what he later calls ideologies. The study of conservative thought, he shows, implies that one must study liberal thought and even socialist thought—*i.e.*, thought which in each case developed along class and party lines. How much this method owed to Marx may be gathered from a brief description of the paradigm Mannheim employed in his analysis.

To understand conservative thought one must begin with rationalism, or the philosophy of the Enlightenment. What accounted for the growth of modern rationalism was the rising capitalist bourgeoisie. Quantitative rationalism, as it appeared in mathematics, philosophy, and the natural sciences, had its parallel in the growth of the capitalist economic system: Commodity production replaced the subsistence economy, exchange-value replaced use-value, and the formerly qualitative attitude toward things and men became increasing quantitative. As Marx had observed, using Carlyle's phrase, it was now the callous "cash nexus" which related man to man. This abstract attitude, Mannheim agreed, gradually came "to include all forms of human experience. In the end even the 'other man' is experienced abstractly." (p. 86.) The situation Marx had described as alienation stood in sharp contrast to the *Gemeinschaft* of the Middle Ages in which—and here Mannheim quotes Marx— "The social relationships of persons engaged in production appear, at any rate, as their own personal relationships, and not disguised as social relations of things, of products of labor." (p. 87*n*.) Conservatism, then, was the political and intellectual reaction against the continuing process which was destroying the older world; it called for a restoration of that world, for a return to the *status quo ante*.

The social "carriers" of this ideological reaction were mainly "those social and intellectual strata which remained outside the capitalistic process of rationalization or at least played a passive role in its development." (p. 87.) These included the peasant strata, the small *bourgeoisie*, and the landed aristocracy. It was primarily in these strata that the older, pre-capitalist relationships prevailed, and consequently, where the older traditions were kept alive. These strata and particularly their intellectual representatives resolutely opposed the philosophy of the Enlightenment, *i.e.*, the intellectual tendencies that accompanied bourgeois capitalism. The Romantic-Conservative movement thus sought to salvage the older way of life and its values: " 'Community' is set up against 'society' . . . family against contract, intuitive certainty against reason, spiritual against material experience. All those partially hidden factors at the very basis of everyday life are suddenly laid bare by reflection and fought for." (p. 89.)

In these terms it was not the socialists but the conservatives who historically were the first opponents and critics of capitalism. The Romantic Conservative opposition strove to preserve, among other things, the nonrational elements of life they considered valuable. And Mannheim suggests that it was the peculiar conditions of the modern proletariat which enabled the left opposition to the bourgeoisie to take over certain ideas and criticisms that originated with the conservative, right-wing opposition. Proletarian rationalism has little in common with the "calculability characteristic of the successful bourgeoisie." (p. 91.) There is always a residual irrational element in proletarian rationalism, since "the capitalist world is only partially rationalized, only partially based on a planned economy." (p. 91.) Ultimately, success in its battles with the bourgeoisie depends on the proletariat's "revolutionary *élan* [which] always remains an uncertain factor." The "social position of the proletariat forces it into irrationalism. The attempt at revolution, however planned and 'scientific' it may be, inevitably produces an irrational 'chiliastic' element. Here lies its essential affinity with the 'counterrevolution.'" (p. 92.)

Conservatism, then, like socialism, is a new or modern phenomenon which arose as a *conscious and reflective* reaction against the advance of capitalism. In these terms it is fundamentally different from mere "traditionalism," from simply clinging instinctively to the old ways of life. Conservatism is the intellectual, political-ideological expression of class interests and values in a dynamic historical situation; it is a style and movement of thought that developed as an antithesis to the conditions and ideology of the capitalistic world. In Mannheim's words, "traditionalism can only become conservatism in a society in which change occurs through the medium of class conflict—in a *class society*. This is the sociological background of modern conservatism." (p. 101.) The "carriers" of the conservative experience and thought express their basic *Weltanschauung* by positively emphasizing all those aspects of life and thought which are antagonistic to the life and thought of bourgeois society. With conservative ideology the qualitative and concrete are opposed to the quantitative and abstract; landed property, not the individual, is the basis of history; and organic groups not "classes" are regarded as the real units of society and history. Conservatism looks to the past, liberalism to the present, and socialism to the future.

The conservative moment, then, arose in conscious opposition to capitalistic conditions and to bourgeois society; and the conservative *Weltanschauung* may therefore be viewed, schematically, as a point for point repudiation of *natural-law philosophy*, the mode of thought most characteristic of the bourgeois-revolutionary epoch. Natural-law philosophy included the following doctrines: the "state of nature," "social contract," "popular sovereignty," the inalienable "Rights of Man (life, liberty, property, the right to resist tyranny, etc.)." (p. 117.) The main methodological principles of this philosophy were:

i. Rationalism as a method of solving problems.
ii. Deductive procedure from one general principle to the particular cases.
iii. A claim of *universal validity* for every individual.

    iv. A claim to universal applicability of all laws to all historical and social
       units.
    v. Atomism and mechanism: collective units (the state, the law, etc.),
       are constructed out of isolated individuals or factors.
    vi. Static thinking (right reason conceived as a self-sufficient, autonomous
       sphere unaffected by history). (p. 117.)

The conservatives attacked each and every one of these articles of faith and
proposed their own to replace them. In opposition to Reason and the
deductive method, they stressed "History, Life, the Nation," and the essential
"irrationality of reality." They repudiated the claim of universal validity and
posited instead the historically unique character of each society. For the
mechanical conception of political and social institutions, they substituted the
organic conception: political institutions, for instance, could not be mechanically transposed from one nation to another. As opposed to the liberal,
atomistic notion of a society, *i.e.*, a sum of individuals who form a contract
with one another, the conservatives insisted that society was an organic
unified whole. Finally, the conservatives attacked the doctrine of static
reason: the norms of reason are in a process of continual historical development. German conservatism, however, developed in a peculiar way because
social conditions in Germany differed in a number of fundamental respects
from those in England or France, for example.

    The key to an understanding of German conservative thought, Mannheim
believed, was to be found in Marx's observation that "Germany experienced
the French Revolution on the philosophical plane." (p. 80.) In France, the
conservative movement was engendered by the reaction to the actual revolutionary events. What was being fought out in the social reality was accompanied by a political and ideological conflict. In Germany, in contrast, the
counterrevolution was of a purely intellectual character. Conservatism in Germany was pushed to a logical extreme; this can be attributed to the absence
of a large and strong middle class which, if it had existed as in England and
France, would have developed a liberal party and ideology and would have
mediated between the existing political extremes. Reminiscent of Marx's
critique of the Left-Hegelians for not inquiring into the relationship between
German social reality and German philosophy, Mannheim writes: "From our
point of view, all philosophy is nothing but a deeper elaboration of a kind of
action. To understand the philosophy, one has to understand the nature of the
action which lies at the bottom of it. This 'action' which we have in mind is
a special way, peculiar to each group, of penetrating social reality, and it
takes on its most tangible form in politics. The political struggle gives expression to the aims and purposes which are unconsciously but coherently at
work in all the conscious and half-conscious interpretations of the world
characteristic of the group." (p. 84.)

    This, then, is Mannheim's general approach. Basing himself on Marx's
Critique of Hegel's Philosophy of Law and on Engels' *Germany: Revolution
and Counterrevolution,* he attempts to explain the specific form of German

conservatism on the basis of German economic "backwardness." Capitalist developments in Germany and especially Prussia lagged many decades behind the other Western countries. "Marx's view is probably correct," writes Mannheim, "and he held that the social condition of Germany in 1843 corresponded roughly to that of France in 1789." (p. 121.) At the time of the French Revolution, Germany was lacking in any real bourgeoisie or proletariat; this condition was still evident after 1848 when Engels suggested that the dismal failure of the revolutions in Germany could be attributed to its economic backwardness. The *Mittelstand* was characterized by so wide a diversity of interests that it was incapable of carrying out concerted political action; its response to the French Revolution was therefore purely ideological. The only strata capable of politically effective action were the nobility and the bureaucracy. If in France, the bourgeoisie had mobilized the third and fourth estates against the Church, the monarchy, and the nobility—in Germany it was the nobility "from below" who struggled against the monarchy, allied with the bureaucracy, "from above." The absence of any *real* popular pressure from below weakened the alliance of the nobility and the bureaucracy so, when the latter initiated certain state reforms in the interest of capitalist development, this evoked a romantic-feudal ideological reaction. The economic, and hence class, structure of German society at the time led to the curious situation in which the bureaucracy employed the rational and mechanistic ideas of the French Revolution as an ideological weapon against the nobility; this class, in turn, sought to preserve and revive the privileges of the estates, and the "organic" and "corporative structure of medieval society." (p. 122.) The result was a peculiarly German way of thinking, which may be termed Romantic and historicist. This became so pervasive an intellectual climate that even its opponents, Mannheim observes, "could never quite free [themselves] from its habits of thought. Heine was a Romantic despite his opposition to the Romantic school; Marx a historicist despite his opposition to the historical school; etc." (p. 123*n.*)

The social strata which participated in this Romantic reaction were mainly the nobility, the *Kleinbürgertum,* and their *ideologues.* They voiced their opposition to the new forces of capitalism and liberalism; they united, in short, against the modern developments, as weak as the latter were. Later, most of the representatives of the Romantic movement were drawn from among the young "unattached intellectuals" who found it difficult if not impossible to make a living *qua* intellectuals. They constituted an economically insecure and socially unstable stratum and more often than not their rebellious and intellectually creative youth was followed by a secure position in the bureaucracy. In general, Mannheim viewed these "free-floating" intellectuals[8] as occupying a unique social position which enabled them to fulfill a correspondingly unique role. Unable to make a living in their "un-

[8] This concept which Mannheim borrowed from Alfred Weber, is one to which we shall later return.

attached" state, they are compelled ultimately to "sell their pen"; they can serve any class and plead any cause. Since they themselves are not a class and hence have no ideology of their own, they can espouse any ideology. Precisely because they are relatively unattached they have "an extraordinarily refined sense for all the political and social currents around them. . . . By themselves they know nothing. But let them take up and identify themselves with someone else's interests—they will know them better, really better, than those for whom these interests are laid down by the nature of things, by their social condition." (p. 127.) Their varied social backgrounds, better education, and *relatively* unattached state, explain, according to Mannheim, the more comprehensive and penetrating view these intellectuals are presumably able to achieve.

Eventually the Romantic impulse is tied to feudal-conservative thought, as seen, for example, in the work of Adam Müller, who drew on both sources and employed them in an ideological struggle against natural-law philosophy. The new *Weltanschauung*, a synthesis of Romantic and feudal tendencies, not only posited a system of counter-values but "different categories of life and experience." (p. 147.) All the categories of rationalism are supplanted by "life," "history," "spirit," "nation," "community," etc. The static and mechanical are replaced by the dynamic and organic. In Germany, three stages could be discerned in the development of this new style of thinking: "(a) thinking in terms of antitheses, (b) dynamic thinking, and (c) dialectical thinking." (p. 150.) The first, exemplified in the work of Müller and deriving from the Romantic heritage, proposed, in opposition to the linear reasoning of the Enlightenment, a method of thinking based on antitheses and polarities. The second, dynamic thinking, insisted that theory must move, live, and grow as do living things and in fact as do social institutions. "The wish to make thought just as mobile as life itself breaks through here." (p. 153.) The final stage, synthesizing the first two, is typified in Hegel's dialectical philosophy. Reason is not abandoned but transformed into a dynamic principle of the entire universe including, of course, the human realm. Thinking must be dialectical in order to reflect adequately the dialectical character of being, life, and experience.

This brief discussion is perhaps sufficient to show just how much Mannheim relied in his analysis on insights derived from Marxism, from the historical school, and from the *Geisteswissenschaften*. The form and content of German conservative thought and the significant ways in which it differed from English and French conservatism could only be understood against the background of the German social structure. While the analysis of social structure could be carried out with a relatively high degree of rigor and exactness, the process of relating given styles and movements of thought to their respective classes and strata required a certain "metaphysical gift." Ultimately, there can be little doubt that Mannheim regarded that gift as an indispensable aspect of his method of ideological analysis.

The Problem of Generations

In his approach to the phenomenon of "generations," Mannheim generalized Marx's conception of *class* and in this way formulated a *sociological* conception of the problem. This enabled him to advance beyond previous conceptualizations. One of these, that of Dilthey for example, had viewed "generation as a temporal unit of the history of intellectual evolution [which made] it possible to replace such purely external units as hours, months, years, decades, etc. by a concept of measure operating from within. . . ."[9] The concept of generation, for Dilthey, facilitated an "intuitive reenactment" of how each generation had experienced and interpreted the world. In addition, he had emphasized that *coexistence* as well as succession were characteristic of the generational phenomenon: The same social and cultural circumstances are experienced "by contemporary individuals, both in their early, formative, and in their later years." (p. 282.) This led him to view contemporaries as *one* generation "just because they are subject to common influences" and in this way he had obscured generational differences.

Another view was that of Pinder, the art historian: It is true that young and old live in the same period of time but the really interesting phenomenon here is *"the non-contemporaneity of the contemporaneous."* For each generation "the 'same time' is a different time—that is, it represents a different *period of his self,* which he can only share with people of his own age." (p. 283.) Pinder's notion was insightful but his concern was almost exclusively with the subjective side of generations and with biological rhythm. In general, then, this and other conceptions of "generation" were wanting in that they had not even alluded to the *social* factor.

This factor, Mannheim suggests, may be grasped through the idea of *Lagerung,* or social location. A "generation" is not a group but a category. A "group cannot exist without its members having concrete knowledge of each other, and [it] ceases to exist as a mental and spiritual unit as soon as physical proximity is destroyed." "Generation" is a social category and what is meant by this term may best be understood by considering another category which shares

a certain structural resemblance to it—namely, the class position *(Klassenlage)* of an individual in society.

In its wider sense class position can be defined as the common "location" . . . certain individuals hold in the economic and power structure of a given society as their "lot." (p. 289.)

This refers to the objective position individuals occupy in the class structure of a society and which therefore tends to determine their "life-chances" (to

9 Karl Mannheim, *Essays on the Sociology of Knowledge, op. cit.,* p. 282. (Further references to this work noted in the text by page numbers.)

use the Weberian term) and fate. A class is not a concrete group like a small territorial community, for example. "Class position is an objective fact," writes Mannheim in straight Marxian terms, "whether the individual in question knows his class position or not, and whether he acknowledges it or not." (p. 289.) What Marx had called "class consciousness" does not necessarily accompany a class position, although in certain social conditions the latter can give rise to the former, lending it certain features, and resulting in the formation of a 'conscious class.' " (pp. 289–290.) Generations, Mannheim notes, have something in common with Marx's conception of objective class position, i.e., the "similar location of a number of individuals in a social structure. . . ." (p. 290.)

There is no denying that this similar "location" is based on the biological rhythm of the human organism: people born in the same year share a common temporal location in the social process. Social generations are ultimately based on this fact. Mannheim is quick to add, however, that "to be *based* on a factor does not necessarily mean to be *deducible* from it, or to be implied in it." (pp. 290–91.) The biological factor has sociological relevance and that is where the sociological problem of generations must begin.

"Social location," as the common characteristic of class and generation, refers in the first place to the limitations imposed by that spatio-temporal location: Individuals are exposed to a specific range of potential and actual experiences and excluded from others. In these terms, just as the "experiential, intellectual, and emotional data" differ for each class, they also differ for each generation. Of course, one must not ignore the stratification and varying locations of members of a single generation. "Even a mental climate as rigorously uniform as that of the Catholic Middle Ages presented itself differently according to whether one were a theologizing cleric, a knight, or a monk." (p. 291.) The category of generation is important, however, because it alerts one to the following characteristics of social life:

(a) new participants in the cultural process are emerging whilst
(b) former participants in that process are continually disappearing;
(c) members of any one generation can participate only in a temporally limited section of the historical process, and
(d) it is therefore necessary continually to transmit the accumulated cultural heritage;
(e) the transition from generation to generation is a continuous process. (p. 292.)

New age groups are continually emerging and it is through this process that the continuity and accumulation of culture is achieved. "Fresh contact" is thus made between the older and the younger generations. Of course, there are "fresh contacts" in many other areas of social life, but the main point for Mannheim is that the generational phenomenon provides for "a radical form of fresh contact." This results in a certain loss of accumulated culture but also in selection and change; "it facilitates reevaluation of our inventory and teaches us both to forget that which is no longer useful and to covet that which has yet to be won." (p. 294.) The first two characteristics therefore point to the conditions in which the continuity and rejuvenation of society take place. The third, however, refers to more than mere chronological contemporaneity, for it becomes "sociologically significant only when it also involves participation in the same historical and social circumstances. . . ." (p. 298.) Obviously such participation is not shared by young people in two distinct civilizations, say, China and Germany in the year 1800. Similarly, not all members of a single generation in the same country share precisely the same circumstances, since they are variously located in the social structure. What follows from this is that though each generation may have its own social-psychological strata of meaning, these are far from homogeneous. The fourth characteristic stresses that the need to transmit the cultural heritage involves both those aspects which are non-problematic, and hence spontaneously and unconsciously learned, and those which have "become problematic and [have] therefore invited conscious reflection." (p. 299.)

Mannheim interjects an observation based on a Freudian principle which is far from established: The "inventory of experience which is absorbed by infiltration from the environment in early youth often becomes the historically oldest stratum of consciousness, which tends to stabilize itself as the natural view of the world." (p. 299.) The final point refers to the fact that the hiatus and occasional antagonisms between the older and younger generations—e.g., the father-son antagonism—is lessened by the existence of "intermediary generations." These serve a mediating function and thus make smoother the process of generational continuity and interaction.

Marx had distinguished the objective and subjective aspects of class, and Mannheim employs this distinction with respect to the category of generation. When one says that the members of a single generation share a socio-historical location, this means that the "location as such only contains potentialities which may materialize, or be suppressed. . . ." (p. 303.) Whether young peasants scattered in the countryside and urban youth are an *actual* generation will depend on whether they participate *"in the common destiny"* of some socio-historical unit. "We shall therefore speak of a *generation as an actuality* only when a concrete bond is created between members of a generation by their being exposed to the social and intellectual symptoms of a process of dynamic destabilization. Thus, the young peasants . . . only share the same generation location, without, however, being members of the same generation as an actuality, with the youth of the town. They are similarly located, insofar as they are *potentially* capable of being sucked into the vortex of social change. . . ." (p. 303.) This is reminiscent of Marx's discussion of whether the peasants are a class and of the conditions in which they might conceivably have allied themselves with the urban proletariat.[10]

10 See Marx's essay, "The Class Struggles in France" in Karl Marx and Frederick Engels, *Selected Works I* (Moscow: Foreign Languages Publishing House, 1950).

Further refining the category of generation, Mannheim notes that even within the same *actual* generation, one must distinguish the separate units which emerge in response "to an historical stimulus experienced by all in common. Romantic-Conservative youth and [the] liberal-rationalist group, belong to the same actual generation but form separate 'generation units' within it. The *generation unit* represents a much more concrete bond than the actual generation as such."[11] The *generation unit* is not necessarily a group, since its members may never come into personal contact with one another. Nevertheless, they respond similarly to the situations in which they participate; they share a certain affinity for certain principles and ways of viewing their common world of experiences. "Thus within any generation there can exist a number of differentiated, [and even] antagonistic generation units."[12]

Clearly, all this is a rather straightforward application of Marx's conception of class to the phenomenon of generations. By thus generalizing a Marxian idea, Mannheim provides the means of refining it: the various generational concepts may be employed, for example, in an exploration of the mutual relationship, in given circumstances, of class position, ideology, and generation. This brings us to the later essays in which the Marxian influence is even more conspicuous.

Ideology and Utopia

Although the principles enunciated in these essays could apply to the general problem of "how men actually think" and to the relationship of thinking to other aspects of human action, in practice Mannheim confines his attention to the narrower question of how thinking functions in the public and political spheres of social life. Now, as earlier, his major working hypothesis is derived from Marx's celebrated idea that it is the conditions of men's social existence which tend to determine their social consciousness. Mannheim adopts this principle in its full conflictive and dialectical sense: Men "act with and against one another in diversely organized groups, and while doing so they think with and against one another."[13]

Depending on the position men occupy in the social structure and their consciousness of that position they join together in groups and strive collectively either to change or to preserve the conditions of their existence. Like Marx, Mannheim protests the separation of thought from action. The unity of theory and action must be recognized and restored in practice so that men may gain a fuller consciousness of the consequences of their acts. For Marx, the function of theory was to guide men in changing the world; for Mannheim, similarly, the *raison d'être* of his sociological theory of knowledge was

11 *Ibid.*, p. 304.
12 *Ibid.*, p. 306.
13 Karl Mannheim, *Ideology and Utopia* (London: Routledge and Kegan Paul, Ltd., 1960), p. 3. (Further reference to this work noted in text by page numbers.)

to provide scientific guidance for action directed toward social change—for what he eventually called *planning for freedom.*

At the very outset he points quite clearly to both the advantages and limitations of his sociology of knowledge; " . . . the ultimate criterion of truth or falsity is to be found in the investigation of the object, and the sociology of knowledge is no substitute for this." (p. 4.) Relating men's ideas to the particular location they occupy in the social structure is a process quite different from assessing their truth and validity. The sociological theory of knowledge can tell us how those ideas emerged but not whether they are true or false.

For Mannheim, the sociological theory of knowledge is a peculiarly modern instrument of analysis and reflection. It accompanied the greater tempo of social change of the capitalist-industrial era, including vertical and horizontal mobility, and the more intense and overt class conflicts of that era. Such a theory never could have arisen in medieval Europe, for example, which was a relatively static society characterized by closed castes or ranks. Nobles, clerics, peasants, artisans, and merchants had their own respective views of the world which merely coexisted as isolated *Weltanschauungen*—a reflection of the relative social isolation of these strata from one another. Only with great social mobility and communication of the capitalist era did a decisive change take place. This becomes evident "when the forms of thought and experience, which had hitherto developed independently, enter into one and the same consciousness impelling the mind to discover the irreconcilability of the conflicting conceptions of the world." (p. 7.) In addition, the greater mobility, communication, and conflict which accompanied capitalist-industrial developments brought in their wake greater democratization. This gave the thinking of the lower strata a greater public significance; one example in philosophy of the attempt to formalize such thinking is pragmatism. All these social changes have resulted in a social system fundamentally different from the *Gemeinschaft* of the Middle Ages and are reflected in the thought of the "free intelligentsia"—also a characteristically modern product. They are "recruited from constantly varying social strata and life situations and [their] mode of thought is no longer subject [as it was in the Middle Ages] to regulation by a caste-like organization." (p. 10.)

The greater understanding which the sociological approach to knowledge facilitates becomes evident by comparing it with others. Historically, one may distinguish at least three distinct approaches to problems of knowledge: (a) the *epistemological,* (b) the *psychological,* and (c) the *sociological.* An example of the first may be seen in the various philosophical controversies between the idealists and materialists, the realists and the nominalists, the empiricists and the rationalists, etc. To take the last dispute, there can be no doubt that the participants raised an important question. Is knowledge a result of immediate sensory experience as Locke, for example, had held? Or is it the outcome of experience mediated by a priori categories as Kant had postulated? Mannheim, like Durkheim, sided with the latter school—but with the important qualification that the categories are *not* a priori. The mind and all its logical categories are a social product, and without this insight the epistemological question could never be adequately resolved. Though epistemology has enriched our understanding by posing certain problems, it needs sociology to solve them.

The psychological approach has also yielded greater understanding of the form and content of certain thoughts. Biographical data, for instance, are often very illuminating since they suggest why a given thinker thought the way he did. Yet, this approach, too, has definite limitations. Studying the life of Jesus or the Apostles, for example, can never adequately convey the full meaning of the biblical saying: "The last shall be the first." A full and adequate understanding of this utterance, Mannheim strives to show, could only be gained by going beyond the strictly psychological approach to consider not only biography but social structure and history as well. Combining ideas of Marx, Nietzsche, and Scheler, Mannheim suggests that the phrase, "The last shall be the first," can only be understood if one becomes aware of "the significance of resentment in the formation of moral judgments." (p. 22.) An analysis of the socio-historical context in which the sentence was first uttered suggests "that it has a real appeal only for those who, like the [early] Christians, are in some manner oppressed and who, at the same time, under the impulse of resentment, wish to free themselves from prevailing injustices." (p. 23.) The merit of the sociological approach, then, is that it sets "alongside the individual genesis of meaning the genesis from the context of group life." (p. 25.)

The conditions of existence and conflict of interests between oppressors and oppressed engender antithetical movements of thought. Mannheim employs what he calls "two slogan-like concepts 'ideology and utopia' " to describe these antithetical thought forms. Early Christian thought, for instance, was "utopian" in that it expressed the resentment of the oppressed. Their weakness led them to deprecate power and to glorify passivity—*e.g.,* "turn the other cheek." The early Christians constituted a "stratum which had as yet no real aspirations to rule," thus the saying, "Render unto Caesar the things that are Caesar's." Their resentment was therefore sublimated into a mere psychic rebellion: "The last shall be the first." All the values of the Roman oppressors ("Ideology") were repudiated in the counter-values ("Utopia") of the oppressed Christians. Both ideological thought and utopian thought are thus "situationally determined"; not only in the sense that each reflects the different conditions of existence of rulers and ruled, oppressors and oppressed, or upper and lower strata, but also in the sense that each reflects the interests of its "carriers."

Two distinct meanings may be discerned in the development of the concept ideology, and Mannheim calls them the *particular* and *total* conceptions. The first refers to the "more or less conscious disguises of the real nature of the situation, the true recognition of which would not be in accord with [one's] interests. These distortions range all the way from conscious lies to half-conscious and unwitting disguises; from calculated attempts to dupe others to self-deception." (p. 49.) The *total* conception of ideology, on the other hand, refers, for example, to the *Weltanschauung* of a class or epoch, or to the ideas and categories of thought which are bound up with the existential conditions of that class or epoch. In the *particular,* or psychological, conception one deals with an individual and attempts to "unmask" him by discovering the true personal interests he deceitfully hides or denies; in this case one designates "only a part of the opponent's assertions" as ideology while continuing to share with him a common universe of discourse and common standards of validity. The *total* conception, in contrast, "calls into question the opponent's entire *Weltanschauung* (including his conceptual apparatus) and attempts to understand these concepts as an outgrowth of the collective life of which he partakes." (p. 50.) Examples of the *total* conception might be "conservative thought," "bourgeois-liberal" ideology, etc. When men express these ideas it is not a matter of deceit or even "interests" in any narrow sense but rather an expression of the outlook of a whole social group or stratum whose existential circumstances they share. Marxism fused both conceptions into one and thus became a formidable ideological weapon in the hands of the proletariat and its spokesmen. "It was this theory which first gave due emphasis to the role of class position and class interests in thought." (p. 66.) Soon afterwards, however, the opponents of Marxism learned to use the weapon of ideological analysis and to turn it against Marxism itself. It was this process that made possible the "transition from the theory of ideology to the sociology of knowledge." (p. 67.)

For Mannheim, then, the *total* conception of ideology requires *sociological* analysis, and here two formulations may be distinguished: the *special* and the *general*. At first a group discovers the *Seinsverbundenheit* or "situational determination" of its opponents' ideas while remaining unaware that its own thought is also influenced by the social situation in which it finds itself. When this is the case, Mannheim calls it the *special* formulation of the total conception of ideology. The *general* formulation, on the other hand, is employed when one "has the courage to subject not just the adversary's point of view but all points of view, including his own, to the ideological analysis." (p. 69). And if this *general form of the total conception* is used in an investigation in a non-evaluative manner—*i.e.,* judgments are temporarily suspended as to the truth or falsity of the ideas in question—then one has a *sociology of knowledge.*

This again raises the question, Does not the sociology of knowledge imply that truth is "relative," *i.e.,* "dependent upon the subjective standpoint and the social situation of the knower?" To this Mannheim replies in the negative; for while the study of history from the standpoint of the sociology of knowledge does not reveal any absolute truths, this implies not "relativism" but "relationism." The probability is great that the perspective of an observer or knower will vary with his social standpoint; but the question, "[W]hich social standpoint offers the best chance for reaching an optimum of truth?" still remains. (p. 71.) Unfortunately, Mannheim never goes much beyond this to clarify further the implications of "relationism" for validity and truth. He was altogether aware that he had not solved the problem and on balance his position seems to have been that the analysis of the social basis of ideas and their validity are two relatively separate questions. Social analysis was not entirely irrelevant for the determination of validity, but what precisely that relevance was, Mannheim never made explicit.[14]

Mannheim did indicate, however, in very general terms what he considered that relevance to be. The student of a given social or historical question, even one who has a truly objective intention, is made aware by the sociology of knowledge that all points of view, including his own, are partial and one-sided. His objective posture leads him to consider carefully the many contending viewpoints, which he relates to their respective social situations. "Through this effort the one-sidedness of our own point of view is counter-acted, and conflicting intellectual positions may actually come to supplement one another."[15] Our knowledge and ability to get at the truth are presumably enhanced by the very fact that one can employ a variety of perspectives through which to study a given phenomenon—and are enhanced too by discovering the social bases of the various perspectives.

To illustrate this by returning once more to Max Weber, there can be no doubt that he regarded Marx's perspective as strategically most important for an understanding of historical change, and his own perspective as supple-mentary to that of Marx. For Weber, it was not a matter of one perspective being true and the other false. Rather, by adding his own to Marx's, a richer and more adequate understanding of the origins of capitalism was presumably made possible. One partial truth supplemented and enriched another. This was also Mannheim's attitude toward historical and even some social questions. He does, however, also provide a pragmatic criterion of validity: Practice or action is the test of a theory's truth. An "ethical attitude is invalid," he writes, "if it is oriented with reference to norms with which action in a given historical setting, even with the best of intentions, cannot com-ply."[16] Or, a "theory . . . is wrong if in a given practical situation it uses concepts and categories which, if taken seriously, would prevent man from adjusting himself at that historical stage."[17] Under no circumstances were the postulates of the sociology of knowledge to be regarded as a substitute for

[14] An excellent critical discussion of this and other problems may be found in R. K. Merton's article, "Karl Mannheim and the Sociology of Knowledge." (Footnote 1.) See *Social Theory and Social Structure, op. cit.,* p. 504 *ff.*

[15] Karl Mannheim, *Ideology and Utopia, op cit.,* p. 76.

[16] *Ibid.,* p. 84.

[17] *Ibid.,* p. 85.

empirical research. "We, too, appeal to 'facts' for our proof, but the question of the nature of facts is in itself a considerable problem."[18] If one accepts the fundamental assumptions of the sociology of knowledge, as Mannheim felt one must, then its main value lies in helping one to overcome the "somnambulistic certainty that has existed with reference to the problem of truth during stable periods of history. . . ."[19]

In the end, Mannheim believed that, however objective an analysis, there was "an irreducible residue of evaluation inherent in the structure of all thought," but that there was perhaps one stratum in society which was more capable than any other of becoming conscious of its evaluations. This was the intelligentsia.

The Intelligentsia

It is going too far to say, as did Merton, that Mannheim found "a structural warranty of the validity of social thought in the 'classless position' of the 'socially unattached intellectuals' [*sozialfreischwebende Intelligenz*]."[20] If the impression of such a "warranty" could occasionally be inferred from Mannheim's remarks in *Ideology and Utopia* and other early essays, he makes quite clear in a later essay, devoted entirely to the subject of intellectuals, that this impression is not the one he had intended to convey and, in fact, a misinterpretation of his thesis. Mannheim's point about the intelligentsia was that they are not a class; *i.e.*, they have no common interests, they cannot form a separate party, and, finally, they are incapable of common and concerted action. They are, in fact, *ideologues* of this or that class but never speak for "themselves."

For Mannheim, the intelligentsia was essentially a "classless aggregation," or an "interstitial stratum" which willy-nilly became "a satellite of one or another of the existing classes and parties."[21] It was "between, but not above, the classes." He is quite explicit on this score: The intellectuals are not a "superior" stratum, nor does their peculiar social position assure any greater validity for their perspectives. Their position does, however, enable them to do something which members of other strata are less able to do. It is true that most intellectuals do in fact share the orientations of one or another of the existing classes and parties. "But," writes Mannheim,

over and above these affiliations he is motivated by the fact that his training has equipped him to face the problems of the day in several perspectives and not only in one, as most participants in the controversies of their

18 Ibid., p. 91.
19 *Ibid.*, p. 91.
20 Merton, *op. cit.*, p. 507.
21 Karl Mannheim, *Essays on the Sociology of Culture* (London: Routledge and Kegan Paul, Ltd., 1956) , p. 104. (Immediately following references to this work cited only by page numbers in text.)

time do. We said he is *equipped* to envisage the problems of his time in more than a single perspective, although from case to case he may act as a partisan and align himself with a class. (p. 105.)

The emphasis here is on the *potential* ability of the educated man to adopt a variety of perspectives toward any given social issue or phenomenon. Intellectuals are *not*, Mannheim reemphasizes, "an exalted stratum above the classes and are in no way better endowed with a capacity to overcome their own class attachments than other groups." (p. 105.) In his earlier essays, he explains, the term "relatively" in the phrase "relatively unattached intelligentsia" which he borrowed from Alfred Weber, "was no empty word. The expression simply alluded to the well-established fact that intellectuals do not react to given issues as cohesively as for example . . . workers do." (p. 106.) Being a member of the so-called intelligentsia, then, provides no structural warranty of validity nor does it make one "privy to revelations." Apparently all that Mannheim wanted to convey in his thesis about the intelligentsia "was merely that certain types of intellectuals have a maximum opportunity to test and employ the socially available vistas and to experience their inconsistencies." (p. 106.) Right or wrong, this is a considerably more modest thesis than his critics have attributed to him.

One of the main points Mannheim wanted to make with the phrase "relatively unattached" was that after the Middle Ages the intellectuals to an increasing degree were emancipated from the upper classes and unaligned as yet with the lower.[22] The institutions in which the intellectuals could first be discerned as relatively free and detached were the *salons* and the coffee-houses. While the *salons* enabled individuals of different social backgrounds, views, stations, and allegiances to mingle, entry to the *salon* required social acceptability and was in that sense restricted. The coffee-houses, on the other hand, were open to all and thus "became the first centers of opinion in a partially democratized society." (p. 138.) Membership and participation were now determined not by rank and family ties but by intellectual interests and shared opinions; the latter being especially true when the houses became political clubs. "Not the common style of living and not common friends, but like opinion constituted now the basis of amalgamation." (p. 139.)

In the modern era, *some* intellectuals at least were able to escape a relationship of dependence on local habitat, institution, class and party. To be sure, they "may have their political preferences, but they are not committed to any party or denomination. This detachment, however, is not absolute." (p. 157.) *Some* journalists, *some* writers, *some* scholars, and *some* scientists "enjoy" this relatively uncommitted position which, however, has for Mannheim negative as well as positive consequences. For while it is true that the "free" intellectual has a potentially wider view, and is potentially less blinded

---

22 However, growing bureaucratization in his time, Mannheim believed, now brought with it a pronounced tendency in the reverse direction.

by particular interests and commitments, he lacks at the same time the restraints of real life. He is more inclined to generate ideas without testing them in practice—that is, in the actions and consequences of everyday life. He may lose touch with reality and forget that a main purpose of thought is the orientation of action. These observations helped illuminate the changing historical role of the intellectual.

More important for Mannheim, however, was the fate of the relatively free intellectuals in the face of the tendency so well described by Max Weber: the growing bureaucratization of all aspects of social life including scholarship and science. Increasingly, Weber had pointed out, not only the workers but the scientists and scholars were being "separated" from the means of "production" (research). This together with specialization, which narrows the compass of thought and activity, discourages the "will to dissent and innovate." (p. 168.) More and more, research, thinking, and scholarship were now carried out in the context of large organizations, private and governmental, and this increasing dependence of the mental laborer led to an increasing "intellectual dessication." (p. 168.) There were now few professions that were "free" in the sense that they could be practiced independently, outside a bureaucratic context.

No matter how small this stratum may be, still it retains an important role at once diagnostic, constructive, and critical. There is nothing automatic about these functions—they do not follow "naturally" from a social position. In effect, it is only by a conscious and deliberate commitment that the intellectual can prevent his affiliation with parties and organizations from resulting in self-abnegation. His conscious posture must at all times be critical —of himself as well as of others. Mannheim recognized that the intellectuals were powerless, but he believed, nevertheless, that they could play an influential role in the preservation of freedom and in the reconstruction of society. With the collapse of the liberal democracies and the victory of fascism, the responsibility of the intellectuals was perhaps greater than ever before. And Mannheim believed he was fulfilling his responsibility in his various studies of that devastating crisis of his time.

Just as earlier Mannheim had adopted a modified Marxian approach in the development of his sociology of knowledge, he now did the same in his analyses of contemporary social conditions and in his prescriptions for social change. It was a modified or *revised* Marxism which he developed during his stay in England under the influence of English thought and experience.

Marx had observed that, particularly since the late Middle Ages, it was changing economic relations which had brought about changes in the other social relations of men and even in their consciousness. Marx's general thesis, Mannheim believed, was "increasingly confirmed with every concrete analysis along these lines."[23] Mannheim also understood the dialectical character of

23 Karl Mannheim, *Essays on the Sociology of Knowledge, op. cit.,* p. 274.

Marx's proposition: When one speaks of the determining influence of economic relationships one must always keep in mind that it is men who form the relationships which in turn form men. Mannheim also clearly comprehended that economic crises, the collapse of liberal democracy, and war must not be regarded as "natural" or "inevitable"; these were "natural" and "inevitable" disasters only under certain social conditions. Under different circumstances men could consciously form their economic and social systems and thus shape their destiny. For Marx, this presupposed the shattering of the class structure of society—thus his sociological theory was advanced to guide the revolutionary action of the working class in their movement toward this goal. Marx was talking primarily to the proletariat.

Mannheim, in contrast, seems to be talking to the élites. The tone of the essays soon to be examined is one of pleading: The élites must recognize the need to plan for freedom, the need to bring the economic system under control, the need to give the masses security. All this must be done if crisis, totalitarianism, and war are to be avoided. It is in these essays that one sees clearly the well-intentioned but naïve character of such pleading—the result of his "technocratic" bias which led him to view social change primarily as a scientific-technical problem. Only occasionally does he seem to acknowledge that he might have gone too far in his revision of Marx's theory; only occasionally does he pause to consider the class structure of society and the tremendous resistance to social change generated by the upper advantaged strata. Throughout these essays Mannheim's panacea is "planning," essentially a technical, not a political, problem for him. He placed his faith in the good will of the various élites whom he hoped to persuade that planning was as desirable as it was necessary. This appeared to be the only real option his analysis of contemporary developments revealed. It is to this analysis that we now turn.

Man and Society in an Age of Reconstruction

The key to an understanding of contemporary industrial society, Mannheim believed, could be found in the works of Karl Marx and Max Weber. Marx had explored the social consequences of the concentration of the means of production and of the separation of the worker from those means. This was an important observation, Weber agreed. But in thus focusing on the sphere of production, he argued, Marx had brought into relief only one aspect of a much more general process. The concentration of the "means of production" and the separation of the "worker" could also be discerned in other institutional orders of society—notably in the political and military spheres, where both the means of political administration and the means of violence and destruction were increasingly concentrated in the hands of élites. Both thinkers thus called attention to the major structural trends of industrial society which tended to preclude "fundamental democratization," as Mannheim referred to it. Writing these essays after the Nazis had taken power[24] and almost two decades after the Russian Revolution, Mannheim perceived that in Germany and Russia, as well as in those countries which remained politically democratic, the growing bureaucratization of the crucial sectors of society seemed to be a virtually inexorable process.

Bureaucratization undermined democracy because it separated the people from the means of power and brought about, in Mannheim's words, "the dominance of small minorities under capitalism as well as communism."[25] In the eighteenth and early nineteenth centuries democracy was based in no small degree on the military power of the people: "[O]ne man meant one gun, the resistance of one thousand individuals one thousand guns." Ultimately the people could use this power to safeguard democracy. In the twentieth century, the growing scale and concentration of the instruments of military power had brought about a basic change; large numbers of people could now be intimidated, terrorized, and killed by an efficient, large-scale means of destruction under the control of dominant minorities. The military significance of small arms and barricades had radically diminished and the power of the people had declined accordingly.

Mannheim understood, of course, that this did not necessarily imply a total impotence on the part of the people: "Suppressed elements learn to adapt their tactics to all manner of threats, including even military ones." (p. 49.) This pointed to the possibility of armed conflict, resistance, and violence. Somehow, then, the various élites—to whom Mannheim is really addressing himself—must learn to win over the people and gain their voluntary cooperation in "the pursuit of some common interest." (p. 49.) Reaching the élites with "sound" advice, as we shall see, was Mannheim's main purpose in these essays. First, however, let us consider other aspects of his analysis.

Bureaucratization, Weber had shown, was a manifestation of the general "rationalization" of social life; yet this rationalization was merely formal and not substantive. Here, again, Mannheim followed the leads of Marx and Weber. Marx had described as a contradiction the rational organization of each enterprise contributing to the economic "anarchy" of the capitalist system as a whole. Similarly, Weber spoke of "formal" and "substantive" rationality, a distinction Mannheim adopted and termed, respectively, "functional" and "substantial" rationality. The first refers, for example, to the type of rationality that prevails in an organization of human activities in which the thought, knowledge, and reflection of the participants are virtually unnecessary; men become parts of a mechanical process in which each is assigned a

24 They were first published in German in 1935; and in 1940, translated into English, revised, and expanded.

25 Karl Mannheim, *Man and Society in an Age of Reconstruction* (New York: Harcourt, Brace and World, 1948), p. 46. (Immediately following references to this work cited by page numbers in text.)

functional position and role. Their purposes, wishes, and values become irrelevant and superfluous in an eminently "rational" process. What they forfeit in creativity and initiative is gained by the organization as a whole and contributes, presumably, to its greater "efficiency." "Substantial" rationality, in contrast, refers to the intelligent insight men gain into a situation, which then enables them to control and shape it in accordance with their conscious purposes.

Bureaucratic organization strives for maximum *functional rationality—i.e.,* it suppresses not only all forms of functional irrationality but substantial rationality as well. Functional and substantial rationality are opposed in principle: The first requires the subordination of one's mind and self to a thing or mechanical process, while the second presupposes that men strive to master a situation and adapt it to their conscious ends. The master trend of modern industrial society—bureaucratization, or increasing formal rationalization—far from raising the capacity of Everyman for independent judgment, is in fact paralyzing and destroying it. The average man has little or no understanding of his condition and, in effect, he has turned over to small dominant minorities "the responsibility for making decisions." Mannheim viewed this trend as the basis of "the growing distance between the élite and the masses, and [of] the 'appeal to the leader' which has recently become so widespread." (p. 59.)

Left with a reduced capacity for independent thinking, and accustomed to following blindly, the average individual is also thereby reduced to a state of "terrified helplessness" and impotence when the functionally rationalized system collapses. Under these circumstances, is it any wonder that economic crises and other disruptions of the social system are accompanied by widespread eruptions of irrational behavior? "Irrationality" from this standpoint is a type of behavior generated under specific social circumstances. Man is inherently neither rational nor irrational and which type of conduct will prevail depends on the situational context. "Uncontrolled outbursts and psychic regressions," for example, were more likely to occur, Mannheim argues, in the mass industrialized society than in small groups. Employing a Freudian notion, he observes that the functional rationalization of human behavior in industrial society brings with it "a whole series of repressions and renunciations of impulsive satisfactions," which remain repressed so long as the system works smoothly. With its breakdown, however, the repressed impulses assert themselves as wild and powerful irrational outbursts, which avail the people nothing but which are successfully harnessed by "the leaders." Irrationality, its sources and its consequences, are thus explained *sociologically.*

With this analysis, Mannheim prepared for a presentation of what appeared to him as the only solution: *Planning!* It was high time, he argued, that the liberal advocates of laissez-faire recognized that their classic doctrine had outlived its usefulness. It is the "planlessness" of contemporary society that is the cause of economic crises and of the breakdown of "social order."

Economic planning is absolutely essential if social stability is to be preserved. Not planning in the formal or functional sense, which tends toward totalitarianism, but "democratic" planning. The liberals must be made to understand, once and for all, that planning need not take the totalitarian form. With democratic, rational planning the irrational can be transformed into a positive force, a "pure *élan*" which "heightens the joy of living without breaking up the social order." (p. 63.) Against the various groups of Marxists, on the other hand, Mannheim argued that class conflict, revolution, and working-class power are not the precondition for a new society in which the substantive needs and wants of all are planned for.

What emerges from Mannheim's general discussion, despite his frequent emphasis on *democratic* planning, is a fundamental ambivalence toward democracy. He relates that during a discussion of the possibilities of planning, someone remarked: "We have progressed so far as to be able to plan society and even to plan man himself. Who plans those who are to do the planning?" And Mannheim confesses: "The longer I reflect on this question, the more it haunts me." (p. 74.) He resolves this ambivalence by placing his faith in "responsible élites." Let them plan for the whole society and bear responsibility for it. It is true that they are small minorities but, after all, he consoles himself, "the masses always take the form which the creative minorities controlling societies choose to give them." (p. 75.) This élitist conception of "democracy" is characteristic of all of Mannheim's work on planning, but especially the essays in *Man and Society*.

Let us take as an illustration, his notion of *social techniques, i.e.*, the various means by which the masses are manipulated in contemporary society and most strikingly in the totalitarian states. Mannheim states that democracies can learn from the "use of social techniques in the totalitarian states." The labor camps of fascism may be "an extremely uncongenial solution" to the problem of unemployment; propagandistic and mass psychological techniques repudiate "the enlightenment of the masses and appeal to the most primitive impulses"; nevertheless, from the standpoint of social technique, the totalitarian states have learned *to deal effectively with the mass*—which seems to appear very important to Mannheim.

Mannheim's reasoning seems to have been the following. The high degree of bureaucratization of the crucial sectors of social life is here to stay; the concentration of power is an irreversible process, though decentralization here and there may be possible. Periodic economic crises and now the most dramatic breakdown of all have weakened and even destroyed the liberal political order. The working class and its leaders are divided among themselves and seem incapable of stopping fascism; and the unemployed restless masses have come under the sway of dictators who threaten to envelop the whole world in a devastating war. The only choice, therefore, is to learn what one can from the totalitarian states, namely, planning and other social techniques, and to apply them as democratically as possible toward the maintenance of order. "How it would simplify our common life," writes Mannheim, "if this power of planned persuasion were used, not for stirring up strife, but for encouraging behavior on which all our hopes of peace, coopera- tion, and understanding depend." (p. 261.) It was not without some appre- hension, of course, that he advocated the use of these "techniques"; he saw the great dangers in giving some men, a small minority, so much power over all the others. But in the end, he saw no alternative.

Since the intellectuals have no power, the only option open to those who refuse to become "mere" ideological spokesmen for one or another of the "parties" is to advise the élites. It is here that we have a concrete example of the so-called "relatively unattached intellectual" which Mannheim, no doubt, fancied himself in this instance to be. The role of the intellectual was to impart scientific-sociological knowledge to the various élites so that they might govern wisely and benevolently. In some cases, the intellectuals would become an integral part of the planning authority. Here one sees an approach to social change, reminiscent of Saint-Simon's, which is at once positivistic, technocratic, and paternalistic. "The planning authority," Mannheim pro- poses, "should be able to decide on empirical grounds what sort of influence to use in a given situation, basing its judgments on the scientific study of society, coupled if possible with sociological experiments." (p. 266.)

Apart from the sinister implications of this proposal—giving scientific knowledge to élites by which they can control the "masses"—it is naïvely technocratic: Planning is simply a matter of applying scientific knowledge; social change requires little more than intelligent social engineering. Some- how, science and the goodwill of the élites would be sufficient to bring about a higher "organic" solidarity, and Mannheim in fact relies on Durkheim's thesis for theoretical support. A new consensus must emerge planned by the scientific and power élites and the sole *raison d'être* of "social techniques" "is to influence human behavior as society thinks fit." (p. 271.) "Society" in this instance quite clearly refers to the élites. Nowhere in these essays, despite his insistence on "democratic" planning, does Mannheim make provision for a genuinely democratic decision-making process by which the members of society may determine their own fate.

Of course, Mannheim knew too much Marx to ignore altogether the existence of classes and class conflicts: "But planning based on the inequality of classes or estates probably cannot last long, because these inequalities will create so great a tension in society that it will be impossible to establish even that minimum of tacit consent which is the *conditio sine qua non* of the functioning of a system." (p. 364.) Moreover, in all fairness to Mannheim one must acknowledge that he quite deliberately said more about techniques than about political issues and tactics because he believed that it was pre- cisely in the former area that sociology could make a contribution. (pp. 364– 365.) He understood quite well that "the 'liberties' of liberal capitalist society are often only available to the rich, and that the 'have-nots' are forced to submit to the pressure of circumstances." (p. 377.) What was really decisive, however, if one wanted to change that condition was that there be "sound thinking" which reached "the ruling élites." (p. 366.) During World War II Mannheim retained the same general view but felt that the wartime experiences presented new possibilities to the democracies for peaceful, planned reform.

Diagnosis of Our Time

As a sociologist who was interested in social change, Mannheim maintained that "Just as the revolutionary waits for his hour, the reformer whose concern it is to remold society by peaceful means must seize his passing chance."[26] Much as Marx, in his speech in the Hague, had considered the *possibility* of peaceful but far-reaching social changes in England and other countries with strong democratic institutions, Mannheim suggested "that Britain has the chance and the mission to develop a new pattern of society. . . ." Developing further his earlier description of the basic structural trends of modern industrial society, he calls attention, once again, to the implications of these trends. The concentration of power and the growing scale of organization were an undeniable tendency. This was true not only of the economic, political, and military spheres but of the media of mass communication as well. Clearly, these changes in what Mannheim called "social techniques" (his term for means of social control) had brought about a new situation in which large masses of men could now be controlled and manipulated by small groups of men in key positions of power. A few men, strategically placed, could make decisions affecting the lives and fate of the vast majority. This meant that "social techniques" had acquired a fundamental importance— perhaps "even more fundamental to society than the economic structure or the social stratification of a given order. By their aid one can hamper or remold the working of the economic system, destroy social classes and set others in their place." (p. 2.)

One could not go back to the decentralized, small-scale social organization of the past. And while it is true that the concentration of power accompanying modern developments often fostered oligarchy and even dictatorship, they were not necessary outcomes of those developments. Techniques "are neither good nor bad in themselves" and that is why Mannheim prefers the term. The scale of social life in the modern mass society requires planning, and this has become evident in the periodic breakdowns of the economic system and in the social upheavals accompanying them. The partial "planning" which is already in effect in the "functional" rationalization of many areas of social life, is clearly not what is required. Planning must be democratic and guided by

26 Karl Mannheim, *Diagnosis of Our Time* (London: Routledge and Kegan Paul, Ltd., 1943), p. ix. (Immediately following references to this work noted by page numbers in text.)

substantial rationality. Mannheim was thus trying to persuade a specific English public that laissez-faire was now a useless and even dangerous doctrine, and that planning need not be totalitarian. There is a "third way" which is compatible with democracy and freedom as these concepts are understood, say, in England.

Mannheim's "third way" is a mixture of Keynesian and social-democratic measures. Now as earlier, he advances his proposals with the hope that the existing élites will recognize their wisdom and act upon them. It had become clearer now than ever before that when "left alone" the economic system generated great inequalities in wealth and income—or in "life chances" generally. Not only was this unjust but perhaps more important for Mannheim was that it led to social tension, conflict, revolutionary upheavals, and dictatorship. Social justice as well as class cooperation and social peace, therefore, could only be achieved by a conscious and deliberate diminution of differences in wealth and opportunity. The wealthy and advantaged will have to be enlightened enough to make some sacrifices; if they are, they may be able to hold on to a "reasonable" amount of their wealth. If not, they may lose all. In this way, Mannheim hopes to appeal simultaneously to the sense of justice and the long-term interests of the advantaged.

"The move toward greater justice," he writes, "has the advantage that it can be achieved by the existing means of reform—through taxation, control of investment, through public works, and radical extension of social services; it does not call for revolutionary interference, which would lead at once to dictatorship." (p. 6.) With these means, moreover, the active cooperation of the liberal and conservative intelligentsia, and the Church, could be enlisted. The realization of this plan would also require the militant and systematic inculcation of the basic values of Western civilization—social justice, freedom, brotherly love, mutual help, decency, respect for the individual, etc.

Although Mannheim was appealing primarily to the élites, he was aware that the implementation of his proposals required more than their assent, even if they could be persuaded to give it. These were wartime essays, one must remember, and he shared the illusions of many at the time that the wartime class cooperation would survive the war. The democracies, notably England, had demonstrated, under the Nazi attack, their courage, viability, and efficiency. Much of this could be attributed to the voluntary cooperation among the classes of English society. The experience of the depression and the war and the fear of totalitarianism would encourage, Mannheim hoped, an even more cooperative and reformist attitude among the workers than already prevailed.

For Mannheim, the most important lesson to be learned from recent history was that revolutionary upheavals are more likely to result in fascism than in a good society. Socialist critics of the existing order, therefore, "will be readier to advocate reformist measures, as it is becoming obvious that recent revolutions tend to result in fascism and that the chances of a revolution will be very slight as soon as a united party has coordinated all the key positions and is capable of preventing any organized resistance." (p. 10.)

Of course, increasing social justice by means of democratic social planning required international peace. Mannheim looked forward to the transformation of the wartime coalition—which included partners with different socioeconomic systems—into a lasting peacetime alliance. What William James had called a moral substitute for war could be found. Thus in an optative mood that was indeed shared by many others at the time, Mannheim wrote: "I think there is a reasonable chance at least that after the horrors of this war the tasks of reconstruction will be so urgent that they will be felt by many to be a unifying issue at least as strong as the war itself." (p. 30.)

Mannheim's proposal for peaceful social change required, therefore, general good will, class cooperation, and the rational mobilization of resources guided by the knowledge of the social sciences. This knowledge is an "aid to those who govern," but it can also aid the governed. Education in general but especially in the "science of society" can help the governed check the arbitrariness of the leaders. The élites must be made to understand that "the uneducated and uninformed masses today are a greater danger to the maintenance of any order than classes with a conscious orientation and reasonable expectation." (p. 43.) Education for democratic planning is essential at all age-levels but particularly for the young. Here something can be learned from the totalitarian states. The point, of course, is not to imitate them but to grasp the fact that the great *élan* of youth can be guided toward constructive goals. Presumably, a nationwide youth movement could be organized with a common *Weltanschauung* that would cut across class lines. Mannheim was calling for a new type of awareness; not the *partial* class awareness that furthers class conflict, but a "total" awareness in which one considers general interests not less than one's special interests. Nevertheless, the new consensus would not preclude class conflict; rather it would lend it a democratic and peaceful form. "Democracy is essentially a method of social change, the institutionalization of the belief that adjustment to changing reality and the reconciliation of divers interests can be brought about by conciliatory means, with the help of discussion, bargaining, and integral consensus." (p. 69.) Under these conditions, class struggle even preserves democracy. "What is needed to make democracy safe is not the exclusion of the social struggle, but that it should be fought out by methods of reform." (p. 70.) The workers, especially, should have learned by now that a "society without a governing class" is an unrealizable fantasy. The realistic aim should be "the improvement of the economic, social, political, and educational opportunities for the people to train themselves for leadership, and improvement of the method of the selection of the best in the various fields of social life." (p. 72.)

There were for Mannheim at least three criteria by which one could judge whether a society was succeeding in the implementation of his proposal: (1) social control, discipline, and repression are steadily reduced to an absolute minimum; (2) controls and prohibitions are democratically decided upon and are above all "humane"; and, finally, (3) institutions are designed to help the individual make his way but also to "come to the rescue of those who have failed. . . ." (p. 82.)

Many of the same ideas and some new ones are developed in his essays collected under the title: *Freedom, Power and Democratic Planning*. Mannheim's "third way" may be viewed as a middle-class ideology which attempts to mediate between extremes: between those who insist on maintaining the same old routine and those who demand fundamental social changes. Speaking to both extremes, then, Mannheim is saying first to the defenders of the status quo: Planning is essential to counteract the dangers of a mass society. He appeals to their sense of justice and attempts to enlighten them as to their long-term interests. To the Marxists, on the other hand, Mannheim concedes that their revolutionary theory may have been appropriate to the conditions of early capitalism—a world of scarcity, ruthless exploitation, and "life-and-death struggle between rich and poor in which the poor had nothing to lose but his chains." Today, however, the situation is different and "there are too many people who could lose by revolution."[27]

Moreover, there is another condition which all should reflect upon seriously, but especially the workers. The "withering away" of the state after a socialist revolution was originally not an altogether silly and quixotic vision. When Marx advanced this idea he was justified in projecting into the future a historical tendency in which absolutist regimes were giving way to increasingly democratic ones. The ghastly experiences of the twentieth century, however, have demonstrated that revolutionary upheavals are followed by a strengthening of the state and that far from "withering" it becomes increasingly totalitarian. The "social techniques," the means of social control in the hands of the dominant minorities, are so efficient and powerful as to render revolution "against any totalitarian power once entrenched . . . nearly hopeless. No established totalitarian regime, whatever its political creed, can be broken from within; it takes an external war to unseat it."[28] In short, the almost certain results of any future revolution make it expedient for everyone to opt for the Third Way.

This appeared as a particularly viable alternative for England and for other societies with similar conditions. In England, the main social base of planning would be the large middle class, the broad center. This base, together with highly developed democratic institutions and traditions, makes it more likely that planning would be acceptable to the majority "excluding both the reac-

27 Karl Mannheim, *Freedom, Power and Democratic Planning* (London: Routledge and Kegan Paul, Ltd., 1950), p. 27.

28 *Ibid.*, pp. 27–28.

tionaries who do not want to move at any price, and radicals who think the millennium is just around the corner."[29]

Since the Third Way is unthinkable under conditions of international tension and war, every effort must be made to preserve peace. The beginnings of the blind drift toward what could result in World War III were already visible when Mannheim wrote these essays and he sensed that this could be fatal for all mankind. He placed his faith in the balance of power between the U.S.A. and the U.S.S.R. The danger of this, he recognized, was that the small powers could become pawns in the Great Power struggle and the main hope of preventing this "rests in *tenacious insistence on fair play* on the part of political forces spread all over the world, who are truly interested in and stand for the transformation of present-day imperialism into a peaceful order."[30] Ultimately, however, it is the super powers which have a special responsibility in this regard: "Just as the Roman Empire established its *Pax Romana* among formerly bellicose peoples, so the rule of the great powers may spare us the guerrilla wars of small brigand states."[31] He did not foresee the possibility that peoples throughout the world would come to regard the "order" imposed by the twentieth century equivalent of the *Pax Romana* more intolerable than their guerrilla wars which were often just struggles against oppression and exploitation.

In the end, Mannheim's new society was quite Saint-Simonian: hierarchic, "organic," and guided by scientific-industrial élites. Since even the best planners and the most "substantial" rationality cannot avoid the situation in which "economic decisions affect some groups and classes favorably and others unfavorably," organic unity requires something more. Just as Saint-Simon had called for a New Christianity, Mannheim now proposed a New Social Philosophy based upon Christian values. There was no getting around this basic requirement of the new planned society: Basic ethical principles, enjoining altruism and self-sacrifice, had to be established. "There will, therefore, in every planned society be a body somehow similar to the priests, whose task it will be to watch that certain basic standards are established and maintained."[32] Mannheim longed so strongly for a different world that this led him to believe that there was "a reasonable chance that after the war the struggle between antagonistic dogmatic systems will have burnt out and there will be a desire to develop potentialities which at present can only be diagnosed as latent tendencies of a Third Way."[33] Any final evaluation of Mannheim's work on planning must take into account the fact that he regarded these writings as *essays* in the literal sense, *i.e.*, as initial tentative efforts.

---

29 *Ibid.*, p. 36.
30 *Ibid.*, p. 71. (Italics mine.)
31 *Ibid.*, p. 75.
32 Karl Mannheim, *Diagnosis of Our Time, op. cit.*, p. 119.
33 *Ibid.*, p. 164.

Epilogue

I have tried in this study to document the thesis that the outstanding sociologists of the late nineteenth and early twentieth centuries developed their theories by taking account of, and coming to terms with, the intellectual challenge of Marxism. Weber, Pareto, Mosca, Michels, Durkheim and Mannheim are just a few of the thinkers who engaged in what was at times a dialogue and at other times a debate with the Marxian legacy.

Some of these thinkers, such as Weber and Mannheim, had adopted a reconstructed or revised version of "Marxism," conceived not as a critical and revolutionary theory but as a scientific method and system of analysis. Other thinkers, Pareto and Mosca for instance, had thought of their work as a definitive rebuttal of Marxism. Their respective sociologies may be read as elaborate efforts to repudiate and discredit certain essential aspects of the Marxian conception of society and history.

Still other sociologists of that period sought to mediate between Marxism and other systems of thought. Thus Émile Durkheim's sociology, as we have seen, may be regarded as an attempt to reconcile two antithetical models of society, the Marxian and the Comtean. How were social order, unity, and peace possible in the face of an increasingly complex division of labor which brought with it a dispersion of interests, social cleavages, and class conflict? Durkheim thought he saw the key to a reconciliation of order and progress—which had always been viewed as antithetical

321

principles—in the work of Saint-Simon, the common intellectual ancestor of both Comte and Marx. Taken as a whole, therefore, Durkheim's work may best be understood as a sophisticated elaboration of basically Saint-Simonian principles.

In this perspective, Marxism acquires fundamental importance in the development of sociological theory—not only for the seminal ideas Marx and the Marxists themselves had advanced, but also for the critical intellectual response their ideas provoked.

The real importance of all these thinkers—both Marx and his critics—lies not so much in whether certain of their specific theories were right or wrong as in the questions they asked, the issues they addressed themselves to, and the ideas they employed to grapple with them. It is for their ideas, or "models" if one prefers, that we continue to respect their work and regard it, in C. Wright Mills' phrase, as "the classic tradition in sociological thinking." Mills has explained rather well, I believe, why these men remain great in spite of their errors.

> . . . [T]he classic sociologists construct models of society and use them to develop a number of theories. What is important is the fact that neither the correctness nor the inaccuracy of any of these specific theories necessarily confirms or upsets the usefulness or the adequacy of the models. The models can be used for correcting errors in theories made with their aid. And they are readily open: they can themselves be modified in ways to make them more useful as analytical tools and empirically closer to the run of fact.
>
> It is these models that are great—not only as contributions to the history of social reflection and inquiry, but also as influences on subsequent sociological thinking. They, I believe, are what is alive in the classic tradition of sociology.[1]

Obviously, not all students of sociological theory would agree on who does and who does not belong in this tradition, which includes, no doubt, more thinkers than were discussed in this volume. Among the latter, moreover, not all are of equal stature and my own opinion is that Marx and Weber stand higher than all the rest. Yet, the others also stand out in terms of their contributions to our understanding of the human condition. What is meant by "classical," then, is that the ideas of the men considered here have stood the test of time; that in fact we still employ them actively in thinking about the social phenomena and problems of today.

Another way of illustrating the importance of these men and their ideas is by means of a *Gedankenexperiment:* substitute for the thinkers considered here an equal number of different theorists who never explicitly participated in the debate with Marx's ghost, and reflect on whether sociological theory would then be of equal quality, better or worse. In my mind there is no doubt as to how I would answer this question: Without the debate between Marx and his critics, sociological thinking would be so greatly impoverished as to be reduced to an ineffectual state.

[1] C. Wright Mills, *Images of Man* (New York: George Braziller, Inc., 1960), p. 3.

Index

Alienated labor, 103ff.
Alienation, 85, 87, 88, 107
Ancient Judaism, 149ff.
Anomic division of labor, 247
Anomy, 250
*Archiv für Sozialwissenschaft und Sozial-
politik,* 112
Aristotle, 19, 90, 202, 203, 205, 206, 212
Asceticism, 129

Bauer, Bruno, 94, 95
Baxter, Richard, 128, 130, 132
Bazard, Saint Amand, 62
Berkeley, George, 8
Bernstein, Eduard, 225
Beruf, 126
Blanc, Louis, 222
Bonald, Louis de, 43–60, 68, 71, 241, 247
Bonaparte, Napoleon, 50
Bourgeoisie, 47
Bousquet, G. H., 160, 194
Brentano, Lujo, 131
Buddhism, 146
Bureaucratization (*see also* Weber, Max),
  311
Burke, Edmund, 37–39, 42, 52, 266

Calling, 126
Calvin, John, 127, 130, 132
Calvinism, 127, 133
Capital, 86, 91, 102, 103ff., 164

Capitalism, 84, 118
Cassirer, Ernst, 4, 7, 12
Catholic, 43
Catholic Church, 47
China, 122
China, religion of, 118, 138ff.
Christianity, 68
Christian thought, 304
Circulation of élites, 168, 229
Class conflict, 204, 250
Classes, 230, 239
Classical economists, 61
Class position, 300
Class struggle, 224, 317
Communism, 88, 91
Communist society, 92
Comte, Auguste, 38, 55–57, 60–62, 66, 68–74,
  76–79, 83, 84, 235, 246–48, 251, 265, 266
Condillac, E. B. de, 6, 26, 45
Condorcet, Marquis Jean Ambroise, 13
Conflict, 92
Confucianism, 142
Conscience collective, 243, 245
Conservatism, 295
Conservative reaction, 43, 53
Conservative thought, 293ff.
Constraint, 262
Croce, Benedetto, 219

D'Alembert, Jean Le Rond, 6
Das Kapital (*see also Capital*), 216

Democracy, 233
Derivations, 170, 173, 182, 184, 189
Descartes, René, 5
Diagnosis of Our Time, 282, 315ff.
Dialectic, 93
Dialectical conception, 90
Dilthey, Wilhelm, 283, 285, 299
Disraeli, Benjamin, 219
Division of labor, 257, 269
Division of Labor in Society, 242ff.
Durkheim, Émile, 16, 19, 20, 54, 55, 60, 62, 64, 68, 234ff., 304, 314
Dysfunctions, 280

Education and Sociology, 257ff.
Elementary Forms of Religious Life, 260, 267, 276ff.
Élites, 167, 168, 176, 187, 190, 310, 317
Enclosure Acts, 86
Encyclopedia, 7
Enfantin, Barthelemy Prosper, 62
Engels, Frederick, 92, 198, 210, 216, 217, 296
Enlightenment, 3, 7, 9, 23, 35, 44, 45, 47, 50, 72, 84, 89, 108, 204, 294
Essays on the Sociology of Culture, 282

False consciousness, 217, 278
Fascism, 193, 194, 316, 317
Feuerbach, Ludwig, 85
Fischoff, Ephraim, 131
Force, 187, 188, 190, 191
Forced division of labor, 249
Fourier, Charles, 234
Franklin, Benjamin, 125, 126, 130, 135, 137
Freedom, Power and Democratic Planning, 282, 318ff.
"Free-floating" intellectuals (*see* Unattached intellectuals)
French Revolution, 5, 35, 37, 47, 49, 57, 63, 64, 83, 84, 294, 297
Freud, Sigmund, 25, 182
Functions, 238, 241, 274

Geisteswissenschaften, 115, 283, 285, 289, 290, 292, 293
Gemeinschaft und Gesellschaft, 180
Generations, 299
German sociology, 282
Germany, 157
Gouldner, Alvin, 236
Guest people, 146

Hamilton, Thomas, 95
Hegel, G. W. F., 38–40, 42, 63, 65, 70, 85, 89, 90, 92–94, 96, 266, 283, 291
Hegelian dialectic, 70
Heine, Heinrich, 297

Helvetius, Claude Adrien, 9
Hinduism, 146
Historicism, 290, 292
Hobbes, Thomas, 26
Holbach, Paul H. D., 9
Hook, Sidney, 95n.
Hume, David, 8, 36
Husserl, Edmund, 292

Idealism, 97
Ideal types, 119, 120
Ideology, conceptions of, 305
Ideology and Utopia, 282, 302ff.
India, 122
India, religion of, 118, 144ff.
Industrial Revolution, 47
Intelligentsia (*see also* Unattached intellectuals), 307ff.
Interests, 171, 173
Iron law of oligarchy, 221
Israel, 122
Israelite prophecy, 118

Jaffé, Edgar, 112
James, William, 317
Jaurès, Jean, 241
Jewish prophets, 143
Jewish Question, 94
Judaism, 129, 150 ff.
Juridical defense, 203, 207–9

Kant, Immanuel, 7, 36, 37, 303
Kolko, Gabriel, 135, 136

Lafargue, Paul, 225
La Mettrie, Julien O. de, 9
Left Hegelians (or Young Hegelians), 85, 94, 296
Leibniz, Gottfried, W., 37
Liberalism, 203
Livingston, Arthur, 161
Locke, John, 8, 28, 303
Logico-experimental, 162, 169
Loyola, Ignatius, 79
Luther, Martin, 126, 127

Machiavelli, Niccolo, 197
Maistre, Joseph de, 43, 44, 50–53, 56, 60, 68, 71, 72, 241, 247
Malinowski, Bronislaw, 182, 183
Man and Society in an Age of Reconstruction, 282, 310ff.
Mannheim, Karl, 281ff.
Marcuse, Herbert, 70, 89
Markham, F. M. H., 60, 62
Marx, Karl, 25, 42, 46, 57, 58, 61, 62, 64, 65, 79–108, 111, 112, 114, 116, 118–22, 132, 138, 146, 150, 159, 160, 164–67, 183, 195,

198, 202, 207, 209–12, 215, 216, 218, 220, 221, 225, 230–32, 234–36, 240, 246, 248, 252, 256, 265, 266, 276, 278, 281, 283, 285, 294, 296, 297, 301, 302, 306, 310, 314, 315
Marxism, 108, 112, 165, 305, 309
Marxists, 113
Masses, 176, 224
Materialism, 97
Materialist conception of history, 165
Mauss, Marcel, 234
Mayer, J. P., 157, 158
Mead, George H., 257
Mechanical solidarity, 237, 244
Meisel, James H., 204, 216
Methodism, 129
Michels, Robert, 217ff.
Middle Ages, 59, 62, 68
Mikhailovsky, Nikolai, 118
Mill, J. S., 79
Mills, C. Wright, 322n.
Mode of production, 98, 100
Montesquieu, Charles, 11, 22, 202–6, 208, 212, 213
Moral Education, 260, 262, 264
Mosca, Gaetano, 195ff., 218, 220, 221
Mussolini, Benito, 193

Naturwissenschaften, 115
Nazis, 311
Negation of the negation, 41
Negative-critical philosophy, 83
Negative-critical principles, 68
Negative philosophy, 70
Newton, Isaac, 5, 8, 36, 59
Nietzsche, Frederick, 156
Nisbet, Robert A., 53n.
Nonlogical, 161

Occupational guilds, 238, 251
Offenbacher, Martin, 134
Organic society, 83
Organic solidarity, 237, 246, 275
Owen, Robert, 234

Pareto, Vilfredo, 159ff., 198, 202, 212, 213, 218–21, 229
Pariah people, 146, 149
Paris Commune, 210, 217
Parliamentarism, 212
Parsons, Talcott, 112n.
Perspectivistic, 293
Philosophes, 3–6, 8, 13, 23, 35, 38, 40, 44, 48, 54, 55, 68, 70, 84, 237, 258, 260, 264
Planning, 310, 312
Political formula, 200
Political parties, 220
Popper, Karl, 216

Popular sovereignty, 210
Positive philosophy, 70, 74
Positivism, 58, 59
Professional Ethics and Civic Morals, 252ff., 264, 270, 274
Proletarians, 83
Prophets, 151
Protestant Ethic, 111, 122, 124, 130, 158
Protestantism, 122
Proudhon, Pierre J., 222
Puritanism, 129
Puritans, 128, 136

Rational ethic, 117
Rationalization of social life (*see also* Weber, Max), 311
Reason, 3
Reformation, 49, 58, 133
Relationism, 306
Residues, 169, 170, 173ff.
Restoration, 43, 47
Rickert, H., 285
Romantic-Conservative conception, 39
Romantic-Conservative movement, 294
Romantic movement, 36
Rousseau, Jean-Jacques, 23–29, 31, 36, 45, 50, 51, 73, 84, 195, 204, 205, 207, 222
Rules of the Sociological Method, 254, 267ff.
Ruling class, 101, 196, 216

Saint-Simon, Henri Comte de, 19, 38, 48, 55–58, 60–69, 71, 74, 197, 234, 235, 236ff., 242, 252, 272, 314, 319
Samuelsson, Kurt, 132–35
Scheler, Max, 283
Sentiments, 161, 162, 168, 171, 172, 182
Sex residue, 181ff.
Simmel, Georg, 283
Sismondi, J. C. S. de, 61
Social contract, 30, 31, 47, 204
Social Darwinism, 200
Social equilibrium, 173, 179, 185
Social forces, 199, 206, 210, 212
Socialism, 91, 166, 235, 295
Social techniques, 313–15, 318
Society, 241, 250, 251, 254, 257–59, 265, 267, 273, 279, 280
Sociology of knowledge, 281ff.
Sombart, Werner, 112, 283
Sorel, Georges, 200
Spencer, Herbert, 244
Standing armies, 214
Suicide, 262, 271ff.

Tawney, R. H., 131
Theological-retrograde school, 75

Thierry, Augustin, 58
Third way, 316, 318, 319
Tönnies, Ferdinand, 222
Totalitarianism, 208, 318

Unattached intellectuals, 297
Universal suffrage, 210
Utility, 161

Verstehen, 283
Vico, Giovanni, 11, 12

Weber, Alfred, 308
Weber, Marianne, 155
Weber, Max, 111–158; methodology of,
112ff.; political sociology and political
values of, 155; 179, 209, 218, 220, 281,
284, 285, 290, 292, 306, 309, 310

Weltanschauungen, 283, 287, 288, 290
Weltreligionen, 111, 118
Wertrationalität, 179
Wesley, John, 129, 130, 132
Western civilization, 124
Western sociology, 10
Wilson, Edmund, 11
Windelband, Wilhelm, 285
Wirtschaft und Gesellschaft, 111

Yahwe, conception of, 152
Young Hegelians (*see also* Left Hegelians),
96

Zeitgeist, 287
Zweckrationalität, 179

27.9.76 — 10.12.76
5.1.77 — 24.3.77
18.4.77 — 1.7.77